Education in the United States

Series in American Studies

Editor-in-Chief: Joseph J. Kwiat
PROGRAM IN AMERICAN STUDIES
UNIVERSITY OF MINNESOTA

EDUCATION

IN THE

UNITED STATES

EDITED BY

NICHOLAS MURRAY BUTLER

Volume 2

With a New Introduction by
TIMOTHY L. SMITH
PROFESSOR OF EDUCATION AND OF HISTORY
THE JOHNS HOPKINS UNIVERSITY

JOHNSON REPRINT CORPORATION
New York and London
1969

EDUCATION

IN THE

UNITED STATES

A SERIES OF MONOGRAPHS

PREPARED FOR THE UNITED STATES EXHIBIT AT THE
PARIS EXPOSITION
1900

EDITED BY

NICHOLAS MURRAY BUTLER

Professor of Philosophy and Education in Columbia University

New York

PUBLISHERS
J. B. LYON COMPANY
ALBANY, N. Y.
1900

96283

CONTENTS

DEPARTMENT OF EDUCATION

FOR THE

UNITED STATES COMMISSION TO THE PARIS EXPOSITION OF 1900

MONOGRAPHS ON EDUCATION

IN THE

UNITED STATES

EDITED BY

NICHOLAS MURRAY BUTLER

Professor of Philosophy and Education in Columbia University, New York

10

PROFESSIONAL EDUCATION

BY

JAMES RUSSELL PARSONS JR

*Director of the College and High School Departments, University of the State
of New York, Albany, New York*

THIS MONOGRAPH IS CONTRIBUTED TO THE UNITED STATES EDUCATIONAL EXHIBIT BY THE
STATE OF NEW YORK

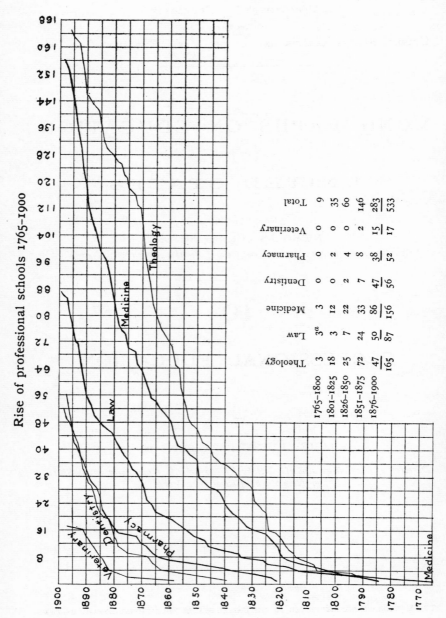

Rise of professional schools 1765–1900

	Theology	Law	Medicine	Dentistry	Pharmacy	Veterinary	Total
1765–1800	3	3[a]	3	0	0	0	9
1801–1825	18	3	12	0	2	0	35
1826–1850	25	7	22	2	4	0	60
1851–1875	72	24	33	7	8	2	146
1876–1900	47	50	86	47	38	15	283
	165	87	156	56	52	17	533

[a] Extinct Litchfield school and first attempts at college of Philadelphia and Columbia.

PROFESSIONAL EDUCATION

I GENERAL

Preacademic, grammar or common school work refers to the eight years of elementary instruction; secondary or academic work, to the four years of secondary instruction between elementary school and college; college work, to the four years of higher instruction, following the four years of secondary. Professional institutions are uniformly called schools.

Authorities — It is impossible within the limits of this monograph to give more than a brief outline of professional education in the United States. For detailed information touching laws, regulations, location of schools, and courses of study the reader is referred to *Professional education in the United States*, published by the University of the State of New York.

Of the many authorities consulted the following have proved most helpful: U. S. education reports; Eliot's *Educational reform;* U. S. census reports; Briggs' *Theological education and its needs;*[1] Dyer's *Theological education in America;*[2] Jessup's *Legal education in New York;*[3] Wellman's *Admission to the bar;*[4] Hammond's *American law schools, past and future;*[5] *Reports of the American bar association;* Toner's *Annals of medical progress in the United States;*[6] Davis' *Medical education and medical institutions in the United States;*[7] *Journal American medical association;* Shepard's *Inaugural address at the World's Columbian dental congress; Proceedings of the American pharmaceutical association.* These and other authorities have been used freely, but limited space makes it impracticable to give in many cases more than this general acknowledgment.

---

[1] *Forum*, January 1892. [2] *Penn monthly*, August 1880. [3] See the *History of the bench and bar of New York.* [4] *American law review*, May 1881. [5] *Southern law review*, August 1881. [6] *U. S. education report*, 1874. [7] *U. S. education report*, 1877.

Assistance rendered by specialists is acknowledged in the chapter relating to each profession.

Growth — At the time of the declaration of independence there were only two professional schools in this country, the Medical college of Philadelphia (1765), now the medical department of the University of Pennsylvania, and the medical department of King's college (1768).[1]

The following statistics, summarized from *Professional education in the United States*, show unprecedented growth :[2]

	Schools 1899	Instructors 1899	Students 1898	Graduates 1898	Students 1899
Theology	165	1 070	8 317	1 693	8 093
Law	86	970	11 783	3 110	11 883
Medicine.....	[3]156	[3]5 735	[3]24 043	[3]5 725	[3]24 119
Dentistry	56	1 513	7 221	1 921	7 633
Pharmacy	[4]52	[4]492	[4]3 525	[4]1 122	[4]3 563
Veterinary medicine....	17	249	368	123	378
[5]Total	532	10 029	55 257	13 694	55 669

In 1898, 286 of the 532 schools reported total property amounting to nearly $50,000,000 (New York 33 per cent),

[1] King's college is now Columbia university.
[2] The 1898 U. S. education report gives the following:

	Schools	Instructors	Students	Graduates
Theology...........................	155	958	8 371	1 673
Law...............................	83	845	11 615	3 065
Medicine...............................	151	4 247	23 433	5 597
Dentistry...............................	50	961	6 774	1 848
Pharmacy...............................	45	401	3 712	1 129
Veterinary medicine...................	14	173	326	109
Total...........................	498	7 585	54 231	13 421

[3] Excluding graduate schools, but including 3 medical preparatory schools.
[4] Including Department of pharmacy, University of Washington, which has suspended temporarily.
[5] In these totals training schools for nurses are not included. The Philadelphia lying-in, charity and nurse school was opened in 1828, but it is said that systematic training in schools for nurses was not given till 1873. The 1898 U. S. education report gives 377 of these schools with 8805 students. The course of study is usually two years in length though nearly 1-4 of the schools now require three years. Most of these schools are connected with hospitals where medical, surgical and obstetric cases are treated. The course of study embraces anatomy, physiology and hygiene, and obstetrics.

Distribution of professional students in 1899

Red, political divisions with professional schools having more than 1000 students

Blue, political divisions with professional schools having less than 1000 students

White, political divisions without professional schools

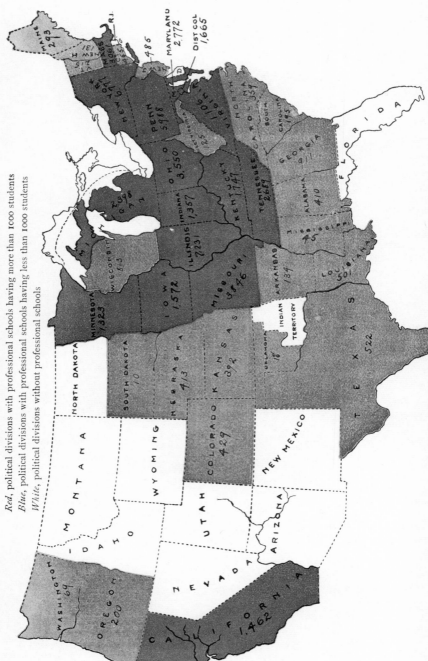

The map does not show Alaska, Hawaii and Puerto Rico which have no professional schools, or Cuba and the Philippines where professional schools are connected with the universities at Havana and Manila respectively.

262 reported receipts exceeding $5,000,000 (New York 31 per cent), 270 expenditures exceeding $4,500,000 (New York 28 per cent). Degrees are granted by 73 theological schools, 82 law schools, 152 medical schools, 56 dental schools, 45 schools of pharmacy and 16 veterinary medical schools.

Distribution of professional schools and students in 1899[1]— 38 political divisions of the United States report professional schools and students as follows :

Division	Theology		Law		Medicine		Dentistry		Pharmacy		Veteri-nary		Total	
Sc. =school; St. =student.	Sc.	St.	Sc.	St.	Sc.	St.	Sc.	St.	Sc.	St.	Sc.	St.	Sc.	St.
Illinois............	18	1 210	9	1 308	16	3 065	5	1 282	2	284	2	82	52	7 231
New York	17	1 039	7	2 202	11	2 415	3	503	4	536	3	82	45	6 777
Pennsylvania......	17	813	3	526	6	2 475	5	1 503	3	619	1	52	35	5 988
Missouri	6	448	3	366	16	2 345	4	485	2	177	1	25	32	3 846
Ohio..............	13	432	6	705	13	1 392	5	589	5	418	1	14	43	3 550
Massachusetts.....	8	514	2	974	4	1 066	2	302	1	178	1	27	18	3 061
Maryland.........	6	561	2	277	8	1 331	3	497	1	106	0	0	20	2 772
Tennessee	8	226	6	211	9	1 876	4	301	3	75	0	0	30	2 689
Michigan	3	102	2	918	6	877	2	346	2	129	2	26	17	2 398
Kentucky	3	401	2	96	7	1 011	1	179	1	60	0	0	14	1 747
District Columbia..	5	105	5	892	5	460	3	135	2	46	2	27	22	1 665
Iowa..............	5	204	2	365	5	631	2	135	3	210	1	27	18	1 572
California.........	5	78	3	323	6	576	4	395	2	83	1	7	21	1 462
Indiana...........	4	161	4	456	4	305	2	258	2	170	1	7	17	1 357
Minnesota.........	8	277	1	446	3	428	1	110	1	62	0	0	14	1 323
Virginia...........	4	194	3	236	3	618	2	36	2	22	0	0	14	1 106
Georgia...........	2	98	4	75	3	449	2	258	1	31	0	0	12	911
Wisconsin	4	160	2	259	2	198	1	135	1	61	0	0	10	813
Texas	1	16	2	176	2	290	0	0	1	40	0	0	6	522
Louisiana.........	1	23	1	72	2	388	0	0	1	18	0	0	5	501
New Jersey........	5	459	0	0	0	0	0	0	1	26	0	0	6	485
Connecticut	3	152	1	194	1	109	0	0	0	0	0	0	5	455
Colorado	2	33	2	93	4	253	2	50	0	0	0	0	10	429
Nebraska	3	59	2	117	3	179	1	58	0	0	0	0	9	413
Alabama..........	3	61	1	27	3	239	1	42	2	41	0	0	10	410
Kansas............	1	9	1	166	3	172	0	0	1	45	0	0	6	392
North Carolina....	3	81	2	86	3	167	0	0	2	25	0	0	10	359
Maine	2	78	1	31	2	171	0	0	1	13	0	0	6	293
Vermont...........	0	0	0	0	1	215	0	0	0	0	0	0	1	215
Oregon............	2	53	2	65	2	182	0	0	0	0	0	0	6	200
South Carolina....	3	46	1	25	1	97	0	0	1	27	0	0	6	195
Arkansas	0	0	1	26	1	108	0	0	0	0	0	0	2	134
New Hampshire...	0	0	0	0	1	131	0	0	0	0	0	0	1	131
West Virginia......	0	0	1	125	0	0	0	0	0	0	0	0	1	125
Washington.......	0	0	1	0	0	0	1	34	2	33	1	2	5	69
Mississippi........	0	0	1	45	0	0	0	0	0	0	0	0	1	45
Oklahoma........	0	0	0	0	0	0	0	0	1	18	0	0	1	18
South Dakota.....	0	0	0	0	0	0	0	0	1	10	0	0	1	10
	165	8 093	86	11 883	156	24 119	56	7 633	52	3 563	17	378	532	55 669

The following report no professional schools : Alaska, Arizona, Delaware, Florida, Hawaii, Idaho, Indian territory, Montana, Nevada, New Mexico, North Dakota, Puerto Rico, Rhode Island, Utah, Wyoming.

[1] Not including students at the University of Havana: law 124, medicine 98, pharmacy 98 (1899), or at the University of Santo Tomas, Manila theology 6, law 558, medicine 404, pharmacy 51 (1897). Grand total, including also 1916 graduate medical students, 58,924.

Illinois leads for the first time in professional students, a fact due to a lack of proper control of the power to grant degrees and licenses. Including students in graduate medical schools, New York and Illinois report about the same number of professional students in 1899.

Varying standards — There is no national authority in the United States that can prescribe standards for degrees or for license to practise the professions. Each state makes its own professional laws. As a result there are almost as many standards as there are political divisions. The desirability of uniform standards throughout the country for admission to professional practice is recognized generally, but varying conditions as to density of population, educational advantages and general development make it impracticable to hope for the attainment of this end for some time to come.[1]

30 years ago the public had little protection from incompetency in professional practice. The bar is said to have been at its lowest ebb. Medical laws were crude and largely inoperative. In several states only were there any acts designed to control the practice of pharmacy and dentistry. There was no law whatever restricting the practice of veterinary medicine.

There has been extraordinary progress, specially in the last decade, in restrictive professional legislation, and in the admission and graduation requirements of professional schools throughout the United States. In view of these facts the growth in professional students is remarkable. From 1888 to 1899 the increase was as follows: theology 24 per cent, law 224 per cent, medicine 84 per cent, dentistry 380 per cent, pharmacy 31 per cent, veterinary medicine 17 per cent.

In 1890, when the last U. S. census was taken, the ratio to population for each given profession was: clergymen 1 to 710, lawyers 1 to 699, physicians 1 to 598, dentists 1 to 3579. The corresponding ratios for 1870 were: clergymen 1 to 879, lawyers 1 to 946, physicians 1 to 617, dentists 1 to

---

[1] See section on Influence of medical societies.

Growth in professional students

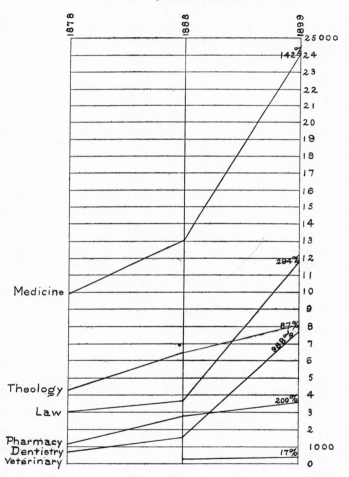

4919.   In each profession there has been a growth which is greater proportionately than the growth in population.[1]

Preliminary general education for licenses — In New York state a preliminary general education equivalent to graduation from a four years' high school course after a completed eight years' elementary course is prescribed by statute as the minimum standard for license to practise medicine. This standard approximates that required in continental Europe. New Hampshire has similar requirements, but they are not as rigidly enforced. The statutes of Delaware, Maryland, New Jersey and Pennsylvania prescribe a "common school education." Louisiana demands "a fair primary education." The rules in Vermont prescribe a high school course; in Illinois and Iowa less than one year of high school work; in Virginia, "evidence of a preliminary education." In remaining political divisions laws and rules are either silent in this respect or so indefinite (Arkansas and other political divisions) as to be of little value.

In New York and Illinois (after Jan. 1, 1900) a preliminary general education equivalent to a three years' high school course is required for admission to the bar. Connecticut demands a high school education or an indefinite preliminary examination. The minimum requirement in Michigan (in case of examination) is less than two years of high

[1] These returns were first given in 1860 when the ratio to population (31,443, 321) was: clergymen (37,529) 1 to 837, lawyers (33,193) 1 to 947, physicians (54,543) 1 to 576, dentists (5606) 1 to 5608. Following are the figures for 1870, 1880 and 1890:

	Population	Clergymen	Lawyers	Physicians	Dentists
1870	38 558 371	43 874	40 736	62 448	7 839
1880	50 155 783	64 698	64 137	85 671	12 314
1890	62 622 250	88 203	89 630	104 805	17 498

Students at these periods were reported as follows in 1897 by the American bar association:

	Theology	Law	Medicine	Dentistry	Pharmacy
1870	3 254	1 653	6 198	257	512
1880	5 242	3 134	11 929	730	1 347
1890	7 013	4 518	16 660	2 696	2 871

school work, in Colorado it is one year of high school work, in Minnesota (in case of examination) it is less than one year, in Ohio it is a common school education. If anything is demanded in other political divisions the requirement is not sufficiently established (excepting a few local cases) to find a place either in statutes or court rules.

The New York law exacts a full high school course as one of the requirements for license to practise dentistry.[1] New Jersey demands by statute "a preliminary education equal to that furnished by the common schools," Pennsylvania "a competent common school education," Virginia a "fair academic education." In other political divisions there is no such requirement.[2] Louisiana, Michigan, South Dakota, Wisconsin, and, in case of examination, California and Texas are the only political divisions which mention in their rules preliminary general education as a requirement for license to practise pharmacy. An elementary education only is prescribed. The completion of a full high school course or its equivalent is one of the statutory requirements for license to practise veterinary medicine in New York.[3] Pennsylvania demands "a competent common school education." There is no such requirement in any other state.

Preliminary general education for degrees — In New York, high standards in preliminary general education are demanded both for degrees and for licenses,[4] and in each case the question of attainments is determined by a central authority, the University of the State of New York. As a rule in other states the professional schools conduct their own entrance examinations, and the tests are often mere matters of form, even though the standards may appear satisfactory on paper.

---

[1] For matriculates before Jan. 1, 1901, 3 years in a high school are accepted. [2] See section on Dental societies. [3] For matriculates before Jan. 1, 1901, 2 years in a high school are accepted. [4] Excepting licenses to preach and licenses to practise pharmacy.

Entrance requirements

In 4 theological schools there are no entrance requirements ; in 24 schools they are indefinite. 19 demand a grammar school education. 1, 6 and 19 require respectively one, two and three years of high school work. 18, 3 and 71 demand respectively one, three and four years of college work.

In 16 law schools there are apparently no entrance requirements whatever; in 8 schools they are so indefinite as to be practically worthless. 26 schools demand a grammar school education. 8, 11, 12 and 3 require respectively one, two, three and four years of high school work. Harvard demands an education equivalent to that required for admission to the senior class. The Columbia law school will be maintained as a graduate department after 1903.

In 2 medical schools the requirements are indefinite; 29 demand a grammar school education; 97, 12, 3 and 12 require respectively one, two, three and four years of high school work. Johns Hopkins requires a college course, Harvard also after Sep. 1901.

In 3 dental schools the requirements are indefinite; 18 demand a grammar school education; 18, 11 and 6 require respectively one, two and three years of high school work.

In 6 schools of pharmacy there are no entrance requirements ; in 4 schools they are indefinite. 24 demand a grammar school education ; 11, 6 and 1 require respectively one, two and three years of high school work.

In 1 veterinary medical school the requirements are indefinite; 9 demand a grammar school education ; 1, 5 and 1 require respectively one, two and three years of high school work.

Professional students with college degrees — The 1894 U. S. education report states that probably nearly one half of the theological students held either B.A. or B.S. degrees (46 1-2 per cent), as compared with only about 20 per cent of law students. The corresponding returns from medical schools were so imperfect that they were not tabulated. Tables in the 1897 U. S. education report indicate that of schools reporting graduate students 49 per cent of the students in theology, 24 per cent of those in law and 14 per cent of those in medicine held either B.A. or B.S. degrees. The corresponding returns for 1898 were 53 per cent in theology, 29 per cent in law, and 21 per cent in medicine.

Following is a classification of schools 1) that report graduate students, 2) that report no graduate students, 3) that do not report this item:

		Schools		Students		Hold B. A. or B. S. degrees		Per cent	
		1897	1898	1897	1898	1897	1898	1897	1898
Theology	1	93	85	5 217	5 086	2 566	2 696	49	53
	2	26	28	635	850	0	0	0	0
	3	37	42	2 321	2 435	1	1	1	1
Law	1	56	41	7 997	6 289	1 932	1 825	24	29
	2	2	2	29	20	0	0	0	0
	3	25	40	2 423	5 306	1	1	1	1
Medicine	1	76	64	10 709	9 969	1 498	2 094	14	21
	2	5	3	160	146	0	0	0	0
	3	69	91	13 508	14 339	1	1	1	1

Courses in theology, law and medicine are naturally graduate courses and will eventually be maintained as such by leading universities. It is believed, however, that it would not be advisable or even desirable for the state to make graduation from college the minimum requirement in general education for degrees even in these faculties. High school graduation is sufficient for the minimum state requirement. Anything farther than this should be left to individual initiative.[2]

[1] Not reported.

[2] There are few graduate students in dentistry, pharmacy or veterinary medicine. In library science, however, which under New York's leadership will develop rapidly throughout the United States, a thorough college training will soon be the usual requirement of all strong schools for admission to the professional course. In 1900 for example all but two of the entering class of 31 at the New York state library school are graduates of colleges or universities registered as maintaining proper standards. In public accounting which was raised by New York to the dignity of a profession in 1896 the New York requirement of a full four years' high school course will doubtless be accepted generally as the standard in preliminary general education. Additional requirements in New York for full C. P. A. (certified public accountant) certificates are three years' satisfactory experience in the practice of accounting (one of which has been in the office of an

Length of professional courses —The following table shows as a rule great progress, specially since 1885, in the adoption of higher standards for graduation.

	Four years	Three years	Two years	One year	Not stated
Theological schools 1875...................	26	77	9	0	11
" 1885....................	26	98	6	0	22
" 1897....................	22	116	7	1	11
" 1898....................	[1]20	117	8	0	10
" 1899....................	[2]41	116	7	1	0
Law schools 1875...................	0	1	30	10	2
" 1885....................	0	5	38	6	0
" 1897....................	0	21	47	7	2
" 1898....................	0	38	36	4	5
" 1899....................	0	44	37	4	1
Medical schools 1875...................	0	[3]3	[3]72	5	0
" 1885....................	0	5	103	0	0
" 1897....................	99	49	0	2	0
" 1898....................	103	42	0	0	[4]6
" 1899....................	141	10	2	2	1
Dental schools 1875..................	0	0	12	0	0
" 1885....................	0	5	13	0	0
" 1897....................	1	47	0	0	0
" 1898....................	1	49	0	0	0
" 1899....................	1	55	0	0	0
Schools of pharmacy 1875...................	0	0	10	3	1
" 1885....................	0	0	21	0	0
" 1897....................	0	5	34	2	2
" 1898....................	1	5	35	4	0
" 1899....................	[5]1	6	38	7	0
Veterinary medical schools 1897...................	0	10	2	0	0
" 1898....................	0	12	2	0	0
" 1899....................	0	14	3	0	0

expert public accountant) and examinations in the theory of accounts, practical accounting, auditing and commercial law. Pennsylvania has a C. P. A. law, and attempts have been made to secure similar legislation in Illinois, Maryland, New Jersey and Minnesota.

[1] Including 4 schools that report courses of five years.

[2] Including 17 schools that report courses of more than four years.

[3] Distinction between medical schools with two and three-year courses not certain.

[4] Including 3 medical preparatory schools.

[5] Department of pharmacy, University of Washington, which has suspended temporarily.

Professional schools now remain in session for a much greater part of the year than formerly:

Length of courses in months, 1899

	Unknown or less than 6	6–7	7–8	8–9	9–10	More than 10	Total
Theology...............	0	3	37	57	54	14	165
Law...................	1	2	6	52	21	4	86
Medicine...............	10	74	45	21	6	0	156
Dentistry...............	12	24	11	4	5	0	56
Pharmacy.....	5	16	11	10	5	5	52
Veterinary medicine	5	5	2	4	1	0	17
Total	33	124	112	148	92	23	532

Evening sessions occur less frequently:

	Day sessions	Evening sessions	Both	Unknown	Total
Law	49	24	7	6	86
Medicine.................	135	5	9	7	156
Dentistry	47	4	0	5	56
Pharmacy	36	9	4	3	52
Veterinary medicine..........	7	0	3	7	17
Total	274	42	23	28	367

University supervision — As long as the public had practically no protection from incompetency in professional practice independent proprietary schools flourished. With proper restrictive legislation such institutions will either die or fall under university supervision.

Many professional schools not under university supervision show a self-sacrificing zeal for high standards and an absence of the commercial spirit that might well be emulated by all institutions connected with colleges or universities. Nevertheless independent institutions are realizing more than ever before the disadvantages of working without university privileges and tend more and more toward university connections or university relations.

In 1899, 257 schools were separate institutions and 275 were departments of colleges or universities as follows :

	Separate institutions	Departments	Total
Theology.....................................	119	46	165
Law.....	16	70	86
Medicine..........	82	74	156
Dentistry.........	20	36	56
Pharmacy.............................	14	38	52
Veterinary medicine	6	11	17
Total............................	257	275	532

Scholarships — Theological seminaries, when not endowed, are supported by funds from the denominations they represent. Tuition is generally free, and in many cases board and lodging are furnished. Additional help is given usually when needed, and generous scholarships are the rule. In other professional schools scholarships are comparatively rare. The 1895 U. S. education report gives 40 law school scholarships and 295[1] medical school scholarships. The largest, offered by College of physicians and surgeons, New York, pays $700 a year and is bestowed to promote the discovery of new facts in medical science.

An examination of 82 law school catalogues for 1899 shows that 48 scholarships are offered definitely. Tuition is free at the law department of Howard university, the law departments of the universities of Kansas, Texas and West Virginia. The Harvard law school and the Boston university law school offer a "limited number of free scholarships." Law students may compete for the 150 state scholarships and the 18 university scholarships offered annually at Cornell and for the 50 city scholarships offered by the University of Pennsylvania. The law department of Centre college offers free tuition to sons of ministers and to all young men of limited means and good character. 3 schools give fellowships annually as follows : New York law school,

[1] "Many of these are not scholarships in a strict sense."— *U. S. education report*, 1895

1 at $500 a year, good for from one to three years; Law department University of Pennsylvania, 1 at $300, good for one year; Pittsburg law school, 1 at $250, good for one year. 32 schools offer cash prizes amounting to $3010 and law and reference books as other prizes.

151 medical school catalogues for 1899 report definitely only 152 scholarships and 11 fellowships. These are offered by 31 schools. 5 other schools refer indefinitely to scholarships. At Cornell and the University of Pennsylvania medical students may compete for state and university, or city scholarships on an equal footing with those who would enter other departments. Tuition is free at the Army medical school, the medical department of the University of Texas and the medical preparatory school of the University of Kansas. 19 schools give cash prizes amounting to $5685; 57 offer hospital appointments as prizes; 47 give gold medals, surgical instruments and other prizes.

56 dental school catalogues for 1899 show that 7 schools offer 58 scholarships.[1] The dental department of the University of Maryland deducts one half from tuition fees of one student from each state on recommendation of his state dental society. The Baltimore college of dental surgery had similar beneficiary scholarships till 1898 when they were abolished. 18 schools offer prizes but their value is not great.

52 catalogues of schools of pharmacy for 1899 show that 5 schools offer 12 scholarships and 2 fellowships. Tuition is free at the schools of pharmacy connected with the Alabama polytechnic institute, Washington agricultural college, Purdue university, and the universities of Kansas, Ohio, Oklahoma, Texas, Washington and Wisconsin. 15 schools offer prizes, usually medals or pharmaceutic instruments. 5 of these 15 schools give cash prizes amounting to $620. The committee on revision of the *U. S. pharmacopœia* has instituted fellowships in the University of Michigan and the University of Wisconsin for the discovery of new facts in pharmacy.

---
[1] See section on Subjects discussed in dentistry.

16 veterinary school catalogues for 1899 show that 19 scholarships are offered by 5 schools, that 1 school gives a fellowship and that 6 schools offer prizes. Tuition is free at the veterinary departments of Cornell and Ohio universities, and of Washington agricultural college. Cornell opens to competition by veterinary students, 18 scholarships and to veterinary graduates a fellowship of an annual value of $500. Veterinary matriculates are eligible for 50 city scholarships offered by the University of Pennsylvania. The veterinary department of Ohio state university offers a scholarship in each county in which the agricultural scholarship is not taken.

Fees — Tuition is free in 132 theological schools. Only 8 have matriculation fees, 33 a course fee and 34 other fees. The average matriculation fee is $5.38, the average course fee $91.61, the average of other fees $22.06.

Tuition is free in 4 law schools. 23 have matriculation fees (average $14), 83 have course fees (average $69.80), 59 have other fees (average $10.86).

Tuition is free in 3 medical schools. 119 have matriculation fees (average $10.68), 153 have course fees (average $82.39), 129 have other fees (average $49.47).

Tuition is not free in any dental school. 40 have matriculation fees (average $8.62), 56 have course fees (average $94.32), 5 have other fees (average $33.48).

Tuition is free in 9 schools of pharmacy. 28 have matriculation fees (average $8.07), 43 have course fees (average $58.90), 50 have other fees (average $37.90).

Tuition is free in 3 veterinary medical schools. 7 have matriculation fees (average $7.85), 14 have course fees (average $81.28), 12 have other fees (average $43.50).

Libraries — In 1898 the U. S. commissioner of education reported 1,360,720 volumes in libraries of 118 theological schools, 243,054 in libraries of 47 law schools, 151,433 in libraries of 72 medical schools, 6901 in libraries of 16 dental schools, 22,156 in libraries of 17 schools of pharmacy. 3 theological schools, 9 law schools, 21 medical schools, 9 dental schools and 2 schools of pharmacy reported that they had no libraries. 34 theological schools, 27 law schools, 58 medical schools, 25 dental schools and 26 schools of pharmacy made no report on this item. Libraries in veterinary medical schools were not reported.

Following were the largest libraries:

Theology

	Volumes
Union theological seminary, presbyterian.............	71 576
Hartford theological seminary, congregational	68 029
Princeton theological seminary, presbyterian..........	61 648
Andover theological seminary, congregational	51 000
Seminary of the Reformed Dutch church in America..	43 700

Law

Harvard university, law department..................	44 000
Cornell university, law department	26 000
Columbia university, law department	25 000
University of Pennsylvania, law department..........	18 904
Yale university, law department.....................	[1] 12 000

Medicine

Hahnemann medical college, Philadelphia	15 000
Hahnemann medical college, Chicago	12 000
University of Michigan, homeopathic medical dep't...	10 000
University of Pennsylvania, medical department......	10 000
Johns Hopkins medical school......................	7 712

Dentistry

Marion Sims college of medicine, dental department...	[2] 2 000
Ohio medical university, dental department...........	[3] 2 000
University of Michigan, dental department...........	[1] 600

Pharmacy

Philadelphia college of pharmacy....................	10 000
Massachusetts college of pharmacy..................	[1] 5 132
University of Illinois, department of pharmacy.... ..	1 800

[1] Approximate.
[2] Only one library for medical and dental dep'ts.
[3] Only one library for medical, dental and pharmacy dep'ts.

Endowments—The 1898 U. S. education report gives the following :

84 theological schools report endowments of $17,977,325. 54 do not report this item. 17 state that they are not endowed.

19 medical schools report endowments of $1,906,072. (In 1897, 14 medical schools reported endowments of $648,262.) 84 do not report this item. 48 state that they are not endowed.

8 law schools report endowments of $752,500. The law department of the University of Cincinnati reports also an endowment that yields an income of $7500. (In 1897, 4 law schools reported endowments of $431,000.) 48 do not report this item. 27 report that they are not endowed.

1 dental school, the Harvard dental school, reports an endowment of $50,000. 20 report that they are not endowed. 29 do not report this item.

2 schools of pharmacy, the Massachusetts college of pharmacy ($13,675) and the Albany college of pharmacy ($2381) report endowments of $16,056. 17 report that they are not endowed. 26 do not report this item.

Following were the largest endowments :

Theology

Princeton theological seminary, presbyterian........	$1 369 000
Union theological seminary, presbyterian...........	[1] 1 350 000
General theological seminary, protestant episcopal...	1 260 987
Chicago theological seminary, congregational	968 820
Andover theological seminary, congregational.......	850 000

Law

Harvard university, law department................	400 000
University of California, law department...........	135 000
Catholic university of America, law department.....	[2] 100 000

Medicine

Columbia university, medical department...........	480 000
Johns Hopkins medical school.................. ..	427 000
Woman's medical college of Pennsylvania	296 772
Yale university, medical department..............	106 000

[1] 1897.   [2] Approximate.

Value of grounds and buildings — The 1898 U. S. education report gives the following values of grounds and buildings :

98 theological schools, $13,863,628.   54 do not report this item.   3 report that they do not own grounds or buildings.

19 law schools, $1,431,000.   58 do not report this item. 6 report that they do not own grounds or buildings.

96 medical schools, [1]$11,264,263.   53 do not report this item.   2 report that they do not own grounds or buildings.

15 dental schools, [2]$1,019,836.   30 do not report this item.   5 report that they do not own grounds or buildings.

15 schools of pharmacy, $656,417.   25 do not report this item.   5 report that they do not own grounds or buildings.

The following report the greatest values in grounds and buildings :

Theology

General theological seminary, protestant episcopal ..	$1 353 000
St Joseph's seminary, Roman catholic	1 100 000
Western theological seminary, presbyterian	780 055
Princeton theological seminary, presbyterian	500 000
Union theological seminary, presbyterian	500 000

Law

University of Cincinnati, law department	350 000
Boston university law school	225 000
Harvard university, law department	150 000
New York university, law department	120 000
Vanderbilt university, law department	100 000

Medicine

Columbia university, medical department	2 000 000
Jefferson medical college	600 000
Hahnemann medical college, Philadelphia	523 763
Cooper medical college	460 000
New York homeopathic medical college	450 000

[1] In 1897, 93 schools reported $7,271,009.
[2] In 1897, 13 schools reported $627,500.

Dentistry

Baltimore medical college, dental department.......	[1] 200 000
Philadelphia dental college.......................	170 000
New York college of dentistry....................	120 000
Detroit college of medicine, dental department	[2] 105 336
Pennsylvania college of dental surgery.............	70 000

Pharmacy

New York college of pharmacy	204 067
Philadelphia college of pharmacy.................	150 000
Northwestern university, school of pharmacy.......	[3] 75 000
Massachusetts college of pharmacy................	68 850
Maryland college of pharmacy....................	37 000

When grounds and buildings are used for several departments, as for example the Columbia law school which is in the library building, values are not always reported.

Total and average property, receipts and expenditures in 1898 — It is interesting to compare with the preceding figures those given in *Professional education in the United States :*

Total

	Schools	Property	Schools	Receipts	Schools	Expenditures
Theology	87	$27 785 997	76	$1 561 516	83	$1 420 921
Law	27	3 053 265	31	565 295	33	540 887
Medicine........	126	15 346 030	111	2 185 216	111	2 022 503
Dentistry	19	1 150 915	23	459 996	22	421 689
Pharmacy	19	981 932	13	167 098	13	173 994
Veterinary med..	8	426 697	8	86 598	8	89 604
	286	$48 744 836	262	$5 025 719	270	$4 669 598

Average

	Property	Receipts	Expenditures
Theology..........	$319 379 27	$20 546 26	$17 119 53
Law..............................	113 083 88	18 235 32	16 390 52
Medicine	137 666 90	19 686 63	18 220 74
Dentistry.......................	60 574 47	19 999 82	19 167 68
Pharmacy.	51 680 63	12 853 69	13 384 15
Veterinary medicine....................	53 337 12	10 824 75	11 200 50

[1] Cost of medical and dental buildings; dental buildings and grounds cost less than $75,000. [2] Includes medical and pharmacy dep'ts. [3] Reported in *Professional education in the United States*, $24,000.

Gifts and bequests — The following made up from Appleton's *Annual cyclopedia* shows the amount of gifts and
bequests for educational purposes (including hospitals), of
$5000 each and upward in value for each year from 1894
to 1898. The extraordinary total of $110,952,199 is divided
as follows : theological schools $1,918,500, law schools
$127,500, medical schools $2,631,000, hospitals $16,593,701,
libraries $14,143,888, general education $75,537,610.[1]

Year	Theology	Law	Medicine		Libraries	Gen. educ.	Total
			Schools	Hospitals			
1894	$554 000	$12 500	$126 000	$1 911 000	$3 927 721	$11 681 262	$18 212 483
1895	570 000	....	755 000	2 722 367	3 602 667	10 817 255	18 467 289
1896	305 000	....	....	5 096 667	2 197 000	13 894 058	21 492 725
1897	244 500	115 000	....	3 394 167	2 341 000	21 224 166	27 318 833
1898	245 000	....	1 750 000	3 469 500	2 075 500	17 920 869	25 460 869
	$1 918 500	$127 500	$2 631 000	$16 593 701	$14 143 888	$75 537 610	$110 952 199

Women as professional students — The 1898 U. S. education report shows that women now appear as students in
professional schools of each class except those in veterinary
medicine. In nursing they are of course in a large majority,
8004 as compared with 801 men. In the other professions
they are reported as follows : theology 198, law 147, medicine 1397, dentistry 162, pharmacy 174. The proportion of
women in regular medical schools is much smaller than in
homeopathic, eclectic and physiomedical schools, showing
that women prefer the medical sects.

---

[1] Including the most notable gifts and bequests for all public purposes the
grand total for these five years is $174,800,000. The ordinary denominational
contributions for educational and benevolent purposes, all state and municipal
appropriations to public and sectarian institutions and the grants of congress for
the relief of suffering in Cuba are excluded.

The following table made up from *Professional education
in the United States* gives the division of professional
schools by sex in 1899 :

SCHOOLS	Men	Women	Both	Total
Theology	101	0	64	165
Law	22	0	64	86
Medicine	69	7	80	156
Dentistry	12	0	44	56
Pharmacy	4	0	48	52
Veterinary medicine	14	0	3	17

Power to confer degrees — Low standards in many professional schools are due to a failure to subject the degree-conferring power to strict state supervision.   In New York and
Pennsylvania the laws now prevent an abuse of the power
to confer degrees.[1]   In Massachusetts and Vermont bodies
formed under the general corporation acts are prohibited
from conferring degrees.   In Ohio and Nebraska the statutes require only the nominal endowment of $5000 for a
degree-conferring institution.   In other states and territories
as a rule any body of men may form an educational corporation with power to confer degrees " without any guaranty
whatever that the privilege will not be abused." [2]

This matter has been under discussion recently in various
educational bodies and there is a strong sentiment in favor
of a strict supervision by the state of the degree-conferring
power.[3]

[1] A similar bill, strongly advocated by educators, was defeated at the last session of the Illinois legislature through the efforts of politicians and others in
favor of low standards.

[2] Edward Avery Harriman, *Educational franchise* (R. Am. bar. ass., 1898).

[3] In 1897 the section of legal education of the American bar association resolved
that the degree-conferring power should be " subject to strict state supervision
to be exercised in a manner somewhat similar to that which is exercised by the
regents of the University of the State of New York."   In an address before the
National educational association in 1897, Pres. Henry Wade Rogers said: " There
should be established in each state a council of education, which should be
intrusted with powers similar to those vested in the regents of the University
of the State of New York, and it should be composed of the most eminent men
in the state without any reference to political considerations.   No degree-conferring institution should be incorporated without the approval of the council of
education."

2 THEOLOGY

Schools, faculty and students — In the United States there
is no connection between church and state. Each religious
denomination establishes such theological schools as may be
required. In 1899 the 165 schools had 1070 instructors and
8093 students. 2 schools were nonsectarian, and the rest
were distributed among 23 religious denominations in the
order of students for 1899 as follows :[1]

DENOMINATIONS	SCHOOLS 1899	FACULTY 1899	STUDENTS 1898	1898 Grad.	1899
1 Roman catholic....................	29	222	1 635	330	1 700
2 Baptist.....	16	102	1 286	171	1 142
3 Presbyterian......................	17	125	1 066	283	1 034
4 Methodist episcopal.....	19	107	1 005	166	981
5 Evang. Lutheran...................	17	73	876	234	851
6 Congregational	12	108	556	133	492
7 Protestant episcopal...............	14	92	460	87	430
8 Christian	8	41	429	40	424
9 Reformed church..................	6	51	180	59	188
10 Lutheran........................	5	19	142	39	143
11 United presbyterian..............	3	10	129	45	121
12 Hebrew.........................	2	15	92	8	104
13 Moravian (United brethren)........	2	11	81	23	92
14 Nonsectarian	2	19	73	7	72
15 Cumberland presbyterian..........	1	7	65	11	65
16 Universalist.....................	3	24	61	18	54
17 Methodist protestant..........	2	6	35	0	51
18 Evangelical association...........	1	2	34	9	44
19 African methodist episcopal.......	1	5	37	5	37
20 Unitarian.......................	1	16	18	4	26
21 Reformed presbyterian............	1	2	28	9	20
22 New Jerusalem..................	1	6	12	2	13
23 Associate reform presbyterian	1	4	14	10	7
24 Seventh day baptist..............	1	3	3	0	2
Total......................	165	1 070	8 317	1 693	8 093

[1] The U. S. census report for 1890 gives 119 denominations associated in ecclesiastical groups (18,841,790 members), 24 which are not thus associated and some
independent miscellaneous congregations (1,771,016 members). The 119 denominations are arranged according to number of communicants as follows:

1 R. catholic (7) [See chart]	6 257 871	8 United brethren (2)	225 281
2 Methodist (17)	4 589 284	9 Latter-day saint (2)	166 125
3 Baptist (13)	3 712 468	10 Hebrew (2)	130 496
4 Presbyterian (12)	1 278 332	11 Friend (4)	107 208
5 Lutheran (16)	1 231 072	12 Christian (2)	103 722
6 Episcopalian (2)	540 509	13 Dunkard (4)	73 795
7 Reformed (3)	309 458	14 Adventist (6)	60 491

Theological schools in 1899

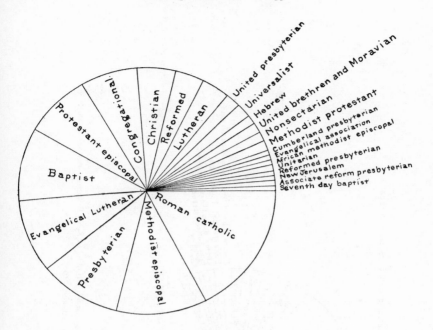

Theological students in 1899

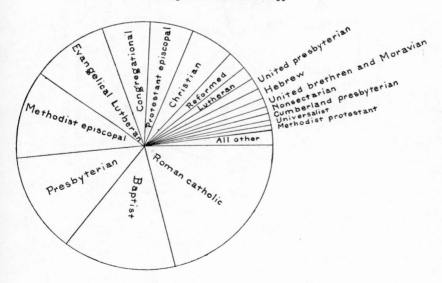

Membership of leading religions, U. S. census 1890

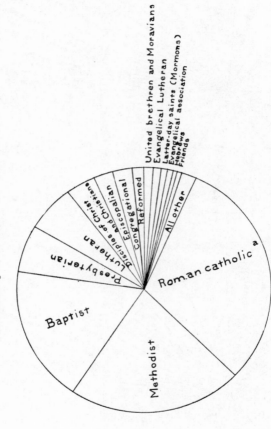

a Includes also Russian orthodox (13,504) Greek catholic (10,850) Reformed catholic (1000), Old catholic (665), Armenian (335), Greek orthodox (100)

In 1878 there were 125 schools with 4320 students. The growth in students in 21 years has been 87 per cent.

The seminaries have increased their requirements steadily so that all the great divisions of theology are now represented in their faculties. In 1899, 1 school had a course of 7 years, 10 a course of 6 years, 6 a course of 5 years, 24 a course of 4 years, 116 a course of 3 years, 7 a course of 2 years and 1 a course of 1 year. 73 grant degrees.

Early theological training — The rise of independent seminaries marked the second step in the development of theological education in this country. A desire to educate candidates for the ministry had influenced the founding of colleges at a much earlier period. In fact our first institutions for higher education owed their origin to this desire. The chief object in the founding of Harvard college (1636) for example was to provide an educated ministry. Cotton Mather in his *Magnalia Christi Americana* gives a list of New England churches in 1696 which shows that of 129 pulpits supplied by 116 pastors, 107 of the clergymen were graduates of Harvard college. The colleges founded at New Haven (1700) and at Princeton (1748) followed Harvard in making education free to candidates for the ministry who could not meet their own expenses.

In England candidates for the ministry usually pursued a university course which included several studies that bore on their future calling. In addition to the college degree they were examined on certain theological books which they

---

| 15 Mennonite (12) | 41 541 | 17 Communistic societies (8) | 4 049 |
| 16 Plymouth Brethren (4) | 6 661 | 18 (River) Brethren (3) | 3 427 |

The independent sects may be classified as follows:

Disciple of Christ	641 051	Universalist	49 194
Congregationalist	512 771	Spiritualist	45 030
Evang. Lutheran	223 588	Moravian	11 781
Evang. association	133 313	New Jerusalem	7 095
Unitarian	67 749	Other	79 444

[Estimates revised to April 1, 1898 give total communicants 26,054,385; Roman catholics (7) 8,410,592, methodists (17) 5,735,898, baptists (13) 4,232,962.]

H. D. Sedgwick jr in the October 1899 *Atlantic monthly* writes that the proportion of Roman catholics to the whole population in 1783 was 1 in 80, in 1829, 1 in 16, in 1844, 1 in 15, in 1890, 1 in 10.

had read either in private or with the assistance of a preceptor. This same scheme was followed in this country in the 17th and 18th centuries. The college faculty included as a rule a professor of Hebrew and a professor of theology and their work was supplemented by the study of theological books either in private or under the oversight of an experienced clergyman.

Rise of independent seminaries — At the close of the 18th century the colleges had departed so far from the special purpose of their creation that it was thought necessary to establish theological seminaries. For more than half a century private theological schools had been in existence. Dr Joseph Bellamy of Connecticut conducted the first of these institutions that attained distinction and some of his graduates opened other similar schools. The theological seminary proper, however, had its origin in this country in the closing years of the 18th century. In England when the universities were closed to those outside of the established church, new institutions sprang up but these included academic as well as theological courses. In this country the seminaries "became a supplement to the college, not a substitute as in England." Undoubtedly the desire to have schools in which their special religious doctrines might be taught influenced the denominations in America that had no secular colleges to found their own theological seminaries, but the necessity for the more definite and systematic training of the theological schools seems to have been felt by all.

The history of the existing institutions that are specially devoted to preparation for the ministry is limited with three exceptions to the present century. The Seminary of the reformed Dutch church in America was founded in 1784. In that year Drs Livingston and Meyer were set apart to be professors of theology and the method of training men for the ministry by any individual pastor whom the student might select was formally discontinued. The succession of classes since 1784 has been continuous with the exception of two or three years. These years were not consecutive so that the work of the professors has been continuous. This work was done first in New York, then at Flatbush, L. I. and since 1810 at New Brunswick, N. J.

St Mary's seminary was founded at Baltimore in 1791 and is under the direction of members of the Society of St Sulpice. Xenia theological seminary is the result of the consolidation in 1874 of the Seminary of the northwest with the Associate seminary at Xenia. The Theological seminary of the associate presbyterian church of North America was located originally at Service, Beaver co. Pa. in 1794, when Dr John Anderson was elected professor of theology by the Associate synod. In 1821 the seminary was transferred to Cannonsburg, Pa. and in 1855 to Xenia, Ohio.

In 1782 the Associate reformed synod was formed by the union of the Associate presbyteries and the Reformed presbyteries. Those who refused to accept this union established the Theological seminary of the associate presbyterian church of North America at Service, Beaver co. Pa. The Associate reformed synod opened a theological seminary in New York in 1805.

In 1808 New England congregationalists united in opening the theological school at Andover. In 1812 the General assembly of the presbyterian church founded the Princeton theological seminary. In 1815 Hartwick seminary, the oldest Lutheran theological school in this country, was opened in Otsego co. N. Y. In 1817 the General convention of the protestant episcopal church established the General theological seminary in New York where instruction was first given in 1819. The seminary was removed to New Haven in 1820 but was reopened in New York in 1822. In 1820 the Baptist education society opened Hamilton theological seminary, the first theological school established by baptists in the United States, since 1893 a department of Colgate university. The Reformed church in the United States founded the theological seminary at Carlisle, Pa. in 1825. In 1839 the methodists founded their first theological seminary " in commemoration of the first centennial of ecumenical methodism." The institution was opened in 1840 at Newbury, Vt., was removed to Concord, N. H. in 1847, to Boston in 1867 and became in 1871 the theological department of Boston university.

Of the 165 existing theological schools 3 were established before 1800, 18 between 1801 and 1825, 25 between 1826 and 1850, 72 between 1851 and 1875, 47 between 1876 and 1900. When the necessity of systematic training for the ministry was recognized theological schools were established. The multiplication of these schools, however, is due to some extent to differences of opinion touching matters pertaining to the Christian faith. When men can not think alike even in details that seem trivial they split frequently into sects which sometimes found theological seminaries to teach their own peculiar views. In an interesting paper on the causes and remedy of the disunion of Christendom the rector of St Andrew's, Rochester, expresses the opinion that the purpose of the church to discipline life, to make men pure and just and kind is often lost sight of in an effort to secure intellectual agreement concerning the most abstruse and difficult subjects that the human mind can entertain. Bishop Whipple of Minnesota emphasizes the other side of this picture as follows : " Never in the world's history has there been such enthusiasm in all humanitarian work as now. Not even in the primitive church have greater victories been won in leading heathen folk to Christian civilization."

Religious bodies vary greatly with regard to the training deemed essential for the ministry. The training of the Roman catholic priest for example begins normally at about the age of 12 when the candidate is secluded in many ways from contact with secular life, living and working constantly under ecclesiastical supervision. On the other hand the protestant candidate for the ministry is usually free to choose his teachers, studies and associates, and he does not begin his special training till he has finished his general education and entered the theological school. Again episcopalians, presbyterians and congregationalists for example have exacted as a rule a comparatively good general and professional education. The methodists on the other hand have not laid so much stress on intellectual training. They did not open a theological school till 1840 and even in 1899 the methodist seminaries did not report so many students as the presbyterian though in the United States there were probably about four times as many methodists as presbyterians. Almost from the date of their organization, however, the methodists have maintained a scheme of systematic theological examinations, and recently progress has been made toward a more thorough training. They now supervise with special care the scholastic work of their higher institutions of learning.

It is commonly asserted that many theological seminaries notwithstanding their comparatively high admission requirements do not maintain the educational standards required by other professional schools, and that students in these seminaries are seldom dropped through failure to reach a satisfactory intellectual standing. As the Rev. W. F. Whitaker of Albany says, however, we should not overlook the fundamental difference between theology and other professions. Physical disease demands everywhere the same skill but intellectual training necessary for the cure and care of souls varies with varying needs.

University relations — Some theologians magnify the advantages that arise from the pursuit of a common purpose in independent seminaries. In their judgment these seminaries accomplish much more thorough work in theology than that done for example at Oxford and Cambridge. Other writers emphasize the fact that " the theologian needs the contact of other minds just as do other specialists," and that it is a mistake to divorce the study of theology from that of the other sciences. In the United States the seminaries long restricted the study of theology to candidates for the ministry ; laymen neglected this field almost entirely and theologians on the other hand were narrowed by the seclusion of the seminary.

The work of independent theological schools is of course much more thorough than that which the secular colleges attempted with the aid of individual clergymen, but the isolation of these schools is a disadvantage when we compare them with some of the great universities abroad in which theology is the leading faculty.

The recognition of this fact marked the third step in the development of theological education in this country. In 1819 Harvard[1] and in 1822 Yale[2] organized separate theological faculties. In 1899, 46 colleges and universities had theological faculties, and 13 independent schools had entered into such relations with neighboring universities that their students were able to enjoy many university privileges. These friendly relations now exist, even between different denominations. The Episcopal theological school at Cambridge, Mass. has for example many of the advantages offered by Harvard university, the Episcopal divinity school at Philadelphia shares advantages offered by the University of Pennsylvania, the Union theological seminary in New York those afforded to the students of Columbia and New York universities.

Present tendencies— Dr C. A. Briggs wrote as follows on theological education in 1892 :

" The course in theology is still very defective in the great majority of the theological schools . . . but no one can deny real and great progress . . . The backbone of theological training is still Hebrew exegesis, Greek exegesis, church history, systematic theology, pastoral theology and homiletics . . . The scientific method is beginning to revolutionize theological education; but this movement is only in its beginnings."

In recent years there has been a tendency to extend the elective system in seminary courses. Some theologians contend that these courses should be entirely elective ; others,

[1] The first professorship established in the university was the Hollis professorship of divinity, established in 1721. The differentiation of the divinity school from the college was very gradual.

[2] The chair of divinity was established in 1755.

that they should require a symmetric training in all fundamental branches, and that the choice of studies should be
limited to those that are demanded by special tastes or by
special lines of work.

In an essay on the education of protestant ministers, published in the *Princeton review* in 1883, and republished in
1898 in *Educational reform*, President Eliot gives the following suggestions touching this matter :

" The subjects which in our day should be set before a
candidate for the ministry are divisible into two classes :
those which every candidate should master, and those from
which every candidate should make a limited selection.
. . . The preliminary subjects which every student of
theology should in my judgment be required to master are as
follows :

1 Languages : Greek (including New testament Greek),
Latin, Hebrew and German

2 English literature, with practice in writing, and study of
style

3 The elements of psychology

4 The elements of political economy

5 Constitutional history, or the history of some interesting period of moderate length

6 Science : botany, zoology, or geology, studied in the
laboratory and the field.

The requisitions in the languages other than English are
the only ones in this list which are now habitually enforced
in theological seminaries."

. . .

" Having finished the preliminary required studies, the
candidate for the ministry is ready to enter upon the advanced
studies which may properly be called professional.   Since
preaching is to be his most important function, he will naturally give a good share of his time to homiletics and the
practice of writing and speaking.   The other subjects which
are now included under the comprehensive term 'theology'
or 'divinity' may be grouped as follows :

1 Semitic studies : linguistic, archeologic and historical
2 New testament criticism and exegesis
3 Ecclesiastical history
4 Comparative religion or historic religions compared
5 Psychology, ethics, and the philosophy of religion
6 Systematic theology, and the history of Christian doctrine
7 Charitable and reformatory methods, and the contest of Christian society with licentiousness, intemperance, pauperism and crime."

.   .   .

"Any three of these seven groups thoroughly studied, in addition to homiletics and the preliminary required studies, would in my judgment give a far better training for the protestant ministers of our day than is now offered in any theological seminary in my knowledge."

In this essay Pres. Eliot deals only "with the surroundings and mental furnishing of the minister, not with his inspiration." He does not maintain that there is no need of uneducated ministers or that men of genius are dependent on systematic training or that "sensibility, earnestness and piety" are not the most essential qualities. He does say, however, that men of genius are rare and that it is not the business of universities and theological seminaries to provide "uninstructed exhorters."

3 LAW

Early law schools — The first American law school was founded at Litchfield, Ct. in 1784 and discontinued in 1833. Though not connected with any university it seems to have made an excellent record. Of 1023 graduates, 50 became members of congress, 15 U. S. senators, 40 judges of the higher state courts, 10 governors of states, 5 cabinet officers, 2 justices of the federal supreme court, 1 vice-president of the United States and several foreign ministers.

A course of lectures in law was delivered in the College of Philadelphia in 1791 by James Wilson who had been appointed professor of law in that institution, but his work was discontinued before the close of the second course. In 1797 James Kent made a similar attempt at Columbia, but he gave only one course of lectures.

The Harvard law school, established in 1817, was the earliest school in the country connected with a university and authorized to confer degrees in law. The course was lengthened to 3 years in 1877. There were no examinations for the degree till 1871, and none for admission till 1877. At the beginning of the year 1897 the rule came into force by which only graduates of approved colleges and persons qualified to enter the senior class of Harvard college are admitted as regular students.

The Yale law school was established in 1824, that of the University of Virginia in 1825 and the Cincinnati law school in 1833.

Development of law schools since 1858 — Law schools had exercised little influence on the legal profession in this country up to the time of the opening of the Columbia law school in 1858. The extinct Litchfield school and the unsuccessful attempts at the college of Philadelphia and Columbia constitute the record up to 1800. 3 of the existing schools were established between 1801 and 1825, 7 between 1826 and 1850, 24 between 1851 and 1875, 50 between 1876 and 1900. The growth of the Columbia law school was quite

steady from the first. In 1859 there were 35 students, in
1876, 573, in 1889, 491. In 1888 the trustees decided to
add a third year to the course to take effect in the fall of
1890. In 1899 they adopted a resolution converting the
school into a graduate department by limiting admission to
college graduates, the change to take effect in the fall of
1903.

Since 1858 the growth in law schools has been most
remarkable. In 1878 there were 50 schools with 3012 students; in 1899 there were 86 schools with 11,883 students.
The increase in students in 21 years has been 294 per cent.
These figures show that the old method of study in the
office of an attorney is rapidly giving place to the systematic
training of the law school. In fact it is impracticable under
existing conditions to obtain a satisfactory legal education
in an attorney's office.[1]

The greatest drawback to efficient work in our law schools
as shown elsewhere, is failure to demand a satisfactory preliminary education for admission. There has been rapid
growth in the belief that the course of study entitling students to the LL. B. degree can not be covered properly in
less than three years. The president of Western reserve
university, Charles F. Thwing writes as follows: "The progress of professional education in the U. S. receives illustration in the fact that a fourth year is now frequently
spoken of as a demand of the law school.[2] Many law
schools are now doing four years' work in three years, and
certain schools are doing three years' work in two years.
The best schools have increased their courses of study from
two years to three, and as they have increased the length of
time they have also increased the number and amount of
the studies."

[1] The ratio of lawyers to population in 1870 was 1 to 946, in 1890 it was 1 to 699.
These figures show a growth somewhat out of proportion to the growth in population, but not by any means as great comparatively as the growth in students
(1870, 1653; 1890, 4518). The explanation is simple. Only students in law schools
have been reported, not those prepared for the bar elsewhere.

[2] The law department of West Virginia university requires four years' work for
LL.B. degree after July 1, 1899.

In 1875 only 1 law school had a course of three years. In 30 schools the course was two years, in 10 one year, in 2 the length of the course was not stated. In 1899, 44 schools had a three years' course, 37 a two years' course, 4 a one year's course. In 1 the length of the course was not stated. Of the 44 schools with three year's course 11 report an absolute requirement of three years' study in a law school for the LL. B. degree; 30 report three years' study in a law school as the regular requirement for the LL. B. degree.

Of the 86 law schools reporting in 1899, 16 are separate institutions and 70 are departments of colleges or universities; 49 hold day sessions, 24 evening sessions, 7 hold both and 6 do not report the item; 82 grant degrees.

Salaries of teachers — Charles Noble Gregory in a paper read before the American bar association in 1897 showed that of 349 law teachers in the United States, 75 or only about 1-5 gave their entire time to the work. The law teachers who received fixed salaries were as a rule somewhat more highly paid than teachers of other topics even in the same university. The report from Harvard law school was most complete. There we found a faculty of 9 men, all but 1 giving their entire time to the school. The salary of an assistant professor was $2250; of a professor $4000 during the first 5 years, $4500 during the next 5 years, and $5000 thereafter. The average salary of the teachers in American law schools who gave their full time to the work, including deans and assistants, was $2564.12. Replies from European law schools indicated that nearly three times as large a proportion of the law teachers gave their full time.

Methods of instruction — Instruction in law schools is given by lectures, by recitations from textbooks, and by discussion and explanation of selected cases. Each of these systems has its advocates. In a majority of the schools instruction is given mainly by lectures. Next in popularity comes the method of recitations on lessons previously assigned. There are only a few schools that depend mainly on the discussion and explanation of selected cases.

Dean Ashley of the New York university law school writes as follows on this subject : " The leading universities repudiate the idea of any fixed method for teaching or studying law." Professor Gray of Harvard says : " In all law schools, I suppose, the students learn from textbooks, cases and oral instruction. At any rate they do so here. Each teacher is free to use these means as he pleases. The different professors do actually use them in different ways and proportions." Dean Keener of Columbia says : " There is no uniform method of instruction in this school. Each instructor is at liberty to pursue the method of instruction which in his opinion will be productive of the best results. At the present time three methods of instruction are used."

The 1898 report of the committee on legal education of the American bar association gives returns from 20 law schools, including the leading schools of the country, on instruction in practice. 2 report that they depend principally on the observations which the students can make in attending actual courts; but in all others the practical importance of school instruction and of practice in moot courts is recognized. The committee recommends as the ideal plan of organization of a law faculty with reference to practical work that provision be made for a professor of pleading and practice, a thoroughly trained lawyer who shall devote his entire time to work of that kind.

Admission to the bar in colonial days — In early colonial days lawyers seem to have been regarded with jealousy and aversion. At the time of the revolution, however, they had gained a position of prominence which they have always maintained in this country. Of 56 signers of the declaration of independence 25 were lawyers and so were 30 out of 55 members of the convention which framed the federal constitution.[1]

There was no particular scheme of legal education in the colonial period but in most of the colonies there were statutes relating to attorneys. In North Carolina the following

[1] Statistics of J. H. Patton jr.

parliamentary provision was in force up to the revolutionary war :

" . . . None shall from henceforth be admitted attorneys in any of the king's courts of record . . . but such as have been brought up in said courts, or otherwise well practised in soliciting of causes, and have been found by their dealings to be skilful and of honest disposition . . ."

In Virginia in 1680 the licensing of attorneys was placed by the general assembly in the hands of the governor :

" . . . no Person or Persons whatsoever, shall practice as an Attorney or appear to plead in the General court, or any county-court in this countrey, but such as shall be first Licenced by his Excellency, or Successors thereunto, and . . . any one that shall presume to plead in the general court, or any county or other court without such licence first obtained, and had ; shall forfeit for every such offence committed in the county-court six hundred pounds of tobacco and in the General Court 2000 pounds of Tobacco."

This act was superseded in 1748 by what seems to be the earliest provision for an examining committee :

" The judges of the General Court shall nominate and appoint such and so many of the council learned in the Law and Attornies practicing in said Court as they shall think fit, to examine into the Capacity, Ability or Fitness of such persons as shall from time to time apply for a licence to practice as Attornies in the County courts and other inferior courts of this colony and shall cause such nomination and appointment to be entered in the Records of their Court ; which persons so nominated shall take oath that they will well and truly examine into the Capacity, Ability and Fitness of such persons as shall make application to them for a Licence to practice as Attornies and that they will not grant a Licence to any person who shall not upon examination to the best of their knowledge be found sufficiently qualified to practice as Attorney aforesaid."

In New Jersey any one was allowed to plead till 1698,

after which date attorneys were licensed by the governor. In Massachusetts, Rhode Island and New Hampshire an oath seems to have been all that was demanded of those seeking admission as attorneys. This was the case also in Delaware up to 1726.

The records of the secretary of state at Albany show that for 70 years just preceding the American revolution attorneys were admitted to practise in New York by the governor without any examination as to fitness, though for admission to practise before the supreme court the usual preparation was "a college or university education and three years' apprenticeship or, without the former, seven years' service under an attorney." [1]

In Connecticut attorneys were appointed by the county courts. In Maryland the justices admitted those whom the governor and council had previously licensed. In Pennsylvania attorneys were admitted by the justices; also in South Carolina till 1721, after which date they were admitted by the chief justice of the general and supreme court at Charleston. In all these cases tests as to fitness, if there were any such tests, seem to have been of a very superficial character.[2]

Admission to the bar after the revolution—The New York constitution of 1777 provided that "all attorneys, solicitors and councellors at law, hereafter to be appointed, be appointed by the Court and licensed by the first judge of the court in which they shall respectively plead or practice; and be regulated by the rules and orders of the said courts."

In 1797 the New York supreme court prescribed a seven years' clerkship with a practitioner as one of the requirements for admission as an attorney except in the case of those who after the age of 14 had pursued classical studies for four years or less, such applicants being permitted to deduct the time so occupied from the seven years' clerkship. After four years' practice the attorney was admitted without

---

[1] William Smith, *History of New York.*

[2] I am indebted to Mr Ashley of the New York state library school for assistance in the study of the colonial records.

further test as a counselor. These rules were modified in 1829 by requiring three years' practice as an attorney and a separate test for the degree of counselor. A few other states had similar requirements.

Under the rules that followed the adoption of the New York constitution of 1846 students were admitted to the bar without any requirements as to period of study or mode of training and without satisfactory evidence as to character. The same laxity prevailed in other states and the law came to be regarded more as an ordinary trade than as a distinct profession. This was the condition of legal education in 1870 when the bar is said to have reached its lowest ebb.

In 1880 most of the states had adopted a system of oral examinations for admission to the bar. These tests were usually held in open court. In about 3-5 of the states any ignoramus could present himself and if successful gain admission to practise before all state courts. The tests at best demanded little knowledge of legal principles; usually they were a farce. 15 states required a definite period of study; 6 gave an allowance in term of study to bachelors of arts; Pennsylvania and Delaware required a preliminary general education; women were admitted in 10 states.[1]

In 1871 admission to the bar in New York was placed under the control of the court of appeals. In 1882 the court adopted a rule requiring all law students unless college graduates to pass an examination as a test of preliminary general education. In 1894 the legislature provided for uniform examinations in all judicial districts, similar in essential features to those adopted in 1878 by the supreme court of New Hampshire. In the latter state from 1812 to 1872 a statute had provided as follows: "*Any* citizen of the age of 21 years, of good moral character, on application to the supreme court, *shall* be admitted to practise as an attorney."

The American bar association has recommended that

---

[1] In 1899 women are admitted definitely in 15 states and by inference in most political divisions. They seem to be excluded definitely only in Arkansas, Georgia and Indiana.

examinations for admission to the bar be conducted by a commission appointed by the court of last resort, according to the system now in force in New York, Ohio and Illinois. Boards with high standards seem to feel that written examinations afford the fairest test. Oral examinations are certainly impracticable when large classes are to be examined. An attempt is now made to select questions that require the application of legal principles to given facts. All progressive boards are abandoning the plan so prevalent in the past of limiting the tests to petty details and questions of local practice.

At the 1899 meeting of the American bar association, the acting president, Charles F. Manderson, spoke substantially as follows: A notable and encouraging sign of the times, presaging much good to the profession and benefit to the public, is the increased interest felt in the proceedings of the local bar associations. Nearly every state has an active, vigorous organization, and very many of the counties and judicial districts have their societies, composed of the best professional material of the vicinity. The standard of qualifications for admission to the bar has been materially elevated by these associations.

Synopsis of present requirements — In the following political divisions law-school diplomas do not now confer the right to practise law, an examination being required by statute in all cases :

Arizona	Indian ter.	Montana	Oregon
Arkansas	Choctaw nat.	New York	South Dakota
Colorado	Iowa	North Carolina	Utah
Florida	Kentucky	North Dakota	Virginia
Hawaii	Maine	Ohio	Washington
Idaho	Massachusetts	Oklahoma	Wyoming

The following require for admission to the licensing examination :

Colorado, one year high school, two years' clerkship or study in school

Iowa, two full years' study in office or reputable school

Maine, two years', after September 1900 three years' study in office or recognized school

Montana, two full years' study of law

New York, three years' high school course, college graduate two years', others three years' study in office or school

North Carolina, 12 months' professional study

North Dakota, two full years' study with practitioner in this state or in reputable school in U. S.

Ohio, a common school education, three full years' study with practising attorney or in school

Oregon, three years' study of law

Washington, two years' regular study of law

Wyoming, two years', after September 1900 three years' study in law school or office

The following require the licensing examination only:

Arizona	Idaho	Massachusetts	Tennessee
Arkansas	Indian ter.	Oklahoma	Utah
Florida	Choctaw nat.	Oregon	Virginia
Hawaii	Kentucky	South Dakota	

The 16 following states require either approval of law diploma or examination by duly qualified authority:

Alabama	Louisiana	Mississippi	Tennessee
California	Maryland	Missouri	Texas
Georgia	Michigan	Nebraska	West Virginia
Kansas	Minnesota	South Carolina	Wisconsin

The following requiring either approval of diploma or examination admit to examination on:

Kansas, two years' study, the last with attorney

Louisiana, two years' study of law

Maryland, three years' study in school or office

Michigan, between one and two years' high school, three years' study of law

Minnesota, about two thirds year high school, three years' study in office or school

Nebraska, two years' study in office of practising attorney

West Virginia, two years' study of law

Wisconsin, two years' study of law

In 10 states, District of Columbia, New Mexico and
Indian territory, Muskogee or Creek nation and Chickasaw
nation, and the Philippines admission is governed by rules
of court not defined in the law as follows:

Connecticut, examination after high school graduation or
indefinite preliminary test, three years' study in a law school
or office, two years' study if a college or law school graduate

Delaware, examination after three years' study of law
under direction of a member of the bar

District of Columbia, three years' study under competent
attorney or in school

Illinois, examination after graduation from three years'
high school course, three years of 36 weeks each in approved
law school or with licensed lawyers who subject the students
to regular examinations in each subject (prior to Jan. 1900
a diploma showing a regular course of two years or an
examination on two years' study in an office)

Indian territory, Cherokee nation, the judge or treasurer
grants a license

Chickasaw nation, supreme court judges issue a license to
any person possessing sufficient law knowledge

Creek nation, a district judge admits to a district court
and a supreme court judge to all courts any person of good
moral character

¹ Indiana, "every person of good moral character, being a
voter, shall be entitled to practise law in all courts of justice." — *Constitution*

Nevada, examination in open court

New Hampshire, examination after three years' study
under direction of a counselor of the court

New Jersey, examination after three years' clerkship with
degree of B. A. or B. S., or four years' clerkship, one year

¹ A constitutional amendment is to be submitted to the people, which provides
that the general assembly shall by law prescribe the necessary qualifications for
admission to the bar.

and a half in a law school may count for an equal period in clerkship (exceptions)

New Mexico, examination after two years' clerkship or diploma of law school

Pennsylvania, to supreme court on motion after four years' clerkship and one year's practice in county court or diploma of certain law schools after three years; to county courts under varying conditions

Philippines, " A strict examination in open court . . . by the justices of the supreme court."   Those admitted to practise in U. S. courts or in the highest court of any political division may be admitted without examination

Rhode Island, examination after three years in an office or a classical education and two years in an office

Vermont, (old rule) examination after three years with attorney, or one year with attorney and two in office, (rules under 98 law not yet approved)

Alaska has no law.   In Cuba and Puerto Rico the requirements are in process of transition.

4 MEDICINE [1]

Apprenticeship system — Before the establishment of medical schools in this country medical students either went abroad to study or served an apprenticeship with some practising physician. The custom of studying with a preceptor was common in view of the expense incident to work abroad, and this custom in a modified form continued till very recently. As a rule the apprentice had little opportunity for study but was forced to depend on what he could absorb by contact with his preceptor. The physicians of the 17th and 18th centuries who had studied abroad were usually classical students and in their preliminary training set an example that it would have been wise to follow.

First public medical lectures — The first public lectures on anatomy before a class of students in this country are said to have been delivered by Dr William Hunter of Newport, R. I. in 1752. It seems, however, that Dr Giles Firmin as early as 1647 delivered readings on human osteology in New England; that Dr Thomas Cadwallader of Philadelphia gave instruction to students in anatomy between 1745 and 1751, and that Drs John Bard and Peter Middleton dissected the human body in New York city in 1750 for purposes of medical instruction. In 1762 Dr William Shippen of Philadelphia gave a course of lectures on anatomy, illustrated by actual dissections. These lectures were continued till the organization of the Medical college of Philadelphia (now the medical department of the University of Pennsylvania) in 1765. Dissections were rarely performed prior to 1760 and even autopsies were seldom permitted.

Early medical schools — At the time of the American revolution, with a population of 3,000,000, there were probably about 3500 physicians in the colonies, of whom it is estimated that not more than 400 had received medical degrees. In New England the clergyman was often the

---

[1] See Toner's *Annals of medical progress in the United States*, and Davis' *Medical education and medical institutions in the United States*.

only available physician.   Two medical schools were organized in the colonies, the Medical college of Philadelphia
(now the medical department of the University of Pennsylvania) in 1765, and the medical department of King's (now
Columbia) college, in 1768.   The first medical degree conferred in this country was that of bachelor of medicine.
This degree was granted to 10 men by the Medical college
of Philadelphia in 1768.   The degree of doctor of medicine
was first conferred in 1770 by the medical school of King's
college on two students who had taken the bachelor's degree
in 1769.   51 medical degrees had been conferred by these
institutions before 1776, when operations were suspended
by the war.   In the colonial period two medical societies
(the State medical society of New Jersey, in 1766, and the
Delaware state medical society, in 1776) and one permanent
general hospital were organized.

Harvard university medical school was organized in 1782,
Dartmouth medical college in 1797, the School of medicine
of the University of Maryland and the College of physicians and surgeons of New York in 1807.   In 1813 the
medical department of King's (the name of which had been
changed to Columbia) college was finally discontinued.
The College of physicians and surgeons became in 1860
the medical department of Columbia university.   Of the
156 medical schools now existing in the United States 3
were established between 1765 and 1800, 12 between 1801
and 1825, 22 between 1826 and 1850, 33 between 1851 and
1875, 86 between 1876 and 1900.

At the time of the organization of the early medical
schools the practice of obstetrics was relegated as a rule to
ignorant midwives; physiology, histology, organic chemistry, pathology and surgery, as now recognized were hardly
known.   The schools at first conferred the degree of bachelor of medicine on those who had studied two years with a
preceptor and attended one course of lectures, the degree of
doctor of medicine after three years of study and two
courses of lectures.   The bachelor's degree was abandoned

in 1813. At first the Medical college of Philadelphia required for admission some knowledge of Greek and Latin, physics, natural history and botany, but the requirement was abandoned about the time of the reorganization of the University of Pennsylvania in 1792. For a century there were as a rule practically no requirements in preliminary general education for admission to medical schools, and even today this is their greatest defect. To the fact that charters for medical schools were to be had for the asking and that those schools were almost wholly self-sustaining is due the multiplication of small schools without facilities for clinical instruction. These schools in their rivalry for fees crowded all instruction into two ungraded lecture courses of from four to five months each. Progressive medical schools were anxious to raise their standards but feared a loss in students. The diploma given as a result of this unsatisfactory instruction admitted to professional practice.

Influence of medical societies — In 1839 the New York state medical society resolved that teaching and licensing ought to be separated as far as possible.[1] In 1837 the same view had been advocated in Philadelphia. Farther discussion of this question led to a call for a convention of delegates from all medical schools and societies in the United States. The convention was held in New York in 1846, and from it sprang the American medical association.

Much has been accomplished by medical societies to elevate the medical profession, specially since the organization of the American medical association in 1846. This national organization, thoroughly representative in character, gave a

---

[1] Results of licensing examinations show the importance of this question. Under the New York licensing laws, for example, 4808 physicians have been examined, of whom 3722 or 77.5% were successful; 916 dentists have been examined, of whom 712 or 77.7% were successful; 67 veterinarins have been examined, of whom 30 or 44.7% were successful. In these statistics each candidate who fails is counted as often as examined, but nevertheless so large a per cent of rejections is astonishing in view of the fact that admission to licensing examinations presupposes the preliminary education required by statute and also graduation with a degree from a registered professional school. Including those unable to meet the requirements for admission to licensing examinations more than 30% of all applicants have failed to secure licenses.

new impetus to medical societies.   In 1876 there was only
one state in the Union that did not have a state medical
society and many affiliated local associations.

The following societies have exercised an important influence in promoting higher standards :

Association of American medical colleges (1890)
American institute of homeopathy (1844)
National confederation of eclectic medical colleges (1871)
Southern medical college association (1892)

The first and fourth of these societies prescribe for admission to medical schools a preliminary general education
equivalent to one year in a high school, the second and third
demand work equivalent to two years in a high school.   All
prescribe four courses of lectures in different years as a condition for an M. D. degree, though they give an allowance
of one year to graduates of reputable literary colleges and
of other professional schools.[1]   All tend to improve facilities for teaching, dissections and clinics.   The schools registered by these societies are 72, 21, 6 and 11 respectively.

At the June 1899 meeting of the American institute of
homeopathy the legislative committee was requested to
draft a model bill with a view to obtaining general uniformity in the laws relating to the practice of medicine,
preparatory to the introduction in congress of a general law
to secure the right of physicians to practise in all states after
being authorized to practise in one.[2]

---

[1] A bill amending the medical law in this respect passed both houses of the New
York legislature in 1897 but unfortunately was not signed by the governor.   This
bill gave the regents power to accept as the equivalent of the first year of medical study "evidence of graduation from a registered college after four years of
general preliminary education in addition to the high school course fixed by law
as a minimum, provided that such college course included not less than the minimum required for such admission to advanced standing in languages, physics,
chemistry and biology."

[2] A uniform standard for admission to practise throughout the United States is
impracticable at present owing to varying conditions as to density of population,
educational advantages and general development.   Weak states can not maintain
the standards demanded elsewhere and strong states can not afford to lower their
standards.   The present needless multiplication of standards, however, is most
unfortunate.   Instead of a separate standard for almost each political division,
two or at most three standards should answer for all.   In the first group should

At the June 1899 meeting of the National confederation of state medical examining and licensing boards the committee on minimum standards for admission to medical schools recommended graduation from a four years' high school course or its equivalent. This committee outlined an alternative examination that represents less than three years of high school work. It also provided for an allowance of the first year of professional study to graduates of reputable literary or scientific colleges after satisfactory examination on the work of the first year.

At the June 1899 meeting of the Association of American medical colleges, a special committee made an interesting report on the condition of medical education in the United States. The committee had corresponded with all the medical schools, 82 in number, which had appeared as members of the association in 1897 and 1898. The replies received from 56 schools show great discrepancy in teaching facilities and in the requirements for graduation. Following are some of the most significant facts :

Laboratory work, including dissections. 1 school makes no report ; 1 gives less than 300 hours of laboratory work in four years ; 5 give between 300 and 500 hours ; 27 between 500 and 1000 hours ; 14 between 1000 and 1500 hours ; 8 over 1500 hours.

Practical work. 5 schools offer less than 100 hours ; 10 give from 100 to 200 ; 13 from 200 to 300 ; 11 from 300 to 500 ; 16 over 500 hours.

---

come the strongest states, and the standard maintained by these states would act as a stimulus to weaker political divisions. In dentistry New York, Pennsylvania and New Jersey have already moved in this direction and in medicine there will be a similar movement when the regents have the statutory power on unanimous recommendation of a state board of medical examiners to indorse the licenses of those whose preliminary education and professional training meet the requirements of the New York law. The Wayne co. (Michigan) medical society has addressed a circular to licensing bodies asking 1) if reciprocity with political divisions that have practically the same licensing requirements would be favored, 2) if statutory amendments necessary to secure such reciprocity would be advocated. Sep. 14, 1899 favorable answers to both inquiries had been received from 30 political divisions. With few exceptions statutory amendments would be necessary.

Obstetric cases.   5 schools offer their students no opportunity to attend obstetric cases before graduation ; 28 give students opportunity to attend personally from one to three cases ; 7 from three to five cases ; 6 from 5 to 10 cases ; 7 over 10 cases.

Clinical cases yearly available.   3 schools furnish no evidence of having even one patient to present to their students before graduation ; 4 have less than 500 patients all told from which to select clinical cases ; 4 have less than 1000 ; 5 between 1000 and 2000 ; 9 between 3000 and 5000 ; 8 between 5000 and 10,000 ; 6 between 10,000 and 20,000 ; 6 between 20,000 and 40,000 ; 3 between 40,000 and 100,000.

Minimum number of hours of clinical attendance by each student.   6 schools offer less than 300 hours of clinical work in four years ; 6 give only from 300 to 400 hours ; 7 from 400 to 500 hours ; 19 from 500 to 800 hours ; 14 from 800 to 1200 hours ; 4 give over 1200 hours.

Didactic work.   2 schools give less than 1000 hours in four years ; 7 from 1000 to 1500 hours ; 22 from 1500 to 2000 hours ; 13 from 2000 to 2500 hours ; 4 from 2500 to 3000 hours ; 8 give over 3000 hours.

Total number of hours' work demanded of medical students.   3 schools demand less than 2000 hours ; 2 from 2000 to 2500 ; 11 from 2500 to 3000 ; 7 from 3000 to 3500 ; 7 from 3500 to 4000 ; 26 over 4000 hours.

The committee recommended a change in the constitution and by-laws of the association by the adoption of the following :

1 After July 1, 1900, and till more stringent rules be adopted, students beginning the study of medicine must possess a diploma from a high school giving a thorough preliminary education, or must pass a thorough examination in all the branches usually taught in such schools.   This examination is to be conducted by a state superintendent of public instruction or some one delegated by him, or by members of the faculty of a university or college, who are not connected with the medical faculty of the school the student wishes to

enter, or by such a body as the regents of the University of the State of New York.

2 Before a student can enter an advanced class he must present certificates from a school whose requirements fully equal those of this association of having successfully passed the examinations in at least three fifths of the branches embraced in the curriculum of the previous years of the school he desires to enter or he must pass examinations on the same ; on the remaining branches he may be conditioned, but these conditions must be removed by taking the work, providing it has not already been taken, and by passing examinations before he can pass on to the succeeding class (that is a man shall not carry conditions for more than one year), providing, however, that this shall not prevent schools from allowing students who have earned the B. A. or B. S. degree and who have had an adequate course in science, or graduates in dentistry or pharmacy, who possess the proper preliminary education, to enter the sophomore class.

3 Before a student can be eligible for the degree of doctor of medicine he must have attended in a well-equipped medical school, four courses of lectures of at least six months each. These courses must embrace at least 3300 hours' actual work in the school, including besides didactic lectures and recitations,

a 500 hours of laboratory work ;

b 150 hours of practical work ;

c One or more obstetric cases personally attended by each student ;

d 750 hours of clinical teaching.

At least 45 months must intervene between a student's matriculation and the date of his graduation. All of the work should be fairly apportioned throughout the four years.

4 No school can be considered capable of giving the requisite instruction that can not command each year at least 3000 hospital or dispensary patients for presentation to its classes.

Medical sects — As commonly understood, regular physicians have no distinctive theory or practice; homeopaths
treat diseases with drugs that excite in healthy persons
symptoms similar to the morbid condition treated; eclectics
make use of what they regard as specific remedies, chiefly
botanical; physiomedicalists use only botanical remedies,
discarding those which are poisonous.   In practice these
distinctions are not always observed.

In addition to the medical sects to which detailed reference is made in this work a number of *pathies* flourish in
many states unmolested under such names as osteopath,
vitapath, electropath, hydropath, divine healer, magnetic
healer, Christian scientist, faith curist, mind curist, sun curist,
etc.   Men and women without preliminary or professional
training treat diseases under these or similar systems to such
an extent that the health of the people is endangered.
These so-called systems are followed with impunity in many
states in what seems to be open violation of laws restricting
the practice of medicine.   This is due largely to the fact that
so many statutes lack specific definitions as to what constitutes the practice of medicine, and without these definitions
the conviction of such practitioners can not be secured
through the courts.[1]

Osteopathy was "discovered" in 1874.   It is based on the
theory that "a natural flow of blood is health" and that the
bones may be "used as levers to relieve pressure on nerves,
veins and arteries."   Osteopathy is now recognized by law
in Iowa, Michigan, Missouri, North and South Dakota, Tennessee and Vermont.   Practice of "the system, method or

---

[1] In Illinois the medical practice act provides special state examinations in
obstetrics for midwives, and in anatomy, physiology, physiologic chemistry, histology and pathology and hygiene for those desiring to practise systems of treat-
ing human ailments in which medicines are not used internally or externally
and operative surgery is not followed.   The act does not apply, however, to any
person who "treats the sick or suffering by mental or spiritual means, without
the use of any drug or material remedy."   It is encouraging to note that notwithstanding this broad exemption Justice Everett of Chicago ruled against "divine
healing" in August 1899.   If his opinion is sustained in the higher court the
"Zion curers" can no longer practise the "laying on of hands."

science of osteopathy" is restricted to licensed physicians
and to graduates of "a legally chartered and regularly conducted school of osteopathy." The use of drugs and operations in "major or operative surgery" are not permitted in
the practice of osteopathy.

In Georgia, Kentucky, Nebraska, New Jersey, New
Mexico, Montana, Ohio[1] and West Virginia there are
stringent laws against non-medical practitioners. In some
other states, like Illinois, they receive such legal protection
that any person may treat "the sick or suffering by mental
or spiritual means, without the use of any drug or material
remedy." Under these conditions any person in Connecticut, Maine, Massachusetts and New Hampshire is free to
practise "the sun cure, mind cure, hypnotism, magnetic healing, Christian science, etc." The greater part of New England[2] seems to be on about the same footing in this respect
with the Cherokee nation, Indian territory, where entire liberty is given to "enchantments in any form." In striking
contrast Hawaii inflicts heavy fines on any person convicted
of an attempt to cure "another by practice of sorcery, witch-
craft, anaana, hoopiopio, hoounauna, hoomanamana, etc."

---

[1] In spite of this the court (6 Ohio Dec. 296) held in January 1897 that an
osteopath was not practising medicine by kneading and manipulations, using only
his hands and no medicines. In Kentucky and West Virginia, however, the courts
have upheld the statutes which provide that manipulations or other expedient
shall constitute the act of practising medicine. In Nebraska the court (40 Neb.
158) ruled in 1894 that the "object of the statute is to protect the afflicted from
the pretensions of the ignorant and avaricious, and its provisions are not limited
to those who attempt to follow beaten paths and established usages." In Ameri-
cus, Georgia in 1899 six prominent citizens, Christian scientists, were sentenced
to fines and imprisonment for refusing to submit to vaccination.

[2] In *Customs and fashions in old New England* Alice Morse Earle tells us that in
"1631, one Nicholas Knapp was fined and whipped for pretending 'to cure the
scurvey by a water of noe worth nor value which he sold at a very deare rate.'"
One is almost tempted to suspect that this whipping took as much out of the New
England officials as it did out of Mr Nicholas Knapp, for since that remote date
scarcely a rumor has reached us of any equally vigorous remonstrance with
unqualified practitioners. As a result New England has been a specially promising field for quacks, not many of whom were considerate enough to follow the
example of the celebrated "rain water doctor." Of this worthy it is recorded that
he "worked wondrous miracles and did a vast and lucrative business" till he
opportunely ended his career by tumbling into a hogshead of his own medicine.

There is much misunderstanding in this country regarding the duty of the state in relation to the health of the people. It does not consist in discriminating between schools or systems of medicine, but in requiring without prejudice or partiality of all who seek a license to practise for gain on the lives of fellow beings a minimum preliminary and professional training.[1]

Midwifery — Special tests for certificates of registration as midwives are required in:

Arizona	Illinois	Louisiana	Puerto Rico
Connecticut	Indiana[2]	New Jersey	Utah
Dist. of Col.	Iowa	Ohio	Wyoming

In the following political divisions the provisions of the medical practice acts do not apply to women engaged in the practice of midwifery:

Alabama	Kentucky	New Mexico	Texas
Arkansas	Maine	North Carolina	Vermont[3]
Florida	Maryland	Rhode Island	Virginia
Georgia	Mississippi	South Carolina	Washington
Idaho	Montana	Tennessee	West Virginia

In other political divisions, though there are some special provisions for certain localities, the general acts regulating the practice of medicine make no reference whatever to the practice of midwifery by women.[4] It would seem, therefore, that these laws restrict the practice of midwifery to

[1] In the November 1898 *Medical record*, W. A. Purrington of New York asks if we are to punish the physician who fails to report contagious diseases and allow a person who boasts his ignorance of medical and sanitary science to treat and conceal such cases. Medical laws provide only, at most, that no person shall practise medicine who has not studied medicine ; a licentiate may practise as he pleases. But there is no reason why unqualified persons should be allowed to pretend to cure disease, by their pretenses deprive the sick of the benefits of science, and yet escape the just consequences of their imposture.

[2] Either examination or approval of diploma.

[3] Those practising midwifery without a certificate can not enforce collection of fee, but this does not apply to the practice of midwifery by women in the town or locality in which they reside.

[4] In Nebraska, North and South Dakota the practice of " medicine, surgery or obstetrics " without a license is prohibited.

licensed physicians. Nevertheless a large proportion of the children in these political divisions are brought into the world by ignorant midwives, and as stated by Dr M. J. Lewi of New York, many women are physical wrecks through their incompetence. Practically the conditions in political divisions where the laws seem to restrict the practice of midwifery to licensed physicians are little better than in political divisions where the practice of midwifery by women without a license is authorized by statute. There will probably be little change for the better till the midwife receives legal recognition and the practice of midwifery is regulated by definite statutory provisions.[1]

Graded system of instruction — In 1859 the Chicago medical college, now the medical department of Northwestern university, was established to test the practicability of a thoroughly graded system of instruction. Students were divided into three classes, and each class was examined at the close of the year. Each of the three courses was six months in duration. Attendance on hospital clinical instruction and practical work in the chemical, anatomic and microscopic or histologic laboratories were required for graduation. In 1871 the Harvard medical school adopted a similar plan. The Syracuse medical school followed and today the graded system of consecutive lectures is the rule.

In 1896 Pres. Eliot wrote substantially as follows : Within 25 years the whole method of teaching medicine has been revolutionized throughout the United States. The old medical teaching was largely exposition ; it gave information at long range about things and processes which were not within reach or sight at the moment. The main means of instruction were lectures, surgical exhibitions in large rooms appropriately called theaters, rude dissecting rooms with scanty supervision, and clinical visits in large groups. The lectures were repeated year after year with little change, and

[1] In New York no agreement has yet been reached regarding a midwifery statute. At the November 1899 meeting of the Federation of women's clubs a resolution favoring the licensing of trained nurses by the University of the State of New York was adopted.

no graded course was laid down. There was little opportunity for laboratory work. The new medical education aims
at imparting manual and ocular skill, and cultivating the
mental powers of close attention through prolonged investigations at close quarters with the facts, and of just reasoning
on the evidence. The subjects of instruction are arranged,
as at the Harvard medical school, in a carefully graded
course, which carries the student forward in an orderly and
logical way from year to year. Laboratory work in anatomy, medical chemistry, physiology, histology, embryology,
pathology and bacteriology demands a large part of the
student's attention. In clinical teaching, also, the change is
great. Formerly a large group of students accompanied a
visiting physician on his rounds, and saw what they could
under very disadvantageous conditions. Now instruction
has become, in many clinical departments, absolutely individual, the instructor dealing with one student at a time, and
personally showing him how to see, hear, and touch for himself in all sorts of difficult observation and manipulation.
Much instruction is given to small groups of students, three
or four at a time — no more than can actually see and touch
for themselves.

Medical schools and medical students in 1899 — In 1899 there
were excluding graduate schools 156 medical schools in the
United States with 24,119 students. The growth in medical students in 21 years has been 142 per cent. Of the 156
schools 125 are regular[1] (21,619 students), 21 homeopathic
(1833 students), 7 eclectic (582 students), and 3 physiomedical (85 students).

Of the 156 medical schools, 135 hold day sessions, 5 have
evening sessions, 9 have both and 7 do not report this item.
74 are departments of colleges or universities, 82 are separate institutions. 152 grant degrees.

In addition to the undergraduate schools there are 8
graduate medical schools which had in 1898, 624 instructors

---

[1] The name commonly applied to the traditional school of medicine. Other
designations are the " old," " allopathic " or " heteropathic " school.

and 1813 students of whom 59 were women.   In 1899 these schools had 1916 students of whom 73 were women.   Nearly half of the students were in the New York schools.

The ratio of physicians to population is 1 to less than 600 in the United States while in foreign countries it varies from 1 to about 1100 in the British isles to 1 to about 8500 in Russia.   We are said to have in proportion to our population four times as many physicians as France, five times as many as Germany, six times as many as Italy.

There are more medical schools in the United States alone than in countries whose total population is six times as great, and yet few of these medical schools in the United States have endowments corresponding to those so lavishly made to other educational institutions or in any way proportioned to their needs.   Fortunately the closing years of this century seem to indicate a change in the attitude of philanthropists toward medical schools.   In 1897, 14 medical schools reported endowments of $648,262.   In 1898, 19 medical schools reported endowments of $1,906,072.[1]   In New York the advanced requirements for license have been accompanied by extraordinary growth in the property of medical schools, specially in greater New York.   A fine building was erected in 1897 by the faculty of the Bellevue hospital medical college.   The College of physicians and surgeons, with the Vanderbilt clinic, doubled in size by the additional gift in 1895 of $350,000, and the Sloane maternity hospital, greatly enlarged in 1897, now make the most complete plant in existence for scientific medical education. The Polhemus memorial clinic has been completed and thoroughly equipped, providing accommodations for the out-patient and medical school departments of the Long Island college hospital.   In the medical division of the Flower hospital, opened in 1896, the New York homeopathic medical college now gives excellent opportunity for the study of practical medicine.   The New York medical college and

---

[1] From 1894 to 1898 the most notable gifts and bequests amounted to $2,631,000 for medical schools and $16,593,701 for hospitals.

hospital for women opened in 1898 its handsome building in West 101st street. An amount reported at $1,500,000 was given in 1898 to build, equip and endow the new medical department of Cornell university in New York city.[1]

Hygiene and state medicine — More attention should be paid in the United States to instruction in hygiene and state medicine. In Great Britain no one can be appointed a medical officer unless he has a special diploma in public health. In this country little opportunity is afforded for general or special sanitary work on broad lines. This subject is now under discussion and doubtless progressive states will soon provide places where medical officers of health or other persons engaged in sanitary work can obtain practical and scientific training. The scientific investigations which would be made in the laboratories of such schools would be of great value to the public.

In *Medical education of the future*, an essay in *Educational reform* which every thoughtful man should read, Pres. Eliot writes : "State medicine has many objects in view. It aims not only to protect the public health, but also to increase it. In state medicine individualism is impracticable for it is impossible for the individual to protect himself. The social cooperation, which in our days the state alone can enforce, is needed to promote security against disease and progress toward better average health and longer life. To take all possible precautions against the spread of infectious diseases is simply an act of good citizenship. Nothing but medical supervision will accomplish the objects of state medicine ; and there are no agents so effective as physicians to spread through all classes of the community an educated sense of sanitary decency. Only the state can guard against dirty milk, corrupted water-supplies, impure ice, adulterated drugs, spoilt meat and fruit, and filthy and over-crowded tenements. Only the state can enforce the isolation of cases of contagious disease, the suppression of epidemics, and the

---

[1] Our medical school will be splendidly housed and endowed. Any statement beyond this is purely unofficial.— *Pres. Schurman*, Sep. 27, 1899.

exclusion of pestilences like cholera and yellow fever. In exercising such control the state needs every aid which medical experts in chemistry, bacteriology, and comparative pathology can place at its disposal. The medical profession itself hardly recognizes as yet how great promise there is in the further study of the connections between diseases in animals and in man — connections which smallpox, scarlatina in cows, tuberculosis in men and animals, and diphtheria already illustrate. Not even the state — that is, a single state or nation — can deal effectively with such a problem as the suppression of cholera or yellow fever. That is an international problem. The evils which the social and gregarious instincts of men create, by inducing the modern crowding into cities, must be socially remedied; and the most effective force which society can exert to this end is the influence of the highly trained medical officer. Every physician should be a medical philanthropist and missionary, zealous to disseminate knowledge of public hygiene."

Present tendencies — Dr Bayard Holmes, secretary of the Association of American medical colleges, writes as follows touching present tendencies in medical education :

" Two stages of educational development are already manifest in the medical schools of the United States. About half the schools have finished the first stage and are entering on the second, while the remainder are laboring tardily to complete the first. In the first stage of development, from the medieval lectures on the 'seven branches of medicine,' the course of study has been lengthened, some entrance requirements instituted and the number of distinct and separate studies greatly increased. Laboratory and recitation work have been introduced, written examinations have been made frequent, once a month or oftener, and a sort of graded medical school established. In this condition are most of the schools that maintain the standard established by the Association of American medical colleges.

Some few schools, however, have already outgrown this system of educational lock-step and are organizing a curriculum adapted to the needs of students of differing tastes or abilities. This curriculum is planned not to instruct but to educate; not from the standpoint of the teacher's convenience, but from that of the student's advantage. The first stage of educational development multiplied the teachers, scattered the energies of the student (in some cases requiring him to go before 10 different professors each week) and dissociated related topics. The second stage of development early introduces the student to the study of the live man, makes continuous clinical study on single cases by each of the students a means of unifying the whole curriculum, and requires thesis work of each student, necessitating on his part clinical, laboratory, experimental and library work on the same subject. This introduces intensity in the place of diffuseness; independence in the place of subordination and original investigation in the place of catechism. To assert that the elective method for any large part of the medical curriculum is already established in any considerable number of medical schools, would be misleading, but this is certainly the tendency of the day.

The growth of medical libraries in the medical schools, the establishment of thoroughly equipped accessory laboratories, the publication of bulletins and theses and the numerous articles on medical pedagogy written by active medical teachers testify to the intense struggle for the liberation of the medical student and the medical teacher from the iron-clad course of study. When this second stage of development has been realized, the medical schools will do more than furnish quiz classes, preparatory to state board and hospital examinations; they will become fountains of original investigation pouring out every year both well-trained medical men, and large and important contributions to medical science, these contributions produced as a means to a rational education."

Early legislation — The earliest law relating exclusively to physicians was passed by Virginia in 1639, but like the later act of 1736 it was designed mainly to regulate their fees.

The act of 1736 made concessions to physicians who held
university degrees. In only 2 of the 13 colonies were well-
considered laws enacted to define the qualifications of physicians. The general assembly of New York in 1760
decreed that no person should practise as physician or surgeon in the city of New York till examined in physic and
surgery and admitted by one of his majesty's council, the
judges of the supreme court, the king's attorney-general and
the mayor of the city of New York. Such candidates as
were approved received certificates conferring the right to
practise throughout the whole province, and a penalty of £5
was prescribed for all violations of this law. A similar act
was passed by the general assembly of New Jersey in 1772.

In 1840 laws had been enacted by the legislatures of
nearly all the states to protect citizens from the imposition
of quacks. Between 1840 and 1850, however, most of
these laws were either repealed or not enforced as a result of
the cry that restrictions against unlicensed practitioners were
designed only to create a monopoly.

Synopsis of present requirements — In the following political divisions medical diplomas do not now confer the right
to practise medicine, an examination being required in all
cases :

Alabama	Illinois	Minnesota	Oregon
Arizona	Indian ter.	Mississippi	Pennsylvania
Connecticut	Cherokee nat.	Montana	South Carolina
Delaware	Iowa	New Hampshire	Utah
Dist. of Col.	Louisiana	New Jersey	Vermont
Florida	Maine	New York	Virginia
Georgia	Maryland	North Carolina	Washington
Hawaii	Massachusetts	North Dakota	West Virginia
Idaho			

In some tables Texas is classed with the states in which
diplomas confer no right to practise, but the Texas laws
conflict.

The following require for admission to the licensing
examination :

Alabama, requirements of State medical association

Arizona, diploma from recognized medical school

Delaware, competent common school education, diploma from legally incorporated medical school

District of Columbia, diploma of school authorized by law to confer M.D. degree

Florida, diploma from recognized medical school

Georgia, diploma from legally organized medical school

Idaho, diploma from legally chartered medical school

Illinois, less than one year of high school work, diploma from approved medical school

Indian territory, Cherokee nation, diploma from reputable medical school

Iowa, less than one year of high school work, diploma from recognized medical school

Louisiana, fair primary education, diploma of recognized medical school

Maryland, common school education, diploma from legally incorporated medical school

Minnesota, four full courses of lectures at recognized medical school

Montana, diploma from legally chartered medical school

New Hampshire, full high school course or its equivalent, diploma from regularly organized medical school

New Jersey, common school education, diploma from legally incorporated medical school

New York, four years' high school course or its equivalent, diploma from registered medical school

North Carolina, diploma from medical school in good standing (after Jan. 1, 1900)

North Dakota, 3 six months' lecture courses

Pennsylvania, common school education, diploma from legally chartered medical school

South Carolina, diploma of recognized medical school

Utah, diploma from chartered medical school in good standing

Vermont, high school course or equivalent and diploma from a U. S. medical school

Virginia, evidence of a preliminary education

The following require the licensing examination only:

Connecticut	Massachusetts	Oregon	West Virginia
Hawaii	Mississippi	Washington	
Maine	North Carolina (diploma after 1900)		

The following require approval of medical diploma by duly qualified boards:

California	Kentucky	Nebraska	Ohio	South Dakota

The following require either approval of medical diploma or examination by state or other duly qualified boards:

Arkansas	Creek nat.	Nevada	Rhode Island
Colorado	Indiana	New Mexico	Wisconsin
Indian ter.	Michigan	Oklahoma	Wyoming
Choctaw nat.	Missouri	Tennessee	

The following requiring either approval of medical diploma or examination, admit to examination on:

Arkansas, a good literary education

Nevada, five years' practice in the state just prior to act or diploma from reputable school without the United States

Oklahoma, full course of lectures

Kansas requires only presentation of diploma or other certificate of qualification to unqualified local officer

Alaska has no law. In Cuba, the Philippines[1] and Puerto Rico[2] the requirements are in process of transition.

The following political divisions have mixed examining boards, that is the boards are composed of representatives of the several schools of medicine:

---

[1] The assistant secretary to the military governor in the Philippines writes Sep. 4, 1899 that " the Spanish law as to admission to practise still governs. In general this requires a diploma from a reputable college, school or university of such profession, or in lieu thereof an examination."

[2] General Davis established Sep. 30, 1899 in Puerto Rico an examining committee for licenses to practise medicine, dentistry, pharmacy, midwifery and professional nursing. Only those with satisfactory credentials are admitted to examination.

Alabama	Kentucky	New Jersey	South Dakota
Arizona	Maine	New Mexico	Tennessee
Arkansas	Massachusetts	North Carolina	Texas
Colorado	Michigan	North Dakota	Utah
Hawaii	Minnesota	Ohio	Virginia
Idaho	Mississippi	Oklahoma	Washington
Illinois	Missouri	Oregon	West Virginia
Indian territory	Montana	Rhode Island	Wisconsin
Indiana	Nebraska	South Carolina	Wyoming
Iowa	Nevada		

The following have separate examining boards for each recognized school of medicine:

California	Dist. of Col.	Louisiana	New York
Connecticut	Florida	Maryland	Pennsylvania
Delaware	Georgia	New Hampshire	Vermont

Alaska and Kansas have no examining boards.

5 DENTISTRY[1]

Independent dental schools — From the earliest times dentistry was practised as a branch of surgery. Herodotus speaks of means of preserving the teeth, and artificial teeth are alluded to by Greek and Latin poets. Within the last half century dentistry has become a distinct profession. John Greenwood who carved in ivory a set of teeth for George Washington is said to have been the first American to establish himself as a dentist. His office was in New York and the work for Gen. Washington was done in 1790 and 1795.

The Baltimore college of dental surgery, established in 1839, was the first institution of the kind in the world. It was the direct result of an agitation to put dentists on a higher professional plane, and followed an unsuccessful attempt to found dental chairs in medical schools. It had been argued that oral pathology and dental mechanics should be taught in the medical schools as branches of medicine and that graduates choosing these courses should receive the degree of M. D. as in the case of other branches of medicine.[2] In the same year the *American journal of dental science*, the first dental periodical in the world, was established.

In 1845 the Ohio college of dental surgery (since 1888 the dental department of the University of Cincinnati), in 1856 the Pennsylvania college of dental surgery, in 1863 the Philadelphia dental college were founded. These separate schools taught at first very little medicine but paid attention almost entirely to mechanical training and to those branches which a dentist must know. All conferred the degree of D. D. S. In 1865 the New York college of den-

---

[1] See Shepard's Inaugural address at the World's Columbian dental congress.

[2] Dr William Carr of New York writes substantially as follows: Dentistry should be recognized as a specialty of medicine, and the dentist should hold a degree in medicine. The education of a physician is as necessary to one who undertakes the treatment of lesions, maladies and defects within the oral cavity as to one whose treatment is confined to the tracts of the nose, the ear and the throat.

tistry was founded with the purpose of educating men to practise dental surgery as a specialty of medicine. The curriculum included the fundamental departments of medicine with operative dentistry and oral prosthetics.

Dental departments — In 1867 Harvard university opened a dental department and began to teach dentistry as a branch of medicine with the special degree D. M. D. (Dentariae medicinae doctor). In 1875 the University of Michigan and in 1878 the University of Pennsylvania followed the example of Harvard in opening dental departments. 36 of the 56 dental schools are now departments of other institutions.

Growth — Since 1878 there has been a most astonishing increase in dental schools and dental students, due largely to the fact that the dental laws in many states now require graduation from a dental school as a condition for license. In 1878 there were 12 schools and 701 students; in 1899 there were 56 schools and 7633 students. The growth in dental students in 21 years has been 988 per cent. Of the 56 dental schools now existing in the United States, 2 were established between 1826 and 1850, 7 between 1851 and 1875, 47 between 1876 and 1900.

47 dental schools hold day sessions, 4 evening sessions, and 5 do not report this item. Degrees are granted to graduates of all schools.[1]

Discoveries and inventions — The discovery of the anesthetic power of drugs, the most important step in the progress of medicine, was made by an American dentist William Jennings Morton, though the honor of this discovery is shared with another dentist Charles W. Wells of Hartford, Ct., who in 1844 rendered the extraction of teeth painless by the use of nitrous oxid. In his *History of European morals* Lecky says: "It is probable that the American inventor of the first anesthetic has done more for the real

---

[1] Graduates of the New York dental school receive degrees through the University of the State of New York which also countersigns the degrees of the New York college of dentistry.

happiness of mankind than all the philosophers from
Socrates to Mill."

Between 1850 and 1860, the use of crystal gold and the
discovery of the cohesiveness of freshly annealed foil
opened a new field for operative dentistry. The next decade
witnessed the introduction of such improved instruments as
the mallet, the rubber dam and the engine. The invention
of the modern artificial crown and the bridge is another
important event of about this period. In the 20 years just
preceding 1893 more than 100 different crowns and bridges
are said to have been invented.

Dental societies — In 1840 the American society of dental
surgeons, the pioneer of the associations to which dentistry
owes so much of its progress, was organized in New York.

The National association of dental faculties, organized in
1884, has done much to strengthen courses of study in dental schools. At the time of its organization only those
schools were admitted which had proper facilities for instruction and a corps of competent teachers. From time to time
standards have been raised by rules governing attendance,
instruction and graduation. There are at present 47 schools
in the association, all of which require three full courses of
dental lectures. The main defect of these schools as a rule
is failure to require a sufficient preliminary general education for admission. The efforts of the association in this
direction have not accomplished much as yet.

The National association of dental examiners,[1] organized
in 1883 to secure higher and more uniform standards for
admission to dental practice voted in 1898 to refuse recognition to any dental school that did not have 1) entrance
requirements equivalent to at least two years of high school
work, 2) attendance on three courses of lectures of at least

---

[1] At its July 1899 meeting this association created an advisory committee to promote uniformity in administering dental laws. Dr H. J. Allen, secretary of the
committee, writes November 15, 1899 for "a comprehensive report from the New
York examiners, as the entire committee regards the New York dental law as the
best in the country." Dr Allen states that boards in about 15 states have agreed
to enter this compact to secure uniform standards.

six months each in different years as a condition for graduation, 3) a faculty of at least six, 4) a course of study embracing operative dentistry, dental pathology, dental prosthetics, oral surgery, anatomy, physiology, general pathology, materia medica, therapeutics and general surgery, 5) suitable chemical and bacteriologic laboratories under competent instructors, 6) suitable lecture rooms, a well-appointed dental infirmary and a general prosthetic laboratory. These rules were not approved by the National association of dental faculties and efforts to enforce them proved unsuccessful.[1]

A joint meeting of committees of these two national associations was held at Niagara Falls in 1899, and it is probable that both will now work harmoniously toward higher standards, the progress to be made by degrees. The committees agreed on one year of high school work as the minimum requirement for admission to dental schools and by vesting the determination of this requirement in the hands of state superintendents of education they recognized the importance of removing this power from those who might exercise it unwisely through a desire to attract students. The motion of Dr Barrett to extend the requirement to two years of high school work after the session of 1901–1902 is to be acted on at the 1900 meeting of the National association of dental faculties. Other requirements of this association, as printed in the new rules, are the same as those given above under the National association of dental examiners except that each course of lectures is to be seven months in duration and general surgery is not mentioned as a special topic.

Subjects discussed — Among the subjects which have attracted much attention recently in dental literature and dental societies are the increasing use of plastics and of porcelain, the modification in practice through laboratory

---

[1] In 19 political divisions the latest prescribed preliminary and professional requirements are those of the National association of dental examiners, in 4 political divisions those of the National association of dental faculties. Differences between these associations having been adjusted their requirements will probably become uniform.

investigation, the germ theory of disease, antiseptics, the uses of electricity and the tendency of prophylaxis to develop along physiologic lines by attention to the laws of health. Among important topics discussed by the National association of dental faculties the undue multiplication of dental schools without proper facilities and detrimental effects of scholarships have been prominent.[1]

The question of interchange of licenses has been discussed frequently during the last few years. The correspondent of the New York state dental society at the May 1899 meeting submitted a proposition that all state boards, members of the National association of dental examiners, use identical question papers prepared by a committee of the national body, and that licenses granted as a result of such examinations be interchangeable among the states represented in the National association. This scheme had been submitted to dental examiners throughout the country and had been approved by most of those from whom replies had been received.

Interchange of licenses is highly desirable and will doubtless be brought about to some extent in the near future. An examination, however, should not be made the only test. A reasonable preliminary general education and a diploma from an accredited school should be required for admission to the final test which should be both theoretic and practical, and should be carefully guarded from danger of fraud or indirection.

An important step toward interchange of licenses was taken in 1898 when the New York dental law was amended so that the regents may now issue their license to any applicant who holds a license to practise dentistry granted by a state board of dental examiners, indorsed by the dental society of the state of New York, provided that his preliminary and professional education meets the New York statu-

---

[1] This association voted August 1, 1899 that no school in the association should grant free or beneficiary scholarships not absolutely obligatory under charter provisions.

tory requirements.   The dental examiners of New Jersey
and Pennsylvania having been indorsed by the New York
state dental society as more nearly approximating the New
York standard than any other state boards, the New York
state dental examiners, at a meeting held Oct. 7, 1899 recommended to the regents the indorsement of New Jersey and
Pennsylvania licenses granted under the new plan, provided the preliminary and professional education of applicants meets the New York statutory requirements.   The
regents will probably act favorably on the recommendation if
the New Jersey and Pennsylvania boards agree to establish
a standard in preliminary general education fully equal to
that required by the New York law.[1]

Legislation — In Alabama in 1841, the first state law regulating the practice of dentistry was enacted.   This was probably the first dental legislation in any country.   The next
state to pass a dental law was New York, but this action was
not taken till 1868.   The English law was enacted in 1878,
and those of other countries about that time or later.

The practice of dentistry is now regulated by statute in
almost all political divisions of the United States.

Synopsis of present requirements — In 23 states dental
diplomas do not now confer the right to practise, an examination being required in all cases :

Alabama	Connecticut	Florida	Idaho
Colorado	Delaware	Georgia	Maine

[1] The New Jersey statute demands "a preliminary education equal to that furnished by the common schools."   The secretary of the New Jersey dental commission writes Oct. 17, 1899 that this has been construed to mean graduation
from a registered four years' high school course.   " We have, however, agreed to
require only a three years' high school course up to Jan. 1, 1901 when the full
requirement shall take effect simultaneously with New York.   This agreement is
made with the full knowledge and approval of the governor and the superintendent of public instruction and you may rest assured that New Jersey will live up
to the spirit as well as the letter of the agreement . . .   We look on the interchange of licenses with New York as the greatest educational advance that has
yet been made in the dental profession, the formation of a nucleus around which
all other states must rally."

Massachusetts	New Jersey	Pennsylvania	Virginia
Minnesota	New York	Rhode Island	Washington
Mississippi	North Carolina	South Carolina	West Virginia
New Hampshire	Oregon	Vermont	

The following require for admission to the licensing examination :

Colorado, diploma from legally organized reputable dental school

Connecticut, diploma from recognized dental school, or three years' instruction or three years' practice

Delaware, diploma of recognized dental school

Florida, diploma from reputable dental school

Georgia, diploma from reputable dental school

Idaho, three years' experience, certificate from another state board, or diploma from legally organized dental school

Minnesota, diploma from reputable dental school, or evidence of 10 years' continuous practice previous to September 1889

New Jersey, common school education, diploma from recognized dental school or a written recommendation from five experienced dentists

New York, full high school course, degree from registered dental school or medical degree with a special one year's dental course

Oregon, diploma from dental school in good standing, or study and practice in Oregon prior to this act

Pennsylvania, good common school education, diploma of recognized dental school

Virginia, a fair academic education

Washington, diploma from recognized dental school or evidence of 10 years' practice

The following require the licensing examination only :

Alabama	Mississippi	Rhode Island	Vermont
Maine	New Hampshire	South Carolina	West Virginia
Massachusetts	North Carolina		

In the following political divisions either approval of dental diploma or examination by state or other duly qualified board.is required:

Arizona	Kansas	Montana	Oklahoma
California	Kentucky	Nebraska	South Dakota
Dist. of Col.	Louisiana	Nevada	Tennessee
Hawaii	Maryland	New Mexico	Texas
Illinois	Michigan	North Dakota	Utah
Indiana	Missouri	Ohio	Wisconsin
Iowa			

The following requiring either approval of diploma or examination, admit to examination on:

Iowa, satisfactory evidence of three years' study

Missouri, three years' study with legally registered dentist or license from another state

Montana, three years' practice or three years' study under licensed dentist

North Dakota, three years' active practice or three years' study with practitioner

Utah, two years' practice or two years' study under licensed dentist

Arkansas requires only a diploma approved by the board

One state, Wyoming, requires only presentation of diploma to unqualified local officers

In Cuba, the Philippines[1] and Puerto Rico[1] the requirements are in process of transition

Alaska and Indian territory have no laws

---

[1] See note under medicine.

6 PHARMACY

Early schools of pharmacy — The first meeting in this country to consider the question of systematic pharmaceutic education was held in Philadelphia in 1821. At this meeting the apothecaries of Philadelphia formed a society to provide a system of instruction in pharmacy and to regulate the conduct of their business. The outcome of this action was the Philadelphia college of pharmacy, which was chartered by the Pennsylvania legislature in 1822. The school opened in 1821–22 with a course of lectures on materia medica and pharmacy, and a course on pharmaceutic and general chemistry. The first class was graduated in 1826. In the early years of the institution committees were appointed to expose adulterations of drugs and a library and cabinet were established. The need of a medium of publication was soon felt. In 1825 the *Journal of the Philadelphia college of pharmacy* was started, which became in 1835 the *American journal of pharmacy*.

The Philadelphia college of pharmacy was followed in 1823 by the Massachusetts college of pharmacy, in 1829 by the New York college of pharmacy, in 1838 by the department of pharmacy of Tulane university, in 1841 by the Maryland college of pharmacy.

Prior to 1840 pharmacists were not recognized in pharmacopœial conventions. In 1850 the chartered schools were invited to send delegates to the decennial convention. In that revision and in the revisions of 1860, 1870 and 1880 pharmacists were well represented. In the convention of 1890, 16 of the 26 members composing the committee on final revision were pharmacists.

Growth — There has been a remarkable increase in schools of pharmacy and students of pharmacy in the past 21 years. In 1878 there were 13 schools with 1187 students. In 1899 there were 52 schools, with 3563 students. The increase in students in 21 years has been 200 per cent. 36 of these schools maintain day sessions, 9 have evening sessions, 4 have both, 3 do not report this item. 14 are separate institutions, 38 are departments of other institutions. 45 grant degrees. 2 of the 52 schools were established between 1801 and 1825, 4 between 1826 and 1850, 8 between 1851 and 1875, 38 between 1876 and 1900.

Apprenticeship — The University of Michigan is said to have been the first institution in this country to graduate pharmacists without any practical experience. In 1898, 24 schools of pharmacy reported that they did not require any practical training. The original object of the early schools of pharmacy was to give a theoretic knowledge of pharmacy as a science and a higher degree of familiarity with botany and chemistry than could be attained in the limited term of apprenticeship. It was not intended that these schools should take the place of an apprenticeship in a pharmacy.

In recent years there has been no little discussion as to whether schools of pharmacy should require work with a druggist as a condition for graduation. The schools that do not exact this requirement admit its necessity to success as a pharmacist, but they claim that it is impracticable to determine whether or not the necessary practical training has been acquired by their matriculates, and that by providing under proper instructors suitable laboratory facilities for actual work with the drugs, they can give more practical experience than that afforded in many pharmacies where the prescription department is of little importance. There is force in this position in the case of schools that give thorough courses requiring the full time of students, specially if matriculation requirements insure a fair general preliminary education. Dr Gregory, dean of the Buffalo college of pharmacy writes as follows touching this matter : " Prior to 1880 the diploma of a school of pharmacy was generally the sole evidence of fitness as a pharmacist. Now the license is demanded. No one denies the value of experience in a pharmacy, but the responsibility of testing its character now rests with boards of examiners, leaving the schools free to attend to the primary function of teaching." [1]

Present tendencies — Dr A. B. Huested of the New York pharmacy board writes as follows touching present tendencies in the teaching of pharmacy :

" These tendencies are all in the line of advancement, in teaching more thoroughly the fundamental subjects of chemistry, pharmacy, materia medica and botany, and including the allied subjects, microscopy, analytic examination of medicines, foods, secretions and excretions of the human system and bacteriology. In the past, the instruction in all schools of pharmacy was confined to evening hours, all the students, and they were few, working during the day in the near by retail and wholesale pharmacies. The establishment of chemical laboratories, where the student practically demonstrated what was taught in the class-room, was the first advance. Next came the pharmaceutic laboratory, devoted to the practical demonstration of the preparation of organic compounds ; then the pharmacognosy room, and the microscopic laboratory, and today analytic and bacteriologic laboratories are being established. These extended courses of instruction demand that more time shall be devoted to the work, so that in place of all instruction being confined to evening hours, most schools now use a part of the day, and some occupy the entire time of the student, in courses extending over nine months in the year. Very many schools afford opportunity for farther work in optional and graduate courses.

Notwithstanding the increase in work and time demanded of the student of pharmacy, the number pursuing this study is greater than during any previous period. It will be

---

[1] " It should be remembered that the schools which led in the abandonment of the apprenticeship requirement did not take this course through any lack of appreciation of the value of actual experience, but because the requirement as frequently enforced was a farce. Very properly the university schools took the ground that their degrees should stand for school work only, and that no institution could honestly vouch for the value of something for which there could be no effective standard and which in many cases was of absolutely no value." *J. H. Beal*

inferred from what has been stated, that those who are now engaged in retail pharmacies are more competent than their predecessors, and have a more thorough knowledge of the agents in which they deal. This is true if the average education is considered, but nevertheless commercial tendencies have exercised a disadvantageous influence. The conditions of trade in the past were such as to allow those pharmacists who were so inclined, to devote their entire time to the study, care and preparation of medicines. Today the greater part of the time of the pharmacist must be devoted to the commercial side of his work, or he will soon find himself without patrons, and therefore without the means to carry on his business. Again, many if not a majority of the agents in which he deals, may and must be had from the large manufacturer. These conditions have attracted the more studious and therefore the better educated pharmacists to those pursuits that foster the educational side of pharmacy, leaving the retail pharmacies in charge of those in whom the commercial spirit predominates. When the educational attainments of the retail pharmacist are considered, I question if he has made the advance that the teaching of the schools would indicate."

Legislation — Apothecaries were organized into a privileged body in civilized parts of Europe in the middle ages, and from that period those who dispense drugs have been required to possess certain qualifications. In the United States there have not been till lately any legal restrictions worthy of the name, but any ignorant boy whom an apothecary chose to employ has been free to dispense drugs.

Georgia seems to have been the first state that attempted to restrict the practice of pharmacy throughout the state to competent persons. The law, enacted in 1825, gave the state medical board power to examine and license apothecaries. The Alabama code of 1852 contained a similar provision. In 1868 a member of the Georgia board reported that he knew of only five licentiates of the board that were then engaged in business in the state. An act was passed in New York in 1839 that applied solely to New York city, in Pennsylvania in 1866 that applied solely to Lycoming county. These early acts had little effect in protecting the public from ignorant apothecaries.

In 1869 a draft of a pharmacy law was recommended by the American pharmaceutical association which required graduation in pharmacy as a condition for license. It was hoped in this way to secure through the schools of pharmacy men better fitted by preliminary education and professional training for the practice of the profession. Rhode Island was the only state which enacted this law (March 1870), and it was amended in the following year. At present there is no pharmacy law in the United States which requires attendance and graduation at a school of pharmacy as a condition for license.

Since 1869 laws restricting the practice of pharmacy have been enacted in almost every state through the efforts of members of the profession. The American pharmaceutical association, organized in 1852, has been a potent factor in the attempt to give pharmacy a professional standing equal to that of other branches of medicine. Its work in this direction has been of special value since the creation in 1887 of the sections of education and legislation. A mass of material on pharmaceutic education and legislation in this country and abroad has been collected and made available through the annual reports of the association.

The 1898 report of the section on education and legislation of the American pharmaceutical association summarizes as follows the fundamental defects in present laws regulating the practice of pharmacy in the United States:

1 Failure to require a sufficient preliminary general education.

2 Failure to demand graduation from a school of pharmacy for admission to the licensing examination or for registration.

3 The privileges accorded to physicians, manufacturers, wholesalers, etc.

4 Failure to provide periods of apprenticeship and courses of study that would make it impracticable for any one to engage in the practice of pharmacy on his own account before the age of 24 or 25 years.

Dr J. H. Beal of the Department of pharmacy at Scio college, Ohio, was appointed by the section on education and legislation of the American pharmaceutical association at its 1899 meeting to draft a model pharmacy law. If approved this law can be introduced simultaneously into the legislatures of all the states. Dr Beal writes November 16, 1899 : " Foreigners are often puzzled to account for the diversity in our legislation. The fact should be emphasized that all matters of internal police control are left exclusively to the several states, so that national laws regulating professional practice can not be enacted."

That a preliminary general education equivalent to graduation from an accredited high school will be required eventually for admission to the study of pharmacy is highly probable, but this demand will not be made for some time to come except by a few progressive states. Present tendencies indicate that graduation from an accredited school of pharmacy will also be required eventually for admission to the licensing test or for registration. The American pharmaceutical association and a number of state associations have within the last year favored this requirement.

Synopsis of present requirements — In 17 states a diploma in pharmacy does not now admit to practise, an examination being required in all cases :

Georgia	Massachusetts	New Hampshire	Pennsylvania
Illinois	Michigan	New York	South Dakota
Indiana	Minnesota	Ohio	Tennessee
Kentucky	Nebraska	Oregon	Wisconsin
Maine			

The following 14 states require for admission to the licensing examination :

Georgia, three years' experience or diploma

Illinois, four years' practical experience in compounding prescriptions; the physician a certificate from state board of health and four years' experience filling his own prescriptions

Indiana, four years' experience, two years in a pharmacy, time spent in approved school may be substituted

Kentucky, three years' practical experience in compounding physicians' prescriptions

Maine, three years' experience in compounding physicians' prescriptions or diploma of regularly incorporated school of medicine or pharmacy

Michigan, grammar school education, three years' experience

Minnesota, four years' experience in a pharmacy

Nebraska, three years' practical experience in pharmacy

New York, four years' experience in pharmacy

Ohio, four years' practical experience in a pharmacy, time spent in an approved school is deducted

Oregon, three years' experience in a pharmacy

Pennsylvania, four years' practical experience

South Dakota, common school education, three years' practice of pharmacy, or diploma from department of pharmacy, state agricultural college, and one year's practice in a pharmacy

Wisconsin, five years' practical experience in a pharmacy, or diploma of approved college and two years' practical experience

The following 4 require the licensing examination only:

| Indiana | Massachusetts | New Hampshire | Tennessee |

The following political divisions require either an approved diploma or examination by state or other duly qualified boards:

Arkansas	Iowa	New Mexico	Texas
California	Kansas	New York city	Utah
Colorado	Louisiana	North Dakota	Washington
Connecticut	Baltimore, Md.	Oklahoma	West Virginia
Delaware	Montana	South Carolina	Wyoming
Dist. of Col.	Erie co., N. Y.		

The following political divisions in case of examination admit to it on:

California, grammar school education, four years' experience in a pharmacy

Colorado, four years' experience in compounding physicians' prescriptions

Connecticut, three years' instruction in pharmacy

Delaware, three years' continuous practical experience in retail drug business

District of Columbia, diploma of respectable medical school, or four years' experience in a pharmacy

Iowa, two years' practical experience in pharmacy, one year allowed for time spent in recognized school, or medical diploma with three years' actual practice of medicine

Kansas, four years' experience in compounding physicians' prescriptions

Louisiana, grammar school education, sufficient knowledge of chemistry and practice of pharmacy

Montana, four years' experience in compounding physicians' prescriptions

New Jersey, four years' experience in a pharmacy

New York city and Erie county, New York, four years' experience in a pharmacy

North Dakota, four successive years' practical experience in a pharmacy

Oklahoma, four years' experience in compounding prescriptions

South Carolina, three years' experience in a pharmacy

Utah, four years' practical experience in a pharmacy

Vermont, practice in pharmacy or served apprenticeship for three years

Virginia, four years' practical experience in a pharmacy

Washington, three years' practical experience in a pharmacy

Wyoming, two years' practical experience in a pharmacy

Vermont accepts also an approved diploma of medical school.

The following grant licenses on examination by state boards and to physicians in certain cases:

Mississippi   New Jersey   North Carolina   Virginia

Alabama and Missouri accept also an approved diploma.

Rhode Island grants license on examination by state board and to practitioners in certain cases.

Idaho requires approved diploma or examination by county board.

Florida requires approved diploma or examination by state board or by local physicians. Authorized physicians are licensed without examination.

In Cuba, the Philippines[1] and Puerto Rico[1] the requirements are in process of transition.

Alaska, Arizona, Hawaii, Indian territory and Nevada have no laws.

---

[1] See note under Synopsis of present requirements in medicine.

7 VETERINARY MEDICINE [1]

Early veterinary schools — Veterinary medicine was pursued as a science by the ancient Egyptians and by the Greeks, but after the destruction of the eastern empire little progress was made in this science till the establishment of a veterinary school at Lyons in 1762. This institution was soon followed by similar schools in other European countries.

Before 1850 graduates in veterinary medicine were almost unknown in America, some of the larger cities only being able to furnish isolated veterinarians who had been educated in the veterinary schools of Europe. The country as a whole, including most of the large cities, had to be satisfied with such service as could be had from the blacksmith, from the physician who sought to apply to animals the principles taught in the medical schools and from the *horse doctor* who, with no basis whatever of medical knowledge, boldly and recklessly administered drugs.

The first step toward systematic veterinary education was the granting of a charter in 1852 by the legislature of Pennsylvania, and the securing of a subscription of $40,000, to serve in the organization of a veterinary school in Philadelphia. This school opened in 1853 but no students responded. In 1859–60 two students were secured, one of whom was a graduate of the Boston veterinary college which had been chartered in 1855. Both of these schools had a short life, but the same cities have now each its veterinary school in connection with the University of Pennsylvania and Harvard respectively. Each of these schools has a matriculation examination and a three years' course of eight months each. In 1857 the New York college of veterinary surgeons was chartered and in 1875 the American veterinary college was opened. These two New York city schools were maintained as proprietary institutions till

---

[1] The historical part of this outline was prepared mainly by Prof. James Law of Cornell university.

1899 when they were placed on a strictly university footing by consolidation under New York university.

In the succeeding years veterinary schools sprang into existence in many of the large cities, Chicago, Kansas City, Cincinnati, Baltimore, Washington, Grand Rapids, Detroit, etc., all like the earlier schools in Boston, Philadelphia and New York, being private ventures, dependent on their financial returns, and with a curriculum of 10 or 12 months representing two years of five or six months each.

Advances made by state schools — The necessity for a fuller, graded course based on matriculation requirements which would be a guaranty of fitness to pursue such course profitably, was first voiced by schools connected with state colleges and universities. As early as 1868, Illinois industrial university[1] and Cornell university instituted 2 veterinary chairs, and filled them with graduates of the Royal college of veterinary surgeons, England. Students were admitted only on the basis of the regular university matriculation and were held to a course of 4 years. Illinois industrial university is said to have turned out several good practitioners, while Cornell graduated 4 veterinarians, 3 of whom have been prominent and valued members of the United States bureau of animal industry, 1 being its chief. These institutions were followed in 1879 by the veterinary department of the Iowa agricultural and mechanical college with moderate matriculation requirements, and a three years' graded course, in 1889 by the veterinary department of the Ohio state university with equal or still greater requirements, and in 1890 by the veterinary department of the university of Minnesota with similar standards.

The important advances made by these state schools of veterinary medicine may be better illustrated by the fact that their academic year extends to eight or nine months, while the year of the private school covered but five or six months. The total curriculum of the state veterinary school therefore extended from 24 to 27 months or in the case of

---

[1] Became University of Illinois in 1885.

Cornell university to 36 months, as against the 10 or 12 months of the private school.

Requirements of American veterinary medical association — The United States veterinary medical association,[1] adopted in 1891 an article providing that all applicants for membership should be graduates of a recognized veterinary school with a curriculum of at least three years, of six months each, and a corps of instructors comprising at least four veterinarians. Nearly all the schools which had not already done so soon placed themselves in harmony with these requirements.

New York's leadership — The next step in advance came in 1895 when the New York legislature enacted that at least a high school diploma representing four years of high school work should be offered for admission to a veterinary school, that the veterinary curriculum should embrace three full years, and that only those who had met both requirements could be admitted to the regents veterinary examination for license to practise in the state. For the present this places New York in the lead. To begin practice in this state the candidate must reach a standard which is not demanded in any other state in the Union. But even within New York state there have been inequalities in the curriculum. In the private veterinary schools in New York city, the old session of six months has stood for a year, while in the New York state veterinary college, Cornell university, a nine-month year is required. To the legal requirement for matriculation, therefore, which is common to all schools in the state, the period devoted to veterinary education in the state school at Cornell is one half longer than that which has been required in the private schools in New York city. Now that these schools have consolidated under New York university, it is hoped that these inequalities will disappear. As a means of extending the benefits of its curriculum to their full legal possibilities, Cornell offers tuition free to all residents of the state, and opens to competition by the

---

[1] Now the American veterinary medical association.

entering veterinary student 18 scholarships of an annual value of $200 and to veterinary graduates a fellowship of an annual value of $500.

Action in Massachusetts — The legislature of Massachusetts has recently appropriated $25,000 for a veterinary laboratory and stable hospital in connection with the state agricultural college. Beginning with Jan. 1, 1899 there is to be an annual appropriation of $1000 as a fund for the maintenance of the veterinary laboratory.

Higher standards — An impartial survey of the entire field shows a marked tendency toward higher standards and, as an important step in this direction, the assumption of the work of veterinary education by the state under such university supervision as will give it character and eliminate the disturbing element of personal pecuniary speculation.

Army veterinary service — The United States army has long had its nominal veterinarians, but many of these were uneducated men, appointed by political influence or advanced from the position of farrier major, and there was little to tempt professional men of character and ability into this service. The army veterinarian had practically no army status, no rights, no prospects. He was not even enlisted, there was no special provision for him during service and no pension if he had to retire disabled. In the last session of congress the first step was taken for the improvement of the army veterinary service by enacting that the army veterinarian of the first grade must enter on the basis of an examination to be prescribed by the secretary of war, and that he shall have the pay and allowances of a second lieutenant of cavalry, while those of the second grade shall have $75 a month and the allowances of a sergeant major.

Veterinary workers in agricultural colleges and experiment stations — A steadily increasing recognition of the veterinary profession is seen in the appointment of veterinarians to chairs in state agricultural colleges and to positions in agricultural experiment stations. Here too the selection thoroughly sustains the growing demand for higher standards.

32 such positions are filled, practically without exception, by men who have passed an exacting matriculation examination and have had a prolonged course of veterinary study. Many add to their veterinary degree the academic B. A., B. S., B. Agr., or the professional M. D.

Municipal, state and national veterinarians — Since its organization in 1882 the United States bureau of animal industry has provided the different states with the funds necessary for the eradication of the cattle lung plague which had been imported from Europe in 1848, the expert and other employees having been made both national and state officers so that they could act as one or the other as the case demanded. It has done most valuable work on Texas fever, anthrax, emphysematous anthrax, hog cholera, swine plague and many other epizootic, enzootic, dietetic and contagious diseases, following the lines of prevention, immunization and serum therapy. It has continued the quarantine of imported animals since it superseded the treasury cattle commission in 1882. It has instituted meat inspection by experts in national employ, at the great packing centers, of meats intended for the export or interstate trade. In a number of states, a state veterinarian and even assistant state veterinarians have been appointed and, though in some instances the old spoils system has retained sufficient vitality to have the inexpert appointed to do expert work, yet in the main the interests of the public and of the profession have been consulted in the appointment of men educated in the duties of the office. In many of the larger cities too, the veterinarian has been recognized in his appointment as municipal meat inspector or as stock inspector. With the continued improvement of the civil service and the imperative demand for public servants who are specially trained and efficient in performing their respective duties, this recognition must soon become the rule.

Indications from veterinary literature — A review of recent veterinary literature shows much thought and research, yet as an indication of the predominant influence of sanitary science and the control of contagious diseases, it need only be said that of papers presented before the American veterinary medical association two thirds have been on such subjects. This indicates a healthful interest in the most vital and promising fields of veterinary research, and speaks well for the supply of experts to work in this field in the future. It is worthy of note that in all strong veterinary schools work in bacteriology is made a first consideration.

Field for educated veterinarians — In 1888 there were 6 veterinary schools with 323 students. In 1899 there were 17 schools with 249 instructors and 378 students. 6 of these 17 schools are separate institutions, 11 are departments of other institutions. 7 maintain day sessions, 3 have both day and evening sessions, 7 do not report this item. 16 schools confer degrees.

There is a broad field in the United States for educated veterinarians, and in view of this fact it is surprising that there are not more veterinary medical students. To assert that this is due to the lengthening to three years of the courses in the veterinary medical schools and to the use of bicycles and electric cars as substitutes for horses is not a satisfactory explanation. Horses will always be in large demand. Furthermore, the close relation between the health of man and that of the domestic animals, specially those that furnish meat and milk, shows the necessity of careful attention to their health. The reports of the department of agriculture give a value of about $2,000,000,000 to the live stock of the United States, and the protection of these enormous interests demands the services of trained veterinarians. The science of meat inspection has not as yet commanded with us the attention it should receive. The work of the national government in this respect is confined to international and interstate trade, principally to the large western packing houses. Local municipal inspection is in its infancy and state legislatures have not as a rule enacted special measures of protection. There now seems to be, however, an increasing demand for scientific work along these lines and the best veterinary schools are recognizing this necessity in their courses of study.

Synopsis of requirements — The first law restricting the practice of veterinary medicine was enacted in New York in 1886. In 1899, 12 states had veterinary medical laws.

In 5 states a veterinary diploma does not admit to the practice of veterinary medicine, an examination being required in all cases :

Minnesota   New York   North Dakota   Pennsylvania   Virginia

The following require for admission to the licensing examination :

Minnesota, diploma from veterinary school

New York, full high school course, diploma of veterinary school with satisfactory standard

North Dakota, diploma from veterinary school

Pennsylvania, competent common school education, approved diploma from legally incorporated veterinary school having a course of three years

Virginia requires the licensing examination only

Illinois requires approved veterinary diploma or 3 years' practice or examination

Ohio requires approved veterinary diploma or examination by state board

California and Maryland require veterinary diploma approved by state board

New Jersey admits on veterinary diploma submitted to unqualified local authority

Wisconsin admits on veterinary diploma or certificate submitted to unqualified local authority, and practitioners five years prior to 1887

Michigan registers veterinary medical degrees without examination and issues certificates of " veterinary surgeon " to those who pass the examinations of the state veterinary board.

The other states and territories have no laws on the subject.

DEPARTMENT OF EDUCATION

FOR THE

UNITED STATES COMMISSION TO THE PARIS EXPOSITION OF 1900

MONOGRAPHS ON EDUCATION

IN THE

UNITED STATES

EDITED BY

NICHOLAS MURRAY BUTLER

Professor of Philosophy and Education in Columbia University, New York

11

SCIENTIFIC, TECHNICAL AND ENGINEERING EDUCATION

BY

T. C. MENDENHALL,

President of the Technological Institute, Worcester, Mass.

THIS MONOGRAPH IS CONTRIBUTED TO THE UNITED STATES EDUCATIONAL EXHIBIT BY THE STATE OF NEW YORK

SCIENTIFIC, TECHNICAL AND ENGINEERING SCHOOLS[1]

The development of the schools of science and technology in the United States is, practically, an affair of the last half of the nineteenth century. In a large measure the same is true of similar institutions in Europe, for although there are isolated examples of earlier foundations both in Europe and America, it is only during the past fifty years that in number and importance they have come to rank with older systems of intellectual and professional training. Their comparatively recent origin is readily accounted for when it is remembered that they are nearly all schools in which science is taught with a view to its practical application and that the admission to the college curriculum of any part of what is now generally included under the term "science" was a rare novelty in the early part of the century. The modern scientific school or engineering college is largely indebted for its being to Archimedes, Galileo, Bacon, Kepler, Newton and a host of others who by creating exact science made applied science possible. The idea of a *school* of science or of a college in which the applications of scientific discovery might be taught was of slow growth at the beginning, and naturally so, for their successful development demanded the evolution of methods of instruction entirely new and often in violation of accepted tradition.

A class of professional schools had existed, indeed, almost as long as education itself, namely, schools for training candidates for the so-called "learned" professions, law, medicine and theology, but it will not be claimed that they had much

---

[1] The author begs to express his appreciation of the assistance generously rendered by officers of many of the institutions referred to in this paper who kindly furnished information in the form of printed circulars, catalogues and other important publications, much of which he has made use of, and much more of which he would have gladly used had the limits of space permitted.

in common, either as to method or material, with the modern school of science.

The earliest technical schools, those of a hundred years ago or more, almost without exception grew out of the industrial demands of the locality in which they were founded. One of the best examples is the famous School of mines at Freiberg which has enjoyed a long and illustrious career and many of the earlier European schools belong to the same class. To these and the more modern schools of science and technology the United States is greatly indebted, especially on account of the generous welcome that has always been extended to American students and for the inspiration with which many of them have returned to take their part in the wonderful educational evolution which the last half century has witnessed.

But in all cases European methods have been adapted rather than adopted. Political, social and material conditions have largely influenced educational foundations, and while the nearly one hundred schools of science and engineering scattered over the United States have many points of resemblance, there is much individuality, particularly among the strongest and best, and it is believed that their several types represent important advances in the direction of scientific and technical education which will not be without interest to educators in other parts of the world.

The limit necessarily put upon the length of this paper makes it impossible to consider historically or otherwise all of the institutions which would properly come under its title. A not very exact classification based on organization easily divides all into three groups, and the end in view will be best accomplished by selecting for more careful description some of the more important representatives of each group. The order of presentation will be, in the main, chronological according to the date of establishment, and this will be departed from only when necessary to include the leading types of the several groups.

In the first group will be included those schools and colleges devoted practically exclusively to science and technology, which have independent foundations and which are not under state or government control. These have almost invariably originated in private endowment, often of one man, and rely for their support upon the income from their endowment and from tuition fees.

The second group embraces those schools which are closely affiliated with other colleges or schools forming universities, sometimes without a distinctly separate faculty or special organization, whose work has been largely individualized, sometimes having a distinguishing name, and not under state or government control. Some members of this group are wholly or partly supported by separate endowments and fix and collect their own tuition fees, while others depend upon sharing the common resources of the larger whole of which they are a part.

In the third group are included that very large and important class of schools supported largely, if not entirely, by state and government appropriation.

The organization of some of these resembles in an important particular that of the first group in the fact that they enjoy a separate existence as schools of science or technology, being independent of any college or university affiliation. The majority, however, are not thus independent, and must be regarded as departments of a college, or schools or colleges of a university. A few of them originated in private endowments and do not rely entirely on the state or national government for support, but yet are so largely dependent on that source of revenue that they fairly belong to the group. Something of the origin, history and development of a few of the principal representatives of these three groups will be given, to be followed by some general statements relating to requirements for admission, courses of study, degrees and other matters of interest or importance.

The first endowment and organization of a school of science in the United States was that of the **Rensselaer**

polytechnic institute in 1824. The founder, Stephen Van Rensselaer, was born in New York November 1, 1765, and died in Albany January 26, 1839. He was known as the "eighth patroon," having inherited his rank and estates from ancestors who had for generations ruled over that enormous feudal estate purchased and colonized early in the 17th century by Killian Van Rensselaer of Amsterdam, Holland. Stephen Van Rensselaer lost his baronial rights on the establishment of the colonial government during the revolutionary war, and the extent and value of the estate, which included the entire territory now comprised in the counties of Albany, Columbia and Rensselaer, were considerably diminished, but after graduating from Harvard college, he took active steps looking to the improvement of the very large property still remaining, and also rapidly became a prominent figure in the politics of the new nation, being in many ways peculiarly fitted for public duties and responsibilities. His early interest in engineering is proved by the fact that he was the first to propose a canal connecting the Hudson river with the great lakes. As a commissioner of the state, he made a personal investigation of the route, and in 1811 a report which was received with favor. The war of 1812 with Great Britain intervening to postpone action upon this important enterprise, he entered the military service as commander of the United States forces on the northern frontier. At the close of the war he again took hold of the canal project and became chairman of the canal commission. In the discharge of his duty as such, he caused to be made by Professor Amos Eaton in 1821–23, a geological survey along the line of the canal from Albany to Buffalo, the examination being also extended some distance into Massachusetts. The importance of the results of this work so impressed itself upon him, together with the lack of men capable of properly conducting such enterprises, as to convince him of the desirability and necessity for scientific and technical education. Professor Eaton, who executed this early geological survey for Van Rensselaer, was a man of many and varied accomplishments, ready to adapt himself to the conditions under which his work was done, and possessed of much ingenuity and skill in inventing and constructing simple devices for taking the place of more elaborate but inaccessible instruments. Such a man was likely to make an impression upon the patroon, who was himself a man of liberal education and broad views. It is to this combination that the Rensselaer polytechnic institute owes its origin. Professor Eaton, its first director, was a native of the state of New York, born in 1776. When fourteen or fifteen years of age, having acted as chainman during a land survey, he determined to become a surveyor. He negotiated with a skillful blacksmith who agreed to work for him at night if he would "blow and strike" during the day. A needle and a good working chain resulted and an old pewter plate, smoothed, polished and graduated, served as a compass circle. At the age of 16 years he did actual surveying with these instruments. Later he entered Williams college and was graduated in 1799. His love for science led him to Yale college in 1815, where he received instruction from Professor Silliman. He gave courses of lectures at Williams college in 1817, developing a remarkable talent for popular exposition of scientific discovery, which resulted in his giving a course of lectures before the members of the New York legislature in 1818 on the invitation of Governor De Witt Clinton, and eventually in the geological survey already referred to at the request of Van Rensselaer. In his first letter to those selected to constitute the board of trustees Van Rensselaer named Professor Eaton as professor of chemistry and experimental philosophy, his office to be designated the "senior professorship."

This was dated November 5th, 1824, and something of the founder's idea of what his school ought to do is shown in "Order 7" of the same communication. He says: "These are not to be taught by seeing experiments and hearing lectures, according to the usual method. But they are to lecture and experiment by turn, under the immediate direction of a professor or competent assistant. Thus by a term of labor, like apprentices to a trade, they are to become operative chemists." The opening of the school occurred on Monday, January 3rd, 1825. It was incorporated in March, 1826, the act providing that the clear annual income of the invested funds of the institution should *not exceed twenty thousand dollars*. It was at first named the "Rensselaer school;" afterward the "Rensselaer institute" and afterwards the "Rensselaer polytechnic institute." Professor Eaton served for seventeen years as the senior professor, and during this period the course of study covered only one year. An important epoch in the history of the institution was the appointment of Professor B. Franklin Greene as senior professor in 1846, who became director on the establishment of that office in 1850. From that time the institute became more distinctly a school of civil engineering. The course of study was lengthened to three years and the corps of instructors was enlarged. The buildings and much of the equipment were destroyed by fire in 1862, but they were replaced by friends of the school and more extensive equipment was provided.

The Rensselaer polytechnic institute offers two courses of four years each, one in civil engineering and one in natural science. Upon those who complete the first it bestows the degree of C. E., and for the second that of B. S. In 1899 its instructors were fifteen in number and its students 143. It has graduated 1219 men, of whom 874 are living. Being the first school of its kind its list of graduates doubtless excels all others in the number of men who have reached distinction in professional life. It is supported by the income from its endowment funds and by tuition fees. Its government is rested in a board of twenty trustees, with the mayor of the city of Troy, *ex-officio*.

The next in order of time and one of the foremost in the country is the **Massachusetts institute of technology** at Boston.

This now famous institution owes its existence to the wise

foresight, the earnest and never-flagging enthusiasm, and the rare personal charm of Professor William B. Rogers, its first president and real founder.   Professor Rogers was born in Philadelphia in 1804, his father, Dr. Patrick K. Rogers, having emigrated from Ireland a few years earlier.   In 1819 Dr. P. K. Rogers became professor of natural philosophy in William and Mary college, Virginia, and there Professor W. B. Rogers was educated.   At an early age he was distinguished for his scientific attainments and for an eloquent and persuasive speech which greatly increased his influence among men.   For a long time he was professor of natural philosophy in the University of Virginia and he also served as state geologist for many years.   It was while still a professor in the university that his mind was turned to the problem of scientific and technical training, and in 1846 he drew up a scheme for a school of technology which some years later and with slight modifications he brought to a realization in the Massachusetts institute of technology. Although not a New England man by birth or education, he had occasionally visited Boston and was greatly impressed with it as a suitable locality for such an institution.   He left Virginia to reside in Boston in 1853, and here, for a period of nearly ten years he worked, wrote and lectured, keeping all the time in mind the organization and development of the school of technology, the plans of which he had so long and so carefully considered.   On April 10, 1861, the act incorporating the Massachusetts institute of technology received the approval of Governor Andrews, just as the nation was plunging into what proved to be a mighty struggle for its existence.   A year later Professor Rogers was formally elected president of the institution, which as yet had no material existence.   Indeed the war for the preservation of the Union delayed the consummation of his desires until February, 1865, at which time instruction in the new school was actually begun.   During these years, as well as during the earlier years of the actual existence of the school, the organization was maintained and the work carried on under great discouragement, mainly through the personal exertions and influence of Dr. Rogers, its president.   He had already attained a high reputation as a scientific man, and to this he added a rare power of lucid explanation and popular exposition of scientific discovery   This, with his simple and engaging manner, enabled him to gather about the young and feeble educational experiment a number of men, many of them distinguished in various walks of life, who loyally put themselves under his leadership in all matters relating to the institute.   The earliest financial support came from two citizens of Boston, Dr. Walker and Mr. Huntington, who contributed $50,000 towards the erection of a building.   When instruction began in 1865 there were enrolled 15 students, but the marvellous material development of the country which followed the civil war was favorable to the growth of the school and its prosperity rapidly increased.   In 1870, owing to ill health, Dr. Rogers retired from the presidency and was succeeded by Professor John D. Runkle, who had been professor of mathematics from the beginning.   In 1878 Dr. Rogers, having partially recovered his health, was induced to return to the presidency, holding that office until 1881, when, on his recommendation, General Francis A. Walker was elected as his successor.   A year later, at noon of May 30th, 1882, Dr. Rogers, in the midst of an address to the graduating class of the institute, in which his hearers were delighted with an apparent revival of the spirit and eloquence with which he was accustomed to enrich every occasion for dignified address, fell upon the platform of Huntington hall, surrounded by the material realization of his dreams of nearly forty years earlier, and by those who, by the closest associations, had learned to love him as few are loved.

Under the able leadership of his distinguished successor, the Massachusetts institute of technology entered upon a new career of growth and development which has placed it in the front rank of its kind throughout the world.

By the act of incorporation of 1861 William Barton

Rogers and his twenty associates were made a body corporate "for the purpose of instituting and maintaining a
society of arts, a museum of arts and a school of industrial
science." The latter has become the prominent feature of
the institute. "It is devoted to the investigation and
teaching of science as applied to the various engineering
professions, namely, civil, mechanical, mining, electrical,
chemical and sanitary engineering, and naval architecture,
as well as to architecture, chemistry, metallurgy, biology,
physics and geology. A course of a less technical nature,
designed as a preparation for business callings, is also provided." There is also affiliated with it the Lowell school
of practical design, established in 1872 by the trustee of
the Lowell institute for the purpose of promoting industrial
art in the United States. The course in this school covers
three years of instruction in the art of design including
technical manipulations; copying and variation of designs;
original designs and the making of working designs.

The institute offers thirteen distinct courses, each of four
years' duration, in civil engineering, mechanical engineering, mining engineering and metallurgy, architecture, chemistry, electrical engineering, biology, physics, general studies,
chemical engineering, sanitary engineering, geology and
naval architecture. It is amply equipped with laboratories,
museums and libraries. Its officers of instruction number
136 in all departments. Students in all departments numbered 1171 in 1899, and the number of graduates from the
beginning is nearly two thousand.

The institute is supported for the most part by the income
from private endowments and from fees received from
tuition. It receives, however, one-third of the income of
the commonwealth of Massachusetts from the national land
grant funds and subsequent national appropriations for land
grant colleges. During the past two years it has received
from private bequests something over one million dollars.
It furnishes free tuition to forty students from the public
schools of Massachusetts from which it is reimbursed by

legislative appropriation. Its government is vested in a corporation consisting of not more than fifty members, including the governor of the commonwealth, the chief justice of the supreme judicial court and the secretary of the state board of education. The corporators, excepting the *ex-officiis* members, hold office for life and vacancies are filled by the corporation. It confers the degree of bachelor of science on the completion of any of the regular courses of study and that of master of science for graduate courses of at least one year.

The Worcester polytechnic institute at Worcester, Massachusetts, was incorporated in May, 1865, only a few weeks after the Massachusetts institute of technology received its first class of fifteen students in rented rooms in Boston. In the latter part of 1864 Mr. John Boynton of Templeton, in Worcester county, a merchant who by thrift and economy had accumulated a considerable fortune, made known to Mr. David Whitcomb of Worcester, who had been his partner and was his most trusted friend, his desire to devote the major portion of his savings to the establishment of a school for training young men for industrial pursuits. He was wisely advised by Mr. Whitcomb, a man of rare sagacity, and Rev. Dr. Seth Sweetser, then pastor of the Central church of Worcester, was also consulted. It developed that a distinguished citizen of Worcester, Mr. Ichabod Washburn, the founder of the great Washburn & Moen steel and wire manufactory, long the leading establishment of its kind in the world, had about a year earlier confided to Dr. Sweetser his own desire to contribute towards the establishment of an institution of like nature. A conference, including among others the Hon. Emory Washburn, President Hill of Harvard university, the Hon. George F. Hoar and the Hon. Stephen Salisbury, resulted in a union of the two schemes, Mr. Washburn contributing the cost of the erection, equipment and endowment of extensive workshops, since known as the Washburn shops, to form a part of the means provided for the proper training of mechanical engineers.

Mr. Boynton's gift was $100,000. The citizens of Worcester undertook to provide for the erection of a suitable building upon a beautiful and convenient site given by Stephen Salisbury, who was also one of the most generous contributors to the building fund. It is interesting to note that many of the subscribers gave small sums, tradesmen and others uniting, to the number of about five hundred, to swell the amount. The corporation organized with the Hon. Stephen Salisbury as president, and in 1868 the first building, Boynton hall, was dedicated and the work of the school inaugurated. Its first president was Dr. Charles O. Thompson, a man most admirably fitted for the development of the new and somewhat novel plans of the trustees and donors. Dr. Thompson made a special study of European technical schools, particularly of the Russian schools, the imperial technical school at Moscow and the institute of technology at St. Petersburg.

In these schools the experiment was first made of combining in the engineering courses the study of text-books, lectures and other exercises long known to form a necessary part of scholastic training, with practical exercises in workshops in which the student was made familiar with machines, their construction and use, and the nature of the materials upon which they worked. Dr. Thompson was especially impressed with this plan as representing very closely the ideas of the founders of the Worcester polytechnic institute, and under his able direction it became the central idea about which the organization of the school crystallized. He remained at its head for fourteen years, during which it developed the distinctive qualities by which it has since been characterized. During the thirty years of its existence it has received numerous additions to its original funds, mostly from citizens of Worcester and especially from the Salisburys, including Stephen Salisbury 2d, the first president of the board of trustees, and Stephen Salisbury 3d, the present (1899) head of the corporation. As the school grew, and with it the demands of new methods of instruction, several large and commodious buildings were added to the original, notably the Salisbury laboratories for physics and chemistry, the gift of the present Stephen Salisbury; the engineering building, with its mechanical laboratories, erected by means of an appropriation by the state of Massachusetts of $100,000; the power laboratory, the hydraulic laboratory, etc.   Perhaps the distinctive feature of the school is the large utilization of workshops in connection with instruction in mechanical and electrical engineering. The constructive principle is dominant in the workshop training, and the student during his course, or sometimes in conjunction with a small group of his fellows, actually produces all the parts of a tolerably complex machine, involving the use of a wide variety of machine tools and of materials used in construction.   The excellence of his work or design is tested as an actual commercial product, which is held to be the final test, and to secure the best results the Washburn shops maintain a commercial side, the greater part of the output of which consists of special machines, appliances and devices originally designed and developed there, representing the results of actual engineering practice on the part of students and professors.

The institute offers five courses, each of four years duration, namely, mechanical engineering, civil engineering, chemistry (including sanitary and industrial chemistry), electrical engineering and general science.   It grants the degree of bachelor of science to those who complete any one of its courses, and the master's degree for graduate study of not less than one year.   Professional degrees of mechanical, civil and electrical engineering are granted upon conditions requiring still further work and several years of successful professional experience.

Its corps of instructors numbers 31 and its students (1899) 236.   Its graduates number (1899) 823.   Its support is derived from the income of its endowment and fees for tuition.   It gives free tuition to forty students from the state of Massachusetts for which it is reimbursed by annual

appropriation from the state. It also furnishes free tuition
to about thirty young men, residents of Worcester county,
for which funds have been provided by donation. Its government is vested in a board of twelve trustees, one being
appointed by the state board of education, and the mayor
of the city of Worcester being a member *ex-officio*. Other
members are chosen by the board and serve for life.

The Lehigh university, at South Bethlehem, Pennsylvania, although by name a university, is and has always been
pre-eminently a technical or engineering college of a high
grade. The original object of its founder was to afford the
young men of the Lehigh valley a complete education, technical, literary and scientific, suitable to fit them for those
professions represented in the development of the peculiar
resources of the rich mining territory in which it is located.

In 1865 the Hon. Asa Packer signified his intention of
providing such an institution by announcing his willingness
to donate to it the sum of $500,000 and one hundred and
fifteen acres of land in South Bethlehem on which the buildings might be placed. Judge Packer was born in Groton,
Connecticut, in 1806, and died in Philadelphia in 1879.
After receiving a common school education he began learning the trade of tanning, but gave it up to serve an apprenticeship as a carpenter. He worked at this trade for some
time, but while still under twenty years of age, on the opening of the Lehigh Valley canal, he established himself at
Mauch Chunk, becoming the owner and master of a canal
boat for carrying coal to Philadelphia. Although entirely
lacking preliminary training, he possessed the instincts of
an engineer, and was soon extensively engaged in the building of locks and boats and in the mining and transportation
of coal. He projected the Lehigh Valley railroad, and
through his varied and extensive operations in mining and
transporting coal became the richest man of his day in the
state of Pennsylvania. He filled important political offices,
was a member of congress and was the candidate of his
party for governor of the state in 1869. He gave to the

newly-established institution more liberally during his life than he had at first announced, and at his death bequeathed to it an endowment of nearly $2,000,000, the total amount of his benefactions reaching over two and a half million dollars.

The institution was incorporated in 1866, and its first class was graduated in 1869. Its first president was Professor Henry Coppee, LL.D. It is well equipped with suitably-appointed laboratories, an astronomical observatory, a museum which is especially rich in minerals, and a large and well-endowed library. While it offers a classical course, its resources are almost exclusively devoted to the school of technology. In this six courses are offered as follows : Civil engineering, mechanical engineering, metallurgy, mining, electrical engineering and chemistry. Its corps of instructors numbers 41 and its students (1899) 325, of whom all except ten were in the technical or scientific courses. Up to 1899 its graduates numbered nearly one thousand.

The Lehigh university is supported by the income from its endowments and the fees charged for tuition, although it has received occasional appropriations from the state. It is governed by a board of ten trustees, together with nine honorary trustees, four of whom are chosen from the alumni to serve for a fixed term of years.

The Stevens institute of technology, at Hoboken, New Jersey, was opened for the admission of students in September, 1871. Mr. Edwin A. Stevens, its founder, was a member of a distinguished family of engineers. His grandfather, John Stevens, had been a member of the continental congress, and his father, also John, had filled offices of trust and responsibility during the revolutionary war, besides being the most famous engineer of his time. At the close of the war for independence he was a man of independent wealth, owning the island of Hoboken on which he lived during the summer, and he devoted practically the remainder of his life to experimental engineering at his own cost for the common good. Through his influence the American patent law was

enacted. He was one of the earliest users of steam and he
made important improvements in the method of generating
it. He was the first to navigate the Hudson by means of a
steamboat, which he did successfully in 1804, and by a vessel propelled by twin screws, essentially the same in form as
those now universally in use, and he was always a warm
advocate of the screw propeller. He established the first
steam ferry in the world, was the first to navigate the ocean
by steam and in 1812 he made the first experiments in the
use of artillery against iron armor, and about the same time
he strongly urged the construction of a railroad between the
seaboard and the great lakes instead of a canal which was
then being talked of. His suggestions were rejected by
the commissioners, who considered them impracticable and
visionary.

His sons, Robert L. and Edwin A., inherited the engineering tastes of their father and added new lustre to the
fame of the family by remarkable achievements in the field
of railroad development and marine engineering. The earliest railroads of importance in the United States were built
under their direction and the two brothers were the joint
inventors of many improvements in track, rolling stock,
power, etc. Both were greatly interested in the application
of engineering to warfare and especially in improving naval
attack and defense, and Robert L. Stevens built the first
ironclad vessel ever constructed. In the will of Edwin A.
Stevens, dated April 15th, 1867, he bequeathed a block of
ground in the city of Hoboken, with $150,000, for the erec-
tion of buildings thereon "suitable for the uses of an institution of learning, and also $500,000 as an endowment
fund for the support of the same. In 1870 Professor
Henry Morton, Ph. D., at that time professor of chemistry
in the University of Pennsylvania and also secretary of the
Franklin institute, was selected as the president of the new
institution for which a charter had been obtained in February of the same year. Dr. Morton, to whom the success
and high character of the school is largely due, has contin-

ued to serve as its president from the beginning.   In 1875
a mechanical laboratory was established under the direction
of Professor R. H. Thurston, who was the first professor of
mechanical engineering in the institute.   The Stevens institute is essentially a school of mechanical engineering alone,
and it offers but one course of study, which requires four
years for its completion.   Much attention is given to practical laboratory and workshop methods.   There is a department of tests in which are undertaken measurements of the
performance of steam engines and other motors, of the efficiency of boilers, electrical and hydraulic apparatus, of the
strength of materials and kindred problems.   Its officers of
instruction are 21 in number and its students (1899) 214.
Since its organization the institute had graduated about 700
students.   It grants the degree of mechanical engineer to
those who have completed its course of study and it has
bestowed honorary degrees of doctor of philosophy and
doctor of engineering.   Since the original bequest of Mr.
Stevens it has received considerable additions to its endowment fund, and its president, Dr. Morton, has been among
the liberal donors.   It derives its support from the income
from its invested funds and from its tuition fees.   Its government is in the hands of a board of twelve trustees, one
of the number being an alumnus.

The Case school of applied science, at Cleveland, Ohio,
was incorporated on March 29th, 1880.   Leonard Case, its
founder, was born in Cleveland on June 27th, 1820.   His
father, also Leonard Case, had come to Ohio from Pennsylvania at the beginning of the century.   By judicious pur-
chases of public lands in and near Cleveland, then a village,
now (1899) a flourishing city of over 300,000 inhabitants,
and by active participation in early railroad enterprises, he
accumulated a large estate, all of which his son, Leonard,
inherited.   The latter was educated at Yale college, being
a member of the class which was graduated in 1842.   He
was, as a young man, inclined rather to literary and scientific pursuits than to business.   He was especially fond of

scientific and mathematical studies, but he possessed considerable real literary ability, as was evidenced by occasional
poems and translations, some of which were published in the
best magazines of the day.   In 1876 he had already determined upon founding a school of science, and in 1877 he
executed a deed of trust setting apart certain real estate for
the support of the institution, to take effect upon his death,
which occurred on January 6th, 1880.

In this he directed the trustees "to cause to be formed
and to be regularly incorporated under the laws of Ohio an
institution of learning to be called 'Case school of applied
science,' and located in said city of Cleveland, in which
shall be taught by competent professors and teachers
mathematics, physics, engineering — mechanical and civil —
chemistry, economic geology, mining and metallurgy, natural history, drawing and modern languages, and such other
kindred branches of learning as the trustees of said institution may deem desirable."   Instruction began in 1881, with
a class of 16 students, the school being carried on from that
time until the summer of 1885 in the old Case homestead.
A commodious building having been erected for the use of
the school, it was occupied at the beginning of the term in
September, 1885.   A year later the building with all that it
contained was destroyed by fire.   It was promptly rebuilt
and occupied in 1888.   Since that time several additional
buildings for laboratory and shop exercises have been
erected.

The Case school of applied science offers eight regular
courses of instruction, each requiring four years.   They are
civil engineering, mechanical engineering, electrical engineering, mining engineering, physics, chemistry, architecture
and general science.   In 1899 there were 21 instructors and
218 students.   From the beginning it has graduated about
230 men.   The degree of bachelor of science is granted to
all who complete one of the regular courses.   That of master of science may be conferred upon graduates who have
devoted at least one year exclusively to graduate study.

Professional degrees, namely, civil engineer, mechanical engineer, electrical engineer and engineer of mines may also be conferred after one year of graduate study or after professional work in positions of responsibility, for three years after graduation. The property left by Mr. Case as an endowment for the support of the school is valued at about $2,000,000, and the amount invested in buildings and equipment is about $350,000. The school derives its support from the income from its endowment and tuition fees. Its government rests with a corporation consisting of twenty men, from whom six known as trustees are selected.

The Rose polytechnic institute, at Terre Haute, Indiana, was organized as early as 1874, but it was not open to students until 1883. The intervening years were spent in the erection of buildings for the accommodation of the school and in the personal examination by members of the board of managers of the leading schools of science and technology in the country. Its founder was Chauncy Rose, born in Wethersfield, Connecticut, in 1794, died in Terre Haute in 1877, having settled in Indiana in 1817. Mr. Rose was a successful business man, made judicious investments in real estate and was active in the early railroad development of Indiana. Throughout his long life he was distinguished for the sturdiest integrity in all business matters and for his generous and philanthropic disposition. An incident of the latter part of his life forcibly illustrates those qualities which made him the founder of schools, orphan asylums, free dispensaries, etc. His brother John lived in New York city and had also become a man of great wealth, concerning the disposition of which, after his death, he had very clear and well-defined ideas. Through a serious error in the preparation of his will, it appeared that if executed under the laws of New York it would fail in accomplishing the evident desires of the testator. Chauncy Rose at once instituted legal proceedings to have the will set aside, in which he succeeded after six years of litigation. He was himself the sole heir, and the estate of over $1,500,000 became his, but he immediately expended the whole in the exact manner desired by his brother, mostly in various charities in New York city.

He carefully attended to the erection of the buildings for the school he was to found, and on his death left an endowment for it of over half a million dollars. The trustees, in their examination of various other institutions, were much impressed with the organization and character of the Worcester polytechnic institute, and accordingly they invited Dr. Charles O. Thompson, its president, to come to Terre Haute as the first president of the Rose polytechnic. He accepted the invitation, and, after nearly a year in Europe, engaged in a renewal of his acquaintance with the leading schools of science and technology to be found there, he began the work of organizing the new institution which was opened to students in 1883. Dr. Thompson's work at the Rose polytechnic was unhappily cut short by his death only a little more than a year after the opening of the institute, but in that time its organization was practically completed, following closely the lines which he had previously established at Worcester, to which full reference has already been made.

The Rose polytechnic institute offers four separate courses of study each of four years' duration. They are in mechanical engineering, electrical engineering, civil engineering and architecture, and in chemistry. Its faculty of instruction (1899) included 15, and its students numbered 100. The total number of its graduates is about 260. It confers the degree of bachelor of science upon those who have completed any of its courses. That of master of science is conferred two years after graduation, at least one of which must be spent in graduate study, approved by the faculty. Professional degrees, mechanical engineer, electrical engineer or civil engineer will be conferred upon those who have already received their master's degree and who have subsequently spent at least two years in the successful practice of their profession. The institute derives its sup-

port from its endowment funds and tuition fees.   Additions
to the endowment fund have been received since the death
of the founder.   It is governed by a board of managers
consisting of nine men, with power to fill vacancies.   By
arrangement one member of the board is an alumnus, elected
by the alumni, to serve for one year.

The Polytechnic institute of Brooklyn, at Brooklyn, New
York, was originally an academy or preparatory school of
high grade, existing since 1854 under the name " Brooklyn
collegiate and polytechnic institute."   Two courses of
advanced study were provided in 1870, and in 1889 it was
reorganized and rechartered under the name it now bears.
One of its courses of study is called the " liberal " course
and leads to the degree of bachelor of arts, but the principal work of the institute is in applied science.   Here three
courses are provided, engineering, chemical and electrical.
Those who complete these courses, which are each four years
in length, receive the degree of bachelor of science.   Post
graduate courses are provided.   In 1899 the corps of
instructors numbered 11, and there were 79 students.   In
its technical and engineering courses it has graduated nearly
a hundred men.   Its income is derived from endowment
funds and tuition fees.

The Armour institute of technology, at Chicago, Illinois,
was founded by Philip D. Armour in 1892, and originally
chartered as " the Armour institute."   Mr. Armour was born
in Stockbridge, N. Y., in 1832.   He received only a common
school training, and after spending some time as a miner in
California, he engaged in a commission business in Milwaukee.   In 1863 he began his career as a grain and pork
merchant, and since 1875 he has been at the head of the firm
of Armour & Company of Chicago, the largest dealers in
dressed meats and provisions in the world.   He has given
generously towards the establishment and maintenance of a
mission in Chicago known as the Armour mission.   His
gifts to the institute of technology which bears his name
already amount to more than $2,500,000.   In the first public

announcement of his gift he said: "This institution is founded for the purpose of giving to young men and women an opportunity to secure a liberal education. . . . It is not intended for the poor or the rich, as sections of society, but for any and all who are earnestly seeking practical education. . . . The institute is not a free school, but its charges for instruction are in harmony with the spirit which animates alike the founder, the trustees and the faculty, namely, the desire to help those who wish to help themselves." Instruction began in 1893, and in 1895 it was somewhat reorganized, full four years' courses were arranged for, and the name changed to the "Armour institute of technology." The principal feature of the school is what is known as "the technical college," to which are allied, under the general organization, the department of domestic arts, the kindergarten normal department, the department of music and the department of shorthand and typewriting. In the technical college five courses of study are offered, a course in mechanical engineering, in electrical engineering, in architecture, in science and in civil engineering. In 1899 the corps of instructors numbered 31. No information concerning the number of students is given in the published yearbook. Its graduates probably number about 60. It confers the degree of bachelor of science. It is especially well equipped in apparatus relating to electric measurements. Its government is vested in a board of six trustees of which the founder is one, as is also the president of the institute.

The limits to which this monograph is restricted will not permit detailed reference to a greater number of institutions belonging to the group of independently organized and endowed schools of technology, although there are several others that, by reason of their excellent facilities and comprehensive courses of study, are quite as important as some of the above which have been selected as types. Within two or three years additions to the list have been made, among which may be mentioned the Bradley polytechnic institute at Peoria, Illinois, and the Clarkson institute of technology at Potsdam, N. Y.   There are a number of excellent schools in the southern states, mostly supported, however, by state appropriations.

Several of the most important schools of science and engineering in the United States belong to the second group, being affiliated with universities and colleges and sharing with other departments the income from private endowments, facilities and faculties of instruction.   Less detailed consideration will be given them here on that account, as they will doubtless receive a large measure of attention in monographs relating to these institutions.   This exposition would be quite incomplete, however, without reference to them, and, at the risk of duplication, a brief description of some of the leading examples will be given.

The Sheffield scientific school of Yale university, at New Haven, Connecticut, was organized in 1847 as a school of applied chemistry.   In 1860 it received its first considerable endowment from Joseph E. Sheffield of New Haven.   Mr. Sheffield was a native of Connecticut, born in 1793.   After receiving a common school education he began, at the early age of fifteen years, a long and successful business career. For more than a quarter of a century he lived in the south, becoming the chief cotton merchant in Mobile, Alabama, but in 1835 he returned to his native state and established himself in New Haven.   He was active in canal and railroad development, both in New England and the west, accumulating a large fortune from which he made munificent donations to Yale college.   In 1860 he provided suitable buildings for the scientific department and made liberal endowments for its support.   The Sheffield scientific school is devoted to "instruction and researches in the mathematical, physical and natural sciences, with reference to the promotion and diffusion of science, and also to the preparation of young men for such pursuits as require special proficiency in those departments of learning."   Instruction is specially planned for two classes of students : 1st, graduates of Yale and other universities or colleges, and others specially quali-

fied for advanced or special scientific study; 2nd, under-
graduates who desire a training chiefly mathematical and
scientific to fit them for higher scientific studies or for such
occupations as demand such training.   The undergraduate
courses extend through three years, but the requirements
for admission are considerably in advance of those in institutions whose courses are of four years.   A number of courses
of study are provided, at least ten being distinctly separate.
They include chemistry, civil engineering, mechanical engineering, electrical engineering, agriculture, natural history,
mineralogy, biology, mining and metallurgy.   There are
also a number of graduate courses.   The degree of bachelor of philosophy is conferred upon those completing any
of the three years' courses of study.   The degree of master
of science is conferred upon those who have taken their first
degree in science and who have had at least one year of resident graduate study, under the direction of the governing
board.   Two additional years are required for the degree of
civil engineer, or mechanical engineer and the degree of
doctor of philosophy is also conferred.   In 1899 there were
59 graduate students, 13 special students and a total of 597.
The total number of professors and instructors is 63.   The
faculty is distinct from that of the academic department
of Yale college, but some of the instructors are connected
with other departments.   The governing board consists of
the president of the university with the director of the scientific school and members of the faculty permanently
attached to the school.   Degrees are conferred by the
president of the university on the regular university commencement day and the corporate control of the school is
that of Yale university.

   The Lawrence scientific school of Harvard university, Cambridge, Massachusetts, was founded by Abbott Lawrence in
1847.   He was the younger of two brothers, born in Groton,
Massachusetts, late in the last century, who were the most
famous merchants in Boston during the first half of this.
He was a graduate of Harvard college and was distin-

guished not only for great success in mercantile and manufacturing operations, but also for the important public services with which he was occupied during the later years of
his life. He was a member of congress, a commissioner
for negotiating the northeast boundary treaty with Great
Britain, and served as minister to England from 1849 to
1852. His first gift for the endowment of the school which
bears his name was $50,000, to which large additions were
afterwards made by himself and members of his family.
The primary object of the institution was to afford an
opportunity for special study and training in science which
the then existing foundations and departments of the university did not offer.   Not the least of the important benefits
it conferred during the earlier years of its existence was the
bringing of Professor Louis Agassiz into close relations with
the university, a special chair of zoology and geology in the
scientific school having been created for him by Mr. Lawrence in 1848. It was originally intended that the Lawrence
scientific school should be independent of Harvard college,
and for many years it was so maintained, but in recent years
it has gradually become merged with it until it now forms a
part of the university, its government together with that of
the college and the graduate school being under the faculty
of arts and sciences. It confers or rather prepares for the
degree of bachelor of science by four years' courses, eleven
in number, including civil engineering, electrical engineering, mechanical engineering, mining and metallurgy, architecture, chemistry, geology, biology, general science, science
for teachers, and anatomy and physiology. These courses
are essentially required, while those of the college are
largely elective. The particular object of the school is
to afford to men of sound preliminary training a liberal-
ized education in various branches of science. So far as
possible the instruction relates rather to the principles of
science than to technical work, the intention being to make
the graduates ready for the apprenticeship of their professions. It avails itself of the great resources of Harvard

university, its museums, libraries, laboratories, etc., these being used in common by students who are candidates for the degrees of bachelor of science, bachelor of arts, or for the several graduate degrees conferred by the faculty of arts and sciences. While there are certain professors whose duties are confined to the scientific school, a great part of the instruction is in common with the college. It is so closely linked with Harvard college that no clear discrimination can be made in the funds which support the scientific school and other foundations. There is considerable election in the subjects required for admission and their range is essentially the same as with the college. In 1899 there were 425 students in the scientific school.

The Chandler school of science of Dartmouth college, Hanover, New Hampshire, was established in 1851 by the trustees of Dartmouth college, on the receipt of a bequest of $50,000, from Abiel Chandler, who left it to them in trust "for the establishment and support of a permanent department or school of instruction in the college, in the practical and useful arts of life." Mr. Chandler was born in Concord, New Hampshire, in 1777. Until he was twenty-one years of age he worked upon a farm but soon after he entered Harvard college from which he was graduated in 1806. For several years he was a teacher but afterwards engaged in business in Boston, retiring with a fortune in 1845. In addition to his bequest to Dartmouth college he distributed most of his estate in charity. The Chandler school was maintained as a separate department of the college for many years but it has recently been formally incorporated into the college and it is now known as the Chandler scientific course leading to the degree of bachelor of science. This course covers four years and is best described as a course in general science, including modern languages, mathematics, history, political science, etc., along with a good representation of the exact and natural history sciences. About 150 students are in the Chandler course.

Affiliated with Dartmouth college is the very important

graduate school of civil engineering known as **The Thayer school of civil engineering.** It was founded in 1867 by Gen. Sylvanus Thayer, U. S. A., who gave a fund of $70,000. General Thayer was born in Massachusetts in 1785. He was graduated from Dartmouth college in 1807 and from the U. S. military academy at West Point, which was then in a very elemental stage, in 1808. He became one of the most distinguished engineers of the army, was sent to Europe to study military works and schools, and on his return in 1817 was made superintendent of the U. S. military academy at West Point, a position which he held for sixteen years. During this time he entirely reorganized the school, putting it upon the same plane as the best military schools of Europe. So important were his services to the academy that his monument at West Point bears the inscription "Colonel Thayer, father of the United States military academy." It was his desire to found at Dartmouth college a graduate school of engineering, exacting in its requirements and complete and thorough in its work. Being a graduate school, its course, which occupies two years, is essentially professional. It devotes itself exclusively to civil engineering in the broader sense, and the high standard of admission has necessarily restricted the number of students. The first class was admitted in 1871, and from that year to 1897, inclusive, 123 have entered, at an average age exceeding 23 years. Of these 79 were graduated with the degree of civil engineer. The government of the school is vested in a board of overseers consisting of the president of Dartmouth college, with four officers of the engineer corps of the United States army, active or retired.

The School of mines of Columbia college, now Columbia university, New York city, began its work in 1864. Its establishment was due, primarily, to Professor Thomas Egleston. Professor Egleston was graduated at Yale in 1854, and at the *École des mines* in Paris in 1860. In 1863 he prepared and published a plan for a school of mines which was the basis of the organization at Columbia college.

Up to that time the enormous mineral resources of the United States were almost unknown; at least there had been little systematic effort towards their development. Such mining as was carried on was mostly under the direction of so-called "practical" miners, whose methods were wasteful and extravagant. A few experts had come from European schools, but the full exploitation of the rich deposits which the country possessed demanded a large number of trained and educated men. This demand the School of mines was destined to supply in a large measure, and it is difficult to overestimate the importance of its work during the quarter of a century following its foundation. The trustees of Columbia college permitted the use of certain rooms in the college buildings for the school and such collections of minerals, etc., as it might obtain. Professor Egleston was made professor of mineralogy and metallurgy, without salary, and he was shortly after joined by Professors Charles F. Chandler and F. L. Vinton on the same conditions, the faculty being expected to depend upon fees for support. The School of mines opened on November 15th, 1864, with 29 students, and its success was a gratifying surprise from the very beginning. The students were generally of somewhat mature age, and many of them were college graduates. Although the college had in no way committed itself to the financial support of the school, small sums of money were granted, and the importance of the school to Columbia college became more and more evident. Early in 1865 the School of mines was formally adopted as a co-ordinate branch of the college, and it is not too much to say that for many years the college was most widely known by reason of this connection. The primary object of the school was the education and training of *mining* engineers and metallurgists. It gathered together a faculty of men distinguished in their specialties, and it was soon evident that it could wisely extend its operations so as to cover other branches of engineering and applied science. Courses of study in civil engineering, applied chemistry, sanitary engineering, geology and architecture were added, although it still continued under the original name, School of mines. In 1889 a course in electrical engineering was added, and later on in mechanical engineering. In 1896 the title "Columbia university" was adopted as covering all the departments of instruction and research previously associated with or forming a part of Columbia college, and the title "School of mines" is now restricted to its original significance. The various engineering and science courses are now collectively directed by the "faculty of applied science," under which are the four schools of mines, chemistry, engineering and architecture. There is also a school of pure science under the direction of a faculty of pure science.

The School of engineering offers courses in civil, electrical and mechanical engineering, all of four years' duration, and corresponding degrees are granted. All of these schools are extensively equipped, and much attention is given to graduate courses and work.

In the School of pure science instruction is given in anatomy, astronomy, bacteriology, botany, chemistry, geology, mathematics, mechanics, mineralogy, physics, physiology, and zoology. The faculty of pure science exercises special supervision over the instruction and work of all candidates for the degrees of master of arts and doctor of philosophy in pure science. The several faculties of instruction in the university are not entirely distinct, but the total number of those giving instruction, in one way or another, in the courses in pure and applied science, is probably not far from 100, including professors, adjunct and associate professors, instructors, tutors and assistants. In 1899 there were registered 470 students under the faculty of applied sciences. The registration in the School of pure science was approximately 100. On January 1st, 1899, the total number of graduates in science was 1172.

Practically all colleges or universities in the United States offer courses in pure or applied science, and while their work may not be differentiated from that of the departments sufficiently to constitute a distinct school, it is often of high quality and the material appliances and equipment, everything that could be desired. Of the older of those giving special attention to science and engineering a few will be briefly mentioned. They will doubtless receive full consideration under another division of the educational institutions of the United States.

The College of the university of Pennsylvania provides, under a foundation known as the Towne scientific school, courses in architecture, mechanical and electrical engineering, chemistry and chemical engineering. They are of four years' duration and lead to the degree of bachelor of science. Ample facilities in the way of laboratories, machinery and apparatus, libaries, etc., are provided. Besides these courses in engineering, there is a course in biology, and all departments are represented in the university curricula and faculty of instruction. The University of Pennsylvania was among the earliest in its class to undertake systematic instruction in science, technology and engineering. In 1852 it was resolved to establish a department of mines, arts and manufactures, and professorships in geology and minerology, and civil engineering and mining, and two regular courses in science were offered. In 1874 John Henry Towne, a trustee of the university, made the university the residuary legatee of his large estate. Whatever sum might accrue from this bequest was to form a portion of the endowment fund of the university, and the income from it was to be devoted exclusively to the payment of the salaries of professors and instructors in the department of science. In recognition of this generosity the department was named "the Towne scientific school of the University of Pennsylvania."

The John C. Green school of science is one of the departments of Princeton university. Mr. Green was a wealthy merchant in New York city, who devoted much of his large fortune to charitable and educational foundations. He contributed generously to Princeton university aside from his

gift of $50,000 to found the school of science in 1873.
This amount was subsequently much increased by the
residuary legatees of his estate.   Instruction is given in
general science, civil engineering and electrical engineering.
The courses are four years in length and lead to the degree
of bachelor of science.   In 1899 the number of students in
the science department of the university was 338.

Union college, at Schenectady, New York, founded in
1795, was one of the earliest institutions to furnish instruction in engineering and general science.   It was among the
first to recognize the importance of modern languages, and
at an early date it added a " scientific course" to the time-
honored curriculum, which included little besides Latin,
Greek and mathematics.   In 1845 it offered courses in civil
engineering, and there has been added recently a department of electrical engineering which will enjoy exceptional
opportunities, owing to the fact that the great manufacturing plant of the General electric company is located at
Schenectady.

Washington university, at St. Louis, Missouri, has long
maintained a school or department of engineering of excellent reputation.   It offers five courses of study, namely, in
civil engineering, mechanical engineering, electrical engineering, chemistry, and science and literature.   They
are of four years' duration and lead to the degree of
bachelor of science.   Advanced and professional degrees
are conferred on about the usual conditions as to study and
experience.   The testing laboratory of the department of
civil engineering is one of the best known, especially for the
large amount of timber testing for the U. S. government
which has been done in it.   The total number of graduates
of the School of engineering, up to 1899, was 186.

The University of Cincinnati, at Cincinnati, Ohio, founded
in 1872 upon a bequest of Charles McMicken, a wealthy
merchant of Cincinnati, provides courses in general science
and in civil engineering.   Instruction is also given in applied
electricity, but no distinctive course in electrical engineering

is offered. The courses are of four years' duration and lead to the degree of bachelor of science. There is also a course in astronomy, instruction in which is facilitated by an excellent astronomical observatory well equipped with modern instruments and appliances. A course in mathematics, announced in 1890, leads to the bachelor of science degree. In addition to the income from the McMicken fund, the university receives annually a considerable sum collected as a tax upon the taxable property of the city of Cincinnati.

The University of California, at Berkeley, California, includes in its departments a college of agriculture, of mechanics, of civil engineering and of chemistry. A course in electrical engineering is offered in the College of mechanics. They are all of four years' duration and lead to the degree of bachelor of science. There is also an astronomical department in which is included the celebrated Lick observatory at Mt. Hamilton.

There is also in California the well-known **Leland Stanford, Junior, university,** which offers courses in the natural sciences and in civil, mechanical and electrical engineering.

The College of technology of Tulane university of Louisiana at New Orleans, Louisiana, is an important school not only on account of the excellence of its courses and facilities for instruction, but specially by reason of its location, and it is destined to be an important factor in the development of the great resources of the southern part of the United States. It offers five courses, namely, mechanical engineering, which includes electrical engineering, chemical engineering, sugar engineering, civil engineering and architecture. The course in "sugar engineering" is unique, and of special value to the sugar producing interests of the region in which the college is located. It includes not only the chemistry and physics of sugar preparation and cultivation, but the mechanics and engineering of all machinery and appliances used in a modern sugar-making plant. The degree of bachelor of engineering is conferred upon all who complete one of the courses of the college of technology.

Vanderbilt university, at Nashville, Tenn., maintains a well-equipped engineering department. In 1888 Mr. Cornelius Vanderbilt, the grandson of the founder, made a donation to the university of $30,000 for the erection of a building for mechanical engineering. Previous to that time, and in fact, from the opening of the institution in 1876, courses of science and civil engineering had been provided and in 1899 mechanical and mining engineering were added. In 1895 a course in electrical engineering was established. Four years are required to complete any of the courses and the degree of bachelor of engineering is conferred upon those who successfully accomplish the work in either course. In 1899 there were 18 students in the engineering department.

There remains to be considered the third group of schools of science and engineering, which includes those depending for support largely upon state or national appropriations, or related to the universities or colleges deriving a large part or all of their income from these sources.

Among the best known schools of engineering in the country are those forming a part of Cornell university, Ithaca, N. Y. Those branches of engineering which depend principally upon mechanics are represented in Sibley college, while civil and hydraulic engineering, geodesy and kindred branches are included in the "college of civil engineering."

The Sibley college of mechanical engineering and the mechanic arts was established through the generosity of Hiram Sibley who had been interested with Mr. Cornell in the great telegraph enterprises out of which grew the Western Union telegraph company. He was born in Masachusetts in 1807 and died in Rochester, N. Y., in 1888. His interest in the telegraph began with the early experiments of Morse, and he was actively engaged in the attempt to connect Europe and America telegraphically by way of Bering Straits. He was also interested in railroad enterprises and in farming on a large scale, being at one time the largest owner of improved lands in the United States. The college of mechanical engineering was begun by a gift from

Mr. Sibley sufficient for the erection of a building and for the support of a chair of "practical mechanics and machine construction." He continued making additions to his first donations, and in 1885 the trustees of the university organized the college under the name by which it is now known. Mr. Sibley's gifts amounted to $180,000, and $50,000 additional have been contributed by other members of the family. The Sibley college includes eight departments; mechanical engineering, experimental engineering, electrical engineering, machine design, mechanic arts or shop work, industrial drawing and art, and graduate schools of marine engineering and naval architecture, and of railway mechanical engineering. Courses of study are four years in length and the degree of mechanical engineer, electrical engineer, etc., are conferred upon those who successfully complete the respective courses. In 1899 the number of students in Sibley college was 492. The laboratories, museums, shops and other parts of the college are very completely furnished and equipped.

The College of civil engineering provides instruction in all departments of that subject and particularly in some of the more advanced developments of the science. Special instruction is given in bridge engineering, railroad engineering, sanitary, municipal, hydraulic and geodetic engineering. Numerous graduate courses are provided, for illustrating which an astronomical observatory or laboratory, a magnetic laboratory, an extensive hydraulic laboratory and other laboratories furnish ample means. The museums of the College of civil engineering are rich in collections of models, instruments of precision, base line and gravity apparatus, together with a large assortment of the usual field instruments, such as transits, theodolites, levels, etc. In 1899 there were registered 186 students in this college.

The University of Michigan, at Ann Arbor, Michigan, was organized by legislative act in 1837, which made provision for instruction in engineering. Regular instruction was not begun, however, until 1853, and the first degrees were conferred in 1860. The engineering courses were included in the department of literature, science and the arts until 1895, at which time the department of engineering was established. Courses are offered in civil, mechanical, electrical and chemical engineering, and four years are usually required to complete any one of these. All lead to the degree of bachelor of science. Advanced degrees are conferred for graduate courses of study. In 1899 there were registered 218 students in the department of engineering.

Purdue university, at Lafayette, Indiana, is in reality the Indiana institute of technology. It was originally organized under the Morrill act, but assumed the name which it now bears in 1869 when, by legislative enactment, the state accepted a gift of $150,000 and one hundred acres of land from John Purdue. It receives support from the state and national government, tuition being free to all residents of Indiana. The university embraces six special schools. They are as follows: A School of mechanical engineering, of civil engineering, of electrical engineering, of agriculture, of science and of pharmacy. Courses of study in these schools are four years in length, except in the School of pharmacy, in which the course is completed in two annual sessions of thirty-seven weeks each. The degree of bachelor of science is conferred upon those completing one of the four-year courses, and that of graduate in pharmacy (Ph. G.) upon those who complete the course in pharmacy. There is an exceptionally large and well-arranged engineering building which accommodates the departments of civil and mechanical engineering, and the equipment of the School of mechanical engineering is excellent. It is provided with a locomotive testing plant and other appliances for railway mechanical engineering. The biological, chemical and other laboratories are well furnished. In 1899 the total enrollment of students was 730, including 130 in the School of pharmacy and in a special class in agriculture, and the total number of instructors was about 65.

The University of Wisconsin, at Madison, Wisconsin, was

established by act of the legislature in 1838, but no action
was taken under the act except the selection of two town-
ships of land as allowed by congress, for the future support of
the institution.   The first meeting of the board of regents for
the purpose of organizing the university was held in 1849,
and the first building was erected in 1851. In 1866 the
university was reorganized to secure the land grant under
the Morrill act, and in the following year the state began to
support the institution by annual appropriations. The College of engineering was opened in 1870, and has established
and maintained a high reputation for the excellence of its
work. The College of "mechanics and engineering," as it
is now called, provides courses of four years' duration in
civil, sanitary, mechanical and electrical engineering, and in
applied electro-chemistry. These courses all lead to the
degree of bachelor of science. Advanced and professional
degrees are conferred under certain conditions as to graduate study and experience. An excellent astronomical
observatory is available for the instruction of students in
civil engineering, and the college is well furnished with
laboratories, apparatus, museums, etc. In 1899 there were
242 students registered in the College of mechanics and
engineering.

The University of Illinois, at Urbana, Illinois, was founded
in acceptance of the national land grant under the Morrill
act in 1862, and named at first the Illinois industrial university. Power to confer degrees was granted by the state
legislature in 1877, and in 1885 the name of the institution
was changed to that which it now bears. The organization
includes four "colleges" and six "schools." The colleges
are of literature and arts, of engineering, of science and of
agriculture. The College of science offers courses arranged
in four groups, including the chemical and physical group,
the mathematical group, the natural science group and the
philosophical group. The College of engineering offers
courses in architecture, architectural engineering, civil engineering, electrical engineering, mechanical engineering and

municipal and sanitary engineering.   There are also graduate courses in science and in engineering.   The degree of
bachelor of science is conferred upon those completing one
of the courses of four years in the College of engineering,
and also in the College of science.

Similar in origin, and in many respects similar in organization, is the **Ohio state university,** at Columbus, Ohio.
The institution opened its doors to students in September,
1873.   From the beginning instruction in science and
engineering has been the most prominent feature of its
work.   As now organized, the university embraces six colleges, the College of engineering being one.   In this college are offered courses in civil engineering, mine engineering, mechanical engineering, electrical engineering, ceramics,
industrial arts, chemistry and architecture.   There is also a
short course in mining, in clay working and in industrial
arts.   To those who complete these courses, which are of
four years' duration (except as explained above), degrees of
civil engineer, engineer of mines, mechanical engineer, etc.,
etc., are granted, and in chemistry and some other courses
the degree is bachelor of science.   The College of arts,
philosophy and science offers a course in general science,
leading to the degree of bachelor of science.   The university
is especially well equipped in its laboratories and museums
of geology, agriculture, mechanics and metallurgy.   In
1898 there were registered 302 students in the College of
engineering.

The University of Minnesota, at Minneapolis, Minnesota,
is another example of an important and extensive development upon the land grant foundation.   Originally organized
in 1851, it dates its real beginning from 1868, when by act
of the legislature it was reorganized as the recipient of the
Morrill act endowments.   Its organization includes a School
of technical and applied chemistry, the College of engineering and mechanical arts and the School of mines.   The
course in the School of chemistry is of four years' duration
and leads to the degree of bachelor of science.

The College of engineering and mechanic arts offers courses of four years each in civil, mechanical and electrical engineering, for which the degrees C. E., M. E. and E. E. are conferred. There is also a four years' course in drawing and industrial art for which no degree is granted. In the School of mines there are two regular courses of study, in mining and in metallugy, leading to the degree of engineer of mines (E. M.) and metallurgical engineer (Met. E.) respectively. In 1898 there were registered in the College of engineering 129 students, in the School of mines 54, and in the School of chemistry 6.

The University of Tennessee, at Knoxville, Tenn., chartered in 1794 as " Blount college," becoming in 1807 " East Tennessee college," in 1840 " East Tennessee university," and finally receiving in 1869 the national land grant endowment, was given the name which it now bears by act of the legislature in 1879. In its College of agriculture, mechanic arts and sciences it provides courses in civil, mechanical and electrical engineering, in chemistry and in general science. Its buildings, laboratories, apparatus and general facilities are well up to the requirements of a high standard of work.

The State college of Pennsylvania, at State College, Pennsylvania, is another institution of pronounced success and high character which owes its origin to the Morrill act of 1862 and in which ample provision is made for instruction in pure and applied science in courses and under conditions not varying greatly from those already set forth in describing other institutions of the same type.

Indeed, the list might easily be extended until it included the entire list of state institutions founded under this act or made the recipient of the income which it provides.

If space permitted it would be profitable to consider in some detail two or three special schools, such as the **Michigan School of mines,** the **Colorado School of mines,** institutions which have grown out of the demands of their respective localities, very much as did the famous school at Freiberg long ago. Much might well be said, also, concerning the efforts made in the United States to establish trade schools, and of their great success in New York, in Philadelphia, and under the direction of the Pratt institute in Brooklyn, and in Cincinnati, and elsewhere, notwithstanding the occasional opposition of trades' unions and other unfriendly organizations.

It is greatly regretted that limitations of space make it impossible to give something of a detailed exposition of the organization and methods of work in a few institutions like the Pratt institute at Brooklyn, the Drexel institute in Philadelphia, each of which is unique, and all of which are doing a most important work.

It will be noted that the leading institutions or departments of institutions in which special attention is given to pure and applied science do not differ materially in their organization, courses of study or degrees conferred. Practically all courses are four years in length, in nearly all the first two years are largely preparatory to the special or professional work of the last two, embracing modern languages, mathematics and a few other subjects, most of which are common to all courses offered. The differentiation begins generally at the opening of the junior or third year, although in some cases it must commence earlier. In the matter of degrees the great majority of schools confer only the degree of bachelor of science at the end of the four years' course, but there are a few that offer the so-called professional degrees such as C. E., M. E., etc., for the mastery of a four years' course. The requirements for graduate degrees are tolerably uniform, being usually a year of resident study with the preparation of a thesis for the master's degree, and in addition to this usually three years' successful professional work with an acceptable thesis for a professional degree.

The requirements for admission are by no means uniform, nor are they extremely varied. Perhaps the typical *average* requirements for admission to schools of science or engineering colleges would include — besides the " common

English branches "— algebra, plane geometry, English literature, history of the United States and either the French
or German language. About two to three years' study of
the latter would be required, and to this list will often be
added solid geometry, plane trigonometry, the elements of
physics or chemistry, and sometimes a year or two of Latin.
There seems to be a growing tendency towards the introduction of a large number of electives among the subjects
required for admission.

It is hoped that a sufficient number of institutions have
been considered and that enough has been said of them to
exhibit in some degree the enormous educational advance
which has taken place during the past fifteen or twenty
years throughout the whole country, and especially in what
is known as the "middle west." At no previous period in
the history of the world has there been so rapid and productive an evolution of educational forces as this period has
witnessed, and it will not escape notice that it has largely
been a development of methods and appliances for the *study
of science, pure and applied*. No sketch of the origin,
growth and present condition of the schools of science and
engineering in the United States would be complete without reference to **the Johns Hopkins university,** an institution
which, although giving little attention to applied science and
technology, has been a very large factor in determining
the character and methods of instruction to which these
schools owe their success. Although not yet twenty-five
years old, it is impossible to overestimate its influence
upon higher education in this country, and especially is
this true in all things relating to science. There is
scarcely a college faculty that has not been enriched by the
presence of one or more of its graduates, bringing with
them at least something of the spirit of that institution, its
respect for exact scholarship and regard for scientific truth.
For the schools of engineering and technology in the
United States are, and are intended to be, something more
than a mere avenue leading to increased money-making

power. They are intended to fit for the responsibilities of citizenship, and, if worthy of the name, their methods of instruction are such as to cultivate independence of thinking and personal responsibility in judgment. Nor are they deficient in that intellectual discipline and culture which constitute a liberal education. Although not specifically organized for original research, their methods of work naturally lead to and encourage it, and during the past quarter of a century they have contributed generously to the advancement of pure science, to which, however, they must always be in debt. As a whole, they represent one of the most important achievements of an age whose chief glory is found in the increase and diffusion of science and its applications.

DEPARTMENT OF EDUCATION
FOR THE
UNITED STATES COMMISSION TO THE PARIS EXPOSITION OF 1900

MONOGRAPHS ON EDUCATION

IN THE

UNITED STATES

EDITED BY

NICHOLAS MURRAY BUTLER

Professor of Philosophy and Education in Columbia University, New York

12

AGRICULTURAL EDUCATION

BY

CHARLES W. DABNEY

President of the University of Tennessee, Knoxville, Tennessee

THIS MONOGRAPH IS CONTRIBUTED TO THE UNITED STATES EDUCATIONAL EXHIBIT BY THE
STATE OF NEW YORK

AGRICULTURAL EDUCATION

The earliest farmers in America had to contend with innumerable and great obstacles ; with the wildness of nature, the attacks of Indians and wild beasts upon their stock, the difficulty of obtaining farming implements and seeds, and with conditions of climate and soil, very different from those of the old countries whence they derived all their methods. The colonial farmer was compelled to use the crudest methods. He cut down, heaped and burned the small trees and undergrowth, and belted the large ones. He scratched the surface a little with a home-made plow, and cultivated his corn and tobacco with a wooden hoe. He harvested the crop that nature gave him in a careless manner and used it wastefully. He cultivated the same field until it was worn out, when he cleared another and moved his family near to it. So long as land was so abundant, no attention was paid to the conservation of fertility of the soil. America was such a vast and fertile country that it took the people over a century to find out that there was any limit to its productiveness. These conditions were quite sufficient to explain the slow progress made in agriculture during the first century or more after the settlement of America.

It was not until the close of the eighteenth century that the attention of practical men commenced to be directed to the discoveries of science, and hopes were excited that immediate benefits would accrue from them to agriculture as they had to the other arts. Lavoisier's discoveries and teachings had aroused the hope that chemistry could do a great deal to promote the advancement of farming. Americans commenced to appreciate their disadvantages as compared with British and continental farmers, and to seek better implements and methods for their work. The newly-

awakened interest in agriculture was marked first by the
formation of agricultural societies.   George Washington
was one of the best technically educated men in America in
his day, and was especially interested in everything pertaining to agriculture.   His various state papers show that he
not only knew the needs of the country, but that he fully
realized that schools for the education of the people and
societies for the distribution of knowledge were necessary
for the safety of the republic.   A few extracts will recall
his strong opinions on this subject.   In his first annual message to congress (Jan. 8, 1790) he expressed the hope that
the "advancement of agriculture, commerce, and manufactures, by all proper means, will not, I trust, need recommendation," and adds, "Nor am I less persuaded that you
will agree with me in the opinion that there is nothing which
can better deserve your patronage than the promotion of
science and literature. * * * Whether this desirable
object will be best promoted by affording aids to seminaries
already established, or by the institution of a national university, or by any other expedients, will be well worthy of a
place in the deliberations of the legislature."   Notice how
agriculture and a national university for the promotion of
science and arts were always associated in Washington's
mind.   He mentions the advancement of agriculture and
the establishment of a national university in the same connection in his first message.   He discusses them together
in many of his writings during eight years, and finally
in his eighth annual message he says, "It will not be
doubted that with reference either to individual or national
welfare agriculture is of primary importance.   In proportion as nations advance in population and other circumstances of maturity, this truth becomes more apparent, and renders the cultivation of the soil more and
more an object of public patronage.   Institutions for promoting it grow up, supported by the public purse; and to
what object can it be dedicated with greater propriety?
Among the means which have been employed to this end,

none have been attended with greater success than the establishment of boards (composed of proper characters) charged
with collecting and diffusing information, and enabled by
premiums and small pecuniary aids to encourage and assist
a spirit of discovery and improvement. This species of
establishment contributes doubly to the increase of improvement by stimulating to enterprise and experiment, and by
drawing to a common center the results everywhere of
individual skill and observation, and spreading them thence
over the whole nation. Experience accordingly has shown
that they are very cheap instruments of immense national
benefits." * * * "I have heretofore proposed to the
consideration of congress the expediency of establishing a
national university and also a military academy. The
desirableness of both these institutions has so constantly
increased with every new view I have taken of the subject
that I cannot omit the opportunity of once for all calling
your attention to them." With marvelous foresight Washington urged the necessity for scientific research and education in America, and he planned at the same time for institutions to discover and collect knowledge, and societies to
disseminate it. He saw also that agriculture was to be the
chief industry in the country, and that it would need the
assistance of science. Thus he appears to have associated
plans for the advancement of agriculture with those for a
national university.

Congress promptly established the military academy, and
some years later the naval academy and the department of
agriculture. But it has not yet established the national university, which was the chief agency in Washington's mind
for the development of all the sciences and arts of peace.

THE FIRST AGRICULTURAL SOCIETIES AND FAIRS

Where did Washington get this conception of the work
of boards of agriculture? The first society for the promotion of agriculture in the United States was organized
at Philadelphia on March 1, 1785; and on the 4th of July

following George Washington and Benjamin Franklin were
elected members.   A similar society was incorporated in
South Carolina in the same year, which proposed, among
other things, to establish an experimental farm — the first
suggestion of the kind in our history.   The New York
society for the promotion of agriculture, arts and manufactures, which had been organized on the 26th of February,
1791, published its first small volume of transactions in 1792.
The Massachusetts society for the promotion of agriculture
was established March 7, 1792, and commenced, in 1797,
the publication of bulletins.   The Society for promoting
agriculture in the state of Connecticut was organized in
1794, and published its first volume of proceedings in 1802.
Washington was evidently familiar with the work of these
agricultural societies; but his knowledge of such agencies
was not limited to his own country.   In Great Britain, the
Bath and the West of England agricultural societies had
been established.   Sir John Sinclair, the "inventor of statistics" and president of the Highland society, had established,
in 1791, the British wool society and the sheep fair at New-
halls Inn.   After agitating the subject for a number of years,
Sinclair secured the establishment of the Royal board of
agriculture, and was appointed its first president in 1793.
Washington's correspondence with Sir John Sinclair shows
that he had the benefit of all the information to be obtained
from the father of the British board of agriculture.

Agricultural societies naturally led to the establishment
of fairs and exhibitions.   A member of the Massachusetts
society suggested first in 1801 that agricultural fairs should
be held regularly at Cambridge spring and fall, and premiums be given for farm products.   No action appears,
however, to have been taken with regard to this suggestion.
Dr. Thornton, the first commissioner of patents at Washington, suggested in 1804 that the sale of agricultural products and of cattle would be promoted by the holding of
fairs on market days, as in England.   As a result of this
suggestion we learn from the "National Intelligencer" of

that year that fairs were held "in the mall on the south side of the Tiber." The first fair proved such a success that the citizens raised an appropriation of $50 for premiums for the next one, which was held in April, 1805. The third fair, held in November, 1805, appears to have been the last.

Governor Edward Winslow, of Massachusetts, is said to have brought to Plymouth, in the ship *Charity*, in 1694, "the first neat cattle that came into New England." It was appropriate that his descendant, Elkanah Watson, of Plymouth, should import the first pair of Spanish Merino sheep into Massachusetts, and should then give notice of an exhibition of them at Pittsfield. This small exhibit led to a larger enterprise and the establishment of stock shows in America. An invitation was published by Watson and some twenty other persons calling an exhibition of stock at the same place on the first of October. This cattle show was so successful that it became a permanent institution in Massachusetts. A number of public spirited citizens of Maryland, Virginia and the District of Columbia had in the meantime formed, in 1809, the Columbian agricultural society, which was for many years actively engaged in the work of educating the farmer through the agency of fairs. From these beginnings agricultural societies have spread all over our country, and agricultural fairs have become a potent agency for the dissemination of valuable information with regard to new crops, implements, stock and improvement in agriculture generally.

Nearly all of the states now have either boards of agriculture or commissioners or secretaries of agriculture in charge of the farming interests. Their work varies, but usually includes the collection of agricultural statistics, the preparation of weather and crop reports and the oversight of the stock interests, and frequently also the inspection and analysis of fertilizers and mixed cattle feeds, the testing and examination of dairy and other food products. Some of the state boards conduct the agricultural colleges, hold fairs, give premiums for fine stock and hold farmers' insti-

tutes.   The boards, commissioners and societies all publish
reports and bulletins and many of them accomplish a great
deal of admirable educational work.

The Patrons of husbandry (Grange) and National farmers'
alliance are organizations with many subordinate branches
and local societies and have exerted great influence especially
in educating the farmers and their families.   The Farmers'
national congress meets once a year for the discussion of
questions of general interest.   For the stock interests, we
have in this country a national live stock association, five
national dairy unions, and fifty-six state dairy associations.
There are fourteen cattle breeders associations representing
the interests of as many different important breeds, eighteen horse breeders associations, twenty-nine sheep breeders
associations, seventeen associations of swine breeders, etc.
Nearly all of the states protect their stock from diseases
through the agency of sanitary boards or veterinarians
under the direction of the state boards or commissioners.

There is a national league for good roads that is doing
much to educate public opinion.   Ten states have forestry
commissions or provide for forest protection and improvement in some way.   There are besides eighteen forestry
associations which are doing much educational work.   Eleven
national or interstate, and fifty-four state horticultural and
kindred societies are at work.   (For the names of these
societies and the addresses of their officers, see the Year-
book of the United States department of agriculture for
1898.)

THE RISE OF AGRICULTURAL SCHOOLS

The origin and development of agricultural schools in
America was a part of a general educational movement
against the old classical college and in favor of scientific and
technical education.   Perhaps the demand for agricultural
education was the first one to be heard ; but it had its origin
in the same causes which gave rise to the demand for the
application of science to all the arts and professions in life.

As the great universities of Europe grew out of monastic

and cathedral schools, so our first American colleges were all the children of the churches. The preachers were in the early days almost the only learned men, and therefore the only teachers. In the case of the rural schools the preacher was both school director and teacher. The institutions for higher education were also founded and controlled by the associations and presbyteries of the different denominations, and the most learned of their clergy became the instructors. Naturally enough, as their founders and teachers were all preachers, these early colleges were devoted almost exclusively to the cultivation of theology, classics and philosophy. Their parson-teachers taught what they held to be the only thing worth learning, and they were right in putting character and culture above everything else. Their methods produced a race of preachers, teachers, lawyers, statesmen, and soldiers scarcely equalled and never surpassed in any country. But a new and rapidly growing country like America needed engineers, chemists, miners, and manufacturers, and an ambitious and intelligent people were not slow to make their wants heard.

Some of the physical sciences, notably chemistry and geology, had already made great progress, and had revolutionized some of the arts. The popular writings of great scientific men, notably Liebig's Letters on chemistry, were eagerly read, and people everywhere cherished bright hopes of the benefits to be derived from the application of science to the industries of life, and especially to agriculture. Discovery and invention were already doing much to develop the material resources of the world and to change the occupations of men. Steam was beginning to be used for the purpose of transportation, chemistry was being applied in working iron, in dyeing fabrics, and in many other arts. Great railroads were to be built, but with the exception of the military academy at West Point, there was no school to train the engineers to survey them. Mines of coal and iron were to be opened, but miners had to be imported to open them. Factories needed to be built, but engineers

had to be brought over from England or Holland to build
them.   Iron works and many other important industries
were calling loudly for chemists, who had to be obtained
from Germany or France.   These influences, but more
especially the need of scientific knowledge in a rapidly
developing country, produced a profound effect on the theories and practice of education ; and thus a vigorous demand
arose for the sciences and their applications to the arts of
life.   The old college was not meeting the new demands ;
but what the new college was to be, and what its methods,
no one knew for a long time.

Columbia college, in the city of New York, appointed, in
1792, Samuel L. Mitchell "professor of natural history,
chemistry and agriculture."   The records of the college do
not show what instruction he gave in agricultural science,
if any, but Professor Mitchell, so far as we know, was, by
title at least, the first professor of agriculture in America.
We are told that he prepared a number of essays on manures
and other subjects for the New York society for the promotion of agriculture, and that his influence in behalf of the
sciences related to agriculture was very evident in the men
he trained.   Many of them became prominent in science,
and some were influential in the movement for agricultural
schools.

The Philadelphia Society for the promotion of agriculture, of which Washington was an honorary member,
appointed a committee on January 21, 1794, "to prepare a
plan for establishing the State society for the promotion of
agriculture, connecting with it the education of youth in the
knowledge of that most important art."   This committee
made a report offering several alternative propositions for
promoting agricultural education.   One suggestion made
was "the endowment of professorships to be annexed to the
University of Pennsylvania and the College of Carlisle, and
other seminaries of learning, for the purpose of teaching the
chemical, philosophical and elementary arts of the theory of
agriculture."   Another suggestion was to use the common

school system of the state to educate the farmer in his business, "the county school masters being made secretaries of the county societies, and the school houses the places of meeting and the repositories of their transactions, models, etc. The legislature may enjoin on these school masters the combination of the subject of agriculture with other parts of education." This is, so far as we know, the first formal effort made in the United States to present the claims of agricultural education to a legislature and to incorporate instruction in agriculture in the common schools.

THE BEGINNINGS OF THE UNITED STATES DEPARTMENT OF AGRICULTURE

The war with England, the expansion of territory, the rapid development of manufacturing and many other causes, contributed to retard the progress of agricultural education for several decades after the beginning of the century. The agitation continued, but little was accomplished until after 1840.

Upon the motion of Elkanah Watson, the Berkshire agricultural society of Massachusetts presented in 1817 a memorial to congress praying for "the establishment of a national board of agriculture in accordance with the original suggestion of President Washington." The bill reported in the house of representatives was promply defeated by a large vote. It was well known that President Madison was opposed to it on constitutional grounds. Others based their opposition on the indifference of the farmers of the country and the idea that such a board was not needed.

The only striking event in the agricultural history of the country during the next decade was the agitation of silk culture, commonly called the "Morus multicaulis" craze from the variety of the mulberry tree which was introduced everywhere to supply food for the silk worm. Congress responded to the popular demand for information on this subject by ordering the preparation and publication of a manual of silk culture, which was done.

The United States department of agriculture grew finally out of the recommendation of President Washington for a national board of agriculture, but more immediately out of the seed distribution originated in the department of state during the presidency of John Quincy Adams. The patent office was first in the hands of the department of state, and the seeds collected by consuls in various parts of the world were turned over to it, as the scientific branch of the government, for distribution. So it came about that when on the 4th of July, 1836, the patent office was made a separate bureau and Henry L. Ellsworth, a practical farmer of Connecticut, was appointed commissioner, he found it one of his duties to distribute seeds and plants. It was a congenial duty and one for which he was well qualified both by education and experience. During his travels over the country as Indian commissioner, Mr. Ellsworth had been deeply impressed with the agricultural possibilities of the western prairies and also with the great ignorance and destitution of the settlers upon them. He believed that what they needed was better implements and seeds adapted to the climate and soils. So deeply impressed was he with the necessities of these people that, without the authority of congress and outside of business hours, he collected seeds and plants, which he distributed to farmers in all sections of the country, but especially to those in the far west, using the postal franks of members of congress for this purpose. This was the beginning of the seed distribution by the United States government, which has since grown to such colossal proportions. Thus also was born the United States department of agriculture. In his first annual report Mr. Ellsworth begged earnestly for an appropriation to continue and enlarge this distribution of seeds and one was made during the last days of the twenty-fifth congress which provided $1,000 from the patent office fund "for the purpose of collecting and distributing seeds, prosecuting agricultural investigations, and procuring agricultural statistics." With the exception of the years 1840, 1841 and 1846 congress made a small appropriation for this purpose each

year from the patent office fund. The first separate appropriation for agriculture, made in the year 1854, was
$35,000, and it has never been less than that sum. An agent
was authorized also at this time to "investigate and report
upon the habits of insects, injurious and beneficial to vege-
tation," and a botanical garden was established. The same
year arrangements were made with the Smithsonian institution for collecting meteorological statistics. The present
United States department of agriculture was established by
an act of congress, approved by President Lincoln on May
15, 1862. This act was chiefly due to the strong plea made
by Commissioner of Patents David P. Holloway, of Indiana.
It is remarkable that the other great act for the promotion
of agriculture in America, known as the land-grant act establishing colleges of agriculture and mechanic arts, was passed
by the same congress and approved by President Lincoln on
July 2nd of the same year, both in the midst of the terrors of
the civil war.

The act of May 15, 1862, did not establish an independent
department of the government. Its chief officer was styled
simply "commissioner of agriculture." He did not become
a member of the cabinet until the 11th of February, 1889,
when President Cleveland approved another act of congress
making the department of agriculture an executive department. The duties of the department of agriculture were
(act of 1862) : "To acquire and diffuse among the people
of the United States useful information on subjects connected with agriculture, in the most general and comprehensive sense of the word, and to procure and propagate among
the people new and valuable seeds and plants."

So much of the history of the United States department
of agriculture appears necessary to this discussion of agricultural education in the United States. Through its surveys and laboratories, its experiment stations and especially
through its numerous and valuable publications it has been
the chief agency of agricultural education in America.

THE FIRST AGRICULTURAL COLLEGES

The demand for scientific and technical education did not cease as the years passed by, but grew louder and louder with the development of the country. The history of the agitation in New York may be taken as an illustration. In 1819 there was published anonymously at Albany a pamphlet on "the necessity of establishing an agricultural college," which has been commonly attributed to that active and intelligent man, Simeon De Witt, surveyor-general of New York. He proposed the establishment of an institution to be called the agricultural college of the state of New York, to be endowed by the state and conducted under state authority. The transactions of the New York agricultural society for 1822 contain allusions to the same subjects, and the matter was never allowed to drop entirely out of sight. About 1825 a private agricultural college or school was undertaken in Columbia county. This was the period (1830 to 1850) of the agitation for the so-called "manual labor schools," and many of the schools of the time took that form. The Oneida institute was one of the first of these schools, and it is said to have had a course of instruction in practical agriculture. These were not manual training schools or technical schools in the modern sense, but schools having farms attached where the students could support themselves by manual labor while pursuing their studies. This plan, which found much popular favor for a time and led to the establishment of numerous schools, was soon found to be impracticable and abandoned.

The demand for agricultural education in New York grew steadily, and by 1838 petitions bearing six thousand signatures were presented to the legislature demanding state aid in behalf of agricultural schools. The committee to whom the petitions were referred deplored in strong language "that there is no school, no seminary, no department of any school in which the science of agriculture is taught," and recommended very strongly the establishment of a school of agriculture. No action was taken at this time, but the matter came up in a different form at each succeeding session of the legislature, and appears to have grown steadily in favor. The State agricultural society helped greatly to advance the interests of the cause, and in 1844 appointed a committee of which Governor Seward, Lieutenant-Governor Dickinson, and James S. Wadsworth, were members, to promote "the introduction of agricultural studies in the schools of the state," and also "for the purpose of selecting books for family and school libraries." It was resolved at the same time, "That this society regards the establishment of an agricultural institute and pattern farm in this state, where shall be taught thoroughly and alike the science, the practice, and the profits of good husbandry, as an object of great importance." This committee co-operated with the association of school superintendents, with the result that that body adopted, in June, 1844, a resolution drawn by Professor Potter, of Union college, setting forth the opinion that "the time has arrived when the elements and scientific principles of agriculture should be taught in all schools." Still the state took no action. Numerous private agricultural schools were established however.

Governor Hamilton Fish first recommended, in January, 1849, in his annual message to the legislature, the establishment of a state agricultural college. During the following session of the legislature Professor Johnson, the great agricultural chemist of Scotland, was invited to Albany and delivered a course of lectures under the auspices of the New York agricultural society. The same year this society established a chemical laboratory at Albany for the analysis of manures, fertilizers, etc. Still nothing was done about the school.

Professor William H. Brewer, from whose writings many of these facts have been derived, thus described the first industrial college established in New York: "In 1850 Mr. John Delafield, a graduate of Columbia college, where he may have received instruction from Professor Mitchell, was

living on one of the best farms of the state, in the town of
Fayette, Seneca county. He was at one time president of
the New York state agricultural society, and originated and
carried out an agricultural survey of Seneca county. He
took a deep interest in the cause of agricultural education,
and owing to his action and energy on April 15, 1853, the
state passed an act establishing an agricultural college.
This act created a board of ten trustees, of which Mr. Delafield was president, but appropriated no money. The college was to be located on Mr. Delafield's farm in the town
of Fayette, but as he died October 22 of the same year
nothing more was done about building a college there."
The Rev. Amos Brown, principal of Ovid academy, situated
fifteen miles south of Fayette, who was to become later the
chief assistant of Senator Morrill in securing the passage of
the land-grant act establishing agricultural colleges, appears
to have gotten his inspiration and information from Mr.
Delafield. At least when the school at Fayette failed, Mr.
Brown conceived the idea of having the charter of the agricultural college transferred to his academy at Ovid. He
secured an act for this purpose from the general assembly in
1856, which provided a loan by the state of $40,000. The
citizens of Fayette and vicinity had in the meantime subscribed about $50,000. The board of trustees was organ-
ized, buildings were erected, and the college was formally
opened as the New York state agricultural college in the fall'
of 1860, with M. R. Patrick as president of the college.
The affairs of the institution appear to have been poorly
managed, however, as it was found to be too heavily in debt
to begin active operations. When the civil war broke out
President Patrick went off with the army, and the college
was closed never again to be opened. Amos Brown afterwards became president of the People's college near Havana,
New York, and after the passage of the Morrill act in 1862
secured an act from the legislature of New York giving
the whole of its share of the land-grant to this college. But
that institution failed to comply with the conditions of the

law, and the land-grant of the state of New York was turned over to Cornell university, which thus became the agricultural college of the state. This narrative has been introduced to show the growth of the idea which led to the establishment of Cornell university, probably our greatest agricultural institution.

The first agricultural college to be actually established and put in operation was that of the state of Michigan. Article 13, section 11 of the constitution of the state of Michigan adopted in 1850, says: "The legislature shall encourage the promotion of intellectual, scientific, and agricultural improvement; and shall as soon as practicable, provide for the establishment of an agricultural school." This was the first state constitution to provide for the establishment of an agricultural school. It is noteworthy, also, that it was the first one to provide that all instruction in the district schools should be conducted in the English language. The act establishing the state agricultural college of Michigan was passed on February 12, 1855. The college was located upon a farm of some 500 acres, situated about four miles east of the city of Lansing; buildings were erected, and the college was formally opened in May, 1847.

The legislature of Maryland incorporated the next agricultural college in 1856, which was, however, in part a private institution. Some five hundred citizens of Maryland, and of the District of Columbia, together with a few from adjacent states, subscribed to a certain amount of stock, which the legislature required should be provided. The stockholders elected a board of trustees, and this body located the college upon the estate of Charles B. Calvert, situated in Prince George county, about nine miles east of the city of Washington. The institution was opened for students in September, 1859, when Professor Joseph Henry of the Smithsonian institution, delivered a handsome oration.

Marshall P. Wilder first urged the importance of establishing an agricultural college in Massachusetts, in an address before the Norfolk agricultural society made in 1849. The state senate of Massachusetts passed a bill in 1850 establishing such a school, but it failed in the house. A committee was appointed to investigate the matter, and they sent Professor Hitchcock to the continent of Europe to visit agricultural schools. His report was transmitted to the legislature by the governor in the following year, with the result that the Massachusetts board of agriculture was established in 1852. Mr. Wilder kept up the agitation, however, and finally in 1856 succeeded in obtaining from the legislature a charter of the Massachusetts school of agriculture. The Massachusetts agricultural college was not regularly opened, however, until 1867.

The general assembly of the state of Pennsylvania incorporated the Farmers' high school, now the State college, in 1854. The act provided that people of different sections of the state might offer land and property and thereby secure its location in their midst. Funds for building and equipment were provided from the state treasury. The State agricultural society made certain donations, and the college was opened for students in the winter of 1859. These were the leading agricultural schools established before the passage of the land-grant act in 1862.

Closely related to these agricultural schools were the scientific schools established at Yale and Harvard between 1840 and 1850, in response to the same demand for a new education. John P. Norton was appointed professor of agricultural chemistry, vegetable and animal physiology at Yale college, New Haven, Connecticut, in 1846. Thus was begun the Sheffield scientific school, which was more of an agricultural institution than any of the other schools of that time. Professor Norton began his lectures in 1847, and for some years wrote voluminously for agricultural journals. He also prepared and published his first work, The Elements of agriculture. Among his first students in the course in agricultural chemistry was the distinguished Professor W. H. Brewer, of the Sheffield scientific school at Yale. The Lawrence scientific school at Harvard, established about the same time, was founded upon an endowment of $40,000, given by the Lawrences, who, being interested in factories, caused this school to direct its attention more to the applications of chemistry to manufactures.

Francis Wayland, president of Brown university, became greatly interested at this time in scientific and technical education, and took a prominent part in the discussion of the reforms needed to adapt the institutions of America to the requirements of the time. In his little book on the Present collegiate system of the United States he argued earnestly in favor of the introduction of scientific subjects into the college curriculum and the adoption of a system of electives. A science hall and a museum of geology were erected at Brown in 1840; but means failed to support the scientific work, and Dr. Wayland was constrained to resign in 1855, when the old classical course was re-established. These changes were all parts of a general movement for the modification of the classical curriculum, and the introduction of scientific and technical study. Wherever this was done the sciences pertaining to agriculture were sure to be introduced.

THE LAND-GRANT COLLEGES

As the plans for the new college education won support in these states, the friends of the cause took courage to conquer new fields. Their activity was soon extended from the halls of state legislation to those of the government at Washington. The agitation first voiced itself there in petitions to congress for national aid for agricultural colleges. After several years the friends of the movement secured the interest and co-operation of Justin S. Morrill, then a member of the house of representatives from the state of Vermont, who was destined to be known as the father of the agricultural colleges and to live to see them firmly established in all the states and territories in the union and well supported by congressional appropriations, made in three acts, secured largely by his efforts extending over thirty years. Mr. Morrill introduced the first bill in the lower

house on December 14, 1857, and saw the last one approved
on August 30, 1890.   His first bill authorized the establishment of colleges in all the states and provided 20,000 acres
of public land for each member of congress for their maintenance.   The committee on public lands, to which it was
referred, brought in an adverse report on April 15, 1858.
The bill however passed both houses at the following session,
but was vetoed by President Buchanan.   Nothing daunted
by this defeat, Mr. Morrill introduced a new bill in the house
in December, 1861, bestowing 30,000 acres of land for each
member of congress upon the several states for the establishment of industrial colleges.   Ben Wade of Ohio introduced the bill in the senate on May 2.   It passed both
houses in spite of an adverse report by the house committee
on public lands, and was approved by President Lincoln
July 2, 1862, the day of McClellan's retreat after the battle
of Malvern Hill in Virginia.   We have shown how President Lincoln approved the bill for the department of agriculture on May 15 preceding.   In the midst of the excite-
ment of the great war little attention was paid to this most
remarkable gift of about 13,000,000 acres of land to promote
the cause of education.   Having been passed during a war,
it is not surprising that the act provided that every college
receiving the benefits of the land-grant should give its students instruction in military science.

This great grant, the greatest ever made to education,
which was the foundation of industrial education in America,
and represented the consummation of a great revolution in
the system of higher instruction in this country, demands
somewhat careful study.   The act was entitled " An Act
donating public lands to the several states and territories
who may provide colleges for the benefit of agriculture and
the mechanic arts."   It granted to each state an amount of
public land equal to 30,000 acres for each senator and representative in congress to which the states were entitled by
the apportionment of the census of 1860.   The object of the
grant is expressed in remarkably broad terms, as follows :

" The endowment, support and maintenance of at least one college where the leading object shall be, without excluding other scientific and classical studies, and including military tactics, to teach such branches of learning as are related to agriculture and the mechanic arts, in such manner as the legislatures of the states may respectively prescribe, in order to promote the liberal and practical education of the industrial classes in the several pursuits and professions of life." This paragraph has been the subject of a vast deal of discussion which must be briefly noticed.   First, let us hear what Senator Morrill himself has said with regard to its meaning.   Says he : " It is perhaps needless to say that these colleges were not established or endowed for the sole purpose of teaching agriculture.   Their object was to give an opportunity for those engaged in industrial pursuits to obtain some knowledge of the practical sciences related to agriculture and the mechanic arts ; such as they could not then obtain at most of our institutions called classical colleges, where the languages, Greek and Latin, French and German, absorbed perhaps two-thirds of all of the time of the students while in college.   But it was never intended to force the boys of farmers going into these institutions so to study that they should all come out farmers.   It was merely intended to give them an opportunity to do so and to do so with advantage if they saw fit.   Obviously not manual but intellectual instruction was the paramount object. It was not provided that agricultural labor in the field should be practically taught, any more than that the mechanical trade of a carpenter or blacksmith should be taught. Secondly, it was a liberal education that was proposed. Classical studies were not to be excluded, and therefore, must be included.   The act of 1862 proposed a system of broad education by colleges, not limited to superficial and dwarfed training such as might be supplied by a foreman of a workshop or by a foreman of an experimental farm.   If any would have only a school with equal scraps of labor and of instruction, or something other than a college, they would not obey the national law.   Experience in manual labor, in the handling of tools and implements, is not to be disparaged ; in the proper time and place it is most essential, and generally something of this may be obtained either before or after the college term, but should not largely interfere with the precious time required for a definite amount of scientific and literary culture, which all earnest students are apt to find far too limited." The chief contention with regard to the meaning of the act has always and everywhere been over the question whether these colleges should be mere schools of practical agriculture and mechanic arts, or institutions for liberal education as well.   This utterance of Senator Morrill, made many years after the bill was passed, should settle this question forever.

In the first place, we learn that the general object of the act was to provide for the scientific and liberal education of industrial classes, who were not sufficiently provided for in the old-fashioned classical colleges.   The new institution was to be a college, that is, an institution of higher education.   It was not to be a mere farm or shop, or even a manual labor school ; but an institution where the sons of farmers and mechanics and of other members of the industrial classes could get, at a moderate cost, both a "liberal and practical education."   By "liberal" education was always meant in those times a literary and classical education.   The act recognized fully the correlation of all knowledge and the necessity of subordinating all to the great objects of the law, by forbidding the exclusion of "other scientific and classical studies."   But it was to be "a college where the *leading* object should be to teach *such branches of learning as are related to agriculture and the mechanic arts*" — not practical agriculture merely, or practical mechanics merely, but *the branches of learning* related thereto.

In the second place, these institutions were to educate, not exclusively, but especially, as has been said, the industrial classes.   At the time they were founded almost the only institutions for higher education were classical colleges patronized by the sons of the wealthy, who usually became literary men, teachers, preachers, lawyers, and physicians. For years the great demand had been for instruction in the branches of learning which qualify men in the industrial pursuits. Therefore these colleges were designed especially to fill this great gap in our educational system and to give the sons of the industrial classes the opportunity to get any kind of an education they wanted. The sons of these industrial classes, however, were not to be limited to agriculture and the mechanic arts, for the law says, they shall receive "a liberal and practical education," which would qualify them for "the several pursuits and professions of life."

These colleges established another new principle in education in America, the principle of free tuition in the highest schools of learning. Liberal education is a necessity in a free government; heretofore only the sons of the rich were able to get it. A government of the people, for the people, and by the people can be perpetuated only by educating all the people. It is not sufficient that we have in America a magnificent system of common schools. The highest education must be within the reach of all the worthy poor. As Butler has said, " The attempt to feed elementary education on itself alone is perpetual motion transformed. Strike at the human heart effectually, and the listless fingers close in death ; strike at the source of scholarship and supply, and every remotest part of this body politic falls back stricken or weak." Or as Atherton has said, " Higher education is as the ocean to the mountain spring, continually sending back the dew and the rain to supply them. It is as the tree to the fruit, continually imparting vitality and substance. It is as the sun to the planets, holding all in their appointed course. From the higher institutions come not only teachers to lead and guide the lower, but that great body of learning and intelligence which creates, molds, and enriches public sentiment, which supports the common school." These national colleges first gave all the people, rich and poor alike, the opportunities for getting the best education.

Thirdly, it is to be noted that these colleges are not class institutions. Though designed to guarantee them these opportunities they are not limited to the industrial classes. They are intended to supplement existing institutions and provide free tuition for all classes, the sons of professional men, as well as mechanics. As Senator Morrill has said in another place, " I should hope that no farmer or mechanic would be so illiberal as to wish to have the monopoly of education in any of these land-grant colleges." They are, in brief, the colleges of all the people, of every class and profession, and they are intended to give all alike the opportunities for the broadest education. As Ezra Cornell expressed it, they are institutions "where any person can find instruction in any subject." This purpose has been wonderfully well accomplished by the majority of them in the thirty years of their existence. By giving the higher education to rich and poor, these colleges have done more to render permanent American institutions than any other institution founded by congress.

American institutions of learning have often been ridiculed for their extravagance in " brick and mortar." The average board of trustees of an American college has a strong disposition to buy land and lay off extensive lawns and parks, and to expend money in large buildings, and then to starve its professors and pinch them in the matter of books and equipment. This was especially true in the earlier days. Seeing how many institutions had ruined their usefulness in the extravagant external management of their affairs, and desiring to stimulate states and local communities to do their share in upbuilding these colleges, the law said, "that no portion of said fund nor the interest thereon, shall be applied, directly or indirectly, under any pretense whatever, to the purchase, erection, preservation, or repair of any building or buildings."

This provision has been the cause of a great diversity of practice as to the manner of providing the necessary buildings and grounds for these institutions. Whether the college should be an independent institution or whether it should be connected with some existing college was the first question raised in every state. The state either had to make large appropriations for buildings and grounds or else connect the new institution with some old one. There were always old institutions wanting the new endowment, and the competition between them was frequently a warm one. The arguments in favor of connecting them with existing institutions were the saving of the cost of buildings and grounds, of museums and libraries, etc., and the difficulty of providing corps of professors in many of the subjects, which had to be taught, especially the literary ones. Other arguments were found in the scarcity of competent professors for the new institutions and in the theory, taught clearly in the act itself, that the new education was to be built upon the old, the practical and the liberal going hand in hand. The arguments in favor of independent agricultural colleges were the danger of having the new fund absorbed for the purposes of the old education, the danger of ill feeling or conflict between the technical and the classical students, and the supposed incompatibility of the study of abstract and applied science.

A very wise provision of the act is the one which makes the exact character of the institution and the nature of the instruction to be given a matter for the decision of the legislatures of the states. The instruction should be adapted to the needs of the people and the character of the industries of the several states. The sciences related to the mechanic arts hold just as important a place in this law as those related to agriculture ; and this term is evidently intended to be interpreted in the same liberal sense in which we have interpreted the terms " agriculture " and " branches of learning related to agriculture." The branches of learning related to mechanic arts comprehend all the sciences not included among those related to agriculture. In some of our states agriculture is the chief industry, while manufacturing is the largest interest in others. Under this provision the state may itself determine which group of sciences shall receive the chief attention. The act has been properly interpreted thus to provide courses of industrial education to suit the needs of the different states and has rarely been abused.

Believing that the time had arrived when the agricultural and mechanical colleges should have additional support, Mr. Morrill and the other friends of industrial education in the United States began in 1889 to formulate plans to secure a second appropriation from the national treasury. Mr. Morrill introduced another bill in congress providing for the further endowment of the colleges, which passed and was approved by President Harrison on August 30, 1890. This act, generally known as the second Morrill act, provides that there shall be appropriated annually to each state out of the funds arising from the sale of public lands, as in the case of the agricultural experiment stations, the sum of $15,000, for the year ending June 30, 1890, and an annual increase by the additional sum of $1,000, to such appropriation for ten years thereafter until the appropriation shall become $25,000, at which figure it shall remain fixed. The act says that this appropriation shall be applied "only to instruction in agriculture, the mechanic arts, the English language, and the various branches of mathematical, physical, natural and economic science, with special reference to their applications to the industries of life, and to the facilities for such instruction." Provision was made at this time for separate institutions for white and colored students in such states as desired to make this arrangement. Being limited in its application this act has done even more than the original one to stimulate industrial education in the United States.

CLASSIFICATION OF AGRICULTURAL COLLEGES

The early agricultural colleges and schools have in nearly all cases been merged into the colleges established under the land-grant act of 1862. The act establishing colleges of agriculture and mechanic arts was a broad one, and was framed purposely so as to permit the states to organize colleges adapted to their particular needs. As a result it is very difficult to classify them. Under this law there have been organized almost all grades of agricultural schools, from those of the high school grade to great universities with extensive departments for scientific research.

According to their type of organization, they may be broadly divided into two classes : First, separate colleges of agriculture and mechanic arts ; secondly, universities having departments of agriculture, and usually also of engineering. Of the earlier institutions having only courses in agriculture, only one remains, the Massachusetts agricultural college, referred to above. All of the other institutions established first as colleges of agriculture, pure and simple, have organized departments of mechanic arts in obedience to the law. Many have become great institutions of technology, with departments for many arts. In some colleges like those of Mississippi and Texas, the agricultural department preponderates largely, as it should always do in great agricultural states having very little manufacturing. The tendency in all the colleges is to multiply the courses of study in sciences applied to the arts and to cover all the technical pursuits of the states. For example, in several of the southern states, where cotton manufacturing is growing, departments have been organized for instruction in the textile industry. Unless large additional appropriations are provided by the states for this purpose, it were better to limit the courses undertaken to a few of the most important ones. The tendency at the present time, however, is to build up all of these technical department schools around the state university or the agricultural and mechanical college having these funds.

Sixty-five institutions have been organized in the several states and territories under the acts of congress of July 2, 1862, and August 30, 1890. At least one institution is now in operation in each state and territory except Alaska. Of the sixty-one colleges having regular courses in agriculture, twenty-seven may be classified as separate colleges of agriculture and mechanic arts, and nineteen as universities having departments of agriculture and engineering. Separate institutions for colored students have been established in accordance with the act of 1890 in eight southern states. Instruction in them has usually been limited for the most part to courses below the college grade and to the industrial arts suited to the needs of the negro. Seven remain unclassified above.

REQUIREMENTS FOR ADMISSION

The requirements for admission to the agricultural colleges vary very much in the different states in accordance with the school systems and the other opportunities for preparation. The western and southern agricultural colleges usually take the students from what is known in this country as the eighth or ninth grade of the public school course. A majority of the institutions require for admission either certificates from the preparatory schools or examinations in the more important subjects.

The average standard of admission to the agricultural colleges is presented in the report of the committee on entrance requirements made to the association of colleges at the meeting in November, 1896. They recommended the following (Rept. of Bureau of education, 1896–97, p. 429):

"The committee holds that it is advisable, as a beginning, to determine the requirements in a few subjects upon which it is possible for all the colleges to agree, and to recommend others, which, although too high at present for adoption by some of these institutions, may yet serve as a standard or goal toward which effort may be directed.

"As a standard series of entrance requirements, to be adopted as soon as possible, we recommend the following:

1. Physical geography.
2. United States history.
3. Arithmetic, including the metric system.
4. Algebra to quadratics.
5. English grammar and composition, together with English requirements of the New England association.
6. Plane geometry.

7. One foreign language.
8. One of the natural sciences.
9. Ancient, general, or English history."

Many of the universities have a much higher standard of admission, some of them requiring a preparation fairly comparable with that for students entering the literary and scientific courses. Candidates for admission at Cornell, for example, must be at least sixteen years of age and pass an examination in English, geography, physiology and hygiene, history of the United States and England, Greece or Rome, plane geometry, elementary algebra, and at least two of the following subjects: Greek, Latin, French, German and advanced mathematics.

COURSES OF STUDY

The courses of study in the separate colleges for agriculture and mechanic arts are not essentially different from those of the agricultural departments of the state universities, with the exception that in most cases the work of the separate colleges begins a little earlier and is not so much differentiated as that in the universities. Many of the separate agricultural colleges have, however, quite as high requirements for admission as any of the state universities, and do as high a grade of work as the best of them. On the whole, it appears that practical agriculture occupies the highest place in the separate colleges, though more research in the sciences pertaining to agriculture is being carried on in the universities. In universities in which departments of agriculture are maintained, it may be said in general that the tendency is to make the four years' course in agriculture correspond in scope and thoroughness with those in philosophy, sciences and engineering. As more means are obtained, instruction in agriculture is divided among an increasing number of specialists, who are provided with separate buildings, laboratories and shops. It is characteristic of American state universities that they are seeing more and more clearly that agriculture and manufacturing are important human interests which may rightfully claim the best efforts of the greatest scientific intellects for their advancement, and that on the basis of agricultural sciences may be built a system of instruction in literature, mathematics and technology which is as well or better adapted to produce scholars, investigators and leaders in civilization as was the old philosophical or the pure science course.

The courses of study in agriculture are variously arranged. Nearly all these institutions maintain a four years' course, which is made up usually of two years of preparatory sciences and general culture studies, followed by two years of more advanced scientific and technical agricultural work, largely elective. At present there is little demand in our country for the all-around agricultural expert, and few colleges attempt to educate them. Such an expert cannot be trained in four years, if at all. When the demand for such a thoroughly-trained expert arises, he will have to begin his training in the preparatory school and carry it up through the college and the university. But this time is far off. At present the agricultural colleges content themselves with giving their students a fair general knowledge of the sciences underlying agriculture, horticulture, and the animal industry, with opportunities to acquire experience in some one line of practical work. The arrangement of this four years' course differs a good deal in different institutions, but the standard for it is laid in the reports adopted by the association of American agricultural colleges at its meetings in 1896–97. The following paragraphs from that report give the plan of this course as at present given in the best institutions :

" Before proceeding to consider in detail the topics which should be included in a course of agriculture, and the methods to be pursued in teaching agricultural subjects, the committee has deemed it essential to determine the general relation of a course in technical agriculture to the other courses of study which should be connected with this to form a four years' course in an agricultural college. This

task was made simpler by the previous work of the committee on entrance requirements, courses of study, and degrees,
whose report, adopted at the last meeting of this association,
suggests certain requirements for entrance and specifies
certain subjects as desirable in all courses given in the colleges in membership with this association.[1]   In the following
suggestions regarding a four years' course in agriculture, this
committee conforms to that report."

That portion of the report of the committee on entrance
requirements, which relates to the subject essential to all
courses, is as follows:

" In the judgment of your committee, it is not too much
to require the equivalent of fifteen hours per week of recitations and lectures, together with ten hours per week of
laboratory work, or practicums, including the time devoted
to military science and drill.   Upon this basis the above-
mentioned general studies should be assigned a relative
importance, approximately, as follows:

	Hours
Algebra	75
Geometry	40
Trigonometry	40
Physics (class-room work)	75
Physics (laboratory work)	75
Chemistry (class-room work)	75
Chemistry (laboratory work)	75
English	200
Modern languages	340
Psychology	60
Ethics or logic	40
Political economy	60
General history	80
Constitutional law	50
Total	1,285

" The total number of hours included in a four years'
course, allowing fifteen hours per week for thirty-six weeks,

[1] See United States Department of agriculture, Office of Experiment stations,
bulletin 41, p. 52.

would be 2,140; with ten hours' laboratory work, or practicums, added, 3,600. In general terms, therefore, the foregoing general studies should comprise about two-fifths of the work required for a bachelor's degree."

"Your committee on methods of teaching agriculture suggests additional subjects to be included in a four years' course in agriculture leading to the degree of bachelor of science, as follows :

		Hours
Agriculture..		486
Horticulture and forestry.................................		180
Veterinary science (including anatomy)		180
Agricultural chemistry (in addition to general requirement).		180
Botany (including vegetable physiology and pathology)....		180
Zoology (including entomology)...........................		120
Physiology		180
Geology		120
Metereology...		60
Drawing		60
Total...................................		1, 746

In reckoning the number of hours, two hours of laboratory work, or practicums, are considered the equivalent of one hour of recitation. In this way the total number of hours in a four years' course is made 2,900, instead of 3,600, as proposed by the committee on entrance requirements."

"Your committee also submits the following suggestions regarding the course of study to be included under the head of 'Agriculture.' In this part of its work the committee has followed the general divisions of agriculture proposed in its previous report. The number of hours to be assigned to each of these general subjects is stated, as well as the main topics to be included under each general subject, and, in some cases, the text-books which may be used in connection with the teaching of particular subjects. These books are, however, named because they are considered by your committee as the best text-books now available on the subjects. They may also serve to show in a general way what would properly be included in the course under the several topics to which they apply. Some notes regarding equipment requisite for teaching the different branches included in this scheme are also given. The number of hours assigned to the different subjects is intended to apply to the average conditions of a four years' course in agriculture. Local conditions will, of course, call for more or less modifications of the scheme here proposed."

"Agriculture (486 hours) shall include:

		Hours
1.	Agronomy, or plant production	132
2.	Zootechny, or animal industry	162
3.	Agrotechny, or agricultural technology	72
4.	Rural engineering, or farm mechanics	60
5.	Rural economics, or farm management	60
	Total	486

Synopsis of Course in Agriculture

Agronomy .... 132 hours.

Texts.

Climate ....⎫
Soils.............................⎬ F. H. King — The Soil.
Tillage, drainage and irrigation....⎭

Fertilizers........ I. P. Roberts — The Fertility of the Land.

Plant production..... ...⎫ G. E. Morrow and T. F. Hunt —
Farm crops...............⎬ Soils and Crops.

Zootechny.. 162 hours.

Principles of breeding .... M. Miles — Stock Breeding.

Breeds of live stock.... G. W. Curtis — Horses, Cattle, Sheep and Swine.

Stock, feeding, care, and management.. H. P. Armsby—Manual of Cattle Feeding.

(Animal physiology to be taught under 'Physiology;' anatomy and animal diseases under 'Veterinary science.')

Agrotechny .... 72 hours.

Butter making.......⎧ H. H. Wing — Milk and its Products.
                   ⎩ H. B. Gurler — American Dairying.

Cheese making..... J. W. Decker — Cheddar Cheese Making.

(Other topics, such as sugar making, wine or olive oil making, may be taught under this head in different parts of the United States.)

Rural engineering............................. ...... 60 hours.
    Roads, drains, irrigation systems, farm buildings, and
machinery.
Rural economics................................ .... 60 hours.
    History of agriculture.
    Farm management, rural law, farm accounts."

The course of study presents the largest problem now
before the faculties of our colleges. The present courses
and methods have been criticised for their lack of "pedagogical form," for the "confusion of studies," and especially
for lack of "orderly sequence in the progress of instruction"
which has made the classical education and to a certain
degree the scientific and engineering courses of our institutes of technology processes commanding the respect of
scholars the world over. These critics are in error when
they speak of agriculture as an independent science, and
propose to formulate the instruction in it as they would that
in chemistry or in biology. The fact is, agriculture is not a
science but an art, and what we are attempting to do in these
colleges is to carry out the injunction of the act of congress
of 1862 and "teach the sciences (chemistry, physics, geology,
biology, vegetable physiology, etc., each including numerous branches), related thereto." For this reason the course
of study in agriculture with good "pedagogical form" must
be made up of a course in chemistry and agricultural chemistry, a course in vegetable physiology, a course in the physiology of animals, a course in soil physics, etc. — many distinct courses. When the student has mastered all these it
would seem to be possible, if he stays at the college long
enough, to teach him in good "pedagogical form," some of
their applications in agriculture. As Professor Jordan,
director of the Maine agricultural experiment station, has
well said (Report of bureau of education, 1896–97, p.
454) : "The real and important need of which the farmer
is conscious is for a knowledge of conditions and not
for methods or for skill in manipulation. When he
clearly understands the reasons for that which goes on

about him, the right method will appear. The difficulties lie with explanations, not with mechanical processes. And besides, agriculture is not a business involving such delicate and intricate mechanical operations that attendance upon a college would be justified in order to learn them, although the modern dairy, the forcing house, and the fruit garden do require skill. But I venture to assert that no machines or practical methods have yet become available to the agriculturist whose use the clear-brained inmates of our farm homes have failed to master. The spraying of fruit with fungicides and insecticides illustrates how readily the necessary manipulation was acquired when the reasons for these operations became evident. It is the explanation of phenomena, then, which the extended course of study should give in order that the farmer may know how to adapt himself to the varying and complex conditions which he meets in his work."

This is the real problem and one which the colleges and universities are working out with marked success.

Perhaps the colleges and universities having departments of agriculture are doing more immediate good to the largest number of persons through their short courses and their special schools for dairying, horticulture, etc., than through the long course. These short courses are designed to meet the wants of young farmers who desire practical, helpful instruction in agriculture after leaving the high schools and before taking up their chosen vocations. A number of the colleges maintain courses in agriculture of twelve weeks beginning the first of January of each year. They usually include lectures on feeds and feeding, breeds of live stock, elementary agricultural chemistry, physics of soils, meteorology, elements of vegetable physiology, the chief facts of veterinary science, dairying, horticulture, and some of the leading facts of bacteriology. Courses are selected from these to meet the needs of special classes of students from different districts. Laboratory practice is usually given in soil physics, stock judging, dairying, vegetable physiology, and practical horticulture. Other short courses are limited, to the chemistry and bacteriology of milk and practical dairying, or to plant propagation, grafting, pruning, and practical horticulture. These courses are more largely attended than the four years' course. The tendency at present seems to be to split up the four years' course into special courses or to distribute among the different short courses students who cannot attend the institution more than a few months at a time. It is encouraging to note that such students frequently return winter after winter for additional training.

MILITARY INSTRUCTION

As has been stated, the land-grant act, establishing colleges of agriculture and mechanic arts, was passed in the midst of the civil war. The supporters of the Union had learned through bitter experience that the great need of the army was trained officers. The chief object of the college was to be, as has been explained, the education of the industrial classes; but the secondary object was the training of young men in military matters who would be ready to serve their country in any future emergency. It will be interesting to notice, therefore, what has been actually accomplished by military departments of these colleges. Forty-two land-grant colleges have fully organized military departments. In the spring of 1898 these colleges had military organizations varying in size from one company to a whole regiment, having nearly 572 officers, 1,456 non-commissioned officers, and nearly 7,000 privates, making a total of about 9,000 cadets under training. It is estimated that about 15,000 young men have completed the course of military instruction in these colleges during the last ten years, and it is evident that a large number of them will be available for military service in case of need. An effort was made by the writer to ascertain the number of officers commissioned in the Spanish-American war who received their education in these institutions. It was difficult to secure complete statistics, but the partial reports received show that 1,092 young men from these colleges were commissioned by the president in the regular and volunteer armies during the last war.

EXPENSES OF STUDENTS

The expenses of students in the agricultural colleges of the United States vary much with the location and advantages offered. The tuition is uniformly free to all students pursuing the agricultural courses. It is customary to charge small fees to cover the actual expenses of material used in the laboratories and shops. Students pay their own board and personal expenses. Some institutions give free lodgings, though a majority charge only the actual cost of the maintenance of the buildings, fuel, lights, etc. Many institutions have special funds with which to pay for student labor, which usually takes the form of a fixed allowance for work regularly performed. The total college expenses of a student will vary from $150 for a session of nine months at a western or southern college, located in the country, to $400 or $500 at a university in one of the eastern states. More assistance and more opportunities for self-support are offered agricultural students than any others in our institutions. The tendency everywhere is to increase these opportunities and to reduce the expense of the students of agriculture, while all the facilities provided them are constantly improved.

EXTENSION WORK IN AGRICULTURE

The farmers' institute is to the adult farmer what the agricultural school is to his son. They were the outgrowth in part of the public meetings of agricultural societies and state boards of agriculture, and in part of the extension work of colleges and universities. The object of these institutes is to bring the workers in the agricultural sciences and the practical agriculturists together for the discussion of questions of mutual interest. Through such discussion the farmer gets the benefit of the information which the scientist has obtained in the course of his investigations, and the scientist learns what the farmer's needs and difficulties are. The results of the practical tests made by the farmer of the scientist's theories are also brought out. By such conferences both classes of workers have their opinions and experiences broadened.

Institutes in the United States are carried on under all conceivable auspices ; most commonly, however, by the state commissioners, the state boards of agriculture, or the agricultural colleges. In some states there is an independent organization with a secretary of institutes in charge. Some states make special appropriations for institutes, others merely allow a limited amount of the funds appropriated for the board of agriculture or college to be used for this purpose. Institutes are held usually during the winter or after the crops are "laid by" in midsummer, when the farmer has most time to spare, and continue in session from one to three or four days. The programs are arranged to promote the interchange of ideas between the farmers and the scientists, every effort being made to draw out a full and free discussion of the topics introduced by the addresses or papers of specialists. The best plan is to secure the assistance of an equal number of scientific experts and experimental farmers, the latter being selected, as far as possible, from the district where the institute is held. A local committee arranges for halls, music, literary and general exercises. The people of the community are usually attracted in large numbers, especially at the evening sessions when more popular subjects are discussed. Subjects connected with good roads, public education, and the interests of the home and farm are also discussed frequently. Those connected with sectarian religion or partisan politics should be carefully excluded, but almost any other topic of interest to the local community may properly find its place on the program of a farmers' institute. In states where institutes have been carefully planned and systematically conducted by competent persons they have become exceedingly popular, with the result that large appropriations are being made for them each year. Something like the farmers' institute is now held in almost all the states in the Union.

Closely related to the farmers' institute are the various

other methods of agricultural college extension work, such
as co-operative field experiments, correspondence courses in
agricultural sciences, reading circles for farmers, and itinerant agricultural schools. Co-operative field experiments
were inaugurated soon after the establishment of the colleges for agriculture. The college or station makes plans
and supplies the fertilizers or gives prescriptions for the
same, with full directions as to methods of carrying out the
experiments. The farmers report upon blanks prepared for
the purpose, and the different results are compared and published. A great deal of good has been accomplished in this
way, especially in educating farmers as to the proper method
of using chemical manures. Similar methods have been
used in testing seeds of field and garden crops, and in testing insecticide and fungicide materials and methods. Such
co-operative experiments have done much to promote the
study of scientific agriculture in the states, and especially to
develop habits of observation among the younger farmers,
who are always the ones to take hold of this work.

Instruction by correspondence and by courses of home
reading in agriculture have been well developed under the
direction of the State college of Pennsylvania. The main
features of the plan are, "first, a carefully prepared course
of reading designed to cover the most important branches
of agricultural science and practice; second, a reduction of
the price upon the books needed; third, personal advice and
assistance through correspondence; fourth, examinations
upon the subjects read, with certificates and diplomas for
those attaining a certain grade of excellence." "This course
has atttacted great attention at home and received numerous applications from farmer students, many of whom have
done excellent work, completed the prescribed courses, and
received certificates." The courses have now been extended
to include five subjects, with five books in each one; namely,
crop production, animal production, horticulture, dairying,
and domestic economy. A supplemental list of fifteen books
is suggested from which students may select reading matter

to form additional courses if they desire. The full course
consists of the thorough study of ten books, followed by an
examination. Lessons are provided from the various books,
and sent the students free of cost, in the form of printed
slips. They give suggestions for study, observation and
experiment, with references to the books recommended.
Each lesson is accompanied by an examination paper covering the particular subject. The students are expected to file
answers to all these questions and discuss them before they
receive the second lesson.

The itinerant agricultural school, a still later scheme, has
been best developed in the state of New York, under the
so-called Nixon bill, "for the purpose of horticultural experiments, investigation, instruction, and information in New
York." This bill placed the sum of $35,000 under the
control of the college of agriculture at Cornell university for
the two years 1899–1900, and has enabled it to inaugurate
a number of most interesting and promising experiments in
promotion of agricultural knowledge, especially of nature
study in the common schools. The itinerant agricultural
school is one only of the plans now being tested by this
institution. The meetings of these schools last two or more
days, at which time certain instructors take up definite lines
of instruction, giving by far the greater part of their attention to underlying principles and not to mere facts or
methods.

AGRICULTURE IN THE COMMON SCHOOLS

From the earliest time it has been the idea of the friends
of agricultural education that instruction in this subject
should be given in the common schools. The subject has
been presented to the legislatures of many of the states, and
by some it has been required to be taught. For evident
reasons, this instruction has, until comparatively recently,
amounted to very little. Any real instruction in agriculture
must be based upon a knowledge of chemistry, geology, and
the physiology of plants and animals. Such a knowledge
cannot be given to young children, and the old-fashioned

school teacher trained to study books and not things, could give no instruction in nature or science. The whole system of education had to be revolutionized to prepare the way for the study of agriculture in the schools. Since the introduction of the natural method great progress has been made. Agricultural colleges have trained the professors, who in normal schools have taught the teachers, who in turn have introduced the new methods in the common schools. This is the only way to promote the study of agriculture among country people who never get to college. The study of nature and of agriculture in the rural and village schools is, as we shall see, one of the latest developments in education in this country.

The following description of the Cornell attempt to introduce nature teaching into the rural schools is condensed from the article on "Popular education for the farmer" by A. C. True, Ph. D., director of the Office of experiment stations, in the Year-book of the Department of agriculture for 1897. p. 284 *et seq.*

"It was conceived that the fundamental difficulty with our agricultural condition was that there was no attempt to instruct the children in matters which will awaken an interest in country life, and therefore that the place in which to begin to correct the agricultural status was with the children and the rural schools. For the purpose of determining what should be done, many rural and village schools were visited during the past year and simple lessons were given on natural objects. The result was that all the instructors were impressed with the readiness with which the children imbibed the information, their keen desire for it and appreciation of it, and the almost universal interest which teachers took in this kind of work. It was clear that the greatest good which could be rendered to the agricultural communities was to awaken an interest in nature study on the part of teachers and children. In order to facilitate teaching in this direction, leaflets were issued to show teachers how nature study should be presented to the pupils, and these have been received with the greatest enthusiasm by educators and many others who have examined them.

"The outgrowth of this work with the schools is that it seems certain that the best way in which to reach the pupils and the teachers is by short and sharp observations upon plants, insects and other natural objects, and not by means of definite lectures of stated lengths.

"Instruction by means of correspondence has been an outgrowth of the last year. There were about 1,600 readers upon the lists at the close of the first three months. It is the plan in this reading course to set the farmers to reading upon certain definite subjects, and then to make them think upon those subjects by periodical questioning. Some months ago the college of agriculture had enrolled under the head of 'university extension work' 15,000 pupils and 10,000 teachers of the public schools and 1,600 young farmers. The pupils and farmers receive guidance by means of printed circulars, and the farmers report progress and difficulties upon special blanks which are furnished. Six instructors are employed throughout the state in conducting university extension work, and special teachers are employed from time to time as occasion requires. These instructors meet the teachers of the public schools in the presence of their pupils and at teachers' associations and institutes for the purpose of illustrating methods for teaching nature studies directly related to agriculture. The leaflets furnished serve as texts for subjects taught. The result of pushing this educational motive into the rural communities has been a most decided waking up of those communities, which, even if the work were to stop at the present time, will continue to exert an influence for a generation and more.

"All this work has been experimental — an attempt to discover the best methods of teaching the people in agriculture. The promoters of this movement believe that the most efficient means of elevating the ideals and practice of the rural communities are as follows, in approximately the order of fundamental importance: (1) The establishment of nature study or object lesson study, combined with field walks and incidental instruction in the principles of farm practice in the rural schools; (2) the establishment of correspondence instruction in connection with reading courses, binding together the university, the rural schools and all rural literary or social societies; (3) itinerant or local experiment and investigation, made chiefly as object lessons to farmers, and not for the purpose, primarily, of discovering scientific facts; (4) the publication of reading bulletins which shall inspire a quickened appreciation of rural life, and which may be used as texts in rural societies and in the reading courses, and which shall prepare the way for the reading of the more extended literature in books; (5) the sending out of special agents as lecturers or teachers or as investigators of special local difficulties or as itinerant instructors in the normal schools and before the training classes of the teachers' institutes; (6) the itinerant agricultural school, which shall be equipped with the very best teachers, and which shall be given as rewards to the most intelligent and energetic communities.

" There is every reason to believe that the plan of 'nature teaching,' as proposed by Cornell university, may prove a grand success and be a very great benefit to farmers' children. The element of education which is at present most lacking in our common schools is the training of the powers of observation. The children need above all things else to be taught to observe carefully and correctly and to state their observations in clear terse language. The ordinary child, whether on the farm or in town, actually sees comparatively little in the world about him. The wonders of the trees and plants in park or meadow, of birds and insects flying about the house, float like shadowy visions before his eyes. 'Seeing, he sees not.' He needs a teacher who can open his eyes and fix his mind on the realities among which his daily life is passed. This accurate observation of natural objects and facts is the only foundation on which scientific attainments can rest. The scientist is chiefly a man who

sees better than his fellow men.   But it is also a great help
in practical life.   Many farmers acquire much of this power
by their own unaided efforts.   And these are the very men
who most regret that they did not have in early life the help
of a trained teacher.   The farmer's child lives where he has
the best opportunity for such training.   It would benefit him
in the practice of his art, and it would add an interest to his
life which would do much to wean him from a desire to
leave the farm for the turmoil and uncertain struggles of the
town.   With proper provision for the training of teachers in
normal and other schools, it would be entirely feasible to
have this nature teaching in all our common schools within
a few years.   It is such teaching that the child mind craves.
With it the school becomes a delightful place and the
teacher an angel of light."

   " Thus far only a few attempts have been made in this
country to provide agricultural instruction of the high school
grade.   It is true that some of the agricultural colleges
receive students directly from the common schools, but the
constant tendency is to raise the grade of instruction in
these institutions to a college basis and, under any conditions,
they very imperfectly perform the duties of secondary
schools of agriculture.   The University of Minnesota has
in recent years maintained a school of agriculture in which
instruction in agriculture of a lower grade than that given
in the college of agriculture has been successfully imparted.
This school has proved quite popular.   Some 300 students
were in attendance last year, and it has been found desirable
to offer courses for girls as well as boys.   The state of
Alabama has recently provided for the maintenance of a
school of agriculture of secondary grade in each of the nine
congressional districts of the state.

   " The establishment of such special schools of agriculture
of high school grade is greatly to be commended.   One of
the best effects of such schools at the present time is to show
the people what distinctions should be drawn between colleges and high schools for agricultural education.   By the

separation of these grades of instruction the colleges will be enabled to do their work more efficiently, and better opportunities will be secured for those students whose pre-vious training only fits them for high-school work in agricul-ture.   But it is not believed that these special agricultural high schools will fully meet the needs of our farmers for agricultural instruction of this grade.   Any school so distant from the farmer's home as to necessitate long journeys and residence at the school for two or more years must neces-sarily be too expensive for most of the farmers' children, especially after they have reached an age when their serv-ices may be more or less utilized on the farm.   What is needed is courses in agriculture in numerous schools to which farmers' children resort, near their homes, to 'finish' their education after they are through with the common schools."

STATISTICS OF THE LAND-GRANT COLLEGES

The statistics of the land-grant colleges have been sum-marized in tables accompanying this paper which were con-densed from those published by the United States depart-ment of agriculture.

In 1898 the numbers of teachers in the faculties of the col-leges of agriculture and mechanic arts was 1,722 ; the officers in the agricultural experiment stations connected therewith numbered 604.   The students in attendance upon them in 1898 were as follows : In preparatory classes 6,593, in collegiate classes 20,466, graduate students, 878, total students (count-ing those in short courses), 31,658.   The graduates in 1898 numbered 2,328 and since the opening of these colleges 34,168.   The number of volumes in the libraries of these institutions was 1,221,226.   The number of acres of land in grounds and farms was 20,713.   (See Table 1 for details.)

The aggregate value of the permanent funds and equip-ment of the 64 land-grant colleges in the United States was estimated in 1898 to be : Land-grant funds of 1862, $10,170,550 ;   other permanent funds, $16,858,712.   The farms and grounds owned by them were worth $6,046,500 ;

buildings, $15,185,476, apparatus and machinery, $3,299,365 ; library and miscellaneous, $3,399,433 ; total, $53,632,852. (Table 2.)

The income of these institutions exclusive of that of the experiment stations was in 1898 : From land-grant fund of 1862 and other permanent funds, $1,232,613 ; from the United States appropriation under act of 1890, $1,108,610 ; from state appropriation, $2,370,719 ; from fees and miscellaneous, $1,306,437 ; total, $6,018,379. The value of the additions to the permanent endowment and equipment of these colleges in 1898 is estimated at $2,796,351. (Table 3.)

Professor Reber of the Pennsylvania state college has made a comparison of the endowments and revenues secured from the land-grant in the several states, using the reports for 1897. The following paragraphs are taken from his paper :[1]

" The great disparity (see our Tables 2 and 3) in the amount of national aid received by the various states is to be accounted for less by the fact that different amounts of land were received, than by the differences in the management and disposal of the lands granted. Kansas, notably, though her grant was among the smallest (90,000 acres), has disposed of her land to such excellent advantage that she is in receipt of one of the best incomes derived from this source. Pennsylvania received 780,000 acres of land, and has from this large grant an income of but $25,637.43. New York received 990,000 acres of land, and from this her university eventually realized $6,662,700, an average of $6.73 per acre. Had Pennsylvania disposed of her land at the same rate her state university would have received $5,249,000 instead of $439,186 (as was the case), and her annual income from this source would have been $314,964. The following figures further illustrate these differences : Minnesota, with 120,000 acres, has an annual income from the land grant of $27,410. California's 150,000 acres yield

---

[1] Comparative view of endowment and income of land-grant colleges, by Louis E. Reber.

an annual income of $43,619.33. Iowa's 240,000 acres yield annual income, $47,729.75. Michigan's 240,000 acres, yield annual income, $31,450. Kansas's 90,000 acres, yield annual income, $50,689. Colorado still holds a large part of her land-grant. Missouri, too, holds a large amount of land (136,000 acres), and this with the condition that it shall not be sold for less than $7 an acre, whereby will eventually be added to her endowment not less than $952,000. Statistics relating to the state of New York have been almost entirely omitted on account of the unique position of Cornell university among the land-grant colleges. She has reaped the benefit of the foresight and philanthropy of Ezra Cornell and others in so large a revenue that she has not (until recently, at least) desired state aid."

" Many of the states, recognizing the munificence of the national government in appropriating so large a sum in the interest of higher education, have ratified their acceptance of the obligation to carry on successfully what the nation has begun, by laying a definite tax for this purpose. This tax yields, in all cases, a maintenance fund only, provision for buildings being made by special appropriation. Other states have assured maintenance to their state institutions by making a fixed annual appropriation. Thirty-nine of the land-grant colleges have, in one way or the other, secured definite annual state aid." (See Table 3.)

" The state of California has given its university over 2,000,000 acres of land, from which is realized $109,000 annually. From a fixed state tax (1-10) this university received in 1897 $128,415.16. These amounts, together with a special appropriation made by legislature, added to those received from the national appropriations, gave her in 1897 an income of over $300,000. In 1898 and thereafter this income will be increased, the fixed state tax of 1-10 of a mill having been changed to 2-10 of a mill. This magnificent provision is independent of special appropriations in which, also, the state of California has been extremely liberal."

"Minnesota gives 23-100 of a mill annually. Colorado gives 6-10 of a mill. Wisconsin divides the tax for her university, giving a certain millage for administrative expenditure, other millage for general instruction and one per cent of the railroad tax to the school of engineering. Her total tax receipts for the state university were, in 1897, $283,000."

"Ohio's millage (1-10) gives at the present time over $177,000, though the amount shown on the chart is only $118,900. This discrepancy is due to the fact that the annual tax rate for the university was increased in January, 1897, and the sum charted is for the college year 1896 and 1897. Nebraska had at one time a millage which yielded an income to the university of $170,000."

THE ORIGIN OF THE AGRICULTURAL EXPERIMENT STATIONS

Research in the sciences related to agriculture was always prominent in the minds of the advocates of agricultural education. After the agricultural colleges were firmly established and the work of instruction was well under way, it became evident that the department of research in these institutions needed a special endowment and to be placed under a somewhat separate management. The funds provided were not sufficient for the purposes of instruction, and research and experiment were in danger of being neglected at the colleges so thronged were they with the young people who came to secure the benefits of this free tuition.

Several of the land-grant colleges early attempted to establish separate departments for scientific research and practical experiments on the plan of the German experiment stations. The act establishing the agricultural college of Maryland, passed in 1856, contained a section requiring the college to establish a model farm and conduct "a series of experiments upon the cultivation of cereals and other plants adapted to the latitude and climate of the state of Maryland, and keep a careful record of the kind of soil upon which they were undertaken, the system of cultivation adopted, the state of the atmosphere, and all other particulars which may be necessary to a fair and complete understanding of the results of said experiments." This work was commenced in 1858 and continued two or three years only, when the civil war stopped all the operations of the college. When Connecticut established her agricultural school in connection with the Sheffield scientific school of Yale college, Samuel W. Johnson was appointed professor of agricultural chemistry, and experimental work was commenced. "To the influence of the professors and pupils trained in this school, more than to any other single cause, is due the recognition of the importance of the establishment of agricultural experiment stations." (True.)

In 1870 the trustees for the Massachusetts society for promoting agriculture granted to Harvard college a sum of money "for the support of a laboratory and for experiments in agricultural chemistry to be conducted upon the Bussey estate." A school of agriculture and horticulture had been founded upon the bequest of Benjamin Bussey. The work of the new institution commenced in 1871. The experiments consisted of field tests of fertilizers, and chemical analyses of commercial manures. The first report was published in December 1871. Other interesting and valuable work was done the next few years, but the commercial crisis of 1873 crippled the institution financially, and it has since been able to make comparatively few original investigations.

At a meeting of the state board of agriculture of Connecticut on December 17, 1873, Professor S. W. Johnson of New Haven, and Professor W. O. Atwater of Wesleyan university, urged the establishment of an agricultural experiment station "after the European pattern." The result of this movement was that the state of Connecticut made, in 1877, an appropriation of $5,000 "to promote agriculture by scientific investigation and experiment." This station was first connected with the chemical laboratory of Wesleyan university, at Middletown, which had been established by Orange Judd and was in charge of Professor Atwater, but after two years it was reorganized under the direct control of the state and permanently located in the neighborhood of New Haven. The state of North Carolina established an agricultural experiment and fertilizer control station in connection with the state university at Chapel Hill, on March 12, 1877. The Cornell university experiment station was organized by the faculty of that institution in February, 1879, without any special appropriation. The New Jersey station was organized in 1880. The Tennessee experiment station in 1882. From these beginnings the experiment stations multiplied in the states until in 1887, when congress passed the experiment station act, there were 17 stations already in existence. This act, known from its great advocate Mr. William H. Hatch of Missouri, as the Hatch act, provided that $15,000 should be appropriated each year out of the funds arising from the sale of public lands in each state and territory, for the establishment of an agricultural experiment station as a department of each of the land-grant colleges. Those states which had established independent experiment stations prior to the passage of the act were allowed, however, to turn over this fund to the stations so established. Section 2 defined the duties of these stations as follows: That it shall be the object and duty of said experiment stations to conduct original researches or verify experiments on the physiology of plants and animals; the diseases to which they are severally subject, with the remedies for the same; the chemical composition of useful plants at their different stages of growth; the comparative advantages of rotative cropping as pursued under a varying series of crops; the capacity of new plants or trees for acclimation; the analysis of soils and water; the chemical composition of manures, natural or artificial, with experiments designed to test their comparative effects on crops of different kinds; the adaptation and value of grasses and forage plants; the composition and digestibility of the different kinds of food for domestic animals; the scientific and economic questions involved in the production of butter and cheese; and such other researches or experiments bearing directly on the agricultural industry of the United States as may in each case be deemed advisable, having due regard to the varying conditions and needs of the respective states or or territories.

The stations were also authorized to publish annual reports of their operations, and "bulletins or reports of progress" at least once in three months, which should be sent to "each newspaper in the state, and such individuals actually engaged in farming as may request the same." The franking privilege was given for station publications. In the annual appropriation bill for the department of agriculture for the fiscal year ending June 30, 1889, congress established the office of experiment stations as a branch of the department of agriculture. This is a clearing house for the experiment stations. It compiles and publishes the results of their work, and aids them in many ways. The following statistics are taken from the last report of the department of agriculture (page 1002 of Experiment station record, 1899):

"Agricultural experiment stations are now in operation under the act of congress of March 2, 1887, in all the states and territories. Agricultural experiments have been begun in Alaska with the aid of national funds, and an experiment station is in operation in Hawaii under private auspices. In each of the states of Alabama, Connecticut, New Jersey, and New York a separate station is maintained wholly or in part by state funds, and in Louisiana a station for sugar experiments is maintained partly by funds contributed by sugar planters. Excluding the branch stations established in several states, the total number of stations in the United States is 54. Of these, 52 receive the appropriation provided for in the act of congress above mentioned. The total income of the stations during 1898 was $1,201,921.17, of which $720,000 was received from the national government, the remainder, $481,921.17, coming from the following sources: State governments, $341,097.94; individuals and communities, $177.20; fees for analysis of fertilizers, $54,977.30; sales of farm products, $65,356.25; miscellaneous, $20,312.48. In addition to this, the office of experiment stations had an appropriation of $35,000 for the past fiscal year, including $5,000 for the Alaskan investigation. The value of additions to equipment of the stations in 1898 is estimated as follows: Buildings, $109,851.65 ; libraries, $11,700.73 ; apparatus, $19,195.43 ; farm implements, $10,800.27; live stock, $13,151.33 ; miscellaneous, $11,972.97; total, $176,469.41.

" The stations employ 669 persons in the work of administration and inquiry. The number of officers engaged in the different lines of work is as follows: Directors, 75 ; chemists, 148 ; agriculturists, 71 ; experts in animal husbandry, 10 ; horticulturists, 77 ; farm foremen, 29 ; dairymen, 21 ; botanists, 50; entomologists, 46; veterinarians, 26 ; meteorologists, 30 ; biologists, 11 ; physicists, 11 ; geologists, 6 ; mycologists and bacteriologists, 19 ; irrigation engineers, 7 ; in charge of sub-stations, 15 ; secretaries and treasurers, 23 ; librarians, 10, and clerks, 46. There are also 21 persons classified as superintendents of gardens, grounds, and buildings, apiarists, herdsmen, etc. Three hundred and five station officers do more or less teaching in the colleges with which the stations are connected.

" During 1898 the stations published 406 annual reports and bulletins. Besides regular reports and bulletins, a number of the stations issued press bulletins, which were widely reproduced in the agricultural and county papers. The mailing list of the stations now aggregate half a million names."

The work of the American agricultural experiment station supplements that of the colleges in many most important ways. It is fully described in the admirable publications issued by the office of experiment stations of the United States department of agriculture, to which the reader is referred for fuller information.

STATISTICS OF LAND-GRANT (AGRICULTURAL AND MECHANICAL) COLLEGES IN THE UNITED STATES [1]

TABLE I—Officers, Students, Graduates, Volumes in Libraries, Acres in Farms, etc.

State or Territory	Post Office	Name of Institution	Date of establishment of institution	Officers: College of agriculture and mechanic arts	Officers: Experiment station officers	Students: Preparatory classes	Students: Collegiate	Students: Post graduate	Students: Total	Graduates: Number in 1898	Graduates: Total number since organization	Number of volumes in library	Number of acres in farm and ground
Alabama	Auburn	Polytechnic Institute	1872	31	11	29	287	23	341	48	500	13 462	240
Alabama	Normal	Normal and Industrial School (for colored)	1891	11	11	440	18		458	33	429	3 500	182
Arizona	Tucson	University of Arizona	1872	15	11	99	57		156	4	10	3 100	
Arkansas	Fayetteville	Industrial University	1872	33	8	62	207	4	478	13	216	14 497	160
Arkansas	Pine Bluff	Branch Normal College (for colored)	.1868	8		129	87	20	319	10	100	3 750	20
California	Berkeley	University of California	1868	72	27	45	1 917	7	2 391	247	3 424	153 500	424
Colorado	Fort Collins	Agricultural College of Colorado	1877	25	18		292		344	13	115	10 984	800
Connecticut	Storrs	Storrs Agricultural College	1881	13	8		113	3	113	14	163	7 000	300
Delaware	Newark	Delaware College	1870	13	6	27	88		101	10	339	18 000	14
Delaware	Dover	College for Colored Students	1892	7		46	19		46	2	2	700	7
Florida	Lake City	Agricultural College	1884	15	7	169	152	2	200	12	49	2 500	140
Florida	Tallahassee	State Normal and Industrial Coll. (for colored)	1887	7			2		218		24	1 140	135
Georgia	Athens	College of Agriculture and Mechanic Arts	1872	21	7	110	105	5	110	11	264	37 005	120
Georgia	College	Industrial College (for colored)	1892	11		161	50		160	7	11	520	86
Idaho	Moscow	University of Idaho	1867	21	11	199	84	3	248	8	17	15 600	112
Illinois	Urbana	University of Illinois	1867	99	10		696	78	1 582	90	1 188	41 088	665
Indiana	Lafayette	Purdue University	1874	64	11	71	693	57	750	72	910	10 952	90
Iowa	Ames	State College of Agriculture and Mechanic Arts	1869	59	21	77	560	5	636	88	978	11 458	840
Kansas	Manhattan	State Agricultural College	1863	42	21	81	669	57	803	69	802	33 040	323
Kentucky	Lexington	Agricultural and Mechanical College	1865	18	12	36	248	9	430	19	191	9 325	100
Kentucky	Frankfort	State Normal School for Colored Persons	1887	5	9		21		147	12	67	883	30
Louisiana	Baton Rouge	State University and Agricultural and Mechanical College	1877	20	20	88		4	250	12		22 000	
Louisiana	New Orleans	Southern University and Agricultural and Mechanical College (for colored)	1880	13		381	62		443	16	116	1 396	104
Maine	Orono	University of Maine	1865	34	12		317	7	324	43	530	20 000	373
Maryland	College Park	Maryland Agricultural College	1859	17	13	23	81	1	105	13	508	2 800	286
Massachusetts	Amherst	Massachusetts Agricultural College	1867	22	22		133	9	142	11	1 960	18 766	404
Massachusetts	Boston	Massachusetts Institute of Technology	1855	54			1 191	7	1 198	193		60 163	
Michigan	Agri. College	State Agricultural College	1855	42	19	164	470	5	475	29	763	25 000	676
Minnesota	Minneapolis	University of Minnesota	1869	58	13		2 551	185	2 890	185	2 540	52 000	300

State	Location	Institution	Founded	1	2	3	4	5	6	7	8	9	10
Mississippi	Agri. College	Agricultural and Mechanical College	1880	21	12	92	200	4	296	15	230	14 177	1 966
Mississippi	Westside	Agricultural and Mechanical Coll. (for colored)	1871	14		224	24		248	1	101	8 320	300
Missouri	Columbia	School of Agriculture and Engineering	1870	30	13		818		818	42			718
Missouri	Rolla	School of Mines and Metallurgy		10			115	2	117	5	88	5 258	20
Missouri	Jefferson City	Lincoln Institute (for colored)				69	51		120	20	126	325	43
Montana	Bozeman	College of Agriculture and Mechanic Arts	1893	18	7	183	18	37	201	4	7	5 500	185
Nebraska	Lincoln	Industrial College of the Univ. of Nebraska	1869	47	19	141	345	4	523	44	241	40 000	332
Nevada	Reno	State University	1873	19	7	92	178	2	328	19	85	877	36
New Hampshire	Durham	College of Agriculture and Mechanic Arts	1866	21	11	7	134	1	143	19	192	10 877	342
New Jersey	New Brunswick	Rutgers Scientific School	1864	33	8	144	151	1	296	41	353	9 346	
New Mexico	Mesilla Park	College of Agriculture and Mechanic Arts	1869	17	15	134	80	166	215	8	21	41 562	200
New York	Ithaca	Cornell University	1865	58	21		1 669	15	1 835	260	4 755	4 316	270
North Carolina	West Raleigh	College of Agriculture and Mechanic Arts	1889		20	29	201	15			87	246 278	500
North Carolina	Greensboro	Agricultural and Mechanical College for the Colored Race (for colored)											
North Dakota	Agri. College	Agricultural College	1890	20	12	175	52	3	237	6	13	9 015	25
Ohio	Columbus	State University	1870	25			59		150	71	876	30 339	640
Oklahoma	Stillwater	Agricultural and Mechanical College	1891	11	11	98	76	15	174	7	16	7 200	345
Oregon	Corvallis	State Agricultural College	1868	26	11		321	3	336	29	291	5 800	200
Pennsylvania	State College	Pennsylvania State College	1855	47	18	40	304	7	347	44	414	13 408	198
Rhode Island	Kingston	College of Agriculture and Mechanic Arts	1888	25	12		144	10	183	10	53	14 250	400
South Carolina	Clemson College	Clemson Agricultural College	1889	29	14	240	227		447	25	62		180
South Carolina	Orangeburg	Normal, Industrial, Agricultural and Mechanical College (for colored)											1 102
South Dakota	Brookings	Agricultural College	1896	21		489	71		560	12	28	750	130
Tennessee	Knoxville	University of Tennessee	1881	19	12	48	352		400	19	133	15 400	400
Texas	College Station	Agricultural and Mechanical College	1794	30	10		251	14	608	31		27 500	231
Texas	Prairie View	Prairie View State Normal School (for colored)	1871	22	15		334	3	337	23	332	8 500	2 416
Utah	Logan	Agricultural College	1888	8			164		190			1 196	108
Vermont	Burlington	University of Vermont and State Agri. College	1865	21	11	279	292	4	447	5	52	8 850	120
Virginia	Blacksburg	Polytechnic Institute	1872	20	13		294	1	575	36	3 174		404
Virginia	Hampton	Hampton Normal and Agricultural Institute (for colored)		31	8			39	333	17	263	3 750	
Washington	Pullman	Agricultural College and School of Science	1865	79		811	309		1 120		987	9 641	795
West Virginia	Morgantown	West Virginia University	1892	23	8	192	162	2	380	11	23	5 166	236
West Virginia	Farm.	West Virginia Colored Institute	1867	38	13	174	322	22	644	45	536		100
Wisconsin	Madison	University of Wisconsin	1891	57	18	91	1 466	23	1 767	164	3 556	68 000	
Wyoming	Laramie	University of Wyoming	1848 / 1887	11	8	272 / 65	112	8	185	11	57	9 750	400 / 356
		Total		1 722	604	6 593	20 466	878	31 658	2 328	34 168	1 221 226	20 713

1 Condensed from the report of "Statistics of Land-grant Colleges and Experiment Stations" for 1898, published by the Office of Experiment Stations, United States Department of Agriculture.

TABLE II—Land-grant and other Permanent Funds, Buildings and Equipment—Value of

STATE OR TERRITORY	Post Office	Number of acres allotted to State under act of 1862	Produced value—land-grant fund of 1862	Other permanent funds	Farm and grounds—value of the institution owned by the institution	Buildings—value of	Apparatus and machinery—value of	Library and miscellaneous—value of	Total
Alabama	Auburn	240 000	$253 500 00		$6 000 00	$144 500 00	$41 040 00	$42 773 00	$487 813 00
Alabama	Normal				10 000 00	50 000 00	5 831 41	1 304 00	67 135 41
Arizona	Tucson		130 000 00		3 000 00	86 600 00	41 000 00	6 533 46	137 133 46
Arkansas	Fayetteville	150 000			9 600 00	230 000 00	28 704 00	15 750 00	414 954 00
Arkansas	Pine Bluff					18 000 00	20 000 00	4 500 00	42 500 00
California	Berkeley	150 000	731 183 30	$2 109 537 90	1 125 554 00	702 110 84		356 384 12	5 024 770 16
Colorado	Fort Collins	90 000	68 612 09	150 000 00	48 468 00	151 709 86	55 306 95	25 752 28	499 849 12
Connecticut	Storrs	180 000	135 000 00	23 000 00	15 000 00	76 000 00	7 500 00	10 000 00	265 500 00
Delaware	Newark	90 000	83 000 00		3 000 00	79 700 00	32 590 00	20 000 00	218 200 00
Delaware	Dover				6 000 00	14 000 00	3 600 00	1 000 00	24 600 00
Florida	Lake City	90 000	151 783 00		7 635 00	31 245 00	11 042 00	14 495 00	216 170 00
Florida	Tallahassee				9 605 00	15 000 00	3 000 00	2 000 00	29 605 00
Georgia	Athens	300 000	243 000 00	912 410 67	7 000 00	300 000 00	110 000 00	60 000 00	720 000 00
Georgia	College		8 000 00		15 000 00	10 500 00	800 00	700 00	35 000 00
Idaho	Moscow	90 000		150 000 00	6 600 00	128 900 00	45 500 00	7 500 00	1 109 910 67
Illinois	Urbana	480 000	464 083 85	150 000 00	150 000 00	800 000 00	150 000 00	75 000 00	1 789 083 85
Indiana	Lafayette	390 000	340 000 00		70 000 00	345 000 00	258 500 00	16 500 00	1 030 000 00
Iowa	Ames	204 000	591 354 01	131 431 45	34 400 00	400 000 00	150 000 00	20 000 00	1 327 185 46
Kansas	Manhattan	82 314	593 478 70	720 00	39 700 00	228 438 66	97 256 55	68 899 16	938 493 01
Kentucky	Lexington	330 000	165 000 00		275 000 00	124 000 00	52 000 00	11 700 00	627 700 00
Kentucky	Frankfort		20 995 00	6 335 00	1 873 25	116 092 74	2 800 00	2 000 00	50 025 00
Louisiana	Baton Rouge								
Louisiana	New Orleans	210 000	118 300 00	100 000 00	22 000 00	45 320 00	7 337 36	7 346 40	82 003 76
Maine	Orono	360 000	219 000 00		9 325 00	200 900 00	56 350 00	44 500 00	529 375 00
Massachusetts	Amherst			141 575 35	45 000 00	216 000 00	14 000 00	29 000 00	664 575 35
Massachusetts Inst. of Techn.	Boston	235 682	115 943 00	1 882 859 59		535 000 00		200 000 00	2 617 859 59
Maryland	College Park	94 000	625 790 98	9 000 00	28 600 00	71 000 00	27 000 00		251 543 00
Michigan	Agricultural College	207 920		88 311 73	47 320 00	297 996 55	79 023 30	86 640 57	1 225 083 13
Minnesota	Minneapolis	270 000	518 000 00	752 839 22	500 000 00	1 000 000 00	140 000 00	125 000 00	3 027 439 22
Mississippi	Agricultural College	275 016	98 575 00	16 814 50	42 605 00	132 655 00	38 842 94	47 370 81	359 448 75
Mississippi	Westside		113 375 00		2 500 00	65 000 00	1 000 00	4 000 00	202 689 50
Missouri	Columbia		349 881 19	77 000 00	153 566 00	205 500 00		118 925 00	904 812 19
Missouri	Rolla		87 472 86	62 000 00	6 000 00	50 000 00	8 000 00	20 000 00	233 472 80

Missouri	Jefferson City				4 300 00	70 000 00	17 000 00	321 00	91 621 00
Montana	Bozeman	90 000		248 000 00	10 000 00	110 000 00	40 000 00	15 000 00	443 000 00
Nebraska	Lincoln	90 000	61 955 15	102 170 34	200 000 00	450 000 00	115 000 00	115 000 00	1 044 125 49
Nevada	Reno	90 000	93 000 00	37 458 75	16 000 00	140 183 67	25 171 03	46 875 13	358 688 58
New Hampshire	Durham	150 000	80 000 00	40 000 00	20 500 00	185 710 85	36 267 58	18 002 57	380 481 00
New Jersey	New Brunswick	210 000	116 000 00	500 000 00	366 500 00			64 880 00	1 047 380 00
New Mexico	Mesilla Park				10 000 00	50 500 00		10 000 00	96 185 00
New York	Ithaca	990 000	688 572 12	5 612 004 72	103 468 91	1 692 903 95	24 785 00	896 403 05	9 232 257 82
North Carolina	West Raleigh	300 000	125 000 00		27 000 00	78 000 00	238 995 07	8 600 00	254 200 00
North Carolina	Greensboro				3 000 00	64 000 00	15 600 00	18 000 00	76 800 00
North Dakota	Agricultural College	90 000		900 000 00	25 000 00	90 000 00	8 000 00	15 500 00	1 044 100 00
Ohio	Columbus	630 000	524 176 30	26 292 97	1 500 000 00	700 000 00	13 600 00	70 000 00	3 220 469 27
Oklahoma	Stillwater				5 000 00	20 000 00	400 000 00	7 500 00	55 500 00
Oregon	Corvallis	90 000	132 430 00	89 709 50	14 500 00	53 000 00	23 000 00	10 000 00	227 930 00
Pennsylvania	State College	780 000	427 290 50		40 000 00	750 000 00	18 000 00	20 000 00	1 387 000 00
Rhode Island	Kingston	50 000	50 000 00		182 000 00	180 900 00	66 000 00	11 625 00	514 990 94
South Carolina	Clemson College		95 900 00	58 539 39	26 286 00	220 000 00	89 565 94	17 000 00	467 719 39
South Carolina	Orangeburg	120 000					50 000 00		
South Dakota	Brookings		396 000 00	1 238 000 00	9 250 00	93 000 00		56 842 94	1 370 259 00
Tennessee	Knoxville	180 000	209 000 00	29 000 00	286 250 00	162 400 00	30 000 00	53 995 45	954 126 44
Texas	College Station				48 320 00	298 065 00	23 633 50		608 480 45
Texas	Prairie View								
Utah	Logan	200 000	135 500 00		10 800 00	145 000 00	37 502 46	5 450 00	198 752 46
Vermont	Burlington	150 000	344 312 00	376 000 00	24 000 00	478 644 95	99 000 00	134 000 00	247 144 95
Virginia	Blacksburg		172 156 00	708 360 00	30 000 00	140 000 00		65 765 50	580 681 50
Virginia	Hampton	300 000			52 000 00	496 000 00	36 000 00	130 000 00	564 516 00
Washington	Pullman	199 000			15 000 00	100 000 00	113 000 00	20 000 00	171 000 00
West Virginia	Morgantown		90 000 00	24 750 00	5 000 00	300 000 00	6 000 00	33 800 00	566 550 00
West Virginia	Farm		302 000 00		2 500 00	45 000 00	266 000 00	32 000 00	56 700 00
Wisconsin	Madison	240 000		255 000 00	300 000 00	1 200 000 00	32 000 00	105 000 00	2 422 000 00
Wyoming	Laramie	100 000			9 540 00	102 000 00		11 325 00	154 865 00
Total		9 559 241	$10 170 549 99	$16 858 712 08	$6 046 500 16	$15 185 476 95	$3 299 365 09	$3 399 433 44	$53 632 852 25

TABLE III — Income from Land-grant Fund, Government and State Appropriations, and Other Sources — Additions to Equipment in 1898.

STATE OR TERRITORY	Post Office	Interest on land-grant and other permanent funds	United States appropriation (act of 1890)	State appropriations, regular and occasional	Fees and miscellaneous sources of revenue	Total revenues	Additions to buildings and equipment in 1898
Alabama	Auburn	$20 280 00	$12 523 48	$9 988 30	$2 968 25	$45 760 03	$8 518 00
Alabama	Normal		10 476 59	4 000 00		14 476 59	1 533 00
Arizona	Tucson		23 000 00	10 700 00	2 539 31	36 239 31	4 286 85
Arkansas	Fayetteville	10 400 00	16 747 30	34 650 00	3 930 00	65 707 30	11 300 00
Arkansas	Pine Bluff		6 272 70	9 000 00	450 00	15 722 70	975 00
California	Berkeley	112 622 79	23 000 00	385 141 39	13 443 64	534 207 82	94 200 37
Colorado	Fort Collins	3 504 12	23 000 00	36 500 00	730 69	63 734 81	45 562 44
Connecticut	Storrs	6 750 00	24 000 00	15 000 00		45 750 00	200 00
Delaware	Newark	4 980 00	18 400 00		2 826 43	26 206 43	3 400 00
Delaware	Dover		4 600 00			4 600 00	
Florida	Lake City	9 107 00	11 500 00	4 355 78	2 543 83	27 506 61	4 107 00
Florida	Tallahassee		12 000 00	4 000 00	389 00	16 389 00	4 000 00
Georgia	Athens	16 954 14	15 333 34		1 050 00	33 337 48	31 415 00
Georgia	College	8 000 00	7 666 67			15 666 67	
Idaho	Moscow	500 00	23 000 00	6 000 00	622 03	30 122 03	12 900 00
Illinois	Urbana	14 366 95	23 000 00	210 000 00	35 545 55	282 912 50	106 570 94
Indiana	Lafayette	17 000 00	23 000 00	81 660 64	29 862 11	151 522 75	65 000 00
Iowa	Ames	47 729 75	23 000 00	45 500 00	2 286 73	118 516 48	20 000 00
Kansas	Manhattan	27 716 59	23 000 00	31 783 54	12 094 04	94 594 17	25 947 61
Kentucky	Lexington	29 616 75	19 655 00	31 675 70	9 358 16	90 315 61	22 650 00
Kentucky	Frankfort	1 255 59	3 335 00	7 404 46	1 944 91	13 939 87	4 911 13
Louisiana	Baton Rouge						
Maine	Orono		11 862 00	9 000 00	200 00	21 062 00	500 00
Maryland	College Park	5 915 00	23 000 00	20 000 00	25 130 52	74 045 52	10 850 00
Massachusetts	Amherst	6 142 30	23 000 00	18 500 00	30 701 73	78 344 03	15 000 00
Massachusetts	Boston	10 976 15	15 333 33	15 000 00	2 183 60	43 493 08	600 00
Michigan	Agricultural College	49 131 37	8 000 00	25 000 00	257 867 03	330 998 40	884 000 00
Minnesota	Minneapolis	46 842 37	23 000 00	11 000 00	18 828 84	99 671 76	93 234 38
Mississippi	Agricultural College	50 277 68	24 000 00	149 000 00	76 216 06	305 493 74	80 401 00
Mississippi	Westside	5 914 50	10 681 41	20 500 00	14 892 80	51 988 71	8 958 41
Missouri	Columbia	17 814 50	12 000 00	10 000 00	1 200 00	51 514 00	5 300 00
Missouri	Rolla	17 594 10	5 679 97	8 000 00	8 465 58	27 159 91	2 600 00
Missouri	Jefferson City	5 010 36	1 233 18	17 275 00	138 50	18 646 68	
Montana	Bozeman		23 000 00	12 000 00	3 000 00	38 000 00	23 000 00
Nebraska	Lincoln	38 500 00	24 000 00	282 000 00	7 500 00	352 000 00	52 500 00
Nevada	Reno	4 253 00	23 000 00	32 500 00	1 250 00	61 003 00	2 933 48
New Hampshire	Durham	7 278 00	23 000 00	5 500 00	14 589 44	50 367 44	8 553 83
New Jersey	New Brunswick	6 480 00	23 000 00		20 439 47	49 919 47	45 729 30

New Mexico	Mesilla Park		23 000 00	4 547 28	1 272 74	28 920 02	21 935 00
New York	Ithaca	375 661 82	23 000 00		170 646 04	569 307 86	288 807 36
North Carolina	West Raleigh	7 500 00	14 936 20	10 000 00	6 048 66	38 484 86	10 000 00
North Carolina	Greensboro		8 414 40		250 00	21 164 40	
North Dakota	Agricultural College		23 000 00	12 500 00	3 277 32	53 277 32	
Ohio	Columbus	32 973 11	23 000 00	27 000 00	220 579 07	462 175 79	2 500 00
Oklahoma	Stillwater		23 000 00	185 623 61		23 500 00	265 887 40
Oregon	Corvallis	12 577 95	23 000 00	500 00	1 161 47	41 739 42	5 993 83
Pennsylvania	State College	25 637 43	23 000 00	5 000 00	10 158 54	98 945 97	2 199 79
Rhode Island	Kingston	2 941 66	23 000 00	40 150 00	12 522 40	59 964 00	3 000 00
South Carolina	Clemson College	9 276 36	11 500 00	21 500 00	3 387 04	74 163 40	21 861 40
South Carolina	Orangeburg		11 500 00	50 000 00			9 100 40
South Dakota	Brookings	5 754 00	23 000 00	10 000 00	1 00	27 255 00	3 000 00
Tennessee	Knoxville	25 410 00	23 000 00	17 500 00	10 603 49	51 103 49	8 000 00
Texas	College Station	14 280 00	17 250 00	20 000 00	10 988 22	59 398 22	
Texas	Prairie View				42 185 00	93 715 00	3 943 59
Utah	Logan		23 000 00	12 250 00	6 175 47	41 425 47	28 655 00
Vermont	Burlington	30 074 15	23 000 00	6 000 00	19 173 62	78 247 77	18 450 00
Virginia	Blocksburg	20 658 72	15 333 34	15 000 00	11 592 97	62 585 93	3 769 50
Virginia	Hampton		7 666 66		99 296 16	146 518 40	8 577 51
Washington	Pullman	39 555 58	23 000 00	27 500 00	9 000 00	9 000 00	275 133 18
West Virginia	Morgantown	6 408 00	18 000 00	36 559 00	12 366 08	73 318 08	5 472 26
West Virginia	Farm		5 000 99	15 000 00	600 00	20 600 00	17 035 06
Wisconsin	Madison	23 999 97	24 000 00	283 287 00	48 798 70	380 076 67	54 200 00
Wyoming	Laramie		23 000 00	8 076 69	1 166 73	32 243 42	58 000 00
	Total	$1 232 613 16	$1 108 610 38	$3 370 719 39	$1 306 436 97	$6 018 379 20	$2 796 350 97

DEPARTMENT OF EDUCATION

FOR THE

UNITED STATES COMMISSION TO THE PARIS EXPOSITION OF 1900

MONOGRAPHS ON EDUCATION

IN THE

UNITED STATES

EDITED BY

NICHOLAS MURRAY BUTLER

Professor of Philosophy and Education in Columbia University, New York

13

COMMERCIAL EDUCATION

BY

EDMUND J. JAMES

Professor of Public Administration in the University of Chicago, Chicago, Illinois

THIS MONOGRAPH IS CONTRIBUTED TO THE UNITED STATES EDUCATIONAL EXHIBIT BY THE STATE OF NEW YORK

COMMERCIAL EDUCATION

No satisfactory exposition of the existing condition of commercial education in the United States can be written at present. Such an exposition would be based upon a full knowledge of the historical development of such instruction as well as upon full and accurate statistics of its present condition. Neither of these presuppositions have been thus far realized. No one has yet devoted the time and attention necessary for a proper monographic treatment of the different aspects of this development. The department of such instruction which has made the most pronounced progress is that of the so-called commercial college, *i. e.*, the elementary technical school intended to prepare pupils for clerical work. It is not known, as will be seen later, exactly when such work was begun in the United States or by whom or where, and the facts about the subsequent development are difficult to ascertain; indeed, one may say it would be impossible for any one person to collect the facts necessary to enable one to treat the subject historically in a thoroughly satisfactory way. On the other hand, the statistics of the present condition of this department of instruction are unsatisfactory.

The bureau of education at Washington has labored faithfully for many years to collect as thorough and accurate information on this subject as possible, but limited as it is in the funds placed at its disposal for collecting and revising and checking up statistics, it is impossible for it to collect information in regard to all the schools which are actually at work from year to year. The statistical reports of the various departments of education in the different states are, if anything, still more unsatisfactory; in fact, they are almost worthless for the purpose in hand, since none of them, with the single exception of those of the University of the State of New York, are of any real value.

It was felt, however, by the authorities having in charge the United States exhibit at Paris that it would be desirable to make the best presentation which under the circumstances might be feasible, trusting that the defects which will be made apparent by this exposition may be remedied at some future time by those in a position to do so.

The opportunities for formal school preparation for a business career which are now offered in the United States may be roughly divided into four classes. First: The "commercial college" of the well-known type, an institution of which the merits have been frequently underrated, but which has already accomplished much good, and which seems to indicate in its constant evolution and advancement the possibilities of a very high grade of usefulness hereafter in the somewhat restricted field which alone it seeks to occupy. Second: The business courses of the public high school, meagre and illiberal hitherto, but growing constantly richer, more popular and more generally introduced, so that there is an early prospect of well-designed, highly attractive and deservedly favored schemes of business instruction in our secondary schools, culminating in our larger cities in distinct and separate high schools of the commercial type, not only fairly comparable to the best schools of similar grade in continental countries, but surpassing them in some respect. Third: Private endowed schools, more or less technical in character, introducing commercial courses which, in their best form, seem tending to realize the desirable standard of secondary business education. Fourth: College and university courses, which promise to embody the conception of higher business instruction in colleges of commerce, the work of which, largely technical, will not be inferior to the ordinary undergraduate courses of our American universities, and which, under favorable circumstances, will parallel for the future business man the advantages which have been hitherto offered in graduate courses for those who are pre-

paring for other careers. When the inherent promise of all
these kinds of business education has been realized, there
will be no failure in this line of work, fairly chargeable
either to the public or to the private system of American
education. We shall have ample opportunities for preparation in business activity open to all young men and women,
looking forward to engaging in any capacity in commercial
and industrial occupation. Lest this judgment of the future
of business education in America seem too optimistic, it may
be best to give not only an account of the present conditions,
but also a *résumé* of the historical development of each of
the four classes of business training, which have been just
now indicated.[1]

If the average American were asked what opportunities
exist in the United States for training toward a business
career, his immediate and unhesitating answer would refer
to the "commercial college," and probably to that alone.
This institution is peculiarly American ; nothing exactly
like it is known in other countries. It embodies the defects
and excellencies of the American character, and typifies in
itself a certain stage in our development. Its almost spon-
taneous origin, its rapid and wide diffusion, its rough adaptation of primitive material to the satisfying of immediate
and pressing needs, its utter disregard of all save the direct
answer to current demand, and then gradually its recognition of present inadequacy, and its determination toward
broader, fuller usefulness, these characteristics of the commercial college mark it as essentially the product of a young,

---

[1] The summaries of statistical tables show the number of students in commercial
courses in each of the five classes of institutions in each state of the United States.
The totals are as follows for the year 1897–98:

In universities and colleges	5 869
In normal schools	5 721
In private high schools and academies	9 740
In public high schools	31 633
In commercial and business colleges	70 950
Total for United States	123 913

— Report of United States Commissioner of Education, 1897-98, p. 2451, Advance Sheets

eager and gradually maturing people. In an older and more developed country the need which was the impulse toward the first commercial school, would not, perhaps, have been so quickly noted, and steps would not have been taken so immediately to satisfy it. The need once apparent, however, discussion and deliberation would have followed in logical order and action would possibly have awaited the maturing of a rational and broadly comprehensive plan, even if only part of this were susceptible of instant realization. Not so under our conditions, and certainly not in the case of the American commercial college ! The man who first noted a need for business instruction waited not to formulate the problem and to discuss the solution, but bent himself straight-a-way to furnish the opportunity and to meet the demand. Who this man was it is not possible now to state. So humble was the beginning of education for business men in the United States, that any one of many men who began practically at the same time to offer instruction in two or three simple subjects of commercial importance, might fairly claim to have aided in the beginning of this work. It is claimed that Bartlett of Cincinnati was the first to assume for his undertaking the name of business "college," and he was unquestionably one of the earliest and most successful workers in this field.[1] He gave commercial instruction to private pupils in the forties.

About the middle of the fifties there were not more than a dozen commercial schools scattered in the large cities from Boston and Philadelphia to Chicago and St. Louis. They had arisen with the idea of facilitating the entrance of young men into minor positions as clerks and book-keepers. The instruction offered was very meagre,— some so-called commercial arithmetic, a little practice in keeping accounts, and a certain amount of ornamental penmanship made up the total. A school of this kind did not require a large force of teachers,— in many cases the entire instruction was given by one man. Nor was the equipment elaborate ; a sin-

---

[1] See address by L. S. Packard in the Practical Age, January, 1897, p. 5.

gle room fitted with chairs and tables frequently sufficed. The tuition fees were proportionate. Forty dollars was reckoned an average charge, not for one term or for one year, but for an indefinite or life scholarship, and that not limited to one school always, but valid at any of a large number, embraced in single "chain." [1]

In those early days there were no text-books for the "commercial colleges;" and arithmetic and bookkeeping were taught by manuscripts prepared by actual accountants engaged in business. As with the text-book authors, or rather manuscript authors, so with the students. These came primarily from the ranks of those already employed at the time in business houses, a fact which necessitated the institution of evening classes. The average time spent in a business college was not more than three months, so that equipment, instruction, fees, time and grade of work were all pretty much on a par. Poor as such education must have been, it evidently filled a need, for commercial colleges throve and multiplied and with success became still more successful. Increased popularity led to higher fees, longer courses, to the preparation of printed texts; life and interchangeable scholarships were abolished; the teaching force was increased; students were no longer adults wearied by daily labor; the commercial school began to draw young men and boys looking forward to employment; day classes largely took the place of evening instruction; school equipment improved and gradually these institutions grew into the apparently permanent place in public favor which they enjoy to-day. [2] Official statistics of the bureau of education report 341 of these schools with 1,764 instructors and 77,746 students, 82 per cent being in day classes. The list does not, by any means, report all the commercial schools of the country and includes principally the larger and more important.

[1] The Bryant and Stratton system of schools numbered at one time more than fifty in as many different cities, and this plan of interchangeable tuition was valid throughout.

[2] See the report of the United States commissioner of education for 1896-7, p. 2257; see Appendix.

One of the leaders in the Federation of business teachers' associations claims not less than two thousand schools with fifteen thousand teachers and an annual enrollment of one hundred and sixty thousand pupils.

Contrast this with the record of forty years ago, when there were fewer than a dozen schools of this kind, with say thirty teachers and a thousand pupils, and the figures become sufficiently impressive. When we add to this numerical increase the considerations of the lengthened course of study, improved teaching and better average preliminary preparation, the development of the business college in the last half century must be admitted as striking. But, after all, the future of this type of institution could not be accounted promising on the basis alone of past achievements. Educational standards are advancing so rapidly that even in the restricted field of the commercial school, radical improvement is the constant price of retaining even the ground already won. Fortunately there is evidence of broadening views and sounder conceptions among the business college teachers and attention is drawn to three or four facts in particular which are pregnant with meaning for this kind of commercial instruction.

In the first place the function of the commercial college has been heretofore conceived in an altogether too narrow manner, even by those who have been its most successful and most progressive managers. It was started with the definite idea of training clerks, bookkeepers, penmen, and later stenographers and typewriters, and up to the present it has remained close to the original conception. The work that has been done in penmanship, in commercial arithmetic and in bookkeeping and business practice and correspondence was intended not only primarily but solely for this class. Merely the absolutely necessary "facilities" of business life were furnished, which include to-day typewriting and stenography, and the possible advance of an individual from a clerkship to some more important position was virtually ignored. Now, even in the very limited field of preparing for subordinate and almost mechanical labor, good work may be done and the business college has, in fact, accomplished excellent results. What is, however, especially encouraging to-day, is the realizing sense on the part of the directors of commercial schools, first, that for clerical positions more technical instruction is necessary; secondly, that a broader education pays, even granting that no higher position is ever won, and thirdly, that while the business college cannot prepare directly for more responsible duties in commerce and industry, it can, in a degree, and should, as far as possible, equip the student through liberal and fundamental studies for subsequent promotion. These ideas are spreading among the teachers and managers of the commercial colleges and are almost insensibly producing their logical outcome, namely, a course of study which is at once broader and more technical. The process is slow but evidences of advance are apparent in the printed announcements of various schools, in the discussions of business teachers' conventions and in the periodicals, weekly and monthly, issued in the interests of business education.[1]

This broadening view of what the business school may do has come hand in hand with a clearer realization that in this phrase the emphasis should rest on the second word; not that the school should not be for business, but that it should not be merely a business. Educational institutions which are run upon the proprietary basis are always susceptible to an excessive and self-destructive regard for receipts. This danger has been recognized in the field of commercial education and emphasized by the failure of hundreds of managers who forgot that a school cannot long "pay" unless it pays the students to attend, unless they be given what they need first of all, and then and only then the tuition fees fixed in proportion. A most hopeful sign for the future of the business college is the growing capacity of the public to judge what schools are worth attending and a growing

---

[1] Cf. address by President J. E. King of the Business Teachers' Association in the Practical Age, January, 1898.

sense on the part of those in control that they must give an increasing *quid pro quo*.

Secondly, the necessity of pedagogical training has been recently forced upon the consciousness of business school directors. In the early history of these schools the advantages of practical business experience for the business teachers were immediately apparent and much popularity was won by wide advertisement of this qualification in the teaching force. Undoubtedly this emphasis was not only shrewd but in a large degree well founded. Experience has, however, laid weight on the need of pedagogical ability and training, and the best schools of this type are now seeking instructors who have skill in teaching as well as theoretical and practical mastery of subject-matter. The change came slowly, but a glance at the list of business teachers shows to-day a large and growing per cent of men and women of collegiate or other special preparation for this work. The business college has been long hampered by the lack of suitable teachers, but the demand is creating a supply, as it will beyond question in other grades of commercial education.

A third favorable influence on the work of the business college has been the recent and marked growth of a new form of competition. Rivalry among schools of the same type has always been springing up, and has had a decidedly beneficial influence in the development of commercial colleges, but this kind of competition has not had the determining force which a new element in the problem bids fair to exert. This additional stimulus to the efficiency of the business colleges comes from the introduction of commercial subjects into the public high schools and the establishment in them as well as in normal schools and academies, of business courses and departments. Free instruction in these schools and frequently instruction of a broader and higher type is putting the commercial college where it must improve or be hopelessly outclassed. This new competition led Mr. King of Rochester in 1897 to address the Federation of Business Teachers' Association in the following pointed words :

" The training which the American commercial college gives its pupils, while good in a way, is extremely narrow and little more than rudimentary. It cannot properly be called business training, it is merely clerical training. While this kind of training may have satisfied the requirements in the past, and while there may continue to be a certain demand for it in the future, I believe the time has arrived when the American commercial school should cease to be a purely clerk factory and educational repair shop, and should assume the duties and position of a real business training school. In order to do this it must raise the standards, broaden and deepen its course of study and lengthen its time requirement.

" Its present standards both for admission and graduation are too low, its course of study too narrow and shallow, and its time requirement too short. It is useless to expect to attract and hold high-grade students with low-grade standards, or thoroughly to train young people for the duties of business life with the present course of study, and in the time now given to this work. The preparation for business life ought to be as thorough as for professional life, and I believe that the time is not far distant when it will be.

" It should be said, and in the same sense, of the graduates of our commercial schools as it is said of the graduates of our best technical schools, viz., ' that the business world not only finds that it can afford to employ them, but that it cannot afford not to employ them.' There is a good demand for thoroughly trained men — not merely clerks — in all departments of business, and the commercial school ought to be able to supply that demand." (*Ibid.*)

The new rivalry of the public high school and the commercial college can prove only to the advantage of each. What effect it will have in detail on the private undertaking is difficult to foretell, but it is not too hazardous a surmise to predict that the commercial college may hereafter be glad to see much of its work go over to the system of public education, thus giving it better equipped students and freedom to evolve a still higher course of instruction.

The probability of this further evolution of the business college into a supplementary educational instrument of a somewhat better type is foreshadowed in a fourth fact favorable to commercial training, and by no means without significance in the history of these institutions; namely, formal recognition as a factor in public education by one of our most influential governing bodies, the University of the state of New York. This recognition is not only honorable in itself, but is important as indicating for this work the beneficent effects which have come to other kinds of educational effort through guidance and supervision by that distinguished corporation. The advantages that have accrued to elementary, secondary and higher education, general and technical, public and private, in New York through state inspection, and in some measure, control, may now be obtained by the commercial schools. Moreover, the standard thus set in one state for business schools will come gradually to be recognized in other parts of the country, and New York can point to another result of adequate supervision.

The regents of the university have established a standard for business schools in confidence that this would further an *esprit de corps* which would create a demand for higher qualifications and lead to a duplicate of the experience with the professional schools of medicine and law, when similar actions led to a large increase in the attendance at secondary schools. They proposed in no wise to discriminate against the smaller commercial colleges, giving on the contrary full credit for the work of these, if of a creditable kind, but ruling out from all recognition the schools of questionable repute. It seemed good to them to omit consideration of all business schools in so far as these gave purely elementary work in the ordinary subjects of business instruction without regard to the previous preparation or the persistency of effort on the part of the students. The conditions of recognition of a business school were in brief : Instruction by at least six teachers giving all their time to the work, an equip-

ment worth not less than $5,000, exclusive of buildings and
fixtures, a satisfactory one-year course, supplementary of the
high school and consisting of at least 500 hours of actual
instruction, in preparation for the state business diploma.
Provisional registration was allowed schools not meeting the
first two conditions, but filling the others satisfactorily. It
speaks well for the character of the New York business
colleges that while the bureau of education reports thirty
schools in the state the regents have granted full recognition
to eleven and provisional registration to thirteen. Besides
granting registration to business schools on these conditions,
an act which, fixing a high standard, will arouse efforts to
meet it, and will be again reactive in raising the standard,
the university decided to issue business credentials, including
a state business diploma and a state stenographer's diploma
and corresponding certificates. The distinction between
the two is the requirement of graduation from a registered
high school, which attaches to the diploma, but not to the
certificate. To obtain the diploma, candidates must be certified as having completed also a full one-year registered
business course, and must pass regents' examinations in
advanced bookkeeping, in commercial law, in business
English, arithmetic, practice and office methods, and in commercial geography and the history of commerce. If the
high school course previously taken did not include United
States history, civics and economics, the regents' examination in these subjects must be passed as well. The value of
these requirements may be best measured by the following
outline, included in a syllabus issued for the guidance of
business schools and supplemented by considerable suggestions in detail :

"**Advanced bookkeeping** — The test in bookkeeping
demands a higher degree of technical knowledge than is
required for the academic examination. It presupposes
ability to open and keep with accuracy the accounts of any
ordinary business, including familiarity, both theoretic and
practical, with books of account.'

"**Business arithmetic** — This test requires a high degree of accuracy and skill in business computations, such as measurements arising in different kinds of business (including a practical and thorough knowledge of the metric system of weights and measures), billmaking, percentage, interest, partial payments, discount, insurance, commission and brokerage, computations arising out of partnership settlements and the operations of incorporated companies, taxes and duties, averaging accounts, ratio and proportion, accounts current, stocks and bonds, domestic and foreign exchange."

"**Commercial law** — The test in commercial law demands a knowledge of those matters of law that have constant application in business life, including drawing up in proper form contracts, articles of incorporation and all business documents. Candidates should have a fair practical knowledge of the laws relating to contracts, negotiable paper, liens, guaranty, interest and usury, sale of personal property, warranty, bailment, agency, partnership, joint stock companies and corporations, insurance, common carriers, attachment and stoppage *in transitu*, real estate, banking, taxes and duties, distribution of estates after death. They should also be familiar with the statute of frauds and the statute of limitations, and have a general knowledge of the interstate commerce law and the national bankruptcy law, and be able to draw in concise legal form any contract or agreement, check, note, bill of exchange, bond, bill of sale, power of attorney, articles of incorporation, insurance policy, charter party, bill of lading, deed, mortgage, lease, notice of protest, will or other document relating to the foregoing subjects."

"**Commercial geography and history of commerce** — The test in geography presupposes some general knowledge of mathematical, physical and political geography, as preliminary to the more detailed knowledge required. Candidates should be able to give the location, physical features, approximate size and population, form of government and prevailing language of the commercial countries mentioned in the following outline, and have knowledge of the relative commercial importance of those countries and of their principal products, routes of travel and transportation, their chief seaports and the ocean routes by which they are connected with the great trading ports of the world.

" In history of commerce the candidate should have a general knowledge regarding the origin and early development of commerce, should be able to trace its influence on the world's civilization, and should be reasonably familiar with the great discoveries, public works, inventions, legislative enactments and other important influences by which the progress of commerce has been affected."

" **Business practice and office methods** — The test demands a practical general knowledge of the manner and methods of conducting ordinary kinds of business, and a ready familiarity with the methods and practice that should prevail in every well-regulated business office. This work is closely correlated with bookkeeping, arithmetic and commercial law, and gives rise in great part to the work in those branches, as well as to much valuable practice in the use of English and in penmanship. The candidate should be familiar with the usual rules and practice in buying and selling breadstuffs and other agricultural products ; meat products, cotton, wool, hides and other raw materials ; lumber, iron and other building materials ; oils and naval stores ; mineral products sold on a commercial scale, stocks and bonds, fruits and groceries, dry goods and all ordinary commodities. He should have a general knowledge of the prevalent customs in the business of transportation on the high seas, the great lakes and navigable rivers, and by canal or railway ; in the business of banking, insurance, and manufacturing ; and should also know something of the important rules and customs governing transactions on the stock exchange, the produce exchange and similar centers of trade.' He should be able to keep the accounts of any ordinary business and to draw up or make out all papers in the regular order of such business. A plain, easy, and above all, legible business handwriting is an indispensable requisite."

"**Business English** — This test calls for such skill in the written expression of thought as every well-equipped business man should possess. It consists entirely of practical exercises in English composition, which are to be rated acording to their character, not only in penmanship, spelling, punctuation, capitalization, and general neatness, but also in the more essential matters of correct use of words, sentence structure, logical sequence of ideas, and paragraphing. The subjects will include letter writing on varied business topics ; drawing up or filling out from rough memoranda, business documents, such as contracts or articles of agreement, descriptions of property in deeds and mortgages, bills of sale or insurance policies ; making reports and abstracts condensing long articles ; writing advertising notices and composing short essays on business topics. No questions in technical grammar will be asked."

The above outline shows how far the business college has advanced from its simple form of forty years ago, since examinations on such a course of study were deemed not too high for a large proportion of these schools in New York. The private commercial school probably cannot without endowment take rank as a higher institution, but with an increasing proportion of high school graduates among its students, it will undoubtedly win its reputation in this field, and give more and more of its energies to work of advanced grade. The example set in one state should be widely followed by commercial schools and the action of the New York regents should be far-reaching in its results. Indeed, it seems probable that the commercial school will be forced more and more to the giving of advanced and supplementary business training by the growth of the second form of commercial instruction, *i. e.*, that of the public high school.

Before leaving this subject of the " Commercial College," *i. e.*, the private, elementary, unendowed, unassisted and uninspected educational undertaking, it is desired to emphasize again how important a function it has performed in our American educational system. It set out to give the girl or boy, man or woman who desired to secure a position as clerk or bookkeeper just such assistance as was needed to prepare for such work. No matter how young or how old, how educated or how ignorant the candidate, the commercial college undertakes to give him an immediate and definite training in book-keeping, commercial arithmetic, penmanship, stenography and typewriting or such portion thereof as is desired. It made of each student a special case; did not hold him back to work along with a class, gave him every assistance in its power, made entrance to the school as easy as possible, rarely requiring any other condition than paying the fee; facilitated the leaving and helped the pupil in finding work.

That it did this work well at least to the satisfaction of its pupils is sufficiently attested by the hundreds of thousands of people who have attended the schools in the last fifty years. Pupils were required to pay fees and in many cases high fees for such instruction. The annual tuition fee varies in the better schools from $50 to $150 and even $200 for a school year of ten months. The payment of such fees by men and women who have to earn their own living at comparatively low salaries testifies eloquently to the value which they themselves set upon the instruction which they receive.

It is perfectly safe to say that in the quality of the work which they do, and in the equipment for this particular work, the American commercial colleges have no rivals. They are as much superior to anything of the sort to be found elsewhere in the world as are the American schools of dentistry to their counterparts,— and for very much the same reason, viz.: that they are engaged largely, one may say chiefly, in the mechanical work in which Americans excel the rest of the world. They are not educational institutions in any broad sense of the term at all. They are trade schools pure and simple, and that in a very narrow sense. They train for facilities. Of course all training has intellectual results, even that of the prize fighter. But the commercial college aims not to train the best bookkeepers, or sten-

ographers, for, to such, a high degree of education is necessary, but to take the boy or man as he is, with or without
education, stupid or bright, and make as good a bookkeeper
or stenographer out of him as is possible, by simply super-
adding a brief technical training.   The limitations of such a
school are perfectly evident to every educationist.   It trains
the clerk, the routinest, the amanuensis, not the manager or
director of business enterprises.   That hundreds of the students of the colleges have been successful business men of
initiative and independent enterprise simply proves that they
had native ability for that sort of thing; not that this sort
of training was especially helpful, though it is only fair to
say that many of these men trace their start in business to
the technical skill in bookkeeping, etc., which they acquired
in the schools.

Many just criticisms might be made on the method,
plan and spirit of these schools, upon the narrow curriculum
characteristic of nearly all of them; of the low grade of
efficiency; of the tendency to decry all higher education,
&c., &c.   But, after all, they have done a valuable service
to our educational and business interests, and the best of
them have become better with every passing decade.

There is another interesting and important phase of this
development of commercial colleges which has not received
the attention it deserves.   The increasing employment of
women in the positions of clerk, bookkeeper, amanuensis,
&c., which is such a marked characteristic of American
business life, could hardly have taken on such dimensions
as at present if it had not been for the opportunities for
technical training which such schools as these offer.

An interesting side light may be thrown on the growth of
the commercial college by noticing for a moment the career
of one of the leaders of the movement, Mr. S. S. Packard,
recently deceased.   Mr. Packard began his work as an
instructor in penmanship in a small school in Cincinnati as
early as 1850.   After teaching in various places — among
others in Chicago — he opened the Packard commercial col-

lege in New York city, in the spring of 1858, as a link in the Bryant and Stratton chain of business colleges.[1]

It was the seventh in the order of evolution, and was intended as the cosmopolitan center. The "chain" eventually embraced schools in fifty of the principal cities of the United States and Canada.

Mr. S. S. Packard was from the beginning the principal and business manager, H. B. Bryant and H. D. Stratton being his associates. In 1867 Mr. Packard bought the interest of his partners, Bryant & Stratton, and changed the name from Bryant, Stratton & Packard's business college to Packard's business college.

The most important result of the change of proprietorship was in doing away with the life-scholarship plan under which the "chain" had been conducted, and putting an end to the interchangeability of tuition. Mr. Packard's lead was followed by the other schools, and thus the foundation was laid for individual — if not competitive — work, which has done so much to advance the character of business education in this country.

During the first year of the existence of the school, Mr. Packard wrote text-books on bookkeeping for the use of the Bryant & Stratton schools, which in revised form are still used. The school was first located in two small rooms in the then new Cooper Union building. It was, in fact, the first tenant of that building. In the fall of 1863 it was removed to the Mortimer block, corner of Broadway and Twenty-second street and Fifth avenue, and in the spring of 1870 to the Methodist building, corner of Broadway and Eleventh street, occupying the entire fourth story of the structure. Here it remained for seventeen years, until it outgrew its accommodations, when its present commodious and elegant quarters were secured.

At present it is located in the college building, formerly occupied by the College of physicians and surgeons, at the

---

[1] This account was prepared from material furnished by the present principal of the Packard school.

corner of Twenty-third street and Fourth avenue, occupying the entire building above the ground floor. It has a floor space of fifteen thousand square feet, with two large assembly rooms, each capable of seating three hundred pupils, and twelve smaller rooms for recitation purposes, offices, etc.

In the early days of the school the students were mature young men, many of them having fought in the civil war, and coming home entered the school as a preparation for clerical positions. The course was intended to cover only about three months, and bookkeeping, penmanship, and business arithmetic only were taught. The school sessions were from nine to four, and from seven to nine in the evening, six days in the week. There were no vacations. No record was kept of attendance, as the students themselves were responsible, being in some cases partially employed during the day. The scholarship plan gave the privilege of unlimited attendance at any school in the " chain."

In 1865 commercial law was added to the course, and later practical English and civics. In 1872 stenography was first taught, in classes only. A very small proportion of students studied this branch, and always in connection with the commercial course. The following year the typewriter was introduced. This was the first school to teach either stenography or typewriting.

At the present an important feature of the work, from which no student is excused, is public speaking without any attempt at elocution. Each student in his turn is required to speak in the morning assembly on some current topic, and always without notes. The object of this exercise is to fit them, as business men, "to think on their feet," to express their thoughts clearly and without embarrassment when occasion demands. Another feature is the character record, a brief history of the student's career from the beginning to the end of his course, showing not only progress in study, but also comments by his various teachers on any special characteristics or performance that is deemed worthy of comment. It has proved not only efficacious as discipline, but is useful as

reference after the student has passed out from the school
and refers to it for recommendation in business. This record is never destroyed. A specimen of the student's work
is also preserved. Faithful work for many years and a strict
adherence to truth-telling in regard to the qualifications
and character of candidates for business positions enable
the management to secure employment for every worthy
graduate.

The commercial course now covers about a year and a
half, or fifteen months, the students entering at any time
and being graduated not in classes, but as they finish the
course, in greater or less time, according to their ability.
The instruction is largely individual. The school graduates
yearly about 150 pupils, the number in recent years being
almost equally divided between the stenographic and commercial departments.

Though the school has the permission of the board of
regents to continue the name "college," it has voluntarily
changed it to the more appropriate name of "commercial
school."

" The history and purpose of this school is written in the
hearts of twenty thousand men and women, who, during the
past forty years, have been of its household. Of this number, at least fifteen thousand have been residents in the city
of New York. Many of them are now important business
men in the city, whose sons and daughters have also been
pupils in the school."

Mr. Packard devoted forty years to the active management of the school and to many plans by which the good
work might be made permanent. He died in October,
1898.

The career of Thomas May Pierce, of Philadelphia, illustrates in a similar way the growth of this department of our
educational system. Starting out in 1865 with the meagre
curriculum then offered, he increased the scope of the work,
improved the equipment, introduced regularity and system

into the instruction until, when he died in 1896, he had built up what might fairly be called a typical school of the better sort. He employed some twenty-five instructors, and occupied quarters in one of the best office buildings in Philadelphia, where he used fifteen rooms containing 10,000 feet of actual floor space. The charge for tuition was $15 per month, or $100 for a course of seven months, showing that he had succeeded in building up an institution which its students at any rate believed in.

Similar careers may be found in all older and larger cities of the United States, all testifying to the service which these schools have rendered the public.

Commercial instruction in the American public school system is only beginning to attract general attention, despite the fact that a certain amount of this work has been carried on for many years. The instruction, however, that has been given was until recently of a very meagre description. A commercial course was not infrequently announced, although it differed from other courses in the same school only by the inclusion of a little typewriting, bookkeeping, and possibly stenography. Of late years a considerable change has come about, and high schools which had offered some business training have improved the course of study. Commercial instruction has been introduced for the first time into many schools, and gradually distinct and separate courses are being established in connection with city systems to give opportunities for the future business man, comparable to the aid already furnished to those looking forward to higher studies of a professional or technical kind. The natural order of development in this matter can be seen in a glance at the course of high school study in some typical cities. Omaha represents one stage, presenting a commercial course in which commercial arithmetic is substituted for elementary science and botany in the ninth grade of the regular English course, bookkeeping for zoology, and mediæval history in the tenth, commercial law and book-keeping for chemistry and French history in the eleventh, and stenography and typewriting for American history and political economy in the twelfth grade. Some question might arise as to the advisability of the substitution in one case or another, yet there remains a fairly liberal plan of study, covering four years and giving an opportunity to young men and women to gain a degree of business preparation along with a general secondary education. Whether or not one be disposed to favor a duplication of business college work in the public high school, there is no doubt of the superiority of the four years' course of Omaha to the one or two years' course in many other cities. Even if the aggregate of special preparation for business does not exceed the ordinary work of a year, it is preferable from an educational point of view at any rate either to place this late in the high school program or to distribute it as indicated above. Fair objection to this may be made on the ground of the inability of many pupils to attend a full four years term, if we admit the need of adding to the public schools a kind of teaching already provided in private institutions. If it seems on the contrary inadvisable to introduce into the public high school a bare imitation of the lower class business college with most of the disadvantages and few of the excellencies of the latter, then the one or two years' course of business training substituted for the first year or two years of secondary instruction can be looked upon with favor only as a transition step. So Boston with a two years' commercial course and little special business training, Pittsburg with one year's work in place of the second high school year, Washington with a two years' course, are all in an early stage of development in this direction. Possibly Washington with a distinct business high school even though the course of study covers only two years, is nearer the final form than Milwaukee with its new four-year commercial course. The evolution of a real secondary business school may come more easily through the addition of suc-

cessive years to the course than through the gradual special-
izing of an ordinary high school curriculum.   Indeed this
view is borne out by the experience of the Hillhouse high
school in New Haven with an admirably outlined three
years' course and by the development in Paterson, N. J., of
a commercial department in the city high school into practically a distinct school operated in a separate building by
an entirely independent faculty, with a special course of two
years, requiring one year of secondary study for admission.

   To attempt any comparison of the relative value of commercial training in the cities mentioned would not be difficult but is perhaps needless.   All of the courses offered
should be judged not alone for what they are to-day.
Rather should they be reviewed from the point of view of
the ultimate standard, for they are changing from year to
year and the best mode of reaching the final form depends
on local conditions.   What is desirable seems perfectly clear.
First of all the course of study should be at least four years.
We cannot successfully defend commercial instruction in the
public high school unless the work is planned as broadly
educative as any other of the secondary courses.   Superintendent Pearse of Omaha struck the right note in an address
before the Business teachers' association, when he insisted
that the student should get as much drill, as much discipline,
as much education, out of a commercial course as he would
get out of other high school courses.[1]   Secondly, the course
should be thoroughly outlined as distinctly commercial.   A
mere substitution of a few business studies in the usual
English course does not make for commercial training and
such action is not only an inadequate provision for
present needs, but it is destructive of future possibilities.   Properly planned, a course of instruction may bear
the stamp of its purpose in every part, and at the
same time lose not a whit, but on the contrary, by unity
and close connection, gain decidedly in general educa-

---

[1] See the Practical Age, February, 1899, p. 36.

tive value. This means necessarily, in the larger cities at any rate, a separate corps of teachers. A separate building is strongly desirable, not only on the ground of superior adaptability for the uses of a commercial school, but for the far weightier consideration of absolute independence in fact, and full differentiation in the public thought.

Secondary education of the manual training type is to-day years ahead of the development which would have been possible if the separate manual training high schools had not been established. Place the commercial course in the ordinary high school largely under the charge of the present teaching force and you rob the new movement of half its possibilities. The problem of working out good secondary business education needs all the freedom that is feasible; it can be solved only by independent faculties with every member intent on the questions of his own department, of course, but also grappling with the problem of the entire scheme of studies. Under these conditions an *esprit de corps* will be aroused, greatly conducive to the final success of this feature in the system of public instruction. When a few such independent schools have wrestled with and solved the problem of commercial instruction, the ordinary schools will have a better basis for "commercial courses." With these considerations in view, we can readily say that between the two-year, strictly commercial course of Washington for example, and the four-year course slightly specialized, of some other cities, the choice should be made not on the basis of what is offered now, but of approximation to the real type, namely, a well-planned, fully-specialized scheme of commercial training covering at least four years of secondary grade.

This standard of secondary commercial training has been more nearly approximated in Philadelphia than in any other American city. In 1898 a department of commerce was established in connection with the Central high school, and the following study-plan was adopted:

SUBJECTS OF STUDY	First year	Second year
I. English	Composition and American literature — 4 [1]	History of English literature — 4
II. Languages other than English	Latin — 4	Latin — 3
		German — 4
III. Mathematics	Algebra — 5	Commercial arithmetic—2
		Geometry — 3
IV. History	Greek and Roman history — 3	English history — 2
V. Science.............	Physical geography, and botany and zoology — 4	Commercial geography—2
VI. Economics and political science.........	Philadelphia and Philadelphia interests — 1	Bookkeeping — 2
VII. Business technique...	Penmanship and business forms — 1	Stenography — 2
	Drawing — 2	

SUBJECTS OF STUDY	Third year	Fourth year
I. English	Readings from English literature — 4	Reviews and thesis writing — 3
II. Languages other than English	German — 3	German — 3
	French (or Spanish) — 4	French (or Spanish) — 3
III. Mathematics		
IV. History	Modern European history — 2	Modern, industrial and commercial history — 3
V. Science..	Physics and chemistry — 4	Industrial chemistry — 2
VI. Economics and political science.........	Political economy — 2	Transportation, banking and finance — 4
		Statistics — 1
		Political science — 3
VII. Business technique...	Office practice — 2	Ethics of business and commercial law — 2
	Stenography — 2	
	Observation of business methods — 3	

For reasons of expedience and economy, the department is housed in the magnificent new high school building, and much of the instruction is given at present by the regular teaching force.   Under a special director, however, the work promises to grow speedily into an entirely differentiated

---

[1] The numeral after each course indicates the number of recitation hours per week.

institution, which may parallel the success of the manual training high schools of that city.

The commercial department in the Pittsburg high school was organized in 1872 for the benefit of those who for any cause were not able to spend four years in the high school and yet who desired some scholastic training in addition to that given in the ward or elementary school, and especially such training as will best prepare for business positions.[1]

It will be seen that the course was recognized to be a shorter one than the other four years' courses. Its commercial studies are essentially those of a so-called commercial college. At the same time it is so far an improvement upon them as it undertakes to give scope for general training. The curriculum is two years, instead of two months or one year. The first year is given up chiefly to general studies, the last to book-keeping, typewriting, stenography. Out of 1,918 students in the school 612, almost exactly one-third, were enrolled in the commercial course and of these 247 were girls and 365 boys. The program declares that the aim of the commercial department is to make the study of bookkeeping in its various branches a mental discipline for the commercial student similar to that produced by the study of higher mathematics in a classical course. A practical department containing various kinds of offices has been established which the students must work through in time.

The commercial courses in the Boston high schools is likewise only two years in length. Commercial arithmetic, bookkeeping, and stenography are begun in the first year, occupying about one-half of the time, while the rest is devoted to general studies like English, history, drawing, music, etc. The second year is much like the first; about one-half the time is given to the study of commercial subjects.

In the Hillhouse high school, New Haven, Conn., while all the other courses are four years each, the commercial course is three years. About five hours a week, approxi-

---

[1] See catalogue of the Pittsburg Central high school, 1897-8.

mately one-third of the time, is given to strictly commercial subjects, the rest are of a general nature. Students who do the regular work well are permitted to take stenography and typewriting extra.

The work in the commercial courses of other high schools is along one or the other of the lines indicated above. It is at present a concession to a popular demand. It does not grow out of a conviction on the part of high school principals and teachers, that it is an essential part of the high school system. It will undoubtedly continue to grow and after a few good commercial high schools have formulated and solved the purpose of this kind of instruction, the average high school, profiting by their experience, will be able to organize commercial courses which will be better than those thus far elaborated.

In the opinion of the writer the technical work of the commercial courses in high schools is not as well done as in the better commercial colleges.

In the two classes of schools giving business training, which we have considered, are to be found nearly two hundred thousand students, a hundred and fifty thousand in the commercial colleges, if we accept the estimate above mentioned, and between thirty and forty thousand in the public high schools.

The third division of business schools or courses embraces the work of private secondary schools and public and private normal schools. There is the usual wide variation in what is here offered, but this class of schools plays something of a role in preparation for business with a total registration of nearly twenty thousand. (See Appendix.) The influence of this form of competition upon the ordinary business college has been already mentioned. How widely it may be felt can, perhaps, best be seen through an outline of what is open to business students in one of the best endowed secondary schools of the country, the Drexel institute of Philadelphia. This is chosen admittedly because its

department of commerce and finance has been strongly
developed, yet we may fairly expect that the example set in
Philadelphia will be widely followed by the schools of similar type which are springing up so rapidly in all parts of the
country. Special departments of such schools and new
endowments by private or semi-public bodies will, we may
expect, play a large part in the work of business training in
the United States, if the experience of other countries be a
good basis for prophecy.

The Drexel institute of arts, science and industry at Philadelphia was founded and endowed by Anthony J. Drexel of
that city. It included from the beginning in the scope of its
instruction courses in commerce and finance. As the school
is well endowed and independent of state control, one may
see from an examination of its work in this department a
type, and, indeed, a very good type, of the best work which
such institutions can do in the field of commercial education.

The department of commerce and finance consists of three
special departments. *First*, the course in commerce and
finance ; *second*, the office course ; *third*, the evening course.

The circular of the institution states that the department
of commerce and finance is founded on a broad and liberal
basis. In its general features it resembles the commercial
schools of Europe, and is intended to place commercial education in its proper relation to other departments of educational work. The object of the course is to train the young
men to do business rather than simply to record business.
It has been organized with a view of meeting these conditions. It provides a liberal, and at the same time, thoroughly
practical course of study, including two years' training in
the knowledge of the world's industries and markets, the
law of trade and finance, and the mechanisms and customs
of business.

The first special department is intended to give young men
and young women thorough fundamental training for the
activities of business which include (1) The production,
manufacture, sale, and transportation of articles of com-

merce; (2) the management of stock companies and corporations; (3) the buying and selling of securities; (4) the importing and exporting of merchandise; (5) the borrowing and lending of money and credit; (6) the advertising of commercial concerns; (7) the keeping of business records.

The work of this course is divided into two years, as follows:

FIRST YEAR

First Term

Language — Composition; letter writing. American classics.

Commercial Arithmetic — Weights and measures; trade standards and prices; wages and pay-rolls; commercial interest and discount; speed practice.

Business Customs — Invoices; commercial paper; bills of lading and manifests; vouchers.

Bookkeeping — Principles and practice of double-entry; simple transactions; business forms.

Penmanship — Typewriting. Correspondence.

Commercial Geography — The earth's surface in its relation to trade and commerce. Commercial geography of the United States.

Civics — Civil government of the United States.

Spanish and German throughout the two years.

Second Term

Language — Grammatical principles; diction. Selected classics.

Industrial Arithmetic — Measurements; builders' and contractors' bids and estimates; scientific measurements; manufacturers' and mechanics' estimates.

Business Customs — Securities; collections; discounts.

Bookkeeping — Principles and practice of double-entry in more complicated transactions. Shipments, consignments and business forms.

Commercial Calculations — Practical exercises for acquiring rapidity and accuracy of work.

Commercial Geography — Natural resources of the chief countries of Europe and the United States in their relation to commercial exchanges.

Civics — History, principles and organization of political parties; civil service reform; ballot systems; municipal government.

Typewriting, Correspondence.

Physical Training in the gymnasium , twice a week throughout the year.

SECOND YEAR

First Term

Language — Rhetorical principles; essay-writing; English classics.

Advanced Bookkeeping — Introducing order-book, cash-book, sales-book, bill-book, etc.; each student is required to keep the entire accounts, for a limited time, of a dozen business concerns, representing the leading industrial and commercial corporations.

Banking and Finance — Outlines of the history of banking and of the national banking system, state banks, saving banks and trust companies.

Commercial Calculations — Practical exercises for acquiring rapidity and accuracy of work.

Commercial Geography — A comparative study of the commerce and industry of the five great commercial nations of the world.

History of Commerce — Outlines of the history of ancient, medieval and modern commerce.

Typewriting — Business forms.

Public Speaking — One hour a week.

Second Term

Language — Historical outlines of English and American literature.

Advanced Bookkeeping — Continued.

Commercial Calculations — Continued.

Banking and Finance — Bank management and practice.

Mechanism of Commerce — Boards of trade; stock and produce exchanges; transportation; interstate commerce; warehousing; importing and exporting; duties; exchange; mercantile agencies.

Commercial Law — Elementary principles of contracts, partnerships, stock companies and commercial paper.

Business Printing and Advertising — Type and paper; printers' estimates; proof-reading; business cards, circulars and catalogues. Modern advertising, including mediums, rates, agencies.

Public Speaking — One hour a week.

Physical Training in the gymnasium, twice a week throughout the year.

Students have also the privilege of attending the special courses of lectures in the chemistry of foods and the chemistry of dyeing and cleansing.

During the second year, visits are made to some of the leading industrial and commercial establishments of Philadelphia.

Diploma —The diploma of the institute is granted to students who complete the work of the course in commerce and finance, and pass the prescribed examinations.

Office courses — In addition to the general course in commerce and finance, described above, and requiring two years for its completion, three distinct office courses are offered. These are thoroughly practical in character, and are designed to prepare young men and young women for entering immediately upon the respective lines of employment to which the training leads.

Bookkeeping course — The object of this course is to prepare young men and young women for positions as book-keepers. It occupies one year and includes the following subjects : Bookkeeping, business forms and customs, typewriting, commercial arithmetic, English and penmanship. The entire course is directed to training in the most approved methods of keeping business records. All the labor-saving devices and checking and recording systems of modern mercantile establishments are thoroughly taught.

The course occupies one year, divided into two terms.

Stenography course — The aim of this course is to train young men and young women for positions as stenographers and typewriter operators. It occupies one year and includes the following subjects : Stenography, typewriting, English, business forms and office practice. There is a growing demand among business and professional men for stenographers who can not only take down and typewrite correspondence, but who have a serviceable knowledge of good English, and who are intelligently trained along general educational lines.

The course occupies one year, divided into two terms.

Private secretary's course — This course has been organized in response to applications that have been made to the institute for clerks fitted to do work of a different character from that required in a purely business office. The subjects included in the course are as follows : Stenography, typewriting, penmanship, English, correspondence, accounts office practice and business printing.   Applicants for admission must show by examination, or otherwise, that they are prepared to meet the requirements of the course.

The course occupies one year, divided into two terms.

Certificates — Certificates are granted to students who complete any one of the office courses and pass the prescribed examinations.

Gymnasium — The gymnasium is a large, airy room, completely equipped in accordance with the requirements of the Swedish system of physical training and with dressing-rooms, and bath-rooms supplied with hot and cold water. All the training is conducted under the immediate supervision of the directors.

Commercial museum — A beginning was made in 1895 towards the formation of a permanent commercial museum, and a large collection of raw and manufactured products has already been secured.   This collection represents quite fully the following industrial products : Flour, wool, petroleum, teas and coffees, sugar, cotton, copper, iron and steel, glass, tobacco, leather, rubber, paper, wood, carpet, linen, spices, aluminum, building stone, brick and terra cotta.   Additions are being made constantly, and the student who is looking forward to devoting his life to trade, shipping, or manufacturing, has opportunity, in connection with his academic work, to make a special study, from both a geographic and an economic standpoint, of the particular industry in which he is interested.

Art museum — The art museum contains extensive collections representing the industrial arts of Egypt, India, China, Japan and Europe.

Library — The library, which contains twenty-five thousand volumes, is supplied with books, periodicals and pamphlets bearing upon the work of the department, and every facility and assistance is afforded for the study of financial, economic and commercial questions.

Admission — Applicants for admission to any of the courses must pass satisfactory examinations in English, geography, arithmetic and United States history.   For admission to the course in commerce and finance, or to any of the office courses, candidates must be at least sixteen years of age. The diploma of high schools of approved standing is accepted in place of an examination.   Application for admission should be made to the registrar, at the institute, between 9 A. M. and 4 P. M., or by letter.

Fees and terms — Course in commerce and finance — *twenty-five dollars* per term.

Office courses — *Twenty-five dollars* per term, each.

Students provide their own text-books and stationery.

Coat-lockers, with individual combination locks, are provided for the men students, giving to each the absolute control of his own property.   Each student is charged *fifty cents* per term for a locker.

There are two terms in the year, beginning in September and February respectively.   Five days' attendance a week is required, from 9 A. M. until 2 P. M.

Evening classes — The department of evening classes is fully organized, and includes the following courses :

   1. Beginners' course in bookkeeping and arithmetic.

   2. Accountants' commercial course.

   3. Office course in stenography and typewriting.

Fee for each of the courses, for the entire season of six months, *five dollars.*

It will be seen that the pup'ls who enter the longer course or any of the office courses must be at least sixteen years of age and must have passed examinations indicating that they have completed the ordinary work of the elementary school, such as the average boy who has been in school from his sixth year could have completed by the time he was fourteen.

The desire of the management, however, is plainly that they shall have done considerably more work, including if possible the first year or two of the high school.   As a matter of fact the average age of the persons who enter upon this course is that of graduation from the ordinary three years' high school course of smaller towns and villages.

The work done in the Drexel institute is paralleled to a greater or less extent by similar work done in many private institutions, such as the Heffley school, formerly of Pratt institute of Brooklyn, the Armour institute of Chicago, and other schools founded by private initiative. Many of these schools have the advantage of ample funds so that they are not as dependent upon the whims of individual students as are the commercial schools described in previous paragraphs, and on the other hand they are independent of the injurious influences at work in many of the public schools.

I think it is not too much to say that the two years' course offered in the Drexel institute forms in its way a model, and furnishes the basis for the elaboration of a curriculum which will compare favorably with the best of the European commercial schools of the same grade. The work done in the evening course of this institution corresponds more closely to the work of the ordinary business college as described above.

When we turn our attention to the fourth class of institutions in which instruction is offered in the field of commercial subjects, namely, the colleges and universities, we are struck by two or three salient facts. In the first place the movement for instruction in these subjects in our higher institutions of learning is of comparatively recent origin. In the second place it has affected but very few of these institutions though in the list are some of the most prominent and influential universities in the country. It is also a matter of interest that the attitude of these higher institutions of learning toward this subject is a radically different one from that of the other classes of institutions which we have been discussing.

It has been very difficult indeed in this whole development to get the so-called commercial colleges, the high schools and other commercial courses of the various institutes in their departments of commerce to give any instruction, whatever, except in the so-called practical subjects, and

of any kind whatever except of the most immediate, technical, special sort.

In the colleges and universities on the other hand, even
where they have been willing to accord a certain recognition
to the necessity of higher education in commercial and business matters, it has been difficult to get them to give any
attention, whatever, to the more practical sides of the work.
While the commercial colleges have felt that political
economy, commercial geography and similar subjects were
too remote and impracticable to make it worth while for
them to admit these subjects into their curricula, the colleges
have felt that accounting, commercial arithmetic, and similar
subjects were too elementary to deserve any attention, whatever, from higher institutions of learning.

The colleges and universities, moreover, have seen scores
and hundreds of young men complete the old-fashioned
classical courses of study, and enter the ranks of business
men with ability and success. They have felt, therefore,
that in a certain sense every man who desired a higher education, even if he should wish to go into business subsequently, would find it worth his while to take the old-
fashioned course. And they were very slow, indeed, to
recognize that there were scores and hundreds of young
men in the community who would take a higher education
if an emphasis were laid upon subjects in which they
were interested and which had to do at some point, at least
with their future careers, who could not be persuaded
to follow out an old-fashioned classical curriculum.

Four institutions in the United States, the University of
Pennsylvania in Philadelphia, the University of Chicago in
Chicago, the University of California in Berkeley, Cal.,
the Columbia university in the city of New York, deserve
special mention for their connection with this subject of
higher commercial education. Some other institutions —
notably, certain of the state institutions — have also attempted
to do something in this department, but their efforts have
been spasmodic, and in some cases futile, owing to the fact,
among other things, that they were not able or willing to

spend the necessary money upon the establishment and maintenance of these courses.

In 1881 Joseph Wharton, Esq., a manufacturer of Philadelphia, gave to the University of Pennsylvania the sum of one hundred thousand dollars in order to establish a department in that institution for higher commercial training. A department was established known as the Wharton school of finance and economy, the object of which was the furnishing of an adequate education in the principles underlying successful business management and in the principles of civil government. The curriculum was two years in length and was made up largely of political economy, political science, accounting, mercantile law and practice, etc. A bachelor's degree was conferred upon the graduates from this school. To enter as a regular student the candidate must have completed the first two years of the regular four years' college course. Many errors were made in the initial establishment of the school, such as assigning instruction in the technical subjects included in the course to men who were already in the university but who knew little about the subject-matter of the courses assigned to them, and cared less. After some unpleasant experience growing out of this circumstance the faculty was reconstructed and enlarged, specialists being added for the newer subjects. After some ten years' experience it was decided to enlarge the course by extending it downward into the first two years of the college course, and at present the course in finance and economy covers four years and is included together with the other courses in arts and science in the so-called school of arts.

The requirements for admission are the same as for other departments and represent the ordinary requirements of first-class American colleges. The faculty is composed of some thirteen members.

A special course intended to give additional facilities for those students who wish to enter journalism is constructed by omitting certain subjects from the regular course and inserting others.

The following is a curriculum of the courses in finance and economy, showing the assignment of subjects among the years and the number of hours per week.

COURSE IN FINANCE AND ECONOMY
Freshman class

SUBJECTS	No. of hours per week	
	1st term	2d term
Composition	2	2
Algebra	2	2
Solid geometry	2	—
Trigonometry	—	2
General chemistry [1]	4	4
German	3	3
Accounting	3	3
Physical and economic geography	2	2
Practical economic problems	3	3
Economic literature	2	2
Newspaper practice [2]	1	1

[1] For students who present solid geometry and plane trigonometry and physics for admission to college. Such students omit solid geometry and trigonometry.

[2] For students in journalism, who omit accounting in second term.

Sophomore class

SUBJECTS	No. of hours per week	
	1st term	2d term
Modern novelists	2	—
History of English literature	—	2
Scientific German	3	3
Business law	2	—
Money and banking	—	2
Business practice	1	1
American history	2	2
Roman history	2	2
Theory and geography of commerce	2	2
Elementary sociology	2	2
General politics	2	2
Congress	1	1
Newspaper practice[1]	1	1
Current topics[1]	1	1

[1] For students in journalism, who omit business practice and history and geography of commerce in second term.

Junior class

SUBJECTS	No. of hours per week	
	1st term	2d term
Constitution of United States.	2	—
Constitutions of Germany and Switzerland..........................	—	2
Congress...	1	1
Modern legislative problems	2	2
Political economy	3	3
Advanced sociology...........	2	2
Sociological field work...............	1	1
Business practice	2	—
Banking.	—	2
American history..	2	2
English constitutional history..................................	2	2
Logic..	2	—
Ethics	—	2
Art and history of newspaper making[1]...........................	1	1
Newspaper practice[1]..	1	1
Current topics[1]...	1	1

[1] For students in journalism, who omit either modern legislative problems, or business practice and banking.

Senior class

SUBJECTS	No. of hours per week	
	1st term	2d term
Public administration..	2	2
Legal institutions...........................	2	2
Municipal government..	2	2
Political economy..	2	2
Statistics..	2	2
Finance	2	2
Transportation...	2	2
History of renaissance and reformation..........................	2	2
Art and history of newspaper making.[1]	1	1
Newspaper practice[1]	1	1
Current topics[1]	1	1

[1] For students in journalism, who omit municipal government, or transportation, or statistics.

It will be seen that this curriculum includes a large number of subjects, and that the nucleus of the course is to be found in the study of economics and politics, supplemented by practical courses in accounting, business law and business practice.

The following table shows the number of students which have been enrolled in the course for the years indicated ·

1892–3	59
1893–4	71
1894–5	113
1895–6.	97
1896–7	101
1897–8	87

The degree of bachelor of science in economics is conferred upon those who complete this course.

The growing demand for higher instruction in commercial subjects, combined with the success of the experiments in the University of Pennsylvania, turned the attention of several institutions toward the subject about the same time.

The University of Chicago, which opened its doors in October, 1892, had included within its plan of work from the beginning a college of practical affairs. But it was not found practicable to undertake the organization of such a department until the year 1898, and students were enrolled in this college for the first time on the first of July of that year. The new department was given the title of the college of commerce and politics, and was organized as a co-ordinate department with the other colleges of arts and literature and science. The purpose of the new college, like that of those already existing in the university, is two-fold. First, it aims at the attainment of general culture; in the second place the weight of work is put in the lines of the courses offered in certain specified departments. In the new college those departments include political economy, political science, history and sociology. In the other colleges the distinctive work is in the classics, modern languages and literatures, and sciences respectively. The courses of study afford instruction concerning the place of America in the general development of civilization, the origin and characteristics of our national institutions, the physical resources, moral traditions, intellectual standards of our country, the commercial, domestic and foreign relations of our industries and our politics, and the principal economic, social and political problems which confront the leading nations of the world.

It is intended by the college of commerce and politics to provide an education for those whose tastes lie along the particular lines indicated, and at the same time to open a way for special training in the direction of certain forms of business, of politics and journalism, and of diplomacy. The college is by no means a technical school, but is intended to give a kind of knowledge and training which may enable those who enter commerce, politics, journalism or diplomacy to begin their work with a certain degree of equipment. Those who develop an especial aptitude for the subject pursued will in many cases continue their work in the graduate school.

The course of study in the college of commerce and politics covers a period of four years. The first two years, however, are essentially the same as the first two years in one or another of the other liberal courses, political economy or political science being the only subject in these two years having a specific relation to the special work of the college. The other studies of the first two years are history, French or German, English, mathematics, science, and a small proportion of the time (about one-sixth) is given to any other subject which the student may desire to pursue from among the courses offered in the university. The admission to the course covers about the curriculum of the typical four years' high school course, including at least four years' work in Latin, two in mathematics, and the usual time devoted to English history, physics, and German or French. It is during the last two years of the work that the special character of the college becomes apparent. The work of the last two years is divided into three groups : Commerce, politics, journalism and diplomacy.

In the first group, commerce, there are four special sub-groups : (a) Railways ; (b) banking ; (c) trade and industry ; (d) insurance.

The student must elect, at the beginning of the third year's work in this college, one of these groups to which he wishes to devote his time. One-third of the course for the next two years must be selected from within the group chosen. Another third may be selected by the student from a list of specified courses. The remaining third may be chosen by the student from any course offered by the departments of political economy, political science, history or sociology. Thus if the student chooses commerce as the main group and banking as the sub-group, he is required to take courses in the financial history of the United States, in money and practical economics, in banking, and in the economic seminar; he must then select an equal amount of work from the following list of courses: Finance and taxation; federal government; government of Great Britain; federal constitutional law of the United States; American administrative law; England under the parliament; contemporary society in the United States outlined, and constructive social philosophy. And from a list of over one hundred courses in the departments of political science, history, sociology, he must choose in addition an equal number of courses.

It will be seen that in this work, as in the University of Pennsylvania, the nucleus consists of courses in economics and politics, using those terms in a large sense. But the University of Chicago has not added special technical courses in accounting, business law, business practice, etc., which forms a characteristic feature of the Wharton school. During the year 1898–9 eleven students enrolled for the courses in the college of commerce and politics. Of these, ten entered upon the work of the first year and one upon the work of the third year. The degree of bachelor of philosophy is conferred upon those who complete this course.

About the same time that the University of Chicago determined to adopt a scheme of higher commercial training, a report was made to the board of trustees of the

University of California, by one of its members, urging the adoption of a similar course there.   After an elaborate discussion, it was decided to erect an addition college in the university, to be known as the college of commerce.   The course extends over four years, similar to that of the other colleges in the university.   The requirements for admission were essentially the same, and correspond to graduation from the typical high schools with the four years' course.

In the first annual report of the president, after work was begun, it was stated that many details were yet to be determined, among others, the question of what degree should be conferred upon students who completed the course.   In the same report the following statement is contained as to the scope of the new college :

" It is the intention of the authorities of the university to place the course in commerce upon a high scientific plane, otherwise it is not justified in claiming a place in the university curriculum beside those advanced scientific, philosophical and literary courses which have already won recognition."

The sciences dealing with the various departments of the world's trade can justly claim such recognition.   The mere arts of the counting room do not belong to the list of studies.   The student will be encouraged to acquire a knowledge of them elsewhere possibly, before entering college.   Thus the college of commerce will supplement, not compete with, the work of the older business commercial schools.

The following list of courses taken from a prospectus recently issued by the university will show more clearly the intended character and scope of the new college :

Economic studies: General theory and analysis — Political economy: General principles and theory. Labor and wages. Theory and practice of exchange; foreign and domestic. Theory of value. Markets: their organization and the determination of prices. Currency: in all countries. Banking: in all countries. Economic features of transportation, by land and water. (A subject in which many special courses should be offered.) Industrial and commercial organization. Corporations and corporation finance. Communication: postal service, telegraph and telephone, newspapers and advertising. Insurance: fire, marine, life, etc. Consumption, and the principles of demand and storage. Commercial usages of different countries. Public finance: Government expenditures, revenues — including taxation, customs, duties, etc.— public debts and fiscal administration. Statistics, mathematical and practical. History, theory and methods: the "movement of population," actuaries' statistics, theory of prices, etc.

Studies in economic history—;The history of commerce in all countries and at every age. (Upon this general subject as large a number of special courses as possible should be offered.) The history of the institution of private property. The history of land tenures. The history of agriculture. The history of industry from the earliest times. The history of manufactures. The history of labor and of labor organizations and other special courses.

Legal studies — Commercial law of different nations. Public international law, and the duties of diplomatic and consular officers. Private international law. Admiralty and maritime law. Roman law. Comparative jurisprudence. Judicial procedure in different countries. Law of private corporations; and other special courses.

Political studies — Constitutional law of different nations. Public law and administration. Municipal government. General political theory. Legislative control of industry and commerce.

Historical studies — The general political and constitutional history of the leading nations, especially during the XIXth century; diplomatic history. (Economic history, that is, the history of industry and commerce, is of such importance as to constitute a separate group; see above.)

Geographical studies — Political geography. Geodesy. Physical geography. Commercial geography. Biological geography: including botany, zoology, anthropology, etc. Meteorology and climatology. Oceanography: Coasts, harbors, etc. Navigation and nautical astronomy. Geology.

Technological studies concerning transportation — Civil engineering and mechanical engineering; construction of roads, bridges, canals, irrigation works, etc.; motors and motor power, etc.; railroad economics, etc.

Technological studies concerning the materials of commerce — Botany: General plant morphology; economic botany. Forestry, and wild-plant products; also wild-animal products. Agriculture: cultivated plant products of all descriptions, including field, orchard, and vineyard products; animal products, such as meats, dairy products, wool, etc., and including agricultural practice, irrigation, etc. Agricultural manufactures, such as sugar, starch, textiles, oils, brewing, tanning, drying, canning, etc. Fisheries, and all the products of the sea. Mining, and mineral products, and building materials. Chemical technology, and chemical products, acids, alkalies, etc. Manufactured products. Decorative and industrial art.

A large number of other special courses in these and other applied sciences connected with the materials and the operations of commerce should be offered.

Mathematical studies — Courses covering all the mathematical principles involved in the above studies.

Linguistic studies — The English language and English literature. The languages and literatures of the nations with which we have commercial relations: American, European, and Oriental.

Philosophical studies — Ethics and civil polity.

No statement of the actual enrollment of students in this new college and of the way in which it has opened up its work has come to the attention of the writer, but the interest felt in the project by some members of the board of trustees and by some members of the faculty justifies the hope that this is the beginning of great things in the department of higher commercial education.

On November 3rd, 1898, the chamber of commerce of the state of New York adopted the report of a committee which had been previously appointed by that body on the subject of commercial education. This report, after strongly commending the establishment of a department of sounder commercial education both in secondary schools and in higher institutions of learning in this country, advised the appointment of a special committee by the president of the chamber of commerce for the further consideration of the subject of commercial education. This committee was appointed and, after various sessions and conferences with authorities of Columbia university, a report was submitted to the chamber of commerce recommending that the chamber assist

Columbia university in the establishment of a collegiate course in commerce by the grant of certain funds.

This report presents in a certain way the most complete scheme of higher commercial instruction which has thus far been submitted for the consideration of the public. It unites the practical elements in the course of the Wharton school with the wider range of the courses and subjects offered at California and Chicago. It was framed upon the plan of utilizing as largely as possible the existing courses of instruction in Columbia university, and supplementing and adding to such courses the subjects necessary to offer a complete and well-rounded scheme of higher commercial instruction.

Although the plan has not been carried into effect as yet and may be materially altered, still, coming from such a source and backed by such a body as the New York chamber of commerce, it seems likely to be of sufficient importance to merit a somewhat fuller notice.

It is intended to be a college course of commerce covering four years of fifteen hours a week. It presupposes graduation from a secondary school, public or private, in which English, mathematics, history and natural science, and one modern language will have been systematically studied to the extent now required for admission to the college department of Columbia university. In form and in content it is adapted to students of college age, namely, sixteen to twenty years.

In addition to the training provided in commercial subjects, the course includes training for two years in writing English, for two years in a modern European language, for two years in European and American history, and for three years in political economy and social science. It offers opportunities for the study of industrial chemistry, of a selection of three modern languages and literature, if any of these be desired.

Of the sixty hours required (four years of 15 hours each) four hours or six and two-thirds per cent are devoted to instruction in writing English; six hours or ten per cent to

European and American history; six hours or ten per cent
to the modern European languages; ten hours or sixteen
and two-thirds per cent to political economy and social sciences, and thirty-four hours or fifty-six and two-thirds per
cent to the study of commerce itself in its various phases.
It will be observed that this curriculum comprises fundamental courses in the principles governing business combined with a detailed course in practice. It is intended that
many of these latter courses, as well as some of the former,
shall be given by men having an intimate personal acquaintance with actual business life. Among such courses would
be those in accounting and transportation, technique of
trade and commerce, commercial ethics, commercial credits,
insurance and commercial business.

Aside from the general subjects included in liberal
courses we note a course of three hours per week for one
year given to accounting and a similar course to economic
geography; a course of two hours a week following a course
in chemistry on the study of commercial products ; a course
of three hours a week upon the technique of trade and commerce, such as weights and measures, currency and banking
systems, customs regulations, markets, fairs, etc. There are
also courses in banking, accounting, commercial geography,
railroad and public accounting, history of commercial theory
and merchant shipping and trade routes, commercial treaties
and insurance.

No degree is to be given for this course for the present,
but a certificate of graduation testifying that the candidate
has completed the work of the four years will be given to
all students who pass the requisite examinations after
attending the courses.[1]

It is plain from the foregoing account that instruction in
commercial subjects is to be introduced into all higher institutions of learning upon a broader scale than ever before.

---

[1] After this account was prepared information comes to hand of a department
of Commerce and Economics at the University of Vermont. A trustee of the
university, Mr. John H. Converse of Philadelphia, has given funds for an endowment, and work will be inaugurated in the autumn of 1900.

It cannot be maintained, however, up to the present that our experience has been large enough to afford any accurate indication of what the ultimate form or purpose of such instruction shall be.   We have as yet established no independent college of commerce in the United States upon an adequate foundation.   We have not even established any institution which may be fairly called a commercial high school, that is, a school with an adequate equipment, with a differentiated curriculum and with an opportunity under favorable conditions to show what it can accomplish in an educational and a technical way.   None of our colleges and universities have as yet been willing to give such departments a fair opportunity to show what they might accomplish in the same directions.   But with every passing year the demand for better facilities on the part of young people who desire to prepare themselves for business careers will force our commercial colleges to improve their work ; will force those who have charge of public education to give a larger space in our secondary schools to this branch of work ; will lead the managers of our private secondary schools to offer better facilities, and will finally compel our colleges and universities to do something for the education of the future business man which may be compared with what they are doing for the future engineer, or lawyer, or physician, so far as the peculiarities of a business career may render such a scheme feasible.

APPENDIX

STATISTICS OF COMMERCIAL AND BUSINESS SCHOOLS
Bureau of education report, 1896–97

In the 341 business schools represented in this report there were 1,764 instructors and 77,746 students. The total number of graduates in the commercial course was 11,728, and in the amanuensis course 8,862. The number of students in the day course was 63,481, or 82 per cent of the whole number, and the number in the evening course was 14,265, or 19 per cent of the whole number. It will be seen by the above figures that the day school contains more than four times the number of students that are reported in the evening schools. The number of students in the various courses of study was as follows:

Course of study	Males	Females
Commercial course	29 216	8 713
Amanuensis course	10 185	12 957
English course	9 653	3 671
In telegraphy	897	312

The total number of students in the commercial and business courses of universities and colleges, normal schools, private high schools and academies, and public high schools was 56,002, and in the commercial course of business schools was 37,929, making a total of commercial students in all the schools in the United States as reported to this bureau of 93,931.

TABLE I — *Summary of statistics of commercial and business colleges, 1896–97*

STATE OR TERRITORY	Number of institutions	INSTRUCTORS			STUDENTS			Day school	Evening school
		Male	Female	Total	Male	Female	Total		
1	2	3	4	5	6	7	8	9	10
United States	341	1 219	445	1 764	51 899	25 847	77 746	63 481	14 265
North Atlantic Division	103	410	197	607	17 797	9 892	27 689	21 444	6 245
South Atlantic Division	22	72	49	121	3 775	1 603	5 468	4 509	959
South Central Division	28	115	30	145	4 906	1 388	6 294	5 494	800
North Central Division	160	517	216	733	20 750	10 479	31 229	26 016	5 213
Western Division	28	105	53	158	4 671	2 395	7 066	6 018	1 048
North Atlantic Division:									
Maine	6	14	10	24	744	467	1 211	1 165	46
New Hampshire	2	5	2	7	100	46	146	106	40
Vermont	1	2	1	3	90	61	151	111	40
Massachusetts	14	56	43	99	1 928	1 540	3 468	2 783	685
Rhode Island	3	14	5	19	323	230	553	496	57
Connecticut	9	27	19	46	1 079	865	1 944	1 622	322
New York	29	129	69	198	6 336	3 361	9 697	7 779	1 918
New Jersey	6	21	11	32	684	401	1 085	708	377
Pennsylvania	33	142	37	179	6 513	2 921	9 434	6 674	2 760
South Atlantic Division:									
Maryland	2	9	1	10	361	135	496	355	141
District of Columbia	5	16	25	41	1 160	768	1 928	1 680	248
Virginia	5	19	7	26	554	166	720	581	139
West Virginia	2	7	2	9	298	169	467	309	158
North Carolina	2	3	0	3	82	6	88	81	7
Georgia	5	15	12	27	1 225	402	1 627	1 401	226
Florida	1	3	2	5	95	47	142	102	40
South Central Division:									
Kentucky	2	11	2	13	567	293	860	750	110
Tennessee	6	22	5	27	949	216	1 165	1 153	12
Alabama	1	2	1	3	195	75	270	220	50
Mississippi	5	32	4	36	668	60	728	693	35
Louisiana	1	9	3	12	368	98	466	354	112
Texas	12	36	14	50	1 939	552	2 491	2 035	456
Arkansas	1	3	1	4	220	94	314	289	25
North Central Division:									
Ohio	29	65	38	103	2 616	1 698	4 314	3 783	531
Indiana	17	72	29	101	2 900	1 605	4 505	3 777	728
Illinois	25	100	36	136	4 289	2 088	6 377	5 508	869
Michigan	15	44	19	63	1 961	1 036	2 997	2 410	587
Wisconsin	15	30	17	47	945	404	1 349	1 088	261
Minnesota	14	35	14	49	1 315	658	1 973	1 637	336
Iowa	16	57	29	86	2 360	1 015	3 375	2 900	475
Missouri	16	74	23	97	2 988	1 463	4 451	3 163	1 288
North Dakota	1	5	1	6	83	38	121	110	11
South Dakota	2	4	1	5	104	57	161	130	31
Nebraska	6	23	5	28	944	260	1 204	1 133	71
Kansas	4	8	4	12	245	157	402	377	25
Western Division:									
Montana	4	20	6	26	689	335	1 024	766	258
Arizona	1	1	2	3	47	25	72	59	13
Colorado	3	5	7	12	387	156	543	376	167
Utah	2	9	2	11	350	77	427	330	97
Washington	2	7	2	9	401	188	589	539	50
Oregon	3	10	7	17	465	265	730	690	40
California	13	53	27	80	2 332	1 349	3 681	3 258	423

TABLE II — *Students in business course in other institutions*

STATE OR TERRITORY	IN OTHER INSTITUTIONS				
	Universities and colleges	Normal schools	Private secondary schools	Public high schools	Total
1	2	3	4	5	6
United States....................	5 056	6 297	11 574	33 075	56 002
North Atlantic Division...............	365	1 445	3 850	15 797	21 457
South Atlantic Division...............	441	627	1 645	1 536	4 249
South Central Division...............	870	947	1 914	1 960	5 691
North Central Division...............	3 075	3 187	3 260	12 109	21 631
Western Division.....................	305	91	905	1 673	2 974
North Atlantic Division :					
Maine.........................	....	34	223	512	769
New Hampshire.................	....	....	257	215	472
Vermont.......................	21	....	377	150	548
Massachusetts.................	....	....	198	3 600	3 798
Rhode Island..................	....	28	323	592	943
Connecticut...................	....	....	103	615	718
New York......................	174	82	1 513	3 691	5 460
New Jersey....................	....	....	118	2 674	2 792
Pennsylvania..................	170	1 301	738	3 748	5 957
South Atlantic Division :					
Delaware......................	....	....	30	216	246
Maryland......................	21	10	151	284	466
District of Columbia..........	26	....	161	202	389
Virginia......................	31	25	279	301	636
West Virginia.................	187	158	98	127	570
North Carolina................	77	99	536	13	725
South Carolina................	8	215	175	76	474
Georgia.......................	13	120	205	201	539
Florida.......................	78	....	10	116	204
South Central Division :					
Kentucky......................	272	368	334	88	1 062
Tennessee.....................	100	133	402	515	1 150
Alabama.......................	88	284	219	228	819
Mississippi	40	88	201	162	491
Louisiana	187	10	287	282	766
Texas	157	64	426	454	1 101
Arkansas	26	....	18	219	263
Oklahoma......................	....	....	....	....	....
Indian Territory..............	....	....	27	12	39
North Central Division :					
Ohio..........................	465	497	131	1 775	2 868
Indiana.......................	14	448	187	634	1 283
Illinois......................	763	341	527	1 486	3 117
Michigan	92	165	144	1 613	2 014
Wisconsin.....................	106	....	507	727	1 340
Minnesota.....................	111	25	564	160	860
Iowa..........................	452	802	441	2 507	4 202
Missouri......................	436	55	442	1 417	2 350
North Dakota..................	50	85	....	95	230
South Dakota..................	50	....	60	82	192
Nebraska......................	61	407	109	730	1 307
Kansas........................	475	362	148	883	1 868
Western Division :					
Montana.......................	....	....	4	171	175
Wyoming.......................	....	....	13	....	13
Colorado......................	....	....	17	362	379
New Mexico....................	....	12	26	17	55
Arizona.......................	15	....	....	11	26
Utah..........................	....	75	277	....	352
Nevada........................	43	....	....	100	143
Idaho.........................	....	....	12	....	12
Washington	51	....	108	72	231
Oregon	11	4	182	29	226
California....................	185	....	266	911	1 362

DEPARTMENT OF EDUCATION
FOR THE
UNITED STATES COMMISSION TO THE PARIS EXPOSITION OF 1900

MONOGRAPHS ON EDUCATION

IN THE

UNITED STATES

EDITED BY

NICHOLAS MURRAY BUTLER

Professor of Philosophy and Education in Columbia University, New York

14

ART AND INDUSTRIAL EDUCATION

BY

ISAAC EDWARDS CLARKE

Bureau of Education, Washington, D. C.

THIS MONOGRAPH IS CONTRIBUTED TO THE UNITED STATES EDUCATIONAL EXHIBIT BY THE
STATE OF NEW YORK

ART AND INDUSTRIAL EDUCATION

Since 1870 the rapidity of the development of art and industrial education in the United States has been so marked and so effective, the rapid increase in the number of special schools and museums of the fine arts so striking, as to make exceedingly difficult a satisfactory survey of this subject within the limits of a monograph.

The movement for the general introduction of drawing in the public schools, and of definite endeavors to promote art education, with a purpose to develop and improve the art industries of a people, seemed alike sudden in England and in the United States. In England it was apparently the definite result of the first world's fair — the exhibition of 1851. In the United States it had its origin in Boston, in 1870, where it was a direct outcome of the English movement.

The Centennial exhibition in Philadelphia in 1876, where the work in drawing of the Massachusetts normal art school, and of the public schools in Boston, was shown, made possible the rapid and remarkable development throughout the United States of the two kindred elements in education, namely, industrial art drawing and manual training. This addition of these two new studies to the regular courses of the public schools has been, perhaps, the most notable characteristic educational feature of the past two decades.

As the English were long held to be a people hopelessly inartistic and devoid of art possibilities, their wonderful development since 1851, in so many lines of artistic manufactures, challenges investigation, especially by a people long similarly accused as being innately inartistic, and for a long period, it must be admitted, apparently deservedly so accused.

The causes of this lack of art development as recited by

Haydon, were the same in both countries. That these causes were amply sufficient to account for this almost entire absence of any national evidence of art consciousness,— without compelling the admission of any inborn lack of mental capactity,— Haydon sought to demonstrate, by an appeal to the art development of England during the thirteenth century : "When England, in her knowledge of form, colour, light, shadow, and in fresco decoration, was in advance of Italy ; and had her progress not been checked by the reformation, would have been at the head of Europe." "Show the people of England fine works," said Haydon ; "give them the opportunity of study and the means of instruction ; teach them the basis of beauty in art, and then give your opinion, if you like ; but you have no right to condemn your fellow countrymen when you give them none of the advantages foreigners enjoy ; when you have no schools for art instruction, no galleries open to public view, no national collections, no schools of design, and when you refuse to allow that art has a public function, and absolutely withhold from it all public support."

However true is his picture of the absence of any opportunities for the people to see works of art, or to enjoy any personal training in the elementary knowledge of art, in the England of his day, the lack of all such opportunities in the United States was tenfold greater. The Puritan immigrants of New England had all the abhorrence of art which marked the followers of the reformation, and for two centuries the bare whitewashed walls of their plain meeting houses were eloquent in protest against the art adornments of ancient church or chapel. Nor did the long hard struggle to wrest sustenance from stony soil and stormy sea afford any space of leisure for those artistic occupations which to the stern puritan were worse than folly.

Such was the situation, alike in England and the United States, during the first half of the nineteenth century. The exhibitions of 1851 and of 1876 seem in turn to have revealed to each people their own artistic deficiencies.

II. PROGRESS OF ART EDUCATION

In 1749, Benjamin Franklin published his proposed " Hints for an Academy," and enumerated as the most useful studies, arithmetic, writing, drawing and mechanics. In this connection drawing is seen to be reckoned with mechanics as a useful study. So, more than a hundred years before Boston had put drawing into its public schools, this Boston boy sought to have his fellow citizens of Philadelphia adopt it in their schools as a required study.

In a Lancastrian school presided over by Mr. Fowle in Boston in 1821, the method prevailed of having the younger pupils taught by those of their fellow pupils a little in advance of them. This method was, in its fundamental idea, successfully adopted by Walter Smith, in his first introduction of drawing as a required study in the public schools of Boston, and has since been followed in many of the public schools throughout the country. This arose from the fact that, as the teachers in the elementary schools were in addition to their duties in teaching other studies unexpectedly to be called on to teach drawing, of which they had before little or no knowledge, it was inevitable that they could then be but little in advance of their pupils in their knowledge of this new study; the teachers could only teach the lessons they had just previously been taught in the weekly lessons given to the public school teachers by the new director of drawing and his assistants.

In the case of the pupils of the normal art school, subsequently established under the director, Professor Walter Smith, and in those attending the various state normal schools, as well as in the fact that drawing has long been a regular study in the public schools, the teachers in the public schools of to-day may fairly be assumed to have as much practical knowledge of this study as of any of the others intrusted to their care.

The arguments for the teaching of drawing in the public schools are clearly and concisely stated by Mr. Fowle in his

introductory words to the third edition of his book on drawing, issued in 1830.   Mr. Fowle also introduced in his school
physical science, music, and, for the girls, needlework.   In
this sewing form of "manual training" Miss Dorothy Dix,
later the noted philanthropist, was his first teacher.   So it
appears that our modern new educational movement was
clearly foreshadowed in this Boston school three-quarters of
a century ago !

In 1838 Henry Barnard, editor of the *American journal of education*, delivered an address in many parts of
of the country on the topic of industrial education and urged
that drawing should be taught in the public schools.   In the
Connecticut common school journal, published in Hartford,
of which Dr. Barnard was editor, he reprinted the report of
Professor Stow on Prussian schools, made to the legislature
of Ohio in 1838.   In occasional numbers during succeeding
years much attention was given to the subject of drawing in
its various phases.   In 1838–9 Miss E. P. Peabody gave a
course of free lessons in drawing in the Franklin school,
Boston, and in 1841–2 a similar course to a class of one hundred teachers of primary schools.   Miss E. P. Peabody and
her sister, Miss Mary Peabody (later Mrs. Horace Mann),
each published an elementary treatise illustrating their
methods of teaching drawing and reading.

Such is a brief summary of a few of the early efforts by
American educators to introduce the study as one of the
essential elementary studies to be taught in all public
schools.   Similar vain efforts to promote the early training
in drawing were from time to time made by leading artists.
Among these perhaps the most notable and earnest attempt
was made in Philadelphia by the distinguished artist Rem-
brandt Peale during the years 1840-1844.

As in Boston and in Philadelphia, earnest efforts to introduce the study or drawing in the schools long preceding
1870, had been successfully thwarted by the opposition
based chiefly on ignorance and lack of appreciation ; so it
resulted in Baltimore, when in 1848–9 Mr. William Minifie,

a remarkable man, taught drawing in that city as a science, and not simply as picture making. This competent master was, however, removed through the influence of an unsympathetic, ignorant committeeman, and so Baltimore lost the opportunity, else within reach, of anticipating the success of Boston by a quarter of a century. Mr. Minifie published his system of teaching, drawing, and perspective and shadows, which has long held its place as a recognized authority. About 1852 this work was adopted as one of the regular text-books, used in the South Kensington art schools of London, England, and which, it may be fairly assumed, Walter Smith studied; at least the underlying principles of the system of Professor Minifie and those of Professor Walter Smith are practically identical. As professor of drawing in the School of design of the Maryland institute in 1852–1854, Professor Minifie delivered and published three public addresses on drawing and design ; in these the teaching of drawing as a regular study in the public schools was eloquently urged.

To one who remembered the ability and methods of Professor Minifie, and the work done by his pupils of the high school, as far back as 1848, the exhibition made of drawings by the Baltimore high school, in the Centennial exposition in Philadelphia, in 1876, was pitiful indeed.

Cleveland, Ohio, seems to have been more fortunate than the cities whose experience has just been briefly recited. In 1849 drawing was put in the schools as a regular exercise, and after a few months was intrusted to the regular teachers of the public schools, who eventually found in the late Professor John Brainerd an enthusiastic instructor, who took such interest in their work that he followed them to the schools and aided them in teaching the pupils; in the end the professor was put in charge of the work in all the schools, and for several years remained with gratifying results. He published a manual for use in the schools. Subsequently Professor Brainerd was for years an examiner in the U. S. patent office in Washington.

In this brief summary of various sporadic efforts in diferent cities and communities to introduce drawing in the schools, it is clear that the desirability of general instruction of the school children in drawing was in the process of becoming a popular belief, and, in American communities, this is usually the precursor of legislative action.

While these efforts, as we have seen, had been confined to no single section or state, and, indeed, in some towns and cities drawing had already secured foothold in the schools. the movement in Boston, and in a degree through the state of Massachusetts, was more pronounced than elsewhere.

In this state certain studies which are required to be taught in all public schools are enumerated in the law, while certain other studies are recorded as permissible at the discretion of the school committee. Thus, the trend of the upward and onward direction in the progress of elementary education is indicated by the appearance of certain studies as "permissible."

In the law of 1860 "algebra, vocal music, drawing, physiology and hygiene" are thus recorded as permissible. This is believed to be the first legal recognition of drawing in this category. In 1869 the board of education is directed to prepare a plan for free instruction of men, women and children in mechanical drawing, applicable to all towns and cities of 5,000 inhabitants or more. In the law of 1870 "drawing" appears as a required study in all public schools, and "any city or town having more than 10,000 inhabitants shall annually make provision for giving free public instruction in industrial or mechanical drawing, either in day or evening schools under direction of the school committee."

The annual reports of the board of education of Massachusetts, about that time, show great interest in promoting the study of drawing, and later in developing technical industrial education with special reference to the manufacturing interests of the state.

In the report of 1870–71 "the Worcester county free

institute of industrial science"[1] in the city of Worcester, incorporated in 1865, is highly praised and pointed out as the only school in the state where such an education can be obtained.

As already indicated, the history of the slow development of the artistic training of youth in this country closely resembled in its several stages that of its progress in England, though, happily, there is here no story of individual effort and failure quite so tragic as that of the unfortunate Haydon, though the story of the last days of Walter Smith in America, just before his return to his native country, where he was gladly welcomed to an honorable career, all too brief, owing to his untimely decease, is not one to be dwelt on by Americans with any especial pride. He brought rare and precious gifts to America, while to his splendid abilities as a great teacher, and to his contagious enthusiasm, which inspired the eager youth who clustered about him, the final success of the new elements in popular education — industrial art and manual training — are more largely due than to any other single influence.

Although, during a century of progress, sporadic efforts were made in various localities to introduce the teaching of drawing in schools there was no permanent or general success. It was not till the system of public schools had become general, and the experiment of teaching the same thing at the same time, to a large number of pupils, had been proved feasible, that the time was ripe for the general introduction of industrial drawing and of manual training. Before this the teaching of drawing had been a personal matter between pupil and teacher, and no conception that it was possible to teach the elements of drawing to large classes at once had dawned upon educators.

The so-called "farm schools," which had a certain vogue in the earlier years of the present century, had proved failures as might easily have been foreseen, since it was not

---

[1] Name changed by act of legislature, in 1877, to " The Worcester polytechnic institute."

found feasible to work young men for remuneration so constantly, as was requisite to make them self-supporting as
well as school-supporting, while taxing them with the mental work essential to their obtaining anything that would
merit the name of an education.

A tendency towards something of this impossible nature
is still occasionally manifested by the over-zealous advocates
of industrial training, pure and simple, but it is to be hoped
that the "farm schools" experience will suffice to restrain
the present movement from like disaster.   Elementary training in industrial art and in manual training has in these
latter years been successfully introduced in many public
schools of country and town.   "Higher education" in each
of these directions, as in all others, must be provided, either
by the community or by individual benefactors.   It is never,
in any form, self-supporting, as the endowed literary and
scientific colleges, the schools of technology and the professional schools attached to the universities witness.

In the first annual report made by General John Eaton,
commissioner of education, in 1870, there appeared an interesting record of the results attained from an effort to ascertain the direct worth to a workingman of the education
given in the common elementary public schools.   The concurrence of testimony showing that even this small portion
of knowledge and mental training was of real pecuniary
value to its recipient, was convincing, leaving no room for
question but that the community was amply repaid for all
the cost of the common schools, by the increased earning
power of their pupils.   If this was true of a course of study
simply giving the elements of knowledge, the inference is
logical, that those forms of education which gave direct
capacity for higher grades of productive work must be so
much the more valuable.   In the progress of the concurrent
educational movement of that time, looking to the development on the one hand of industrial facility, and on the other
to that of artistic power, the commissioner was greatly interested, especially in the Massachusetts experiment of intro-

ducing the study of elementary drawing — essential to both phases of the movement — in all the public schools of the state.

It was with the purpose of recording for the information of the educators of the country, the progress of this Boston experiment that the preparation of the "Circular of education, No. 2, 1874,"[1] was undertaken by the present writer in 1873.

This movement was begun in Boston by the well-known educator, long the city superintendent of schools, the late Hon. J. D. Philbrick, and the late Hon. Charles C. Perkins, — the latter, the leading authority in the city in all matters relating to the fine arts,— in connection with some of their associate members of the city board of education.

Their purpose was to introduce the study of drawing as one of the required studies in the common schools of the city and state.

They were fortunate in securing, in 1870, the services of a leading English art master, the late Walter Smith, who was made "art director," in charge of drawing in the schools of the city and the state.

In this pamphlet, of some 56 pages, brief statements of the desirableness of such elementary art training in our American schools, and of the efforts made by European countries to promote such art training among their people, were given. Especial mention was also made of the English efforts both to develop artistic industries and to extend the teaching of drawing throughout their schools by means of the South Kensington institution. In addition it was sought to give a brief account of such art institutions and collections as were open to the public in the United States; to take an inventory, as it were, of the means at hand for the development of art education in this country. No list of such public art collections existed, and the attempt to secure such a list was undertaken with all the resources of the United States bureau of education. The trivial result

---

[1] Circular of Education. Drawing in the Public Schools. The Relation of Art to Education.—Washington, 1874, pp. 56.

of all this effort, as shown by the four pages of scattering statistics at the end of the circular, was ludicrous, while the poverty of the United States in art treasures available for the public, as thus exposed, was appalling. The interest taken by educators and the public generally in this small pamphlet, in view of the world's fair to be held in Philadelphia in 1876, in which coming event increasing interest was shown, and its efficacy in securing information, before so difficult to procure, led to the plan of further publications in the same line, and to the preparation by the present writer, as author and editor, of the special report upon the world movements in the development of artistic and industrial education and of like movements throughout the United States, since issued by this bureau in four large volumes.[1]   As there was little literature available concerning this comparatively new educational movement, and none at all within reach of the majority of the teachers of the country, copious appendices were added to each volume of this report. Those in Part I, given to "drawing in public schools," were made up largely of occasional addresses and lectures delivered to teachers by American and foreign leaders of the movement; of practical papers with programmes of courses in drawing ; of historical papers relating to the movement, and of abstracts showing the aid given to this form of education by foreign governments, and especially by that of Great Britain.   Each volume had in its appendix similarly appropriate papers, and was thus designed to be, in a measure, an encyclopedia relating to its subject.[1]

---

[1] Titles of the volumes of the special report already issued, "U. S. Department of the Interior, Bureau of Education, John Eaton, Commissioner.

"Art and Industry. Education in the Industrial and Fine Arts in the United States. By Isaac Edwards Clarke, A. M. Part I. Drawing in Public Schools. Washington: Government Printing Office. 1885. Pp. CCLIX, 1–842."

Part II. W. T. Harris, U. S. Commissioner. Industrial and Manual Training in Public Schools. 1892. Pp. CXLVIII, 1–1338.

Part III. W. T. Harris, U. S. Commissioner. Industrial and Technical Training in Voluntary Associations and Endowed Institutions. 1897. Pp. LIII, 1–1145.

Part IV. W. T. Harris, U. S. Commissioner. Industrial and Technical Training in Schools of Technology and in U. S. Land Grant Colleges. 1898. Pp. LVI, 1–1020.

Parts V & VI. Relating, severally, to Public Art Schools and to Public Art Museums. (In preparation.)

In view of the later development of the movement, attention is called to the title of the circular "Drawing in public schools — the relation of *art* to education," as indicative of the purpose of those who introduced the new study into the curriculum of public school studies.

In view of the marvelous progress in providing educational facilities for art and art industrial development, that has gone on in the United States since the publication of this little pamphlet in 1874, I venture to quote from it a couple of pages showing the author's belief in the American possibilities of such development a quarter of a century ago.

AMERICAN FACILITIES FOR GENERAL INTRODUCTION OF ART TRAINING

While, in the countries of Europe, whatever relates to the people in education, as in other matters, is in the control and general direction of the central government, so that what the central power decides to do is readily and immediately set in motion throughout the entire country, in the United States there is wisely no such central control. This power inheres to the states and to the local communities within the states. This very circumstance though somewhat, it may be, delaying the adoption of useful measures, yet renders the wise adaptation of training to the peculiar industries and needs of the various parts of the country far more probable. It is readily seen that the kind of special technical training would vary, as it was applicable to a manufacturing, a farming, or a mining community.

INFLUENCE OF LOCALITIES ON ART DEVELOPMENT

Indeed, this has already been exemplified in a marked degree in the different developments of the schools of science in the several states, adapting themselves in their chief courses of instruction to the industrial demands of their localities. So we may hope to have in the art future of this country, as have the different European countries, art capitals famous for their peculiar developments, and queening

it over their own states, as do Dresden and Munich and
Florence, and the other famous homes of art. San Francisco, Saint Louis, Cincinnati, Chicago, Cleveland, Pitts-
burgh, Philadelphia, New York, Boston, New Haven, Worcester, and many other prosperous cities and towns may
become in time great centers of beauty as well as of commerce, each having its own special development, varying in
architecture according to the building material most conve-
niently accessible, and in art production and artistic manufactures according to their special industries and resources ;
but all alike affording to their children thorough technical
training, and all attractive, because, everywhere, the eye
rests on noble buildings ; when the homes of industry shall
also be homes of beauty, and to walk through the city
streets shall be of itself an art education, as of old in
Athens, as it was in many a mediæval town, and is still, in
many an ancient city of France, Germany, Italy, and far-off
Spain.

Now, drawing is the very alphabet of art (for art is but a
language), the one essential requisite preliminary to any
artistic or technical training ; and, if it is desirable that the
children of the public schools shall be fitted to become, if
they wish it, skilled workmen in any branch of industry, it
is necessary that they shall be taught to draw correctly. To
those to whom art means higher things, as they suppose,
than its application to every-day utensils and mere manufactures ; who look for grand galleries of pictures and statues,
and to all the higher refinements of cultured art, it may be
a suggestive reflection that, among a people ignorant of
drawing, and whose daily surroundings, as is true of most of
the American people, afford few suggestions of art in any
of its forms, high art must ever remain an exotic, and
native artists be rarer than the fabled phœnix.

A country's art, like all its other developments, must be
based primarily upon the characteristics of its people.
Where all are judges of art, great artists arise, just as great
warriors among nations of soldiers, so that until the com-

mon people know the language of art, and can comprehend
the meaning of line and color and form, the artist is as
much out of place and as little to be looked for as a great
author would be among a people ignorant of reading.

Nor has it ever been otherwise.   The history of art is the
history of peoples.   Nor is there anything little or common
in the eyes of art.   The people that produced great buildings, fine paintings, and noble statues, had also the most
exquisite household utensils.   Their commonest articles,
whose fragile beauty has outlasted the centuries, to-day,
with subtle grace and perfect form, tease the eye of the
artist and challenge in vain our most skilled artisans to
reproduce them.   The antique eastern dish of burned clay
is held by the modern *connoisseur* as of more worth than its
weight in silver ; yet it was once in as humble and universal
use as the commonest crockery of our kitchens.

Great collections, museums, art galleries, much as they
may contribute to the self-satisfaction of cliques and cities,
will be of the slightest possible value and barren of results,
either upon the industries of the people or their art culture,
so long as drawing is not generally understood.

Whoever succeeds in having all the public school children
of the country properly trained in elementary drawing will
have done more to advance the manufactures of the country, and more to make possible the art culture of the people, than could be accomplished by the establishment of a
hundred art museums without this training.   Just as libraries are worthless to those who cannot read, so are art collections to those who cannot comprehend them ; just as all
literature is open to him who has learned to read, so is all
art to him who has learned to draw, whose eye has been
trained to see, and his fingers made facile to execute.   We
have begun at the wrong end ; we asked for art galleries
when we needed drawing schools.   But the evil is not irreme-
diable.   Let drawing be generally taught, and our art galleries and museums, poor as they are, will at once grow more
and more valuable, for they will then begin to be of use.

MASSACHUSETTS THE FIRST STATE TO ACT

The legislature of Massachusetts, moved thereto by the persistent efforts of a few cultured and public-spirited citizens, who realized the imperative need and demand for such training in the public schools, passed an act in 1870 making drawing one of the studies of the public schools, and also making the establishment of free drawing classes for adults obligatory upon all towns and cities containing over ten thousand inhabitants. In pursuance of this law, Mr. Walter Smith, "art master, London, late head master of the Leeds school of art and science and training school for art teachers," was invited, both by the city of Boston and by the state of Massachusetts, to come from England and introduce the new study into the schools of the city and of the commonwealth. Mr. Smith was highly recommended by the Kensington school authorities. He was appointed state director of art education, and has been unremitting in his efforts to introduce drawing into the public schools, and to foster the establishment of classes for adults. Mr. Smith was also appointed general supervisor of art in the Boston schools.

He published, in 1872, a large illustrated work upon art education,[1] which is indispensable to a thorough investigation of the subject, and will be found full of practical suggestions to those wishing to introduce the study into the schools.

SUMMARY OF THE CONDITION IN THE UNITED STATES OF EDUCATION RELATING TO ART IN 1874

It is only necessary for the American people to be convinced that a want exists to cause them to supply it. Believing the lack of provision for industrial and general art training in our present system of public education to be such a want, I have sought to show

---

[1] "Art Education, Scholastic and Industrial, by Walter Smith, art master, London, late head master of the Leeds school of art and science, and training school for art teachers, now professor of art education, Massachusetts," with illustrations. James Osgood & Co., Boston, 1872, pp. 398.

First. The need of preliminary instruction in drawing, its utility, and the practicability of its introduction into all grades of the public schools.

Secondly. What steps have been taken towards introducing it and how it can best be done.

Thirdly. The present condition oɩ the means for industrial art training in technical schools, including the schools of science.

Fourthly. The means possessed by our higher institutions of learning for giving general knowledge of art.

Fifthly. The special schools existing for training professional artists.

Sixthly. The steps that have been taken for founding great art museums in connection with art-training schools.

We find that in one state, Massachusetts, drawing has been by law introduced into all the public schools, and a state normal art school established ; that in many cities and towns in other states drawing has been more or less taught in the public schools ; that in all the "schools of science," where engineering is taught, mechanical drawing is of necessity taught.

SCHOOLS OF DESIGN

In schools for the practical teaching of art, as applied to industry and manufactures, the free industrial classes for adults in Massachusetts, the Lowell free school of industrial design at the Boston institute of technology, the schools of Cooper union, the Philadelphia school of design for women, and the school of design of the University of Cincinnati complete the short list.

SCHOOLS OF ART

For the special training of artists we have the schools of the National academy of design, New York, the Yale school of fine arts, New Haven, and the new college of fine arts in the Syracuse university, which comprise all at present existing. The San Francisco school is soon to open. The school of the Pennsylvania academy of fine arts will resume active operations on the completion of the new building.

ART DEPARTMENTS IN COLLEGES AND UNIVERSITIES

Of the colleges possessing any special collections or facilities for giving any instruction in art, even the most general, we find, excepting Yale and Syracuse, with their special art departments, only Harvard, University of Michigan, Cornell, Rochester university, the college of Notre Dame and Vassar college, out of the hundreds of colleges of the country, that either give any art training or possess any art collections, however small or incomplete.

PUBLIC ART MUSEUMS AND GALLERIES

There remain, then, but the public art institutions which we have already described; there are four of these in the whole land: at Boston, New York, Washington and San Francisco.

The Metropolitan museum of New York, the Brooklyn art association, the Boston art museum, the Corcoran art gallery and the Art association of San Francisco are admirable instances of the methods by which communities and individuals in this country voluntarily provide those institutions for which, in other lands, the government alone is looked to.

An important means of art culture, and the only one which has appealed to the general public, is found in the public art exhibitions. To those of the Metropolitan museum, National academy, the Boston athenæum, the Yale art school, the San Francisco art association, and the permanent exhibitions of the Corcoran art gallery, I have already referred.

LOAN EXHIBITIONS

It would not be difficult to obtain collections of fresh works of the artists for exhibition and sale in connection with the loan exhibitions of works of art belonging to citizens that have been already suggested.

The popularity of exhibitions of good pictures, as attested by the throngs of visitors that attend them and the crowds that visit the saloons of the leading picture dealers in the large cities, who hold perpetual exhibitions in a small way, sufficiently shows the public interest in art. Indeed, with the multiplicity of American tourists in Europe in these days, it would be strange if the love was not awakened. There are quite a number of well-known private art collections in the leading cities which, separately, would make a desirable public gallery, and from which, as the Metropolitan museum has shown, a loan collection of rare works can be made for public exhibition.

While I have recorded the paucity of institutions capable of giving a thorough art training and the few public art collections now in this country, it is, nevertheless, apparent that there already exists in all the leading cities the material which needs only to be made available, to afford all necessary facilities for general and technical art training; and if it shall be undertaken in earnest, there is possible in this country a development, both in industrial art and in what are called the higher branches of art, which, at the end of twenty-five years, will render obsolete the verdict passed upon us at the World's fair in 1851 and never yet reversed. Here there is opened a field of honorable rivalry between the several states, cities, and towns of the Union. What England has done in this direction we can do, and the more readily that we have the advantage of her experience. No time or force need be wasted. We have but to adopt and modify the methods so thoroughly tested there to the different conditions that may exist in our several communities.

I commend this subject of the relation of art to education to the consideration not only of all educators but to all who are interested in the varied mauufacturing industries of our many states. Skill is the modern secret of success. Science becomes ever more certainly the measure of prosperity. Science underlies and must precede art; it is the strong substructure upon whose fixed foundations she builds her palace walls. In the common schools the children of America must be trained to draw if her artisans are to hold their own in the world's contest, and if her artists are to enshrine her history.

If they but will it, the "republic of the people" shall become the home of an art as noble and as enduring as that which glorified the "republic of princes," whose palaces for so many centuries have lifted their stately walls above the waves, guarding for mankind, not the trophies of her warriors nor the wealth of her merchants, but the priceless work of her humbler artists.

Tintorretto, Titian, and Veronese are still fresh in men's memories, though the names of doge and patrician have faded from recollection.

In the tables of statistics of "museums of art and archæology for 1873," given in the circular, there were but thirteen institutions in all. Of these the two since reckoned among those having the leading art collections of the country, were but at the beginning of their history. The Corcoran art gallery of Washington, D. C., founded in 1869 by the late W. W. Corcoran, Esq., and by him richly endowed, had about one hundred paintings, mostly the private collection of the founder, and a collection of nearly two hundred casts of antique sculpture.

The Metropolitan museum of art of New York, founded in 1870, by a few citizens, lovers of art, had but a small endowment contributed by citizens and had, in its first modest home down town, as the nucleus of the magnificent and varied collections which now, in 1899, crowd the stately halls and galleries of its majestic palace in Central park, the Cesnola collection of Cyprian sculptures, ceramics and glass, and a small collection of paintings, the latter mostly loaned.

In the 25 pages of statistics of art institutions for 1881–82, given in Part I of the special report, are recorded 37 "institutions affording art instruction, including all training in industrial art," and 30 "museums of art." Of these 37 schools, 24 were established in, or since 1869, and of the 30 museums 14 had like dates of foundation. These statistics

show the unusual activity then existing in the art development of the people, nor has this ceased ; new art institutions
are being opened from time to time, either founded by
liberal individuals, or by the community, and continual and
important additions are constantly being made to the art
collections of the several institutions.

The development of popular interest in the new features
of education, from 1870 to the opening of the centennial in
1876, was very rapid, and its progress immediately following
the centennial was surprising in its universality.

Up to the time of the centennial there were, in the United
States, literally no books on artistic industries, and few on
the fine arts, either published in this country or to be found
in the ordinary public libraries.

In view of the present abundance here of this class of
literature, native and foreign, this statement seems almost
incredible ; it is, however, strictly accurate.

Save occasionally in three or four of the older cities, there
was in the United States, during the first half of the 19th
century, little public opportunity for seeing any works of
art, so that, on the part of the people generally throughout
the land, there was neither knowledge of, nor interest in,
anything relating to art.   The world exhibitions at the centennial first revealed to the great mass of American visitors
the wonderful attractiveness and power of art, in creating
and shaping the industries of the world.   The wide-reaching
influence of this world-view upon American educational and
industrial development, thus effected by the centennial of
1876, can hardly be exaggerated.   Its beneficent results were
charmingly illustrated throughout the Columbian exposition
in Chicago, in 1892–93.

In fact, the great eras of that triumphant progress of
modern civilization which characterizes our present century,
are marked by the splendid milestones of the " World's
fair," beginning with the one set up in London in 1851.

A "straw," showing the wide-spreading interest in all matters relating to art, now existing in this country, in marked

contrast with the absence of such interest before 1870, may be seen in the fact that in 1899 a book is issued by " The Mac-Millan Company, publishers, New York and London," which gives for the United States and Canada similar information concerning art matters and artists to that which has long been given for Great Britain in their English issue, entitled "The Year's Art" — a directory of all art schools, museums, etc., etc.

The American volume[1] is a handsome well-printed book, illustrated with 52 full-page reproductions of the works of living artists. The varied contents of this work, when contrasted with the few pages of statistics in the circular of education of 1874, give more striking evidence of the general diffusion of knowledge of and interest in matters relating to art throughout the United States than could be given by many pages of mere description.

As the volumes of the special report, to be given to the history and present conditions of the schools and museums of the fine arts, though finished as to the early histories, are not yet completed ; and, as there has not been opportunity to collect and compile the present statistics of these institutions in time to be available for this monograph, I have been glad to avail myself of the statistics gathered by Miss Levy, editor of the volume just referred to, showing, as they do, the continued growth and prosperity of the public art institutions. For the 30 "museums of art," as given in the art and industry report statistics for 1881–82, Miss Levy shows, as existing in 1898, 41 "art galleries," an increase of eleven, while for the 37 art schools of 1882 Miss Levy records 117. She also gives a total of 159 art societies in the United States and 9 in Canada. No such societies were recorded in the special report. Reference to the U. S. bureau statistics, as given in the preceding pages, show a notable increase in art collections and schools from 1869 to 1882. The statistics, as now given by Miss Levy for 1898, show

---

[1]American Art Annual, 1898. Florence N. Levy, editor, New York. The Mac-Millan Company, 1899, pp. 540. Price $3.

most emphatically that the interest in art education and in public collections of the fine arts, as contrasted with that shown by the earlier statistics, is still a growing and continuing interest. The good seed planted in Boston in 1870 has brought an abundant harvest !

III. THE MOVEMENT FOR MANUAL TRAINING

This movement which was so suddenly developed had its immediate origin in the demonstration given by the successful introduction of the new study of drawing in the public schools, showing conclusively that it was feasible to teach at one time, a single subject to a large number of pupils.

The following immediate paragraphs are taken from the opening pages of the introduction to " Part I of the art and industry report " published in 1885, by the present writer, in which the history of the introduction of industrial drawing in the educational systems of the country is given in detail.

One of the most striking and significant results of the experiment, begun in Boston in 1870, by the teaching of industrial drawing to the public school children of that city, has been the widespread interest awakened throughout the United States in the further development of the industrial training of children. No sooner was it shown that it was possible to give to the children in the public schools, some elementary training of the hands and eyes, than a movement began in many places, to teach actual trades and handicrafts to the children while in school.

Though there might be danger that overzealous promoters of this so-called " practical education " would in their earnestness, overstep the true province of education, overstrain childish muscles, and overtax the mental as well as bodily strength of the growing children, still the public good sense may be trusted to restrain and modify such extremes ; while the intellectual activity, which has been aroused and stimulated by this new departure in education, if wisely directed into practicable channels, can hardly fail of accomplishing desirable results.

KINDERGARTENS AND OBJECT TEACHING IN PUBLIC SCHOOLS

The substitution of a knowledge of the thing, in place of a verbal account of the thing, which is characteristic of the kindergarten methods, has begun to be introduced in the schools and mechanic's classes of England, and, also, so notably here in the schools of Quincy, Massachusetts, that it now goes in the United States by the name of the "Quincy method." * * *

"Object teaching" so far as it tends to awaken the intellectual faculties of the child, and to encourage improved habits of study and observation is to be commended and fostered.

RESULTS OF THE INTRODUCTION OF DRAWING AS A PART OF ELE-
MENTARY EDUCATION

It is referred to here only as one evidence of the rapid progress of the "evolution" of the principle embodied in the introduction of industrial drawing into the elementary public schools of the country. The practical bearing of this study upon the industries of the country, is shown in the tendency to begin the technical training of the future workman or workwoman, at a far earlier age than had been before thought practicable. The danger, as already suggested, lies in not recognizing the limitations set by nature. While the kindergarten method avails itself of the natural curiosity and wonderful activity of very young children, and in its educational processes closely follows the leadings of nature; the attempt to teach handicrafts to young boys may very easily go contrary to nature, by imposing tasks unfit for untrained minds and undeveloped muscles. No such objection can, however, lie against the study of industrial drawing. Weak indeed must be the hand that cannot lift a pencil, weaker the mind that, beginning at the beginning, cannot follow the graded and orderly steps, by which Walter Smith, basing his teaching on the everlasting truths of geometry, has arranged his progressive studies.

RESULTS TO BE ANTICIPATED FROM GENERAL INTRODUCTION OF
DRAWING IN SCHOOLS

When the study of drawing is regarded in all public
schools as of the same importance as the study of reading
and spelling, and as much time in the week is given to teaching drawing, as is given to either of these studies — which
has nowhere yet been done, for even in Boston this study
has been admitted largely on " sufferance "— then, judging
from the results already secured, it is reasonable to antici-
pate an increase in the numbers, as well as superior expert-
ness in the skill of American-born workmen.   It is by reason
of its direct bearing upon the development of skilled labor
that this subject of the introduction of the study of elementary drawing based on geometry, and with a direct view
to its application to industries, is of the national and general importance which seems to justify the preparation and
publication of the present report.   Accounts of the experiments in introducing "manual training" in the public
schools, as well as the reports of the special schools for such
training and of the technical industrial schools, will be found
in their appropriate connection in Part II of this report.

THE LAND GRANT ACT OF 1862 THE RECOGNITION BY CONGRESS OF
THE ADVENT OF SCIENCE AS A FACTOR OF EDUCATION

The passage by congress of the law establishing the
" colleges of agriculture and the mechanic arts " as long ago
as 1862, is proof that the need of some form of educational
training, other than the purely literary courses which then
comprised all that was given in the higher schools and colleges, was widely recognized.   *   *   *

DRAWING A REQUISITE PREPARATORY STUDY FOR ALL SCHOOLS OF
SCIENCE

A knowledge of drawing is so essential to any progress
in many of the studies comprised in the regular courses of
the schools of science that, in view of the almost total
neglect at that time of this study in the public, or private

elementary schools, it is little wonder that when the new colleges, created by the national land grant act, were first opened, there were frequent complaints that, for want of this indispensable preliminary training in the element of drawing, nearly a year's time was lost in teaching the pupils that which should have been taught in the primary schools. While there were doubtless other studies in which a lack of suitable training was observed, drawing was both the most important of these preliminary studies, and the one in which deficiency was most common and most disastrous.

It is because this knowledge is indispensable as a preparation for the courses in the schools of science, that the teaching of the study of drawing in all the public schools of the country is of importance to the colleges created by the national land grant of 1862 ; and it is in this connection that one element of the practical value and importance of this training of the public school children in elementary drawing can be readily seen.

THE COMMON SCHOOLS ARE THE PREPARATORY ACADEMIES FOR THE AGRICULTURAL COLLEGES

The public schools are the academies that fit the students for the national agricultural colleges, and, therefore, it is of importance to these colleges that the studies taught in the public schools shall be such as are preparatory to their own courses of study.

*   *   *   *   *   *   *   *

UNIVERSAL TEACHING OF ELEMENTARY DRAWING ESSENTIAL

The fundamental idea of the present report is, that universal teaching in all public schools of the elements of "industrial drawing" — meaning by that an orderly progressive course of drawing based on geometry — has become an essential part of any general system of the public education of a people, and is equally necessary, whether the after-training of the child is to be that of an artisan, an artist, or a citizen engaged in any productive pursuit, or whether the child is to be so situated as to be removed from the ranks of producers to those of consumers.

The subject naturally separates into two main divisions; on the one hand, that embracing all matters relating to the technical industrial producing arts and artistic industries; on the other, those relating mostly to the fine arts; this last division properly includes three distinct subdivisions, relating, separately, to the theory and history, to the study and practice, and to the enjoyment and patronage of art. The first of these minor divisions includes such a knowledge of the historical development of art as must hereafter be implied in the term "liberal education," such as, within the past few years, has been taught in some of the classical colleges and universities; the second includes the special art schools and academies for the technical training of artists, architects, sculptors, painters and engravers, preparatory to the actual production of works of high art; the third comprises the various means of promoting that general information and art culture of the public, which is derived largely from the opportunities of seeing choice works of art in the collections of art museums and art loan exhibitions; the latter, having, perhaps, as important, if not as manifest, an influence upon the development of the industries and arts of a people as the former; for the industries and arts of a people are determined by their needs, their desires, and their intelligence.

So long as individuals and communities have never seen the added attractions given to buildings, furniture, clothing and household implements, by the application of art to such articles of prime necessity, so long there is no demand for the production of similar artistic articles; but let once their eyes be opened by a sight of the wonders of a "world's fair," or an "art loan collection," and immediately the demand is created. There is at first no ability, owing to lack of knowl-

edge and skill on the part of the home workmen to produce
similar articles, consequently this demand must be met by
importation.   An increase of imports with no corresponding
increase of exports is an evident disadvantage for the importing country.   It is, therefore, of importance to any community or country to ascertain by what methods other countries
have trained skilled artists and artificers, in order to adopt
similar means ; hence, an account of the experiments,
expenditures and systems adopted by foreign countries, for
these purposes, is directly demanded in such a report as this.

The origin of the educational form of manual training,
as introduced in the public schools of the United States, and
as presented in the technical manual training schools, is by
some definitely assigned to the year 1876 as being the direct
outcome of the object lessons of the "work in metals,"
shown by the Strogonoff school in the Russian exhibition at
the centennial.   The work of this Russian school was
enthusiastically set forth to educators by Professor Runkle,
of the Boston institute of technology, and by Professor
Woodward, since director of the manual training school of
St. Louis.   Several other educators, interested in industrial
education, as shown in the exposition, by the work in wood
in the Swedish department, and by other like experiments,
heartily favored the movement.

THE NEW DEPARTURE IN EDUCATION IN PUBLIC SCHOOLS. THE
INDUSTRIAL PHASE OF THE MOVEMENT

This movement is, in the opinion of the writer, as stated
in the opening sentences of Part I of the art and industry
report, simply the logical outcome of the experiment of
introducing instruction in industrial art drawing in the public schools, initiated by the calling of Walter Smith to Massachusetts in 1870.   It is, therefore, germane to the purpose
of the report, although not solely artistic in its present
development.   *   *   *

As this is a new departure in educational methods, it has
seemed desirable to show the growth and changes of opin-

ions, for the movement is necessarily based upon the percep-
tion, by the educators and the public, of the desirableness
of some changes in methods, while the nature, extent, and
manner of the changes are all in question and proper subjects of discussion.   So, that it seems desirable that the various steps by which conclusions have been arrived at in such
communities as have taken some decided action, should be
given at length, for the information of others contemplating
action in similar directions.   For this reason public official
reports, as well as direct communications made to this bureau,
are freely quoted at length in the appendices.   It is hoped
that sufficient material for tracing historically the inception and progress of this important educational movement
in the United States will there be found, as well as an adequate showing of the arguments used by both parties to the
discussion.   Fullness and accuracy, rather than brevity, have
been sought in the compilation from the various authorities
there given.

It has been said, by one experienced in observing the
results of legislation, that the unforeseen, indirect and far-
reaching influence of any law was much greater, and often
far other, than the intentional results sought by its enactment.   Perhaps the recent "interstate commerce" law may
be instanced as in point.   However this may be as applied
to man's enactments, it is unquestionably true in relation to
the results of his discoveries in the realms of nature, when
he has once set his new-found servitors to work!   Who, for
instance, could have foreseen that Galvani, experimenting
with the legs of frogs in his laboratory in Italy; Watt,
dreamily watching the tea kettle by the cottage hearth in
England; Franklin, kite-flying in the Philadelphia fields;
Fulton, whittling out the model of the strange, sailless craft
he was to launch on the Hudson; or Morse, stringing wires
around the walls of his studio in New York, were, each and
all of them, more busy with that which would affect for ages
all the after development of civilization; and influence the
lives of men and the destinies of nations to a far greater

extent than did the decisive defeat and victory of Waterloo?
Yet the discovery and utilization of the powers of steam
and of electricity have not only revolutionized the world of
matter, but of ideas !

ADVENT OF THE INDUSTRIAL ERA

The era of industrial democracy was made possible by
these modest, patient students of nature. As soon as the
advance in material development due to their discoveries
began to be realized, the male inhabitants, either of king-
doms or republics, who had hitherto been regarded only as
possible soldiers, began to be respected as producers —
active factors in the production of the resources of wealth
and power of the country. The new contests between countries gradually became contests between the art, skill and
industry of their respective peoples. Not that wars have
ceased, or that arms are laid aside, but that the arts of
industry, the avocations of peace, begin to be recognized as
legitimate fields in which the interests of nations are to be
contested. The rulers are alert to impress all discoveries in
the arts into the service of war, and are prompt in utilizing
all inventions in the industries for warlike preparations.
Nevertheless, it grows more and more apparent that the
skilled artisan is rising in the scale of importance, while the
warrior is valued more and more because he may be the pro-
tector of the workman, and of the precious things his art
has produced. The world's fairs are recognized as the arenas
in which the most brilliant triumphs of nations are to be
won. The moment that it was seen that commercial
supremacy was based upon industrial superiority, the new
era was inaugurated. This was first clearly seen at the first
great "world's fair," which was held in Hyde Park in 1851.
National efforts to promote technical industrial education on
a large scale date from that event. The rise of the mediæval
renaissance does not more clearly date from the discovery
of the classic manuscripts than does this modern era of the
European renaissance of artistic industries from this great

fair. The traditions of art industries had, it is true, never been wholly lost in France, but the beginning of that general movement, which embraces all the European states, which led Russia to recreate Byzantine art, and England to discover new regions of art, and which has begun to be felt even in these United States, can be definitely traced to that time of the uplifting of the strange, gleaming, crystal dome above the elms of the London park.

DRAWING IN AMERICAN SCHOOLS

The beginning of the modern art educational movement in the United States can be as definitely assigned to the year 1870.

By a melancholy coincidence which groups the termination of the lives of the three remarkable men by whom this great educational reformation was begun, within a few short months of each other, the close of the first period of this movement, destined to exert immeasurable influence over the future of America, can be fixed as in 1886.

In common with Dr. Philbrick and Mr. Perkins, Professor Smith regarded the introduction of industrial art drawing in the schools as but the beginning of the movement for the industrial art education of the American people, as his published addresses testify.

The great movement in the United States which these three men definitely organized, and of the development of which they had a far-sighted, comprehensive view, may be said to have already fairly entered upon the second period of its development, no longer by any means confined to the public schools.

THE RELATION OF DRAWING TO THE PRESENT MOVEMENT

It is because all training in industrial education that can be given in the public schools as they now exist, or in any new class of schools that may be established with that direct purpose, must, of necessity, be based on the thorough grounding of the pupils in the knowledge and practice of elementary industrial art drawing, of like character with that first successfully taught in the public schools of Massachusetts under the directorship of Professor Walter Smith, that the present widespread movement is termed a second step in the new educational advance. * * *

What these three men in Massachusetts did was to demonstrate beyond cavil, that it is as possible in the same time to teach a subject, by means of drawings and objects shown and explained by a teacher to a class, to many pupils simultaneously, as it is to teach the same thing to a single pupil. The effect of this discovery was at once to multiply indefinitely the power and capacity of the public school. For not only was this true of instruction in drawing and in writing, the studies which before had been thought to need particular devotion of the teacher to the individual pupil but it was found applicable to many other studies and to afford great facilities to teachers in illustrating many topics.

If industrial art drawing had no other value than to have furnished this proof of the facility of general instruction to classes, instead of to individual pupils, it would have fully justified all the cost of its introduction in the schools in money, time and effort. Much besides this was effected by the proof that the study of industrial art drawing demanded no special faculty on the part of either pupil or teacher, but could be taught to all by the regular teachers of the schools after a little preliminary training of the teachers themselves in classes. It was long before the popular impression that drawing merely meant picture-making, and that the ability to draw was a special gift of genius, could be corrected ; but this was gradually effected by repeated public exhibitions of the work done by all the pupils of a school, or of all the schools of a town or city, where it was shown that every child whose eyes and fingers were uninjured could learn to draw. The object of the study, which was to train the eye and the hand — the one to accuracy of seeing, the other to facility of execution and exactness of statement — began slowly to be understood.

The value of a thorough training in industrial art drawing has at last become so generally recognized as to call for little argument. It is taken for granted in the discussions about the further development of industrial education that the pupils have been taught the elements of drawing, just as, in discussions about new text-books, their ability to read is assumed. It was far otherwise in the beginning. All through the early years of the decade, from 1870 to 1880, there were very few individuals, and fewer school officials in cities and towns, who were in the least aware of the usefulness of this study. The very places in which the most zealous advocacy for manual training in schools, and for the adoption of all forms of industrial education is now found, were only, after long-continued efforts, led to allow the experiment of teaching drawing in their public schools to be tried. However, the centennial exhibition in Philadelphia, in 1876, worked wonders in the general diffusion of a knowledge of the possible value of this industrial art education ; for the American people then first saw into how large a share of the manufactures and arts of mankind this application of art to material enters ; first learned how values were enhanced by art, and began to realize how art ennobles labor.

They saw, also, at Philadelphia, in the collections shown there of the industrial art drawings made by the school children of Massachusetts, by what methods, and with what results, the teaching of this new study could be effected. More than this, the pupils' work in applied mechanics, shown by the Russian schools, illustrating the results of giving definite instruction, in a systematic course, to artisans, was there first seen, and the idea of the " manual training school," since so admirably exemplified in the St. Louis and the Boston schools, modelled after the Russian plan, was familiarized to American educators. Thus, the sure foundation for a further advance in the development of industrial education was laid.

As soon as the success of this attempt to begin the elementary training of the eye and hand in the public schools was satisfactorily established, it was evident that a new and valuable means of education had come into use. Educators eagerly adopted and experimented with the new methods, some looking at them only with a view to their application in the art of teaching, their pedagogic value; others, the majority, seeing in them the means of giving a more directly practical turn to the training in the public schools. The demand for this more practical education has been rapidly growing, and in these new studies were found the first practical suggestions for so modifying the old methods of school education as to adapt them to the new demands. In common with all germinal ideas, they were found capable of various applications and of indefinite development. It was the recognition of this potentiality that led Dr. Philbrick and Mr. Perkins to desire and secure their introduction.

When it is seen how truly the present interest in industrial training is the legitimate result of the introduction of industrial art drawing in the public schools of Massachusetts, and that, but for this pioneer work in thus clearing the way, and laying the sure beginnings of general technical training in this country, the great Philadelphia exhibition must have failed of any direct practical bearing upon our education, or our industries, other than to greatly stimulate the buying of foreign art manufactures ; the magnitude of the services rendered to the whole country by the three men who originated the plan, and effected the introduction of the practical study of industrial art drawing in the common schools of Massachusetts in 1870, begins to assume larger and grander proportions.

That the practical value to the people of the United States of the opportunities afforded by the splendid displays of their art industries by the nations of the world at Philadelphia, was greatly enhanced owing to the direct interest in industrial art training, begun in Boston six years before and rapidly developing in Cincinnati, St. Louis, and elsewhere, may safely be assumed ; because the industrial value to a people of the sight of such varied museum collections as

were shown at the centennial, is not mainly derived from the
pleasure given to the mere sight-seer, but is owing to the
opportunities thus afforded to practical designers and artificers for thorough study of the works shown ; for, as Emer-
son sagely says, "No matter how much facility of idle seeing
a man has, the step from knowing to doing is rarely taken."
It was in this exhibition that the utility of such training in
the artistic industries was first made known to large numbers
of Americans ; it was here, also, that the methods of successful teaching in the elements of these arts were first shown
to the whole country.   It is of interest thus to be able,
sometimes, as in this instance, to trace great results to
their causes.

This movement was the true dawn of the new era of the
industrial art development of America, which was apparently
ushered in by the centennial exhibition ; nor, if the movement, which has gone steadily forward from those early days
in Boston, meets with no unforeseen interruption, will the
term "era" seem inappropriate.

That the purpose of the early promoters of the introduction of the teaching of drawing in the public schools of the
country, was to develop and promote the knowledge and
love of art throughout the community may be inferred from
the fact that, in the same year that Walter Smith, himself a
sculptor by profession, was brought to Boston, Mr. Charles
C. Perkins,— at whose suggestion some two years before, the
American social science association had sent to Europe for
a number of casts of classical statues and busts to be placed
in the new building of "The Newton street girls' high
school,"— superintended the placing of these works of
high art in position ; the architect having provided for
them in his plans.   The purpose of this collection was two-
fold, both to provide fitting decoration for the building, and,
"as a simple but efficient means of introducing an æsthetic
element into the educational system of the United States,"
by offering to the pupils, an opportunity to see and comprehend, some of the works of the great masters of art.   With

this intent Mr. Perkins, himself an acknowledged authority on all matters relating to this subject, gave to the fortunate pupils of that school, a series of lectures on classic art as exemplified by the works before them. This collection comprised casts of ten famous antique statues and eleven busts. In addition to these single examples a portion of the wonderful frieze by Phidias, from the Parthenon, was put in place on the walls.

The Museum of fine arts, though incorporated in this year of 1870, was not opened for several years; so that the casts of the girls' high school collection comprised the most of the works of classic art then accessible to the public in the city.

This, then, seems to have been the first instance in this country of the definite undertaking of the artistic adornment of the interior of school buildings, though for many a year, here and there, in some wayside country schoolhouse, a few wild flowers, or garden posies, brought by loving scholar to the youthful teacher, and set in honor upon her desk for all to see, had given unwonted charm and color to the dingy room, with unconscious suggestion of the beauty waiting to transform, at a touch of the magic wand of art, those too often repellant dens of ugliness, the common school rooms of the country, with their desolate, naked walls, into bright attractive homes for the happy children; such as are to be found to-day in city and town, and along country hillside, all over the land.

As the origin of the present somewhat widely extended movement for beautifying the school rooms, has been attributed solely to the movements begun in France and in England, a decade later (see report of Boston school committee on drawing and music for 1883) — it has seemed well to refer here to the inauguration in 1870, of this earlier Boston idea of placing examples of antique art in the school. For a full account of this Boston experiment, and of other later similar efforts elsewhere, as well as for several papers of interest in this connection, see chapter I of part II, "Art and industry report," pages 1–11, and Appendix " K," part II, pages 709–731.

Mr. Perkins, and his associates, sought to give to the young girls, many of them about to become teachers in their turn, some definite knowledge of classic art, so that not only should they see for themselves these objects of ideal beauty, but that all literature should be thus for them illumined — since the literature both of Europe and America, springs so largely from that of Greece and Rome. Of course the cost of such a collection of casts of ancient art, would preclude any such undertaking in most schools, public or private, but, fortunately, beauty is not to be held a captive, even in golden chains, and, just as the cheaper plaster casts, as in this instance, take the place of costly marbles and bronzes, so engravings and photographs, afford admirable and inexpensive reproductions of plastic and pictorial art ; while in our large cities are now publishers who make a specialty of providing such artistic illustrations, for the use of students, or for the adornment of the study walls, and the halls and assembly rooms, of the schools ; adapted to all needs and to all purses. However, unless the living teacher shall bid these dry bones of art to live, shall unseal the closed eyes of the children so that they can recognize their beauty, and shall awaken their eager curiosity to learn the meaning and the message of these silent ministers of art, they will fail of their mission.

The initial movement in Boston, in 1870, for artistic adornment of school rooms, as well as for the art instruction of pupils, was soon followed by similar undertakings in some of the neighboring towns and cities of Massachusetts ; and, later, when the English and French movements became generally known, in many places all over the country.

In New York, Brooklyn, Providence, New Haven, Philadelphia, Chicago, Milwaukee, Denver, San Francisco, and doubtless in many other cities, the movement has made good progress. Long since, in Baltimore, in the Maryland normal school building, under Superintendent Newell, and in Washington, D. C., in the Franklin school building and the high school building, under Superintendent Wilson, many artistic works had been placed in the halls and school rooms, which are constantly added to, under the supervision of their successors. In Boston, in November, 1894, there was held under the auspices of " The public school art league " " The New England conferences of educational workers " and " The Boston art students' association," a fine exhibition of works suitable for school-house decoration, and in Brooklyn, New York, in the spring of 1896, a similar exhibition in charge of the art education section of " The Brooklyn institute of arts and sciences."

This direct outcome of the movement for industrial art training in all public schools, and inspired by the same leaders, may serve to show that the art idea was ever in the plan of the founders of this important movement, which, unfortunately for awhile, was in great danger of being wholly divorced from any idea of art.

The Boston movement for putting the study of drawing into the regular curriculum of the public schools, attracted the attention of educators all over the country, and during his first year in Boston, Professor Smith was invited to attend the convention of state school superintendents held in Washington, to explain the nature and purpose of the innovation of which he was in charge. The strong personality of the man impressed all who listened to his impassioned pleadings and aroused a contagious enthusiasm, so that even before the showing of results at the centennial in 1876, the fundamental principles of the movement were well known throughout the educational centers of the public school systems of the several states of the union.

THE CULTURE OF THE ÆSTHETIC FACULTIES FORMS NO FEATURE
IN MOST OF THE MANUAL TRAINING SCHOOL COURSES

This failure of the art idea in the manual training schools is so evident that some of those who started enthusiastically with the industrial art drawing movement, but were led away by the more sudden popularity of the industrial training movement to the hearty indorsement and support of the latter, begin to realize the evil they have helped to bring upon the most hopeful educational movement ever begun in these United States, and feebly point to a single manual training school in which — thanks to the fact that the superintendent of that city was once thoroughly in touch with Walter Smith, and had mastered the underlying principles of art training which inspired the teachings of that great master — some reachings out for æsthetic culture are indicated, as the ground for their hope that in the future, art training in manual training schools "must come as a necessity!" So, for ages, men have pointed forward to some anticipated millenium!

Neither in the theories, wishes or methods of the people who most actively advocate the manual training movement can the present writer see promise of any valuable development or training of the æsthetic nature of the public school children of the United States.

"The 'industrial training' and 'manual training school advocates are entitled to much credit for what they have accomplished, and there is much of value in the work they seek to do; but there is no evidence that they comprehend, or desire, any such art training as Messrs. Philbrick, Perkins, Smith, and their wise and enthusiastic coadjutors, hoped to add to the educational forces of America." * * *

'Had these three men been spared to instruct and to inspire, it seems possible that the hopes they aroused might have met fruition." * * *

"The prolonged study of these schools, as well as of the arguments of manual training advocates, incident to the preparation of this volume, has led to the reluctant conclusion that, however desirable the development of art among the American people may be, no such development is directly, or indirectly, to be anticipated from the efforts of the advocates of industrial education; while the methods of the manual training schools are, of necessity, mostly occupied with the kind of drawing specially adapted to mechanical processes."

" It is to be remembered that Professor Woodward, the foremost advocate of the manual training school, has never made any claim for it on the ground that it was an art training school. He bases the claims of this class of schools on far other grounds. It is rather to those who began as advocates of 'industrial art training,' and who, perhaps, finding 'industrial training' more immediately popular, and seeing that it was the outcome of the first movement, hoped to blend the two, that any artistic claim for the latter movement is to be attributed."

" In the early chapters of the present volume it was argued that the two ideals and methods were by no means incompatible, nor is there any insurmountable reason why they should be; but it remains that, almost without exception, the training in these schools under the influence of the industrial education ideals, is away from art, and more and more towards mechanics; while the advocates seem long since to have forgotten that there was ever any idea of introducing any art training in the public schools,— the drawing they would have taught is practical, mechanical. All this is good, excellent for the purpose sought, but it is *not*, and has nothing to do with, 'industrial' or any other 'art.' "

THE SCOPE OF THE INDUSTRIAL EDUCATION MOVEMENT

The industrial education movement is far more wide embracing in its scope, than would be implied by the present prominence of the manual training school feature; it includes the girls, as well as the boys; it considers the needs of children in the remote country schools, no less than the wants of those in the crowded cities; it is busy with the problem of a logical system of training, beginning with the kindergarten and ending only with the high schools. It is a vital movement full of interest and of enthusiasm, and has drawn to its support wide-awake educators all over the land. It has also aroused great interest on the part of the public, and some outspoken advocates, inexperienced in the practical work of education, have in their enthusiasm, made many statements in regard to existing methods of education which are fairly open to criticism.

As stated, the general awakening of interest in the educational industrial possibilities caused by the rapid extension of the movement for the adoption of drawing as one of the required studies in all public elementary schools, had a marked tendency to eliminate the art idea. So little was the knowledge of, or interest in, art in any community, that the first advocates of drawing, though, as has here been clearly indicated, they valued the study chiefly for its relation to the arts, spoke to the public mostly of the industrial value of drawing, seeking thereby to recommend the new study.

The enthusiastic efforts of the advocates of drawing, the remarkable personal influence of Professor Walter Smith, the showing made at the centennial exposition of the successful work of the students of the Boston normal art school, and of the work of the Boston school children, gave a great impetus to the development and spread of the industrial art movement throughout the country, so that it seemed to be on the point of complete success, and of being adopted in all the public schools of the states. Suddenly, however, a change came. After twelve years of devotion to his important work of supervision, Mr. Smith resigned as art director of the state, as principal of the normal art school, and as in charge of the art training of the Boston public schools, and returned to England.

The marked change that followed in the direction of the educational movement from industrial art training to manual training and the teaching of trades, was doubtless somewhat to the general indifference to art felt by a large part of the public; but, more largely, to the failure of intelligent support of the art ideal, due in part, as suggested, to the return of Walter Smith to England — driven out by antagonisms, but in a greater degree to the almost simultaneous removal by death of the able early promoters of an art pur-

pose in the study.   To the concurrence of these lamentable
events may fairly be attributed the almost total eclipse of any
art idea in the study of drawing which for a time prevailed.

At this period the purpose which inspired the early promoters of the new study of drawing seemed hopelessly lost
in the new-born zeal for mechanical drawing as relating only
to "manual training"— to making things; and to the pre-
posterous, though popular, idea of graduating from the public schools boys of fourteen and eighteen years of age as
thoroughly-trained expert mechanics!

The simplest principles of educational and technical
industrial standards are alike violated by such claims and
endeavors.

Since statistics show that the vast majority of children in
the United States remain in the public schools only five
years — the period varying somewhere between the ages of
five and of twenty years — no argument seems called for to
demonstrate that the skill requisite for a competent, self-
supporting mechanic can hardly be acquired during those
few years of youthful, immature development.

The not uncommon exhibition of steam engines and other
complex machines, as having been designed and built in the
school, by boys of only fifteen or eighteen years of age,
needs no comment.

The claim that the simple mechanical processes can be
taught; some knowledge of the use of tools acquired, and
much given that will serve to prepare the boy for the subsequent technical training which is essential to his success, but
suitable only to one of added years and maturer physical
development, is perfectly tenable; so that manual training, as
elementary preparation for the technical study of future life-
work, or, as giving some desirable general knowledge of
mechanics, is to be warmly commended and encouraged, but
it is not to be taught as antagonistic to the elementary instruction in drawing, the alphabet of art as well as of mechanics.

It is an evidence of the common sense of the community
that such waves of feverish interest in educational experi-

ments are but of short duration.   Inevitably somewhat later
the new study, which at first was to revolutionize all former
educational theories and methods, gravitates to its proper
place in the general scheme of education, according to its
proved relative importance.   This was strikingly illustrated
a few years since, in the schedule of studies in the Massachusetts institute of technology.   When manual training
was there first introduced a large workshop in a separate
building was given to it, and pages in the catalogue were
devoted to the outline courses of the new study, but, in a
year or two, the grand common sense of General Francis A.
Walker, while retaining it in the institute, had quietly relegated it alike in building and catalogue, to its rightful
position as a subordinate feature among the varied courses
taught in that practical university.

So, within the past few years, a similar reaction has come
in connection with the public schools, and the art quality of
drawing is again recognized.

It is to be hoped that the essential difference between the
educational value of a study as a method of developing and
stimulating the intellect, and that simple iteration of thought
and movement, essential to the production of technical
facility in mechanical operations, will not again be lost sight
of by the educators or the public.

OFFICIAL STATISTICS SHOWING THE GROWTH AND PRESENT CON-
DITION OF MANUAL TRAINING IN THE UNITED STATES

In the statistical tables of the annual reports of the commissioner of education, the facts in relation to the various
public schools, and educational institutions of the country,
are carefully tabulated ; and occasionally, at intervals of
several years, full chapters of the report are given to the
consideration of one or more of the several classes of educational institutions.

In the annual report for 1893–94, issued in 1896, were
published full tables of statistics of manual and industrial
training in city public schools, and other educational institutions, in the United States.

These comprised full details of courses given in the public schools of ninety-five towns and cities; in forty-nine institutions of collegiate grade; in nineteen normal schools, and in seventeen manual training schools. In addition, there were the industrial statistics of sixty-three colored schools; fifty-five schools for the deaf; twenty-six schools for the blind; nineteen for the feeble minded; fifty-three reform schools; eighteen charity schools; six trade schools, and twenty-seven United States Indian schools. This report also contains a most interesting chapter on "the rise and progress of manual training," by C. M. Woodward, director of the manual training school of Washington university, of St. Louis, Missouri. (Volume I, pages 877–949.)

In the annual report for 1895–96, issued in 1897, were published several chapters relating to "industrial" and "industrial art" training. Chapter xvi, relating to "typical institutions offering manual or industrial training," (see vol. II, pages 1001–1152), treats of city public schools in eighteen leading cities; manual training schools in five cities; trade schools, six; normal schools, five; schools for defective classes, eight; schools for colored pupils, five; miscellaneous institutions, many of them endowed, sixteen. These represent all varieties of typical training schools, and of schools in which industrial training is an important feature.

In the annual report for 1896–97, issued in 1898, Statistics of schools for manual and industrial training (vol. 2, pp. 2279–2294) are given for public schools in ninety-nine cities, and in 359 institutions, other than city schools. There are sixty-six manual training schools and twenty-four industrial schools for Indian children.

In the annual report for 1897–98, issued in 1899, chapter xlviii, volume 2, is given to detailed statistics of manual and industrial training, References are given to similar statistics in the several annual reports from 1888–89.

Statistics for 1897–98 are given for 114 manual training schools, an increase of 15 over the preceding year. Of these, 24 are industrial schools for Indian children.

No attempt was made to collect statistics of manual training given in other schools. Such statistics were given in the report for 1893–94.

The following statistics show the steady growth of this training in public schools : In 1890, reports were given of 37 cities ; in 1894, of 93 cities ; in 1896, of 121 cities, and in 1898 there were 146 cities in the schools of which manual training was taught.

A BRIEF SUMMARY OF THE INTENT OF THE VOLUMES ALREADY ISSUED OF THE ART AND INDUSTRY REPORT

As reference has been freely made to the "special report on art and industry," issued by congress, and the United States bureau of education, I briefly recapitulate here the main divisions of the three first volumes, before coming to the general consideration of the present condition of the country, both in its art development and in its facilities for education in art, and in the technical application both of art and of science to industry, which precedes the main body of part IV, the final volume of the report yet issued.

The first two volumes of this report dealt mostly with the elementary public schools — these last two with the artistic and industrial training in other schools, and classes, for older pupils, and are given more directly to the methods of industrial training, though, in each volume, the art ideal, which inspired the Boston promoters of the new education, is ever kept in view, and it is to be hoped may not seem to have been neglected. This was the absolutely new element added to our American methods of public education, an element to us of priceless value. The universal Yankee Nation had shown no inferiority in the application of mechanical invention to industry, and there seemed no especial need of increasing educational activity in that direction. "Necessity" had, early in New England, proved a prolific "mother of invention," and the increasing peoples in other parts of the land showed no falling off in mechanical ingenuity. It was far otherwise in all matters relating to the fine arts.

As the first volume of the art and industry report was given to an account of the introduction of drawing into the regular courses of study in the public schools, so the second volume was devoted to a similar account of the widespread movement for putting "manual training" and industrial education in its various forms in the public elementary schools.

The third volume was given to an account of the voluntary associations, by mechanics and others, in the several cities and towns, for mutual improvement by means of reading rooms, libraries, courses of lectures, etc., and which, also, in most instances, began with elementary common schools and, as rapidly as public free schools were established by the community, grew into special, technical trade schools, in some cases of a high technical or artistic character; as new educational demands, not as yet met by the public schools, were recognized.   These furnish a most interesting class of schools, varying with the local needs of their communities, and are admirable examples of the practical working out of educational and industrial problems by a voluntary effort of self-help by independent citizens.

These were, in many places, eventually supplemented by the efforts of liberal individual citizens, who founded schools and institutions with similar purpose, namely, to give to youth, otherwise unable to secure them, educational facilities to fit them to become self-supporting citizens.   This ever-growing throng of public benefactors, led by McDonough, Franklin and Girard, nigh a century ago, is one of the proudest glories of the American people.   Space fails here to record the names already inscribed on this golden book of fame.   Accounts of a number of these admirable institutions, mostly of superior technical character, are given in volume three.

In the fourth volume, the last of the series as yet issued, accounts are given of the typical manual training schools; of five leading technical mechanical schools; of some trade schools; of a most interesting educational experiment under-

taken by the Baltimore and Ohio railway under the auspices
of President Robert Garrett, in 1885–87; and of the schools
of science and engineering of the land grant colleges of
agriculture and the mechanic arts. No attempt is made,
however, to give a complete view of these latter institutions; the accounts of these colleges are limited to notices
of those departments which give instruction in drawing and
the industrial arts.[1]

These two volumes thus continue the accounts of the
development of industrial art education, begun in part I, by
the history of the introduction of the study of drawing in
the public schools and continued in part II, by accounts of
the surprisingly rapid development of manual training, as a
part of public school education in the United States. A
phase of educational activity and enthusiasm which, for a
season, seemed to threaten the extinction of any idea of
artistic development; and to substitute for the æsthetic culture of the youthful mind, simply a certain amount of manual
dexterity in the manipulation of mere mechanical movements, with a limited training in the elements of common
industries. All of these practical bits of manual training
are useful in their turn, but the sum of this training furnishes but a pitiful substitute, as an element of education,
for that æsthetic industrial art training which those far-see-
ing educators, Walter Smith, John D. Philbrick, and Charles
C. Perkins, so successfully began in Boston in 1870.

At that era it was evident to all intelligent observers that
the one element absolutely lacking in all American education
was the æsthetic. Art as an essential feature of education
was unknown. It is true that the literary arts, poetry and
oratory, received some little attention in the higher institutions, and that instruction in elementary music was not wholly
neglected in the public schools; but, so far from any attempt
to give even the most cursory knowledge of the graphic
and plastic arts, being made generally in the higher educa-

---

[1] For current statistics of these colleges see latest annual reports issued by the
United States commissioner of education.

tional institutions of the country, they were simply ignored, while æsthetics were only thought of as forming a subordinate branch of metaphysics.

This absence of any knowledge of, or training in, the fine arts, held true in all American public educational institutions, from the district school to the college. There were then no true universities, though several small but ambitious colleges were incumbered by the grandiose title.

While this statement as to the absence of any general opportunity for seeing examples of the fine arts, and as to the lack of any attempt to give a knowledge of the arts of painting and sculpture in the public schools and other public educational institutions in the United States is not exaggerated, it is nevertheless true that the fine arts were not wholly ignored in America, and that, as early as the latter part of the 18th century, the names of some few American artists were known to the world, while early in the present century efforts were made by a few people of culture to establish art centres in several of our cities. Facts relating to the early history of these sporadic efforts to form art academies and public art collections, have been most eagerly sought and collected for the present work. These interesting histories will be given in parts V and VI of this report. In view of the later developments, especially of the growing general interest in, and knowledge of, art matters since the beginning of the movement in Boston for teaching elementary drawing in the public schools, and the vastly greater impulse to public interest in everything pertaining to art, given in turn by the holding of the Centennial and the Columbian expositions, the story of these early efforts acquires added interest. To the self-denying efforts of a few artists and art enthusiasts, were suddenly added the enthusiasm and the active support of an awakened public.

In view of the many collections of casts of antique sculpture, and of the private and public art galleries, rich in examples of the work of the leading modern artists of Europe and America, which, as the result of this "awakening," are

to be found in the United States in the year 1898, and of
the special art classes and art schools now in our cities, with
the very general interest shown in the literature of the arts,
and, further, in view of the present easy access by the public
to the before-mentioned art collections, the statement concerning the scarcity in America, as recently as in 1870, of
similar opportunities, would seem almost incredible.   It is,
nevertheless, the fact that, at that date, there were but four
or five small collections of casts of classic sculpture in the
whole country.   Boston, New Haven, New York, Philadelphia and Washington, had each a few examples of such
casts ; but all the casts of sculpture then in the country, both
in public and private possession, would not equal in numbers or value, the casts now possessed by the leading art
museum in any one of these cities ; while in towns, cities,
and colleges, all over the land, are to be found valuable and
interesting collections of casts and paintings.

Two statistical tables in part I of this report, show clearly
the poverty of this nation in public art collections, and in
opportunities for learning art, as recently as 1873.

There were then but eight colleges which gave any instruction whatever in art, or that had any collections of art works,
while there were but five public art museums in the whole
land.   (See tables on pages 502–507 ; part I of this report.)

The Centennial exposition in Philadelphia, in 1876, was
a revelation to the American people, not only of the glory
of the graphic and plastic arts, as shown by the world's
great living artists, sculptors and painters ; but, also, of the
variety and beauty imparted to articles of usefulness and
ornament by the wonderfully artistic weavers, potters, and
metal-workers of the Orient, and by the skilled art workers
of Europe.

The impulse then given to public interest to art, in
America, may perhaps be most readily realized by a glance
at the table of statistics of institutions giving art instruction, and of the public art museums, existing in the United
States in 1883, given in part I of this report.   (See part I,

pages 385–411.)   Thirty-seven institutions, which give some
form of art instruction, and thirty museums of art, are
recorded in these tables,— certainly a remarkable increase
in the opportunities for art culture provided for the public
to have been effected in the short time of ten years!

The increase of such opportunities since 1883, by the
opening to the public of similar facilities for art culture,
both by the founding of public art galleries, the making of
private collections of art, and the general dissemination
of information on all matters relating to the arts, by the
press, and by lectures and addresses, have been no less
remarkable, stimulated as all this interest has been by the
holding of the exhibition in Chicago, in 1892–93; for,
wonderful as were the revelations of the Centennial, to the
public of 1876, the marvellous showing of the Columbian
exhibition, or world's fair, at Chicago, in 1892–93, completely overshadowed them.

In this latter exhibition of the world's industries and arts,
was shown not only the striking advances made since 1876,
by all the world, in every field of human activity, knowledge and enterprise, in art and industry; but, also, more
impressively if possible,— at any rate more significant educationally,— than these myriad treasures from all the earth, was
the revelation of the marvellous beauty of that white city
by the inland sea; with its classic peristyle, worthy of the
Athens of Pericles and Phidias; its lofty pillared fronts
and swelling domes — its vast palaces stretching in seeming endless procession.   The beautiful transitory treasure
houses America had built for the world's richest offerings!
These stately structures — which filled every beholder with
wonder and delight — proclaimed to the world that, in the
intervening years following the Centennial, the young nation
of the west had given birth to a race of great builders —
architects, sculptors, painters and decorators, worthy to rank
with the world's worthiest!

As the American architects had, as a body, early undertaken to secure thorough training in that art, for the young

men aspiring to enter their profession, this demonstration of
the grand results of thorough artistic training in architecture
and its kindred arts was in the nature of a triumphal verdict
in favor of definite education — of special training — in art,
as well as in science, or in the so-called " learned professions."

Thus, while these temporary buildings by their variety,
fitness and beauty of proportion, won the admiration of all
beholders, they were, in fact, but a great object lesson, illustrating on a gigantic scale what education in architecture,
art and artistic decoration could effect.

The noble building of the Boston public library, since
erected, and the stately marble palace of the National
library, so recently opened in Washington, are enduring
monuments, showing what the art of American architects,
builders, sculptors and painters can accomplish, in these
closing years of the nineteenth century, in the construction
and adornment of a great public library.

The exterior walls and sculptures of the National library,
the interior halls and grand stairways, and, above all, the profusion, variety and general excellence of the sculptured and
pictorial art works enriching walls and ceilings within, remind
us that we are, even now, in this nineteenth century, living in
the years of that " renaissance " which did not pass away, as
we once thought, with the passing of Angelo, Raphael, De
Vinci, and their peers, but which is still vital with inspiration,
so that here, on this to them unknown continent, opportunities are beginning for the future art masters of the world.
When Hunt, painted his two great allegorical pictures on
the walls of the legislative chamber in the state capitol
at Albany, that great artist " builded better than he knew,"
though, alas ! his own works so quickly passes ; for, by that
single precedent, he opened up all wall spaces of public
buildings to the future artists of America ; so that hereafter,
in this land, it shall be held — just as it was in Europe centuries ago — that the walls and ceilings of all palaces,
churches, and other public buildings are to be considered
but as the durable canvass of the painters.

That "rebirth" of the past, which came with the discovery of a few of the art wonders of Greece, occurring almost simultaneously with the regaining of some of the intellectual glories of Greece and Rome, in the unearthing of a few manuscripts which gave to us moderns a glimpse of their glorious intellectual triumphs — as yet unsurpassed and seemingly unsurpassable — gave to our conception of the capacity of the human intellect a new ideal, and woke the world to life!

What the wonders of the classic age, in art and literature, must have been, we can faintly imagine, contemplating the works of the intellectual and artistic giants of Italy in the middle ages, who sprang into being at the magic call of a few scattered fragments of the words and works of the mightier ancients; just as, in Holy Writ, we are told, the chance touch of the bones of the prophet Elisha woke the dead to life!

So, to-day, as Homer, Aeschylus, Demosthenes, Aristotle and Plato, dominate the world of letters in poetry, eloquence and philosophy, Phidias, Ictinus, Appelles, and their compeers, lead the worshippers of art.

In art, in our own day, have been repeated similar discoveries to those which in literature, four centuries ago, aroused to new activities the mind of Europe; for the revelations of Etruscan tombs, the patient explorations by Layard, Schliemann and Di Cesnola, the unearthing of the terra cotta figurines in Tanagra, the later work by English and American enthusiastic scholars in Greece, in these very days, have brought home to us moderns a comprehension of the vitality of classic art; which, contrary to our earlier impressions, we now find to have been busied not only with the ideal images of the Olympian divinities, but also with the every-day life of the people, all testifying to the solidarity of the human race; for, quickened by the life-giving touch of their artists in those far-off centuries, the little figurines of the graceful maidens of Tanagra, reveal, in their unconscious attitudes, the same love of dress, the same delight in free movement and flowing robes, in short, the same irrepressible joy in life, and the same marvelous beauty of youth, which meets us to-day on every hand, a-foot or a-wheel, in the blushing maidens of 16 years in this fair land, the unknown "ultima thule" of the ancients! So past and present meet and blend, taking no thought of the thousand intervening years! Here to-day, the thought, the art, of Athens and Rome, shape our thoughts and arts; so that we, consciously or unconsciously, are the children of that elder civilization.

The most recent illustration of this influence of classic examples upon our modern American art ideals, to which reference has been made, occurs among the buildings of the exposition held in Nashville, Tennessee, in this summer of 1897, where the crowning architectural charm is found in the striking restoration of the Parthenon of Athens, which is the model taken for the art building of the exposition. This reproduction is spoken of as full of grandeur and beauty.

It is also remarked that the government building erected for showing the governmental exhibits, has, fortunately, been modelled after the Chicago exhibition art building; so that, instead of being externally, as was the one at Chicago, a hideous enormity, in contrast with the artistic buildings surrounding it, this copy in little, of the beautiful construction designed by Richard M. Hunt for the art building of Chicago, is not out of harmony even when brought into contrast with the world renowned *chef d'œuvre* of Ictinus and Phidias.

This is all the more to be rejoiced in, because it began to seem that, under the stress for room in our modern cities, all ideas of beauty in architecture must, perforce, be wholly subordinated to the frenzy of piling stories upon stories, till the builders seemed to have no ideal other than that of the Tower of Babel.

This epidemic of many storied buildings has had a most unfortunate effect, in many instances, in degrading the architectural aspect of our older cities. Perhaps some of the

most striking examples of this incidental evil, are to be
found in the city of New York, where the ever beautiful old
familiar landmark of Trinity church steeple has been elimi-
nated from the once attractive view of the city as seen from
the bay. In addition to this misfortune must be reckoned
the recent belittling of that charming example of palace
architecture, the New York city hall, formerly so well shown
standing as it did in the ample open square given to it in
the heart of the town, now, seeming as if at the bottom of
some mountain valley, towered over by the clustering cliff-
like business buildings that crowd about the square, shutting
out all views save of their own precipitous walls.

In Washington, an impertinent modern apartment house,
towering in apparent emulation of the Washington monu-
ment, obtrudes its awkward outlines and gigantic bulk in
every possible view of the capital city, once so beautiful as
seen from every point of vantage and uglifies it all.

In some, at least, of the cities of Europe, the observer
can hardly fail to notice that, while the residences and business buildings in the streets of the city may make no pre-
tence to any display of architecture — often being notice-
able rather by reason of excessive plainness — care has been
taken to secure for the public buildings of church or state
— the cathedral and the civic palace — ample space, where
no private erections could ever destroy the harmony of proportion, or impair the true architectural effect of the building.

In this country, notably in the very instance of the New
York city hall, this effect was supposedly secured by the
generation who built it only to be thrown away by a later
generation of ignoble or careless successors.

In the situation of the capitol building of the United
States in Washington, D. C., and in those of the state capitol buildings in Albany, New York; in Boston, Massachusetts; in Hartford, Connecticut; in Nashville, Tennessee,
and in many another state capital, the sites are commanding,

It is to be hoped that in the choice of the situation of the
new buildings of Columbia college and the new cathedral

on Morningside heights, New York city, the relative position of those several buildings have been so chosen as to be architecturally isolated, so that no such misfortunes can affect them, as have recently relegated Trinity church and the city hall to comparative obscurity.

If, hereafter, American towns and cities, take pains to secure ample room and effective positions for their chief architectural buildings, the lesson to be learned from the humiliating experience architecturally, of New York city, may not be without compensation.

In a republic, it seems eminently fitting that the powerful effects of great architecture should be reserved for the public buildings of church and state, rather than be lavished on the comparatively humble dwellings of private citizens, however wealthy, or personally powerful, they may chance to be ; for the individual passes, but the state remains.

In a country like ours, where, fortunately, there is no hereditary class, it is absolutely wasteful for any private citizens to build palaces for their residences, only to leave them to be enjoyed by strangers, as has been, and seemingly must continue to be, the history of many of the costly private dwellings built by ostentatious millionaires in the United States, during the past few decades.

It is well that this should be so. Great art is for all the people, and can no more be limited to a few, than can the blessed sunlight ; which floods alike the hut of the hind and the palace of the noble.

The present volume of this report, as well as the one immediately preceding, is mainly given rather to a consideration of the opportunities afforded in these United States, for acquiring technical industrial and scientific training, than to the facilities for acquiring knowledge of, and skill in, the so-called fine arts ; though, in view of the intimate connection which exists between the industrial and fine arts, and of the fact that much of the elementary training is essentially the same in both, the consideration of either is in place in each and every volume of this report ; though the given

volume may be mostly occupied with the other. It is with
this thought that the foregoing pages have been given to
the brief summary of the recent remarkable development of
the fine and decorative arts, in connection with the forward
movement in the architecture of public buildings, so strikingly illustrated in the recently erected library buildings, in
Boston and Washington. The just completed building of
the Chicago public library, though on a smaller scale than
the others, and, in further contrast, making larger use of
merely decorative marbles in wall surfaces than of the work
of the artist painters, is, nevertheless. unmistakably of the
renaissance period.

The wonderful wealth in decorative carvings and grandiose stairways, in the as yet uncompleted state capitol at
Albany, suggests some of the undesirable features of the
later renaissance, in which in the interiors, costliness of
material and work, seemed to take the place of artistic
inspiration; while the ostentatious piling up of costly stone
exteriors, suffocated all efforts of living art. A heathen
apotheosis of mere material wealth, against which gothic
art was a religious protest; and concerning which John
Ruskin has so earnestly and eloquently warned the men of
his own day. Coldly inhuman, these towering piles of quar-
ried stone, frowning above our city streets, seem as menac-
ing as hostile fortresses.

The grand marble stairway of the capitol building in
Albany, designed by Richardson, and said to be the most
beautiful and costly example of elaborate carved work in
the country, which has taken more than twelve years in its
construction, seems to repeat, in the lavish profusion of its
carving, something of the extravagance of the later renaissance. It is due, however, to the architects of this great
building, Messrs. Fuller, Eidlitz and H. H. Richardson, to
state that its exterior in nowise recalls the characteristics of
those ostentatious buildings referred to; while it is well to
remember that, if anywhere profusion of art decoration is
fitly employed, it is in enriching and dignifying the impor-

tant public buildings designed for the uses of the people. In considering this particular people's palace, all who love art must ever remember that it was in this building, as has already been here stated, that William M. Hunt, the great painter, set to the American artists and builders of our time the striking lesson of noble art decoration so fortunately followed in the great public library buildings just completed.

In the zeal of this new awakening on the part of American architects and their employers to a practical recognition of the value of art in the decoration of the interior wall surfaces of public buildings — the most recent examples of which I have instanced — it should not be forgotten that, decades before these later buildings were planned, those who had charge of the construction of the grand building of the nation's capitol at Washington had freely availed themselves of the works of the American painters of their day, beginning as early as 1837, to illustrate memorable and pivotal events in the history of the republic ; so that, on entering the grand rotunda, the visitors found themselves encircled by a series of large historical paintings, of a size in harmony with the colossal proportions of the encircling walls which supported the upspringing arches of the crowning dome ; while in the dome itself, in a blaze of allegory, dear to the heart of Italy, was given the Italian artist's conception of the great powers essential to the prosperity of a people, and, though diplomatically disguised in appellation, a glimpse of the crowning triumph of the nation in its latest terrible struggle for existence.   From the landing of Columbus to the coming of Lincoln,— he who runs may read ; in the paintings, the bas-reliefs and the encircling frieze, " *in tempera* "— (though little can be said in praise of the artistic excellence of the relievos and the frieze) — the dramatic events of the centuries which have resulted in giving to the world the republic of these United States of America.

Our legislators called not only on the painters, but also

summoned the sculptors, to the adornment of this, the chief
building of their country, and gradually important works by
Greenough, Powers, Crawford and Rogers were secured.
In addition to these works by native artists, the services of
Italian artists, as decorators, were largely availed of in the
halls, galleries and committee rooms of the building ; while
in the wings, occupied, respectively, by the legislative cham-
bers of the House of Representatives and the Senate, later
American artists have added many fine works illustrating
the history, or the scenery, of the country.

It has been a fashion with many writers, posing as art
critics, to speak contemptuously of the historical paintings
in the rotunda. However true their criticism may have
been, if comparison of these paintings with the *chef d'œuvres*
of the world's great artists — Titian, Tintoretto, Veronese,
Velasquez, Rubens, and other great art masters in historical
painting, either in their conception of the subject or mastery
of technique, are concerned ; it should not be forgotten, in
endeavoring to estimate the value of this art work to the
country, that, a half century or more ago, few American
citizens who entered that building had ever before had the
opportunity to look upon a fine work of art of any kind.
It followed, therefore, that the sight of that grand rotunda,
with its uplifting dome, its great paintings, was an event
never to be forgotten ; and the grandeur and inspiration of
the scene gave to many their first realization of the meaning,
the power, and the possibilities of art.

There have been American artists, before and since these
works were painted, who justly rank as artists far in advance
of Trumbull (though few have left works which can surpass in
brilliancy his small, jewel-like originals of these large paintings, long the pride of the Yale college art gallery), Weir,
Chapman, Vanderlyn, and Powell, the painters of the works
in the rotunda ; but it may well be questioned whether, before
1870, any other American artists have given to so many of
their fellow countrymen their first appreciation of something
of the glory of art !

A debt of gratitude is due to the legislators who author-ized and the artists who executed these works.

Nor, taken as a whole, are the art adornments of this, the noblest legislative building in the world, inferior to those of similar modern public buildings in European countries. Art in the early part of the nineteenth century, so far as shown in statuary on the exterior of buildings, was in nowise gen-erally superior to the grandiose sculptures by Persico, which stand in the east portico of the rotunda; while the group by Greenough is far superior to the ordinary statuary of that day. Nor, in painting, was Trumbull so greatly inferior to his master, West! In fact, the era of the reign of the fourth George of England, and his immediate successor, was, nowhere in Europe, memorable as illustrating the highest ideals of art. Early in this century America had, in Allston and Stuart, art masters equal to their contempo-raries of any other nations.

In view of this long-continued example of the possibilities of the artistic use of interior wall surfaces, as shown by the pictorial illustrations in the rotunda, of the history of the country, by well-known artists; and, also, by decorative paintings on minor wall spaces, which adorn the interiors of the nation's capitol building; the fact of the almost entire absence throughout this period of similar wall paintings and decorations in other civic public buildings in the land, as well as in churches, and private dwellings, so that the paintings by Hunt, in the state house, at Albany, can be accurately designated as marking the definite beginning of the present era of the general artistic interior decoration of buildings, civic and religious, public and private; — fur-nishes a convincing proof of the utter lack, on the part of the American people as a whole, of any general knowledge and appreciation of the value of art in its application to the buildings, and the furnishings, of life, prior to the holding of the Centennial exposition, in Philadelphia, in 1876.

It may well be urged that, up to that time, this busy peo-ple were too fully occupied in completing the physical conquest of a vast territory, in subduing forests, bridging streams and opening virgin prairies to cultivation ; in providing for the transportation, housing, and feeding of the ever-surging incoming tides of eager emigrants ; were in short too busy in their imperative task of *making* history ; to find time, or thought, for its artistic record ! When, at last, they found time to pause and study the lessons of that Centennial, they proved apt students ; as the Columbian exposition has shown !

Yet notwithstanding this later surprising and artistic evolution of the American people, so widespread and rapid has been the development of technical training in its application to industrial and fine art manufactures throughout the leading countries of the continent of Europe, and also, though begun later, in Great Britain, that, although the development in elementary artistic training and its facilities for the acquisition of advanced instruction in these arts, in the United States, has been wonderfully increased since the beginning in Boston, in 1870, of the movement for school instruction in drawing, and the holding of the Centennial exposition in Philadelphia, in 1876 ; still, in the opportunities offered for the training of skilled youthful workers in the industries of applied art, the United States, to-day,— in view of the persistent efforts and great advances made during the past twenty years, by European countries, in providing such educational facilities,— are relatively, hardly in any better position to contest successfully with the products of the trained workers of Europe, than they were in 1870.

Nevertheless the efforts made in this country by leading educators, and by liberal patrons of artistic and technical education, have been notable, and most worthy of honor ; while the great advance since the Centennial, as shown in the art qualities of American manufactures, in jewelry, in glass, in art fabrics in silk, in woolen and in cotton, as well as in architecture, and in all material pertaining to the decorative arts, has been simply marvellous.

So far, also, as affording requisite opportunities for acquiring thorough training in the fine arts of painting, sculpture and architecture, the few art schools in the United States compare most favorably with those of the older countries; so that it is no longer essential — though it may often be, for other reasons, desirable — for the ambitious young painter, sculptor or architect, to exile himself in order to obtain needed opportunities for instruction in those several arts.   Nor are our leading technical schools of science inferior in equipment or in quality of instruction to the similar schools in Europe.   These schools in the United States are, however, so few in number, in proportion to our increasing population as compared to the number and variety of those offered to the citizens of the leading art industrial European countries of Germany, Switzerland, Belgium and France — not to mention Great Britain, Austria, Italy and Russia — that the inadequacy in numbers of our schools for training the captains of industry, not to mention those merely technical trade schools designed for creating a force of trained workers, impresses itself painfully upon the investigator in these fields.

With the increasing knowledge of the forces of nature acquired by the patient investigations continually carried on by scientists of every class, in chemistry, in geology, in natural philosophy, in mining, both in the methods of mechanical operations and in the reduction of ores; in short, in the general application of the discoveries of science throughout the various realms of nature, to the needs of man, which so constantly revolutionize former methods and create ever new demands; for example, in the endeavor to secure the economic production of electricity and to contrive the best methods for its application to human uses, not to speak of the similar needs in other fields, the demand on the community for the founding of institutions for giving thorough training in these latest discoveries of science is imperative.

In all these ever-recurring demands for the invention and application of methods by which to make these discoveries of science available in the industries of life, a knowledge of,

and practical facility in, the art ot   mechanical drawing,"
becomes absolutely indispensable; consequently, this elementary branch of industrial art clearly forms an essential
factor in modern industrial education, and, of necessity,
holds place in all the elementary and higher schools of technology; hence, though its relation to the so-called "high
arts" may at times seem somewhat remote, its claim to a
place in this report on art and industry is unquestionable.

To close this sketch of the beginning and progressive
development of this important educational movement, without making honorable mention by name of some, at least,
of the many enthusiastic supporters and earnest co-workers
with the three men who were literally the pioneers in this
momentous experiment, is to leave it incomplete, indeed.
To give here a complete list of the many educators and
lovers of beauty who gave it warm welcome; of the modest teachers who shrank from no labor in the effort to fit
themselves to teach the unfamiliar lessons, were an impossible task.   Great effort was made, however, by the writer
in the volumes of the art and industry report, to secure
full record of the names of all workers for this special
branch of education.   It may be said, greatly to the credit
of our countrymen, that while there was at first, on the part
of many, great and freely outspoken opposition to the movement, yet very many of the acknowledged leaders in educational circles — state or city — school superintendents, with
professors in colleges and normal schools, gave instant and
hearty welcome to Walter Smith and his methods; that the
press generally gave support to the efforts to put both drawing and manual training in the schools, and that, as rapidly
as the purpose and methods of industrial drawing were generally known, that movement won for itself popular support,
while the movement for manual training in the schools was at
once heartily welcomed by the great majority of the people.

One movement, almost cotemporary, for promoting
instruction in the fine arts, both in the institutions of learning and in the community at large, met with cordial response

from many of the colleges and from numerous liberal citizens. As the result of generous gifts, public collections of casts from the antique became accessible in many institutions of learning and in many localities where, before 1870, they were absolutely unknown.

To patronize artists, and also to make art gifts to public museums and to colleges, became a fashion, so that great numbers of examples of the best modern art masters of Europe, are now in this country, either in the hands of private owners or in public art galleries. Meantime numbers of young American painters and sculptors are winning favor in Europe and America, while the art schools in this country are thronged with eager aspirants. Enough has been cited of American art accomplishment to convince us that one would no longer be justified in saying of this "era" of 1899, as was said of another era at the opening of this chapter, that "the one element absolutely lacking in all American education was the æsthetic!" Industrial art proves its worth to a country by its results, as shown in the industrial output. To record the amazing variety and exquisite charm of the countless productions of art work in metals, ceramics, and fabrics by Americans of *this* "era" would demand volumes.

DEPARTMENT OF EDUCATION

FOR THE

UNITED STATES COMMISSION TO THE PARIS EXPOSITION OF 1900

MONOGRAPHS ON EDUCATION

IN THE

UNITED STATES

EDITED BY

NICHOLAS MURRAY BUTLER

Professor of Philosophy and Education in Columbia University, New York

15

EDUCATION OF DEFECTIVES

BY

EDWARD ELLIS ALLEN

*Principal of the Pennsylvania Institution for the Instruction of the Blind,
Overbrook, Pennsylvania*

THIS MONOGRAPH IS CONTRIBUTED TO THE UNITED STATES EDUCATIONAL EXHIBIT BY THE
STATE OF NEW YORK

EDUCATION OF DEFECTIVES

Systematic care of the defective classes began in America in 1815, when a young theological student, Thomas Hopkins Gallaudet, started for Europe to study methods of teaching the deaf and dumb. A school for this class was opened in 1817, one for the blind in 1831, and one for the feeble-minded in 1845 — practically fifteen years apart. In each case the first schools were in New England, the second in New York, the third in Pennsylvania; and these schools followed one another quickly. All started in the face of more or less distrust as to their feasibility. At first all were experimental, being started through private initiative. A few pupils were taught and exhibited before the amazed public, when in the case of the deaf and the blind private funds in abundance were contributed and the schools quickly established as private corporations. In the case of the feeble-minded the first school to be incorporated was a public organization — that is, it was supported by the state. Before 1822 the state had not been educated to the point of supporting schools for the special classes, but by 1848 it was ready to see its duty towards even the idiotic, though wealthy people were by no means prepared to contribute directly to schools for them.

The three states named having led the way, the movement spread quickly into Ohio, Kentucky, Virginia and Illinois — in almost identical order for each special class. Here, however, the schools for the three classes arose as state institutions. It had become an accepted part of public policy for the state to provide a means of education for all her children. The superintendents of the early schools for the deaf and dumb were generally clergymen; those of the blind and the idiotic, generally physicians. The institutions were necessarily boarding schools; and the early ones were

established as a rule in or near the state capitals, chiefly
that their achievements might be kept before the members
of the legislatures, on whose practical sympathy the continuance of the schools usually depended.

The large private or semi-public institutions are confined
to the eastern states, where the movement began. Their
support comes chiefly from private bequests and the interest
on invested endowment funds. All, however, receive what
is termed state aid, and all make annual report to the state
legislatures, to the commissioners of public charities or of
public education, as the case may be. All these institutions
are governed by honorary boards of trustees or managers,
who appoint the superintendent or principal. In the semi-
public organization the managers form a self-appointing,
close corporation; in the public, they are appointed usually
by the state governor, by whom they may also be removed.

The semi-public institutions are usually well endowed.
Their expenditures are, therefore, not limited by legislative
grant; and, moreover, these institutions are free from political interference, an interference which, in the case of several
of the state organizations, has seriously affected from time
to time the efficiency of the institutions themselves. As a
rule, the institution plants are large and well equipped.
Even when within the built-up cities the buildings are surrounded with ample lawns and playgrounds. The appropriations of money are generous, whether the schools are
public or semi-public. The earlier institutions were built
on the congregate plan; the later and those that have
been rebuilt have generally adopted the segregate or cottage plan.

The pupils are not committed to these institutions, but
are admitted or rejected by the boards of trustees on the
recommendation of the superintendents.

The early institutions for all three classes of defectives
began purely as schools. And all those existing to-day,
except those for the feeble-minded, discharge or graduate
all pupils after these have completed the course of instruc-

tion. With the feeble-minded this plan was found to be inexpedient, for reasons which will be stated later.

A very recent movement, started by the instructors of the deaf, is the affiliation of the educators of the defective classes with those of the national education association. It is being more and more recognized that the line between a defective and normal child cannot be drawn hard and fast, and that many a child who appears dull and stupid in school is in some measure defective. Hence, these special schools afford fields of most helpful suggestion to teachers of ordinary children. All persons intending to make teaching a vocation should become acquainted with these schools and their methods.

It is interesting to note that systematic work for the deaf and dumb, the blind, and the feeble-minded began in France, and that to France America sent its early teachers to study methods and ascertain results.

THE DEAF

About the middle of the last century three schools for the deaf and dumb were opened in Europe, one in France, one in Germany, and one in Scotland. Though they sprang up at about the same time they were yet wholly independent in origin. In Paris the Abbé de l'Epée having observed two deaf-mute sisters conversing by means of gestures, seized upon the idea that in gesture language lay the secret of instructing the deaf and dumb. He therefore elaborated a system of gesture signs and made it the medium of instruction in the school which he started. Heinicke in Dresden and Braidwood in Edinburg simply adopted articulate speech as the language of man and taught their pupils through it, requiring them to speak and read the lips of others. Thus arose the two important methods of deaf-mute instruction.

Reports of the successes, chiefly in the British school, having reached America, several parents of deaf-mutes sent their children to Scotland to be educated. These deaf children returned no longer as mutes; they were able to converse readily by speaking and lip reading.   One of these parents was so delighted with his boy's schooling that he published a book in London and wrote articles for the New England periodicals, with the intention of arousing interest in the new work.   This man also took steps to ascertain the number of deaf-mutes in Massachusetts.   Another man in Virginia, some of whose relatives had attended Braidwood's school, even opened a little school for deaf and dumb pupils in his state, employing as its teacher one of the Braidwood family, who had come to America for the purpose of continuing in the profession of his family here.   This was in 1812. The school was the first of its kind started in America. However, it was soon given up, as was a similar effort in New York, where a clergyman undertook to instruct several deaf children whom he found in an almshouse.

Though the events above touched upon seemed to result in little, they yet had great effect in directing intelligent attention to this field of work.   They constitute its preliminary stages.

It happened in Hartford, Conn., that there was a physician, one of whose little daughters had become deaf.   Why could not this child be educated as well as her hearing sisters? With this thought he spent some eight years in agitating the question of starting a school for deaf children.   In 1815 money enough was raised in a single day to defray the expenses of sending a teacher abroad to study methods.   A young graduate of Yale college and of a theological seminary was chosen as the teacher to go.   This was Thomas Hopkins Gallaudet, who was destined to become the founder of deaf-mute instruction in America.

Of course he went to Great Britain.   He proposed to study the only method that Americans knew about.   But the doors of the British schools were closed to him.   He found the science and art of teaching the deaf regarded as a business monopoly, whereas he had expected to find it conducted from his own motive of philanthropy.   After wandering about there for nine months he gave up hope of acquiring the Braidwood method and accepted an invitation to study methods at the Paris school.   At this school he spent the three remaining months of the year, a time far too short in which to acquire the special language of gesture signs.   Hence, he induced a deaf-mute, who was teaching in the school, to accompany him to America.   This man was the brilliant and accomplished Laurent Clerk, who became an engine of power for establishing schools for deaf-mutes in our country.   Thus was the French method or the sign-language method brought to America.   It was improved and further systematized by our early teachers and in this form was the basis of instruction in all our schools for half a century.

During the absence of Dr. Gallaudet, influential men of Hartford had secured from the state legislature the incorporation of the Connecticut asylum for the education and instruction of deaf and dumb persons.   Upon his return he and Mr. Clerk traveled for eight months among prominent cities in behalf of the cause of the deaf.   The exhibition of Laurent Clerk alone helped the cause as nothing else could have done.   On April 15, 1817, school work began at Hartford with seven pupils.   During the year 33 pupils came. This was the first permanent school in the country.   While in other countries similar schools had no reliable basis of support, the founders of our schools immediately established theirs on a permanent basis.   Private aid was necessary at first, but no sooner had the feasibility of the work been shown than public moneys were granted.

In this year the Connecticut asylum changed its name to the American asylum at Hartford for the education and instruction of the deaf and dumb ; for it was then supposed that one school could accommodate for many years all the pupils of the country who would attend school.   But interest in the schooling of deaf-mutes had been aroused in other places.   In 1818 a school was opened in New York under a teacher from Hartford ; and in Philadelphia, where Dr. Gallaudet and Mr. Clerk had gone to obtain aid for the Hartford school, an humble storekeeper by the name of Seixas began to teach, in 1819, a little class of deaf pupils, and he was so successful that an institution was organized in 1820 with Seixas as first teacher and principal. In a very few months he was succeeded by a permanent principal from Hartford. Back in 1819 Massachusetts had provided an appropriation for the education of 20 indigent pupils at Hartford, and in 1825 New Hampshire and Vermont adopted the same policy. " Other states soon followed this good example. Thus, through the efforts of the founders of this [the Hartford] school, the humane, just and wise policy of educating deaf-mutes at the public expense was firmly established in this country, and has been adopted by almost every state in the union. In some of the western states means for the education of deaf-mutes are secured by constitutional provision. This has put the schools for deaf-mutes in the United States on a better basis, financially, than those in any other part of the world."[1]

Only two years after the founding of the Pennsylvania school, Kentucky followed with its institution, being the first to be supported by a state. The act establishing it limited the pupils at any one time to 25, and their term of instruction to three years. In fact limits of this kind are usually prescribed in all the early institutions. (The Illinois school now has 612 pupils, and the New York schools allow a term of 17 years.) The first principal of the Kentucky school went to Hartford for a year to study methods. Ohio and Virginia soon followed in the good work. Both received their first superintendents from Hartford. Thereafter institutions sprang up rapidly in the south and west, taking their early superintendents or teachers either from the parent school at Hartford or from one or another of the older schools.

In 1857 there was incorporated by the national congress the Columbia institution at Washington, D. C., which requires

_____
[1] Histories American schools for the Deaf.— American asylum, 1: 13.

special mention. Though originally intended as a school
where the deaf children of government beneficiaries could
be educated, circumstances of which not the least influential
was the energy of its principal, Dr. Edward M. Gallaudet,
son of the pioneer, soon brought about a change enabling
the institution to confer collegiate degrees. The institution
was then divided into two departments, the advanced department taking the name of the National deaf-mute college.
Thus, in 1864, America had taken a step "unprecedented
in the history of deaf-mute instruction."

Most of the deaf and dumb are either born deaf or
became so before acquiring language. They are dumb
because they are deaf, and without special instruction can
never know any but a gestural language. The pioneer educators of the deaf in this country were all "broad-minded
men of liberal education," and they set a high standard at
the outset for the work. A language of signs they saw
was the key to the instruction of their pupils, who, indeed,
were allowed so few years of schooling, that no time was to
be lost in laboring over the extraordinary difficulties of
teaching them speech. Moreover, these teachers saw with
great satisfaction the development of their pupils through
the language of signs.

This language is ideographic — "being readily expressive
of ideas and emotions," rather than of phraseology. Put
into words their order is entirely different from the natural
order, thus, " Let it be supposed that a girl has been seen by
a deaf-mute child to drop a cup of milk which she was carrying home. He would relate the incident in the following
order of sign words: Saw-I-girl-walk-cup-milk-carry-home-
drop." [1] The late superintendent of the Illinois institution,
Dr. Gillett, writes : " When reduced to a system they [signs]
form a convenient means of conveying to one mind the ideas
conceived by another, though not clothed in the language
in which a cultured mind expresses them. One addressed
in the sign language receives the idea and translates it into

[1] Encyclop. Brit. (9th ed.) Am. reprint— Art. Deaf and dumb.

English without any intimation of the phraseology in the mind of the speaker, so that a dozen persons familiar with the sign language, observing the gesticulations of a speaker, would each translate correctly the thoughts given forth, but no two of them would be in exactly the same phraseology. It is a concrete language, in which the expression of abstract ideas is exceedingly difficult."[1] As the ideas are given out chiefly by means of hand gestures, schools using the sign language as a means of instruction are said to follow or use the manual method.[2]

Among the manually-taught deaf this language early becomes the vernacular. As it is a language of living pictures, such deaf people think in pictures and dream in them. The sign language is said to be to the deaf what spoken language is to the hearing; and yet its use in the school room is deemed by many teachers extremely detrimental to the acquisition of the English language, and, therefore, unwise.

All our educators of the deaf agree that giving to their pupils the ability to use the English language is their chief end and aim. They differ widely, however, over the use of signs. The greater number believe a moderate use of them to be economical of time and extremely useful to the deaf in the acquisition of knowledge. There is a small but growing number who dispense with signs *in toto* just as soon as possible. These latter teach by the intuitive, direct or "English language method." They teach English by and through English, spoken, read and written.

It is extraordinarily difficult to get started by the oral or English language method. But teachers of this method claim that once well started their pupils advance more

---

[1] Gillett. Some notable benefactors of the deaf. Pp. 14–15.

[2] The simple sign for *cat* well illustrates the graphic nature of the language. In order to teach this sign, a sign teacher " would show the child a cat, if possible, or a picture of a cat, which would be recognized by the child. The next step would be to direct attention to the cat's whiskers, drawing the thumb and finger of each hand lightly over them. A similar motion with the thumb and finger of each hand above the teacher's upper lip at once becomes the sign for cat. The instructed deaf child will be expected to recall the object, cat, on seeing this conventional sign." Gordon. The difference between the two systems of teaching deaf-mute children the English language. Pp. 1–2.

logically, more surely, more precisely, and finally more swiftly than the pupils of those permitting the intervention of signs. Advocates of using the signs together with other means claim that the minds of most of their new pupils are sluggish from want of language to think in, and that they need to be aroused by the quickest method ; that their pupils have already lost too many years of youth, and that to cause them to lose more because of a theory is wrong and wicked. This school asserts that " A large percentage of the deaf under proper methods can obtain a very use-ful amount of speech and lip-reading, but [that] there is also a large percentage of them that would be greatly restricted in their mental development, if allowed no other means of instruction," and continues :

"We are striving to take the golden mean, placing first in importance mental development and a knowledge of written language, and adding thereto in the case of every child speech and lip-reading to the degree that his capacity and adaptability allow him to acquire them." [1]

And again, " For rapid and clear explanation, for testing the comprehension of the pupil, for lectures and religious instruction before large numbers of pupils, there is no other means equal in efficiency to the sign language. Its proper and conservative use always tends to mental development, saves time, and is the most efficient aid known in the acqui-sition of written and spoken language." [2]

The other school affirms that the two methods or systems are mutually exclusive, saying : " Of course no pupil can be taught under the intuitive and the sign method at the same time, and it is impossible to combine into one system a method which is dependent upon the 'sign' language at every stage of instruction with a method which dispenses absolutely with the 'sign' language at every stage in teach-ing the English language. In the 'sign-language' method instructors aim to teach the vernacular language through

---

[1] Third Biennial Report American school, p. 12.
[2] First Biennial Report American asylum, p. 17.

the intervention of signs, but their deaf-mute pupils acquire a mixture of natural signs, pantomime, conventional signs and finger spelling which becomes the habitual vehicle of thought and expression, wherever it is possible to use a gestural language, to the exclusion of the English language. The intuitive method dispenses entirely with the crutch of the 'sign-language' in the mastery of English."[1]

A form of the English language method, taught at the Rochester (N. Y.) institution, substitutes finger spelling for signs as these are used in manual schools, and is called the "manual alphabet method." Superintendent Westervelt says of it, " It is the principle of our method of instruction that the child has a right to receive instruction through that form of our language which he can understand most readily, with the least strain of attention, and the least diversion from the thought to the organ of its expression."[2]

So much for the rival methods, which, however, it is absolutely necessary to understand if we would comprehend the history of deaf-mute education in America.

The history of the rise of the oral method is interesting. As has been said, the manual method reigned supreme for the first fifty years of the work. In 1843, Horace Mann, secretary of the Massachusetts state board of education, and Dr. Howe, director of the Perkins institution for the blind in Boston, made a tour of Europe. In his next annual report Horace Mann praised the oral method as taught in Germany, stating that it was superior to the method employed in America. The report was widely read, and caused no little commotion among our teachers of the deaf, several of whom went abroad to see for themselves. These gentlemen did not agree with Horace Mann, and little change was then made in American methods. Still as a result of their recommendations, classes in articulation were introduced into several schools. Later, in 1864, the father of a little deaf girl in Massachusetts began to agitate for the incorporation of an

---

[1] Gordon. The Difference between the two systems of teaching, etc., p. 3.
[2] Histories of American schools for the deaf, West. New York inst., 2: 11.

oral school in that state. A small private school of the kind
was soon opened near Boston. In the nick of time — for the
opponents of opening an oral school were active — a Mr.
Clarke of Northampton offered to endow a school for the deaf
in Massachusetts. The project being favored by the governor
of the commonwealth, and by Dr. Howe, who was then secretary of the state board of charities, the legislature incorporated in 1867 the Clarke institution at Northampton, which
was opened as an oral school. In the same year a former
teacher of an Austrian school opened in New York what
soon became the New York institution for the improved
instruction of deaf-mutes.

This invasion of the field so long occupied by the silent
method of signs occasioned much controversy. Dr. Edward
M. Gallaudet, president of the Columbia institution, at once
went abroad to examine schools and their methods. Upon
his return he reported that if the whole body of the deaf
were to be restricted to one kind of instruction, he favored
results to be obtained by the manual methods of America;
but he maintained "the practicability of teaching a large
proportion of the deaf to speak and to read from the lips,"[1]
and advocated the introduction of articulation into all the
schools of the country. As a result a conference of principals of American institutions met at Washington, which
adopted resolutions in the line of President Gallaudet's
recommendations. Classes in articulation were then very
generally introduced.

During the next few years a gradual movement abroad
towards the abolition of signs was evident; and at the second international conference at Milan, in 1880, an over-
whelming majority of the delegates present voted in favor
of the oral method. Even the French delegates were found
to have abandoned the method that originated with them in
favor of the oral method. At the various conventions of
the American instructors of the deaf, more and more atten-

---

[1] Quoted in Gordon's notes and observations upon the education of the deaf,
p. xxix.

tion came to be paid to the question of methods. Then, conventions of articulation teachers were held. In the meantime Dr. Alexander Graham Bell had introduced to teachers his father's system of visible speech, a system of written characters devised to show the position taken and the movement made by the tongue, teeth, lips, glottis, and other vocal organs in articulation. A similar but simpler system of visible speech symbols had been independently worked out by a Mr. Zera Whipple, of Mystic, Connecticut; and more recently the Lyon phonetic manual has been devised, which is founded on the principle of visible speech and may be written in the air by the fingers. In 1888 the royal commission of the United Kingdom voted " that every child who is deaf should have full opportunity of being educated on the pure oral system," but that those found physically or mentally disqualified " should be either removed from the oral department of the school or taught elsewhere on the sign and manual system." [1] In 1890 the American association to promote the teaching of speech to the deaf was incorporated, with Dr. Alexander Graham Bell as president. Dr. Bell immediately endowed the association handsomely.

Ever since Horace Mann stirred up the waters in 1843, they have remained in more or less agitation. And this fact has had a grand effect upon the work. It cannot be denied that at times the controversy over methods has been bitter; to-day, however, it has been reduced to a generous rivalry, in which the champions of the various methods and systems are striving with might and main to find out the best means of instructing the deaf and to pursue it. The majority of our schools do not limit their teaching to any one method, but are eclectic, calling themselves " combined system " schools. Satisfaction with the original uniformity of method would not have meant progress; and certainly the work for the deaf in this land of opportunity has progressed remarkably. No other country has so many deaf pupils under instruction as this has, none has provided so

---

[1] Quoted in Gordon's notes and observations, p. xlii.

generously for them, and there is none in which their educators are more alert to test new inventions and appliances that may bear upon the methods of instruction. And yet, unquestionably, the education of the deaf is still in its youth.

The early principals saw the need of exchanging ideas, and soon after the beginning of the work started an organ of communication. This organ, " The Annals of the deaf," is now in its 44th volume. It is a quarterly magazine,[1] conducted under the direction of a committee of the conference of superintendents and principals of American schools for the deaf. It is a high-class, much-prized periodical, and is said to be the leading publication of its kind in the world. In the pages of the Annals have been published articles on all manner of questions relating to the deaf. Its editor, Dr. Edward A. Fay, has made a most thorough investigation into the results of marriages of the deaf. His data and conclusions have appeared in a volume published by the Volta bureau.

The Volta bureau is a unique institution. The Volta prize of 25,000 francs awarded by the French government to Dr. Bell for his invention of the telephone, he applied to the founding of a bureau for the purpose of collecting and diffusing knowledge concerning the deaf. This is the Volta bureau of Washington, D. C. It has already published a large number of papers, studies, and books.

The influence of Dr. Bell upon the work for the deaf has been deep and lasting. The invention of the telephone itself resulted from his experiments upon a device which he hoped would enable the deaf to read the vibrations of the human voice. Though a Scotchman by birth, he is practically an American, and has devoted his best energies and his means to furthering the work which he has made his profession. His great efforts have been towards the promotion of speech-teaching to the deaf.

" The instruction of the deaf is one of the most difficult

---

[1] It now appears six times a year.

fields in the entire department of education for achievement
at once successful and satisfactory to the teacher." [1]   For
many years the parent school at Hartford was parent in the
sense of providing principals and teachers for other schools.
The New York institution has also furnished schools with
many officers and teachers.   It is only within comparatively
recent years that normal classes, as such, have come to exist
in a few of the schools.   Among others, the Clarke institution, the Wisconsin phonological institute, the school at
Bala, Pa., and Gallaudet college have them — the latter
announcing that it has opened to a limited number of college graduates annually, normal fellowships of $500, tenable
for one year.   Thus has the standard of deaf-mute teaching
come to be in line with modern university methods of training teachers.

Public day schools for the deaf have sprung up in various places.   The Horace Mann school of Boston is a notable example.   They fill an unquestioned need, as many
parents refuse to send their deaf children off to an institution.   A still further movement towards decentralization
has come to pass in Wisconsin.   Wherever in this state a
few deaf children can be gathered near their homes, state
aid will be given to pay teachers sent there to teach them.
And this movement is tending to become more and more
general.   All these day schools spread the oral method.
An important effect of the rise of this method has been the
lowering of the age when deaf children are received, and of
lengthening their term of instruction ; also of largely increasing the number of women teachers employed.   The Home
for the training in speech of little deaf children before they
are of school age, at Bala, takes children at the age when
normal children learn to talk and teaches speech by talking
to them and having them talk back as if they heard.   There
are several private oral schools for the deaf in this country
where the pupils pay tuition.   One of the best is the Wright-
Humason school in New York.

---

[1] Gillett.   Some notable benefactors of the deaf, p. 3.

With the lowering of the age of pupils, kindergarten methods have been made use of more and more; though no true kindergarten can be conducted in schools where language comes so hard and so late, where even natural signs are arbitrarily interdicted, and where there can be no music. But the occupations and the games are widely applicable and are now universally used.

From the above discussion it is seen that the deaf child comes to school with almost no language to think in, his only means of expressing his wants being crude natural signs. Such being the case, the first duty of the teacher is to establish communication with him and thereafter, during his whole course at school, more than in any other kind of educational work, to make language the end of training and other subjects the means of varying language teaching. This statement is strictly true only of elementary education, but then the majority of deaf pupils do not advance far beyond the elementary stage; not because they cannot, for they can, but because so very much time is absorbed in language work that their progress in other things is slow; then, too, parents are prone to call their boys away from school as soon as they believe these can help sustain the family. A few of the brighter and more ambitious pupils from the schools take the course at the National deaf-mute college, now called Gallaudet college, where they have "an opportunity to secure the advantages of a rigid and thorough course of intellectual training in the higher walks of literature and the liberal arts." Occasionally we hear of deaf pupils taking high school work in schools with hearing pupils, and even of being graduated from colleges of the hearing.

The course of training at American schools for the deaf has always been practical. Indeed, industrial training is almost essential for those young people who would form industrious habits and facility in the use of tools that will put them on their feet when they enter the world of labor; for most deaf pupils will have to work for their living. Their educators have a magnificent incentive in the knowledge that the trained deaf are not at all disqualified from earning a living by simple inability to hear. In their schools general manual training is followed with a pupil until, for one reason or another, he chooses his trade or it is chosen for him. The general equipment for trade teaching is excellent. Printing is an extremely useful occupation for the deaf, especially in the acquisition of idiomatic language ; and every institution for their instruction publishes one or more papers.

Our educated deaf people form a quiet, well-behaved, self-supporting part of the community. They have formed local and national societies for mutual benefit. The convention of the deaf that met in 1893 at the Columbian exposition at Chicago was the largest meeting of the kind ever held. Their speeches and deliberations and social gatherings occupied several days. That a convention so great and so remarkable could have been held was a source of great pride and satisfaction to those engaged in educating the deaf.

Within the grounds of Gallaudet college at Washington stands a beautiful memorial statue of Gallaudet teaching a little deaf and dumb girl. It was presented to the college by the deaf of the whole country. In this memorial the deaf have made fitting recognition of their indebtedness to education.

THE BLIND

When it is stated that prior to 1830 the blind of America were to be found "moping in hidden corners or degraded by the wayside, or vegetating in almshouses," it is the adult blind that is meant. Still blind children were occasionally found in these places, though it could scarcely be said that they were vegetating, as could be said of the untrained deaf children. Their ability to hear and speak does not cut off the blind from the education of communion with friends and associates. The needs of the blind, then, were not so evident or so early forced upon people's attention as were those of the deaf and dumb children. Blind children were less

often seen than deaf children, for the simple reason that
there were and always are fewer of them. This fact was
not then realized. The British census of 1851 first showed
the world that over 80 per cent of the blind are adults. Our
schools for the blind were started, *first*, because of the widespread interest in the results of educating the young deaf
and dumb, which furnished inspiration for new fields of
educational endeavor; *secondly*, because the country was
coming to the conviction that all the children of the state
should receive education both as a matter of public policy
and as a private right; and *thirdly*, because reports of what
had been accomplished abroad in schools for the blind were
being promulgated in our land.

By 1830 the more progressive states of the east were
ready to give their blind children school training. In that
year the government first included in the national census
the deaf and dumb and the blind. The work of the blind
was to begin with scientific foreknowledge as to their
number.

Private ardor to begin the work had been smouldering
for several years, when in 1829 certain gentlemen in Boston
obtained the incorporation of the " New England asylum
for the blind." This was before they had selected either
the pupils or a teacher for them. By a most fortunate circumstance, the interest and services were obtained of a
graduate of Brown university, Dr. Samuel G. Howe, who
after finishing his medical studies had chivalrously gone to
the aid of the Greeks. This gentleman became the American father and Cadmus of the blind. He went at once to
Europe to study methods of instruction. Upon his return,
in 1832, the school was opened with six pupils. In New
York the act of incorporation of the New York institution
for the blind was passed in 1831 ; but funds were needed
and no one went abroad to study methods. This school
opened in March, 1832, antedating by a few months the
school at Boston. In the very same year a German teacher
of the blind, a Mr. Friedlander, most opportunely came to

Philadelphia, in the hope of starting a school for the blind there. The way the enterprise was put through is typical of many other beginnings of special schools in America. Having trained certain blind children he exhibited their accomplishments, *first*, to a few influential people, *secondly*, before a large audience among whom he distributed a leaflet, "Observations on the instruction of blind persons." A meeting of public-spirited citizens followed, funds were liberally contributed, fairs held, and the success of the cause was assured. The Pennsylvania institution for the instruction of the blind was opened in 1833, fully ten months before an act of incorporation was obtained.

The three schools at Boston, New York and Philadelphia are called the pioneer schools. All sprang from private effort and private funds. All were incorporated as private institutions, and remain so to this day. Two similar institutions for the blind have arisen in this country, that at Baltimore and that at Pittsburg.

The origin of the state schools differs from that of the type above given only in that classes of trained pupils from the earlier schools were exhibited before the state legislatures, as well as before the people. State appropriations followed and the institutions were inaugurated as state institutions. The new schools sprang into being with astonishing rapidity. There are now in 1899 40 schools for the blind in the United States, and every state in the union makes provision for its blind of school age either in its own school or in that of a neighboring state.

In our sparsely-settled country, especially west of the Alleghenies and south of Maryland, great efforts had to be made to find the children and still greater efforts to persuade the parents to send them to school; and in many regions similar conditions of parental ignorance exist to-day. In certain states where the amount of the public fund seemed to preclude a special grant for the blind, pupils of this class were brought together in connection with a school for the deaf and dumb, forming "dual schools," as they are called.

These institutions could not help being unfair to their blind contingent; for in nearly every such case the blind came to a school already established as a school for the deaf, and under the superintendence of a man especially interested in the education of the deaf; moreover, the number of the deaf pupils usually far exceeded that of the blind. There are still a few of these dual schools, but wherever possible they have been divided into two distinct institutions.

In northern schools the colored blind are educated with the white; in southern schools it is best for the colored to have schools of their own. Both the whites and they prefer this arrangement. The first school for the colored blind was opened in North Carolina in 1869.

All the institutions for the blind were in their very inception schools. The pioneer schools imported literary teachers from Paris and handicraft teachers from Edinburg. At first only the brighter class of pupils came under instruction. Teaching them was easy. They progressed with amazing strides; all was enthusiasm; exhibitions were called for and widely given (Dr. Howe's pupils gave exhibitions in 17 states); large editions of the various annual reports were exhausted. Soon, however, less bright pupils came to be admitted; then the curriculum of studies began to sober down to the practical and comprehensive one prevailing to-day. Whatever occupation the boy or girl expects to follow after leaving school, it is assumed he will follow it better and thus live more happily and worthily if he has a general education. When, as was formerly the case, the period or term of schooling allowed pupils was shorter than it is now, they were not admitted before the age of eight or nine. Now that kindergarten departments have been universally added to the schools, the pupils are urged to enter at an early age; because experience has shown that at home these little blind folks are coddled rather than trained, so much so in fact that by the time many of them come to school their natural growth of body and mind has been so interfered with by inaction, that all the efforts of the schools cannot make up for lost time and opportunity. The principle of periodicity of growth has now come to be understood and the importance of applying the proper stimulus at the period most sensitive to it, comprehended. Children with good sight and hearing have got along without kindergarten training, and so have blind children, but of all the useful means of reaching and developing the average blind child none is so effective as the properly-conducted kindergarten. It is not easy to overestimate the importance of hearing as giving the child language and all that this means, song and the joy it brings and the deep feeling it inspires. The practical knowledge of things comes to the blind through the hand, their fingers being veritable projections of their brains. Thus must their hands not only be trained to sensitiveness of touch but to be strong and supple, so that they may, indeed, be dexterous; for as their hands are so are their brains. The kindergarten cultivates ear and heart and hand and brain as nothing else does. Even color is not wholly omitted in kindergartens for the blind. Many see colors, and those who do not love to talk about them and certainly derive some indirect value from considering them. Kindergartens for the blind may be true kindergartens in every sense of the word. A kindergartner of fully-sensed children would miss here only the brightness coming from the untrammeled ability to run and play and observe all that sight brings into view, the quick response of "I know," "I have seen this," and "I have been there." But, then, kindergartens for the blind have as their end and aim this very arousing of the children and the putting of them in touch with their surroundings.

Blind children with kindergarten training are more susceptible to instruction than those without it. Above this department the course of studies in American schools requires from seven to eight years, which means a primary, a grammar and a high school education, or instruction in object lessons, reading, writing, spelling, grammar, composition, arithmetic, history, physiology, botany, zoology, geology, physics, algebra, geometry, civics, English literature, typewriting and sometimes Latin and modern languages. Not a few pupils have fitted for college where they took the regular course with the seeing students, and from which they were graduated usually with distinction. Formerly much of the teaching was oral, which, in many cases, was apt to be more pleasant than profitable to the pupil. Since the general introduction of the embossed text book and tangible writing, the pupil has been forced to depend more and more upon himself, obviously with better results. In fact, the work has been growing more and more practical. The methods of teaching the blind correspond in general to those of teaching other hearing children. The common appliances have but to be raised and enlarged as in maps and diagrams, or simply made tangible, which may be done, for example, by notching an ordinary ruler so that the graduations can be felt. A successful teacher of the seeing readily adapts herself to the instruction of the blind. She learns to write their punctographic systems and to read them with the eye.

Industrial training has been an integral part of the school course from the beginning. Recently educational manual training has been generally introduced as preliminary to the trades. Sloyd has been found especially adapted to the blind. The handicrafts — chair-caning, hammock-making, broom-making, carpet-weaving, and a few others, alone remain of all the many trades taught at one time or another in our schools. Manual occupations of some kind will always be taught, even were it evident that none of them would be followed by the blind as trades ; for it is by doing and making that the blind especially learn best. Then, it is essential that they be kept occupied. They are happier so and far better off. In the past, before the introduction of such varieties of labor-saving machinery as the last half century has seen, many of the discharged pupils followed some manual trade and succeeded in subsisting by it. To-day this is less and less possible. The mind itself of the blind is least trammeled by the lack of sight ; hence some pursuit where intelligence is the chief factor would seem to be best adapted to his condition.

Music, of course, opens up his most delightful field. It is said that all the force of the superintendents of the early schools was required to prevent the institutions from becoming mere conservatories of music. To-day only those pupils pursue music in regular course who have talent for it; but even those are not allowed to neglect other studies for it. It is the experience of the American schools as of the European, that the profession of music offers to the educated and trained musician who is blind, a field in which he can work his way with least hindrance from his lack of sight, and many are they who have found in it a means of livelihood for themselves and their families. A few in nearly every school fit themselves to be tuners of pianos.

The importance of physical training was early recognized; for the blind have less vitality and more feeble constitutions than the seeing; besides, those of our pupils who most need exercise, are least apt to seek it of their own accord. At first the schools had no gymnasiums; of late years such have been pretty generally added, and systematic physical exercise is carried out.

The American schools for the blind were founded upon embossed books. Dr. Howe states somewhere that the simple reading from embossed print did more to establish the schools in the country than any other one thing. Extraordinary pains were taken by Dr. Howe and his assistants to perfect a system which should be at once readily tangible to the fingers of the blind and legible to the eyes of their friends. The result was the small lower case letter of Dr. Howe, the Boston line print, as it is often called. To this the jury gave preference before all other embossed systems exhibited at the great exhibition of the industry of all nations, in London, in 1852. Backed by such indorsement and all the authority of Dr. Howe the system was rapidly adopted into the American schools. It was then the theory that the blind would be further isolated from their friends

if their alphabets were dissimilar. The blind of themselves
had devised a writable system — arbitrary and composed of
dots or points — one which they could both read and write.
But the early superintendents would not countenance it.
However, many of the blind failed to read the line letter
system ; because to read it requires extreme nicety of touch,
which all the blind by no means have.   Characters composed
of points not of lines are scientifically adapted to touch reading.   In the 33rd report of the New York institution, Supt.
Wm. B. Wait wrote : " Now, which is the more important,
that all the young blind should be able to read, thus being
made, in fact, like the seeing, or that they should be taught
an *alphabet which in some sort resembles* that used by the seeing, but by doing which only 34 per cent of them will ever be
able to read with any pleasure or profit ? "   This attitude of
the New York school was the outcome of statistics gathered
from seven institutions, in which 664 pupils were involved,
and of experiments made by Mr. Wait with his own pupils,
using a system scientifically devised by him, composed of
points in arbitrary combination.   This was in 1868.   At
the next convention of the American instructors of the
blind, it was resolved " That the New York horizontal
point alphabet as arranged by Mr. Wait, should be taught
in all institutions for the education of the blind."   Not long
afterwards a national printing house was subsidized, from
which the schools obtained free books, both in the point
and in the line systems.   In a very few years the point
books were in increasing demand, and to-day most of the
schools prefer them to those in the line print.
     The acceptance of the point was due to several things,—
first of all, to its writability and superior tangibility, and
secondly, to the extraordinary energy of a few of its advocates.   The old world was a long time accepting a writable
point system.   That of Louis Braille, devised in 1829,
though much used by individuals, was not officially adopted
into the Paris school where it originated until 1854.   In
contrast, America devised, printed, spread, and resolved to

accept its writable system in less than one-half the time. The benefits of a tangible writable system are vast. It puts the blind more nearly on a par with the seeing, particularly as pupils in school. Its adoption here, next to that of tangible printing, makes obtainable the ideal of American schools for the blind.

Every tangible system has its defects. French "braille" as adopted into England has antiquated abbreviations and contractions for the use of adults; and is involved with rules allowing much bad use, like the omission of all capitals. The New York point as printed also laid itself open to much criticism as to "good use." The American braille, the latest system, combining the best features of French braille and of New York point, was devised by a blind teacher of the Perkins institution. It takes full account of "good use," and those who use the system deem it very satisfactory. In 1892, when the American braille system was adopted into several schools, a typewriter for writing braille was invented, and this was followed by the invention of another machine for embossing braille directly on plates of thin brass from which any number of duplicates could be struck off on paper.[1] Here was a means of creating a new library at once. But the chief value of the invention lay in the fact that as the machine was simple and inexpensive and could be operated if necessary by a blind man, any institution could have a printing office of its own. And several schools immediately established such offices, from which they issued at once whatever their school classes demanded. By co-operating in the selection of the books to be embossed these schools have created in the space of seven years a library of books in American braille than which there is no superior in any system in any country, and they have added an immense amount of music in the braille music notation, which is the same all over the world. A typewriter, and a machine for embossing brass plates in the New York point system, have also appeared.

---

[1] For these inventions, which have been of the greatest recent service to the education of the blind, the work is indebted to Mr. Frank H. Hall, sup't of the Illinois school.

The production of books in both point systems is going on parallelly. Whether this is wise or not it is certainly wasteful. And yet the antagonism of the advocates of the rival systems is so great that the race may continue for some years yet. The matter is, however, not so " stupid " as it would seem to be. There is nothing like competition to eliminate defects and bring out excellences. Moreover, there has been evolution in systems of ink print as there has been in systems of embossed print. In either case that which eventually survives will be the fittest and will be worth all the trouble it caused to make it survive.

Excellent embossed libraries exist in all three of the systems. Books in all three may be obtained from the National printing house for the blind at Louisville, Ky., where many of the plates have been made and where most of them are kept. This printing house was subsidized by congress in 1873, and since that time has spent $10,000 annually in the production of books in the various systems, music scores in the New York point notation, and tangible apparatus, each school ordering from the published list, books, etc., to the value of its quota or part proportional to the number of its pupils. The printing office of the Perkins institution at Boston is the largest private enterprise of its kind in the world. It has been running almost continuously since 1834, and has put forth a splendid list of books in the Boston line print.

American generosity to its defectives has not only provided institutions unsurpassed in their general appointments elsewhere, but the proverbial American ingenuity has supplied the classrooms with appliances and mechanical aids to instruction unequaled in any land. The interest in the work for the blind taken by those actually engaged in it may be seen by a reading of the annual reports of the superintendents, which have served as a means of communication among the schools and between these and the public. France, Germany and Italy have been publishing for many years, magazines or periodicals in the interest of the blind.

For four years this country produced "The Mentor," a monthly which was so excellent and timely that it ought to have been kept up. However, it was supported but poorly and was stopped for that reason. America, then, has no organ of communication among workers for the blind. The superintendents and teachers engaged in this work first met in convention in 1853. The Association of American instructors of the blind was formed in 1871, and has met biennially ever since, usually as the guest of one or another of the institutions. The proceedings of each convention have been published.

The principles underlying the scheme for educating the blind being to make them as little as possible a class apart from the rest of the community, it has not been deemed wise to attempt to establish a national college for the higher education of those capable of taking it, but efforts are making towards enabling the brighter and worthier pupils to attend one of the colleges for the seeing, at the expense of the states or the schools from which they come. The school instruction of the blind is comparatively an easy matter. The work is less of a science than the more difficult task of instructing the deaf and dumb. But if we consider the results, it must be admitted that it is far easier to fit the intelligent deaf to be self-supporting than it is to fit the blind to be so. The world of practical affairs is the world of light; and if the blind succeed in that world it is certainly to their credit. And yet we expect them to succeed in it; and having given them the best preparation we can devise, we find that many do succeed, some brilliantly. Just what proportion "succeed" is not known; for in the vast areas of our large states the majority go out and are lost to view. Many — especially the girls — go home to become helpful in the family, and these live on there as centers of light and culture, and so what was once deemed a calamity, may become to the family a blessing in disguise.

In 1878 an exhaustive census of the graduates from all over the country was compiled. It revealed the following

encouraging facts : 16 became superintendents of other institutions ; 214 became teachers or were otherwise employed
in institutions ; 34 became ministers of the gospel ; 84
authors, publishers or lecturers ; 310 were engaged as teachers
of music or were vocalists outside of institutions ; 69 had been
organists in churches ; 125 piano tuners ; 937 had been
engaged as teachers, employees, and workers in handicraft ;
277 were storekeepers, etc. ; 45 became owners and managers of real estate ; 760 (mostly women) were employed at
housework at home or in families, or at sewing with machines,
or by hand, and 78 were in homes of employment.[1]   Fur
ther, according to the 10th census of the United States
(1880) when there were 48,928 blind in the land, but 2,560
were found in almshouses.[2]   What proportion of these
ever attended our schools, will never be known, but it must
be remembered that blindness is an affliction of old age.

According to statistics printed in the report for 1879 of
the New York institution, " More than 1,200 persons have
been instructed, and have gone out from the institutions
for the blind in this state [New York], only 21 of whom
were found to be in almshouses on the 30th of October, 1879.   Such facts give great force to a statement made
by the board of state commissioners of public charities upon
this subject.   They say : " As observation shows that educated blind persons seldom become a public charge, it would
seem important, not only in its social bearings, but as a
question of political economy, to bring *as many of the blind
as practicable under proper educational training.*"[3]

THE DEAF-BLIND

" Obstacles are things to be overcome " is the motto
given by Dr. Howe to the Perkins institution for the blind.
When this remarkable man learned in 1837 that up in the
mountains of New Hampshire there was a little girl not only

---

[1] Proceedings fifth bien. conv. of the American association of instructors of the
blind, p. 21.
[2] Compendium 10th census, 2, 1702.
[3] Pp. 32–33.

blind but also deaf and dumb, he eagerly sought out the child and obtained the parents' consent to take her to South Boston to be educated.   He had already formed a theory as to how he would reach a mind thus doubly shut in, and with the finding of Laura Bridgman came the wished-for opportunity to test this theory.

It should be noted that Laura Bridgman saw and heard until she was two years old.   She had been rather a delicate child, however, having enjoyed only about four months of robust health, when she sickened, her disease raging with great violence during five weeks, " when her eyes and ears were inflamed, suppurated and their contents were discharged." [1]   Her sufferings continued for months, and it was not "until four years of age that the poor child's bodily health seemed restored." [2]   She was intelligently active, following her mother about the house, seeming anxious to feel of everything, and thus to learn about it ; and she developed signs for her father and her mother, and for some things.

She was eight years old when brought to the Perkins institution.   Dr. Howe writes : " There was one of two ways to be adopted : either to go on and build up a language of signs on the basis of the natural language, which she had already herself commenced, or to teach her the purely arbitrary language in common use ; that is, to give her a sign for every individual thing, or to give her a knowledge of letters, by the combination of which she might express her idea of the existence, and the mode and condition of existence, of anything.   The former would have been easy, but very ineffectual ; the latter seemed very difficult, but, if accomplished, very effectual ; I determined, therefore, to try the latter." [3]   After the child had become adjusted to the change of homes, Dr. Howe began teaching her by means of common articles with which she was familiar — spoons, forks,

---

[1] From reports of Dr. Howe on Laura Bridgman, appendix C, 48th annual report, Perkins institution for the blind, p. 160.

[2] Same source and page.

[3] Same source, pp. 162–3.

keys, etc., on which labels with their names printed in raised letters had been pasted. Similar detached labels were given her to feel. Her touch was acute enough, hence she was able to match labels, placing that for book on the book, etc. She did this easily and willingly because she received approbation for so doing; but the idea that the printed word stood for the name of the object had not entered her brain. Then other detached labels were cut up into their component letters. These her memory soon enabled her to build into wholes or the words she had felt. Such exercises continued for many weeks to be only a meaningless play to the poor child. The success had been " about as great as teaching a very knowing dog," when suddenly the idea flashed upon her that " Here was a way by which she herself could make up a sign for anything that was in her own mind, and show it to another mind, and at once her countenance lighted up with a human expression; it was no longer a dog or parrot, — it was an immortal spirit, eagerly seizing upon a new link of union with other spirits! I could almost fix upon the moment when this truth dawned upon her mind, and spread its light to her countenance; I saw that the great obstacle was overcome, and that henceforward nothing but patient and persevering, plain and straightforward efforts were to be used." [1]

Next, she was given metal type each bearing some embossed letter, and a frame with holes to receive them. With this appliance Laura readily wrote the name of any object she knew and by writing them fixed in mind an extensive vocabulary of common names. Then the less cumbrous manual alphabet was taught her. Here was a means by which she could both write and read; she could spell to her teacher and read what her teacher spelled into her hand.

Dr. Howe's reports teem with interesting psychologic material. At the end of the year he writes: " She is nine years of age, and yet her knowledge of language is not

---

[1] Same source, p. 164.

greater than a common child of three years. There has been no difficulty in communicating knowledge of facts, positive qualities of bodies, numbers, etc. ; but the *words expressive of them*, which other children learn by hearing, as they learn to talk, must all be communicated to Laura by a circuitous and tedious method. In all the knowledge which is acquired by the perceptive faculties, she is of course backward ; because, previous to her coming here, her perceptive faculties were probably less exercised in one week than those of common children are in one hour." [1]

And so her instruction went on. Through it all the child showed, an eagerness to learn and to put herself in touch with the world that was a powerful aid to the teacher. In a few years, when Oliver Caswell, also deaf, dumb, and blind, came to the institution, Laura naturally took great interest in teaching him, and thereby profitted much herself. As she approached womanhood her education was already good. Laura had learned to sew, to knit, and to do fancy work, and so employed her time when not reading or conversing with her many friends. She often visited her home but her true home was the institution. There she lived to her 60th year and there she died, the first case of any one so afflicted made capable of leading an industrious and happy life, and as the first case, historically the most remarkable.

Popular interest in Laura Bridgman, both in this country and abroad, was naturally very great. The printed reports of her progress which were eagerly awaited were as eagerly absorbed. Distinguished foreigners coming to Boston visited her. Charles Dickens wrote in his American notes a sympathetic account of his impressions of her. Naturally enough in succeeding cases of the deaf-blind that from time to time came under instruction in one school or another, much less interest was shown. The way to give liberty to the imprisoned mind had been made plain.

In the year 1887, however, something like the old interest

---

[1] Same source, p. 167.

was aroused by the publication of accounts of the brilliant deaf, dumb, and blind child in Alabama, Helen Keller. This child had lost sight and hearing at 19 months as a result of a serious illness. Like Laura she kept actively interested in all that surrounded her, and like Laura she developed her own little language of signs. When she was six years old, her friends, who knew of Laura Bridgman's case, applied to Boston for a teacher. In the following year Miss Annie M. Sullivan was sent. This lady was able to put herself in touch with Helen in a very short time and in a marvelous way. In fact, she has proved herself to be a most remarkable teacher. Following in general the methods adopted in teaching Laura, Miss Sullivan began her work by putting Helen in possession of the manual alphabet. A doll was happily chosen to begin with; and with the doll on the child's lap, the teacher formed in Helen's hand the finger letters *d-o-l-l*. Other familiar objects were similarly introduced, and strange as it may seem, that which had taken three months to reach in Laura's case in Helen's took but a few days;[1] or, in Miss Sullivan's words, "it was more than a week before she understood that all things were thus identified."[2] Her teacher writes: "Never did a child apply herself more joyfully to any task than did Helen to the acquisition of new words. In a few days she had mastered the manual alphabet and learned upwards of a hundred names."[3] After teaching verbs and prepositions through action and position Miss Sullivan made a departure. She began to use new words in connection with old words, letting Helen understand them if possible from the context. The child adopted these words "often without inquiry." In this way she became familiar with the use of many words whose meaning never had to be explained to her.

As to the letters of the raised alphabet, Miss Sullivan writes: "Incredible as it may seem, she learned all the let-

---

[1] See 56th an. rep. Perkins inst. for the blind, p. 82.

[2] Same source, p. 101.

[3] Same source, p. 101.

ters both capital and small in one day." [1]   Then came the
primer; then pencil writing than which there is scarcely a
more difficult exercise for the blind to learn; and yet Helen
"wrote without assistance a correctly spelled and legible
letter to one of her cousins; and this was only a little more
than a month after her first lesson in chirography." [2]   Braille,
or tangible point writing, became a constant delight to her.

Words like *perhaps* and *suppose* and those indicative of
abstract ideas she learned more through association and
repetition than through any explanation of her teacher.
The child had the language sense largely developed.   Much
of the time when no one was talking with her she was reading in books printed in raised letters.   Dr. Bell in trying to
account for Helen's wonderful familiarity with idiomatic
English, considers of great significance the statement of
Miss Sullivan that, "long before she could read them [the
books] . . . she would amuse herself for hours each
day in carefully passing her fingers over the words, searching for such words as she knew." [3]

In 1888, when Helen was 8 years old her teacher took her
to South Boston where she could have the advantage of all
the appliances and embossed books that a school for the
blind affords.   Thenceforth an account of her progress
reads like a romance.   It was no more difficult for her to
learn a new word in German or in Greek than in English;
and she took great delight in picking up and using French
or Greek phrases.   And when later she came to study these
languages, she seemed to advance without effort in the
knowledge of them.

The educators of the deaf, who have good reason to comprehend the exceeding difficulty of teaching their pupils to
articulate intelligibly, feel that Helen Keller's rapid mastery
of speech is by all odds her most wonderful achievement.
After she had been in South Boston some little time she
heard of a Swedish girl afflicted like herself, who had learned

[1] Same source, p. 103.
[2] Same source, p. 104.
[3] Amer. annals of the deaf, April, 1892, p. 134.

to speak, and she said, "I must learn to speak." Miss Sullivan took her to Miss Sarah Fuller, principal of the Horace Mann school for the deaf, and though Helen's only means of learning the position of the vocal organs in speech was to put her fingers on the lips, tongue, teeth, and throat of the speaker, she learned in ten lessons[1] to articulate so well that she could carry on an intelligible and audible conversation, having communication addressed to her spelled into her hand by the manual alphabet. She has learned since that time to read from the lips and throat of a speaker by placing her fingers lightly on them; so that any one sitting near her can converse with her just as though she could both hear and see. She spent a winter at the Wright-Humason private school for the deaf, where she improved her articulation.

When Helen was sixteen years old she entered the Cambridge school for girls, Miss Sullivan accompanying her. There, under the guidance of Mr. Arthur Gilman, the director of the school, she took the course preparatory to entering Radcliffe college. At the end of one year she took the regular required examinations in the history of Greece and Rome, in English, in Latin, in elementary French, in elementary German, and in advanced German. As the questions and other matter were read into her hand by Mr. Gilman himself, Helen wrote her answers and translations on an ordinary typewriter. Her papers were read by the regular examiners. She passed the tests in every subject, taking "honors" in English and German. Mr. Gilman writes: "I think that I may say that no candidate in Harvard or Radcliffe college was graded higher than Helen in English."[2]

There are still other children afflicted like Helen who are doing splendid work, but, "taking this child all in all," says Dr. Job Williams, principal of the American school for the

---

[1] See Sarah Fuller's article How Helen Keller learned to speak, Annals of the deaf, Jan. 1892, p. 26.

[2] Miss Helen Adams Keller's first year of college preparatory work. American Annals of the Deaf, November, 1897.

deaf at Hartford, "and making due allowance for every possible aid that has been given her, and for all unconscious exaggeration due to friendly admiration, there yet remains so much that is marvelous as to place her beyond comparison with any other child of whom we have ever heard. The whole history of literature reveals nothing equal to her language productions from one of her years, even among those possessed of all their faculties. She is a genius, a prodigy, a phenomenon." [1]

The other deaf-blind children under instruction are some at schools for the blind, some at schools for the deaf. They must always have a special teacher, and use embossed books and adapted appliances. All are being taught on principles used in teaching Helen. In South Boston, where there are several, they attend classes with other pupils, the special teacher acting simply as interpreter and companion.

THE FEEBLE–MINDED

The term feeble-minded is now used to embrace all classes and grades of the mentally defective, excepting the insane, who, properly speaking, are mentally sick. Idiocy was the term formerly used to cover the same range. Idiocy or feeble-mindedness may be defined as "mental deficiency depending upon imperfect development, or disease of the nervous system, occurring before, at or after birth, previous to the evolution of the mental faculties." [2] At the time the feeble-minded were first taught, it was supposed that their growth of body and mind, which was seen to be but partial, had simply been stopped by malign influences, and that in many cases all that was needed was proper environment in order to start the growth again ; it was hoped that the improvable cases at least could be educated and trained to approach in capacity the normal-minded individual.

With the end in view of so educating idiots, as they called them, the first attempts to train them in this country were

---

[1] Annals of the deaf, April, 1892, p. 159.
[2] Quoted in Fernald's Feeble-minded children, p. 2.

made in 1848. Before then idiots who were not кept at home were to be found in almshouses or in insane asylums, where they were sadly out of place. Kind-hearted physicians who saw this "rubbish of humanity" cowering in terror before lunatics or abused by almshouse associates, agitated for their relief, care, and training. The movement began in New York and Massachusetts in the year 1846. Massachusetts was more ripe for the work; for the matter had no sooner been presented to the legislature than this body appointed a commission to report upon the number, condition, and the best means of relieving the idiots in the commonwealth. Dr. Samuel G. Howe, the director of the Perkins institution for the blind, was made chairman of the commission. Its report made in 1848, and widely known as " Dr. Howe's report on idiocy," was exhaustive, and ended by recommending the opening of an experimental school. One was opened at the expense of the state and under the guidance of Dr. Howe himself. The results were so favorable that in three years' time the state doubled its appropriation, and founded in South Boston the Massachusetts school for idiots, the first state school for them. The state of New York followed, establishing its school similarly, or experimentally, in 1851, and permanently in 1853.

Between the appointment of the Massachusetts commission and its report, a country physician, Dr. H. B. Wilbur, had opened a small private school for idiots at Barre, Mass., really the first school of its kind in America. Dr. Wilbur was soon called to take charge of the New York state school. The Pennsylvania school followed in 1852, and was established in Philadelphia as a private corporation in 1853; then in 1857 came the Ohio state institution at Columbus; in 1858 the semi-public school in Lakeville, Conn.; the Kentucky state school at Frankfort in 1860; the Illinois state school in 1865; the Hillside home, a private school at Fayville, Mass., in 1870. "Thus up to 1874, twenty-six years after this work was begun in America, public institutions for the feeble-minded had been established in seven states.

These institutions then had under training a total of 1,041
pupils. There were also two private institutions in Massachusetts, . . . with a total of 69 inmates."[1] Applications for admittance were numerous and pressing. At first
it was the theory that only imbeciles, the improvable idiots,
should be taken into the institution, that the institution
should be a school and should graduate its pupils into the
world. Still, it was but a few years before most of the
superintendents recognized that the pupils would always be
children though adult in years; and that as children they
needed guidance and protection always; that for obvious
reasons girls and women of child-bearing age should not be
discharged — for no girl is so exposed as the simple, weak-
willed, feeble-minded girl — and finally that practically all
cases would have to be retained within the protection of the
institution. Physiology and pathology now teach that "mental deficiency generally, if not always, is the result of a definite cerebral abnormality or defect, or the result of actual disease or damage to some part of the central nervous system ;"[2]
that feeble-mindedness is practically a permanent condition,
and that it cannot be cured. From the time this fact came
to be realized the institutions began to change in character
There arose two distinct departments — the training school
and the asylum.

The school was, is, and ought to be the fundamentally
important department. Education is just as much a right
of the improvable imbecile or feeble-minded child as it is of
any child ; and what are always acknowledged to be the
benefits of an education are no less benefits to the one than
to the other. It is in the school that the feeble-minded
child is to be aroused, developed and trained to lead a useful and a happy life. The aim in the education of an ordinary child is to give a liberal all-round training, fitting him
for anything in life he may choose to take up. With our
feeble-minded child the aim of his education, which is to

[1] Fernald, The history of the treatment of the feeble-minded, p. 8.
[2] Fernald, Feeble-minded children, p. 2.

lead a useful life within the institution, is kept ever in mind. He is happiest when occupied. Hence, his education is principally a practical education. The difference between a normal person and a feeble-minded person after training is that the latter has no initiative, no power to resist the seduction of stronger minds. He may be useful and even self-supporting, but he can become so only under guidance and direction.

When they come to school these children have extremely weak will power. In fact the feeble-minded as a class have been divided according to the attention, thus :

" 1. Absolute idiocy.   Complete absence and impossibility of attention.

" 2. Simple idiocy.   Attention feeble and difficult.

" 3. Imbecility.   Instability of attention." [1]

With all these the condition of the hand indicates that of the brain. The "idiotic hand" is proverbial. Many imbeciles see but do not perceive ; hear but do not understand. They rarely make a purposive effort, but need to be directed in everything. When it is comprehended that though they love games they do not even play of their own accord, it will be understood how their teachers must begin at the very bottom rung in the ladder of education. The special senses of seeing, hearing, and feeling, actually have to be aroused and developed, *first*, as simple physiological functions ; *secondly*, as intellectual faculties. Calisthenics in classes, marching to music, military drill — movements and exercises of all kinds — exert a most salutary and energizing influence, and are in great use in all the schools.

The normal child does not need to be taught each step ; his power of attention, his will, his desire, his originality enable him to fill the gaps in instruction from his own daily experiences. In fact he often learns more out of school than in. On the contrary, the feeble-minded child has to be taught each step, hence, his education is extremely slow.

---

[1] Sollier: Psychologie de l'idiot et l'imbecile, Paris, 1891.   Quoted from G. E. Johnson, Pedagogical seminary, 3, 246.

The simple occupations of the kindergarten fit these children of eight to twelve years of age as they do bright
children of four and five.   The teacher devises all manner
of busy work for them, generally using coarse materials;
the stringing of spools; beads; buttons; spool-knitting;
plain knitting; braiding with broad leather strips, with shoe-
strings, with straw; and block building from the simple
cube to the forms that are more complex.

No instruction is in more general use and is more helpful
to the children than that of the kindergarten.   After this
all their education continues on a very elementary plane
beyond which it is impossible for them to go.   Many learn
reading, writing, and arithmetic.   The brightest read simple
stories with pleasure, and go as far in arithmetic as multiplication.   Division is beyond them.[1]   Calculation in the
abstract they cannot master.   The greater part of their education is, therefore, of a purely practical kind.   They are
taught a good deal of fancy work, like knitting, crocheting,
embroidery and lace-making; but chiefly domestic work,
sewing, washing and ironing, baking, farming, housepaint-
ing, shoemaking, brushmaking, etc.

Entertainments flourish at these institutions.   One is got
up on every possible occasion; and the "men and women
children" are always present.   No discrimination as to age
or capacity is permitted.   Happiness prevails because, in
direct contrast with what happens in the world, the simple
are not scoffed at and driven to a corner, but are made to
feel that they are as good as any one.

The institution is a small community.   It must have a
given number of employees, one or more to each section or
department.   But the stronger grown up children do the
bulk of the work: baking, laundry work, shoemaking, sewing, mending, dressmaking and tailoring.   Each institution
aims to have as many acres of land as it has children, and
on the grounds a barn, cattle, horses and all the parapher-
nalia of a farm.   This farm is worked by the boys, their

---

[1] See Fernald.   Feeble-minded children, p. 14.

cows producing all the milk the institution can consume, and the farm hands raising all their own vegetables and fruit, selling what they cannot store. By utilizing the energies of the pupils in profitable labor the average *per capita* expense may be reduced to $125 or $150 a year. Supt. Doren of the Columbus institution has said that if the state will provide him 1,000 acres of good land he will care for all the custodial cases in Ohio free of expense to the state. When an old school has moved to a new site as the Massachusetts school has recently done, the labor of the boys has been utilized in clearing the land and ditching it, in building the roads, etc. Where the grounds contain suitable clay soil, as at Fort Wayne, Indiana, the boys have made the bricks with which to build new structures as needed. But in all this care is taken that there is no overwork. The work of an average laboring man more than supports himself — it is generally reckoned to support three people. If the feeble-minded man does one-half or one-third of a man's work, and does it every day, his support costs only that which will pay for his superintendence and care.

The lowest cases of the unimprovable idiots, whom nearly all the institutions have been forced to admit, are termed the "custodial cases," and are kept by themselves. They are profoundly helpless, can neither speak nor attend to their bodily wants, but must be cared for like babies which they are. However, they must be attended to — washed, fed, and kept as decent as may be. Attendants willing to do this work are not easily found. But trained feeble-minded girls are delighted and flattered at the privilege of taking care of those more helpless than themselves. And it has been found that they make the best attendants for such cases.

So far, then, as methods of instruction go, American teachers have but broadened the physiological methods of the Frenchman, Seguin. The distinctive results of our schools lie in training the pupils to be helpful, especially in the way of labor for the institution which harbors them.

A distinctive result of work for the feeble-minded has been the gathering of statistics of causes. It has been known that a very large percentage of cases, variously estimated from 50 per cent to 70 per cent, are of congenital origin; that of all classes of defectives the feeble-minded most surely tend to transmit their defect; hence, that the feeble-minded must be sequestrated for life. It has been shown that there is a strange but strong correlation between the forms of degeneracy, i. e., the criminal, the inebriate, the prostitute, and the feeble-minded. Of late years the energies of charitable and sociologic organizations " Have turned towards combating the causes of degeneracy, thereby protecting posterity." [1] The United States census for 1890 gives in round numbers 95,000 feeble-minded and this number is undoubtedly short of the actual number. Still but one-twelfth or about 8,000 of those returned in the census are cared for in special institutions. Here is a terrible problem ahead for the sociologists to work out. Those who have most thoroughly studied the feeble-minded are convinced that, as prevention is cheaper than cure, so the gathering of all this vast army into institutions and especially colonies where fifty per cent of them can be taught to be at least partly self-supporting, and where their multiplication can be cut off, is, by all odds, the most economical and the best policy for the states to pursue in the future. It should not be forgotten that for every idiot cared for we restore at least one productive person to the community; some writers say more than one. The whole matter is receiving widespread and intelligent attention. A large number of our colleges offer courses in practical sociology, and the number of students taking these courses is constantly increasing.

The work for the feeble-minded is considered by those in it as being still in a tentative stage. Nearly all the superintendents are physicians; they do not agree on the different questions involved. They meet regularly in convention, and

---

[1] Powell, Care of the feeble-minded, p. 10.

have an organ of communication, called "The Journal of psycho-asthenics."

As the methods of teaching the feeble-minded and the other defective classes have become understood, they have modified the old methods of teaching children of normal intelligence. Child study is now interesting teachers, and already has led to the sending of many feeble-minded children to special schools for their training. The city of Providence, R. I., has recently led the way in a new movement, that of teaching in special classes the dull or backward pupils of the public schools. The movement is slowly spreading elsewhere, and, in justice both to the dull and the bright children, is of inestimable value, and, as such, is a hopeful sign of the times.[1]

BIBLIOGRAPHY[2]

The deaf

American annals of the deaf. Washington, D. C.

Arnold, Thos. The education of the deaf and dumb. London, 1872.

—— The .anguages or the senses. Margate, 1894.

Bell, A. G. Condition of articulation teaching in American schools for the deaf. Boston, 1893.

—— Deaf-mute instruction in relation to the public schools. Volta bureau, 1884.

—— Education of the deaf. The little aear child, vol. 2, no. 2, 1898.

—— Growth of the oral method of instructing the deaf. Boston, 1896.

Bell, A. M. English visible speech. Volta bureau, 1899.

Clarke institution. Addresses at the 25th anniversary of. Northampton, 1893.

Encyclopædia Brittanica. Art. deaf and dumb.

[1] NOTE: A very radical experiment is being tried, particularly at the Kansas institution. The operation of castration has been performed on several boys, after which they have been found to be so improved that some were transferred from the custodial to the school department, some sent home.

[2] The bibliographies here printed constitute but a small part of what might be given.

Fay, E. A. Index to American annals of the deaf. Vols. 31–40 (1886–1895), and previous indexes.

—— Marriages of the deaf in America. Volta bureau, 1898.

Gallaudet, E. M. The combined system of educating the deaf. Volta bureau, 1891.

—— The deaf and their possibilities. Chicago, 1898.

—— Values in the education of the deaf. Colorado Springs, Col., 1893.

Gillett, P. G. Some notable benefactors of the deaf. Rochester, N. Y., 1896.

Gordon, J. C. The education of the deaf, being evidence of Drs. Gallaudet and Bell, presented to the royal commission of Great Britain. Volta bureau, 1892.

—— Notes and observations on the education of the deaf. Volta bureau, 1892.

—— The difference between the two systems of teaching deaf-mute children the English language. Volta bureau, 1898.

Green, Francis. Vox oculis subjecta, part 1. Boston, 1897.

Histories of American schools for the deaf. 3 vols. Volta bureau, 1893.

Hubbard, G. G. The story of the rise of the oral method in America. Washington, 1898.

Johns, Rev. B. G. The land of silence and the land of darkness. London, 1857.

Kitto, John. The lost senses. New York, 1852.

Mann, Horace. Life and works of. 3 : 244. Boston, 1891.

Proceedings of American association to promote the teaching of speech to the deaf.

Proceedings of conferences of principals and superintendents of the deaf.

Proceedings o. conventions of American instructors of the deaf.

Reports of American institutions for the deaf.

Seguin, E. Education of the deaf and mute, in report on education. Milwaukee, 1880.

The blind

Anagnos, M. Education of the blind. Boston, 1882.

Armitage, T. R. Education and employment of the blind. London, 1886.

Cary, T. G. Memoir of Thomas Handasyd Perkins. Boston, 1856.

Diderot. An essay on blindness. London reprints, 1895.

Education of the blind, from "The North American Review," vol. 37.

Encyclopædia Brittanica. Art. The blind.

Hauy, V. An essay on the education of the blind. London reprints, 1894.

Howe, Julia Ward. Memoir of Dr. S. G. Howe, Boston, 1877.

Howe, S. G. 43 annual reports of the Perkins institution. 1833–1875.

Jubilee celebration, Yorkshire school for the blind. London, 1884.

Kitto, John. The lost senses. New York, 1852.

Mell, A. Encyclopädisches handbuch des blinden-wesens. Wien und Leipzig, 1899.

Prescott, W. H. The blind, in "biographical and critical essays." Boston, 1846.

Report of the conference of the blind and their friends. Royal normal college, July, 1890.

Reports of the biennial conventions of American instructors of the blind.

Reports of American institutions for the instruction of the blind.

Robinson, E. B. F. The true sphere of the blind. Toronto, 1896.

Rutherford, John. William Moon and his work for the blind. London, 1898.

Sizeranne, M. de la. Les Aveugles par un Aveugle. Paris, 1891.

Sturgis, Dinah. The kindergarten for the blind. New England magazine, December, 1895, p. 433.

The Mentor. Boston, 1891–94.

Wickersham, J. P. History of education in Pennsylvania. Lancaster, Pa., 1886.

The deaf-blind

Anagnos, M. Helen Keller; a second Laura Bridgman. Boston, 1888.

——. Reports of the Perkins institution. 1887–98.

Chamberlain, J. E. Helen Keller, as she really is. Annals of the deaf, June, 1899, pp. 286–301.

Chappell, Jennie. Always happy, or the story of Helen Keller. London.

Fuller, Sarah. How Helen Keller learned to speak. Annals of the deaf, Jan. 1892, p. 23.

Dickens, C. An account of the Institution for the blind at Boston. "American Notes," vol. 1. London, 1842.

Gilman, A. Miss Helen Adams Keller's first year of college preparatory work. Volta bureau, 1897.

Hall, G. S. Laura Bridgman, from "Aspects of German culture." Boston, 1891.

Howe, S. G. Education of Laura Bridgman; extracts from reports of. Boston, 1890.

Lamson, Mary S. Life and education of Laura Dewey Bridgman. Boston, 1878.

Sullivan, Annie M. How Helen Keller acquired language. Annals of the deaf, April, 1892, p. 127.

The language of the deaf-blind. Annals of the deaf, April, 1899, p. 218.

The feeble-minded

Association of medical officers of American institutions for idiotic and feeble-minded persons. Proceedings, 1876–98.

Barr, M. W. Children of a day. Phila., 1896.

——. Mental defectives and the social welfare. Popular science monthly, April, 1899.

Doren, G. A. Our defective classes. Columbus, O., 1897.

Fernald, W. E. Feeble-minded children. Boston, 1897.

——. The history of the treatment of the feeble-minded. Boston, 1893.

Henderson, C. R. Dependent, defective and delinquent children. Boston, 1893.

Howe, S. G. Report on idiocy. Boston, 1850.

Indiana bulletin of charities and correction. Indianapolis, 1898.

Johnson, Alexander. Concerning a form of degeneracy. American journal of sociology, November, 1898.

——. The mother-state and her weaker children. Boston, 1897.

Johnson, G. E. Contribution to the psychology and pedagogy of feeble-minded children. Pedagogical seminary, 3 : 246.

Kerlin, Isaac N. Feeble-minded children. West Chester, Pa., 1879.

——. The mind unveiled. Philadelphia, 1858.

Powell, F. M. Care of the feeble-minded. Boston, 1898.

Psycho-Asthenics, journal of. Faribault, Minn.

Report of 10th anniversary and annual meeting of the association of the New Jersey training school for feeble-minded children. Vineland, 1898.

Reports of commissioner of education. Washington, D. C.

Reports of institutions for the feeble-minded throughout the country.

Seguin, E. Education of idiots and feeble-minded children from report on education. Milwaukee, 1880.

——. Idiocy and its treatment by the physiological method. New York, 1870.

Shuttleworth, G. E. Mentally deficient children. London, 1895.

Sollier, Paul. Psychologie de l'idiot et de l'imbecile. Paris, 1891.

Tuke, D. Hack. Modes of providing for the insane and idiots in the United States and Great Britain. Medical rec., 1887.

Warner, A. G. American charities. A study in philanthropy and economics. Crowell & Co., pub.

Wilbur, W. B. Suggestions on principles and methods of elementary instruction. Albany, 1862.

Statistics of schools for defective classes

Compiled from report commissioner of education 1896–77, 2 : 2335–60

	Blind	DEAF			FEEBLE-MINDED	
		State public institutions	Public day schools	Private day schools	Public institutions	Private
Institutions................	36	54	22	19	18	10
Volumes in library.........	95 879	90 184	....	....	....	....
Value of scientific apparatus	$13 300	$21 394	....	....	....	....
Instructors	387	877	60	83	190	58
Pupils	3 630	9 391	506	532	8 177	357
Expenditures..............	$920 224	$2 461 402	$42 827	....	$1 362 791	....
Value of grounds and buildings....................	$6 183 538	$11 373 873	....	....	$4 631 917	....

Public schools for the deaf

From report of commissioner of education, 1896–97, 2 : 2346–9

STATE	City	No. of pupils	Value of lands and buildings	Expenditures for support
Alabama	Talladega	143	$125 000	$30 222
Arkansas	Little Rock	228	100 000	43 500
California	Berkeley	171	450 000	59 650
Colorado	Colorado Springs	78	220 894	25 266
Connecticut	Hartford	157	250 000	43 100
D. C.	Washington	132	700 000	70 858
D. C. Kendall school	Washington	65		
Florida	St. Augustine	45	25 000	4 648
Georgia	Cavesprings	139	80 000	22 000
Illinois	Jacksonville	534	455 000	97 000
Indiana	Indianapolis	312	526 000	62 059
Iowa	Council Bluffs	316	500 000	61 700
Kansas	Olathe	250	250 000	46 500
Kentucky	Danville	323	200 000	48 061
Louisiana	Baton Rouge	93	300 000	16 500
Maine	Portland	69	30 000	14 000
Maryland	Baltimore	40	35 000	[1] 10 645
Maryland	Frederick	96	255 000	26 588
Massachusetts	Northampton	155	135 149	43 756
Michigan	Flint	417	426 255	63 558
Minnesota	Faribault	227	271 625	45 455
Mississippi	Jackson	114	75 000	16 430
Missouri	Fulton	345	310 000	92 000
Montana	Boulder	18	30 000	[1] 6 250
Nebraska	Omaha	143	120 000	55 240
New Jersey	Trenton	149	100 000	40 000
New Mexico	Santa Fe	14	6 000	4 000
New York	Buffalo	152	154 560	30 720
New York	Fordham	355	509 236	92 994
New York	Malone	87	89 586	22 936
New York	904 Lexington ave., New York	211	360 000	48 753
New York	Washington Heights	465	506 000	112 216
New York	Rochester	199	130 000	46 647
New York	Rome	137	125 000	39 612
North Carolina	Morganton	186	160 000	35 000
North Carolina	Raleigh	70	30 000	10 000
North Dakota	Devil's Lake	47	22 500	9 638
Ohio	Columbus	484	650 000	84 000
Oregon	Salem	51	25 000	12 000
Pennsylvania	Edgewood Park	209	257 137	50 134
Pennsylvania	Bala, Philadelphia	42	48 431	12 869
Pennsylvania	Mt. Airy, Philadelphia	509	1 000 000	135 940
Pennsylvania	Scranton	71	160 000	16 237
Rhode Island	Providence	60	60 000	19 000
South Carolina	Cedar Springs	96	55 000	[1] 17 288
South Dakota	Sioux Falls	43	60 000	12 250
Tennessee	Knoxville	259	150 000	30 800
Texas	Austin	262	225 000	43 114
Texas	Austin, colored d. and b.	36	37 500	8 500
Utah	Ogden	67	200 000	20 000
Virginia	Staunton	105	80 000	[1] 21 000
Washington	Vancouver	66	100 000	29 000
West Virginia	Romney	128	85 000	[1] 25 737
Wisconsin	Delavan	221	118 000	39 800

[1] Includes the blind.

Public day schools for the deaf

From report of the commissioner of education, 1896–97, 2 : 2350.

STATE	City	No. of pupils	Value of land and buildings	Expenditures for support
Illinois.................	Chicago (six schools)....	120	....	....
Indiana	Evansville........... ...	10	....	$1 000
Massachusetts	Boston	123	$98 000	21 569
Michigan...............	Detroit.	15	....	650
Missouri	St. Louis...............	35	....	....
Ohio	Cincinnati..............	36	20 000	3 600
Ohio	Cincinnati..............	6	....	800
Ohio	Cleveland	38	....	2 500
Wisconsin	Eau Claire.............	6	....	585
Wisconsin..	Fond du Lac	7	....	630
Wisconsin........... ...	La Crosse	9	....	525
Wisconsin	Manitowoc	9	....	1 019
Wisconsin	Marinette	6	....	522
Wisconsin..	Milwaukee	54	12 000	6 291
Wisconsin	Oshkosh................	13	....	1 000
Wisconsin	Sheboygan	7	....	875
Wisconsin	Wausau	12	....	1 261

Private schools for the deaf

From report of the commissioner of education, 1896–97, 2 : 2351.

STATE	City	No. of pupils
California	North Tamescal	27
Connecticut	Mystic	29
Illinois..........................	Chicago (three schools)	146
Iowa.	Dubuque.........................	5
Louisiana	Chincuba.........................	56
Maryland	Baltimore	26
Massachusetts	Beverly	24
Massachusetts....	West Medford.......	10
Michigan........................	North Detroit	36
Missouri	St. Louis (two schools)............	80
Nebraska	Omaha......	9
New Mexico.....................	Santa Fe	8
New York.......................	Albany...	15
New York..........	New York	18
Ohio	Cincinnati	12
Wisconsin.......................	St. Francis.......................	31

Schools for the blind

From report of commissioner of education, 1896–97, 2 : 2340–1.

STATE	City	Number of pupils	Value of land and buildings	Expenditures for support
Alabama..................	Talladega	70	$55 000	$15 000
Arkansas......	Little Rock..............	......	....	....
California	Berkeley	50	450 000	57 616
Colorado..................	Colorado Springs........	55	220 894	17 944
Florida	St. Augustine...........	7	20 000	8 507
Georgia..........	Macon......	126	125 000	18 000
Illinois	Jacksonville.............	220	225 000	52 000
Indiana..................	Indianapolis.............	137	548 870	26 130
Iowa.....	Vinton	186	300 000	32 847
Kansas..............	Kansas City.............	137	100 000	20 570
Kentucky..............	Louisville................	127	100 000	24 522
Louisiana.............	Baton Rouge	33	40 000	9 577
Maryland..................	Baltimore	99	350 000	25 992
Maryland colored b. and d.	Baltimore	25	35 000	8 000
Massachusetts.............	South Boston...........	251	517 027	[1] 30 000
Michigan	Lansing	106	165 484	25 098
Minnesota	Faribault	70	50 000	17 074
Mississippi................	Jackson.......	30	60 000	3 600
Missouri...................	St. Louis...............	117	150 000	29 100
Montana..................	Boulder	6	....	1 800
Nebraska	Nebraska City.	77	45 000	20 103
New York.................	Batavia................	130	375 000	41 500
New York..................	New York................	227	384 957	76 001
North Carolina............	Raleigh	157	150 000	30 000
Ohio......................	Columbus	301	550 000	42 936
Oregon..	Salem...................	24	17 000	7 150
Pennsylvania..............	Philadelphia	192	157 306	53 683
Pennsylvania	Pittsburg................	68	260 000	15 226
South Carolina....	Cedar Spring............	48	55 000	17 000
Tennessee.................	Nashville................	102	100 000	18 000
Texas.	Austin..................	169	75 000	39 350
Texas colored b. and d....	Austin...........	40	37 000	8 200
Virginia..................	Staunton	48	80 000	15 000
Washington...............	Vancouver...............	14	100 000	....
West Virginia.............	Romney................	56	85 000	11 260
Wisconsin	Janesville	125	200 000	23 000

[1] State grant.

Public institutions for the feeble-minded

From Powell: Proceedings of the 24th national conference of charities correction, 1897, p. 290

STATE	City	No. inmates	No. in school dept.	No. custodial dept.	No. epileptics	Value of land and buildings	Expenditures for support 1
California	Eldridge	470	256	154	98	$400 000	$75 000
Illinois	Lincoln	642	171	137	124	300 500	101 139
Indiana	Fort Wayne	554	320	233	135	375 000	79 560
Iowa	Glenwood	690	331	359	178	350 000	102 080
Kansas	Winfield	118	63	36	26	60 620	17 988
Kentucky	Frankfort	123	115	......	6	80 000	25 000
Massachusetts	Waltham	423	228	195	60	250 000	63 377
Michigan	Lapeer	200	127	38	4	75 000	35 000
Minnesota	Faribault	574	210	310	138	359 720	98 767
Nebraska	Beatrice	220	112	60	60	200 000	36 500
New York:							
Children	Syracuse	532	400	133	45	421 330	90 112
Women	Newark	386	......	386	16	179 011	51 876
Custodial	Rome	327	......	327	11	271 733	....
Randall's Island	New York	364	......	......	......	....	....
New Jersey:							
Children	Vineland	217	......	......	......	100 000	46 609
Women	Vineland	94	......	......	33	....	20 000
Ohio	Columbus	973	......	......	......	698 582	143 231
Pennsylvania:							
East	Elwyn	1 028	402	516	197	560 639	163 137
West	Polk	225	......	55	30	500 000	....
Washington	Vancouver	41	41	......	......	20 000	....

1 From report of the commissioner of education, 1896-97, 2 : 2353-4.

Private schools for the feeble-minded

From report of the commissioner of education, 1896-97, 2 : 2355.

STATE	City	No. of pupils
Connecticut	Lakeville	168
Illinois	Godfrey	3
Maryland	Ellicott City	32
Massachusetts	Amherst	10
Massachusetts	Barre	49
Massachusetts	Fayville	4
Michigan	Kalamazoo	30
New Jersey	Cranbury	17
New Jersey	Haddonfield	19
New Jersey	Orange	25

DEPARTMENT OF EDUCATION

FOR THE

UNITED STATES COMMISSION TO THE PARIS EXPOSITION OF 1900

MONOGRAPHS ON EDUCATION

IN THE

UNITED STATES

EDITED BY

NICHOLAS MURRAY BUTLER

Professor of Philosophy and Education in Columbia University, New York

16

SUMMER SCHOOLS
AND UNIVERSITY EXTENSION

BY

HERBERT B. ADAMS

Professor of American and Institutional History in the Johns Hopkins University, Baltimore, Maryland

THIS MONOGRAPH IS CONTRIBUTED TO THE UNITED STATES EDUCATIONAL EXHIBIT BY THE STATE OF NEW YORK

SUMMER SCHOOLS AND UNIVERSITY EXTENSION

CHAUTAUQUA SYSTEM OF POPULAR EDUCATION

The place — In America the name " Chautauqua " stands for a place, an institution, and an idea. The place is a summer town on Lake Chautauqua, in southwestern New York. It is a popular educational resort, during the months of July and August, for several thousand people, who go there from all parts of the country to hear lectures and music, to attend class courses of instruction, to enjoy college life and open air. Chautauqua is a well-nigh deserted village during nine months in the year, but in the summer season it has a cottage and hotel population ranging from 3,000 to 10,000 people.

It is a kind of educational Bayreuth for the people; indeed it has become a center of musical and social-economic training of no mean order. It is a vast summer encampment or *cantonnement*, 165 acres in territorial extent, on the upland terraces of a beautiful lake 18 miles long and from 1 to 3 miles wide, the highest navigable water on the continent, 730 feet higher than Lake Erie and 1,400 feet above the sea level. Chautauqua was the Indian name for this lake, the shores of which are a natural " divide " between waters which flow northeastward with the St. Lawrence from the great lake district and waters which flow southwestward to the Mississippi river and the Gulf of Mexico. Chautauqua is one of the highlands of New York, although it lies in the lowly southwest corner of the state, 70 miles south of Buffalo, 200 miles north of Pittsburg, and 450 miles west from New York city. Chautauqua is connected with the Lake Shore route to Chicago and easily reached by railroads from the east.

Von Holst on Chautauqua — When Von Holst, the German historian of the United States, was asked what are the

most characteristic American sights, he replied: " Go to
Niagara Falls and then around the corner [of New York
state] to see Chautauqua." It is certainly a better thing to
see than the stock yards and pig-sticking of Chicago. Chautauqua is beautiful for education but not remarkable architecturally. The academic village has some useful school
buildings; a few hundred decent cottages in the woods; a
fair hotel called " The Athenæum ;" a few shops or "stores ;"
a plain college building on a hilltop, with a beautiful lake-
environment; a so-called "hall of philosophy," which is a
wooden temple with supporting pillars, open to the summer
breeze and seating three or four hundred people; and a
vast amphitheatre, like a Greek theatre dug out of a hillside, but well roofed, well lighted by electricity, and capable
of seating five or six thousand people. It is an inspiring
sight to see a large Chautauqua audience in the afternoon
or evening.

The Chautauqua salute — When the presiding officer
wishes to show special honor to some foreign visitor or distinguished lecturer, the audience is requested to give the
so-called " Chautauqua salute." Immediately thousands of
white handkerchiefs are waved in the air and suddenly the
vast amphitheatre seems full of life and motion. The effect
is picturesque in the extreme. It appeals only to the eye,
but it surpasses any noisy applause. The custom had a
natural origin, which is thus explained by Chancellor Vincent : In the early days of the Chautauqua lake assembly,
Professor Green, a deaf-mute from Canada, was giving a
lecture in pantomime, illustrating certain incidents in the
life of Christ. The performance was so good that the audience applauded vigorously by clapping their hands. Chancellor Vincent, realizing that the professor could not hear the
applause, suggested that the people wave their handkerchiefs, which was done amid great enthusiasm. This
"Chautauqua salute" is now given at many Chautauqua
gatherings in various local assemblies, but the honor is
reserved at the central Chautauqua for very rare occasions.

Governor Roosevelt at Chautauqua —At a recent visit (August 19, 1899) of the warrior, statesman and historian, Governor Roosevelt, of New York, to Chautauqua, where he has long been known as a public historical lecturer, he was welcomed by the Chautauqua salute in the presence of 10,000 people assembled in the vast amphitheatre. In response he said from the platform that he came to preach the gospel of intelligent work. It is good for everybody, for parent and child. He appealed to the presiding genius of Chautauqua : " Bishop Vincent, nothing has interested me more in reading the history of the growth of the west than to read what Peter Cartwright and other Methodist clergymen did to tame the shaggy wilderness and instill a love of the higher spiritual life into the minds and heads of the tamers of that wilderness. They worked hard. They had no easy life. We should emulate them. Look back at your own career. Do you not take the greatest pride in that portion of your life when you manfully labored with all your might? This Chautauqua did not come by chance. It is the result, obviously, of years of work. * * * You here have had to work long and hard, and now there is no institution more fraught with good to the nation than this one at Chautauqua. * * * I am going to speak soon at the Catholic Chautauqua [at Plattsburg] and hope next year to speak at the Jewish Chautauqua. Recognize the good qualities of any man, south or north, Jew or Gentile, provided he is a good American."— *New York Tribune*, August 20, 1899.

This is certainly the spirit of Chautauqua, which is something more than a New York local institution. It is national and even international in its influence. Governor Roosevelt emphasized at Chautauqua the gospel of work, which is as old as the motto of the Benedictine monk who said " *ora et labore.*" Andrew Carnegie once told the students of Union college "An honest day's work well performed is not a bad sort of prayer."[1]

---

[1] Andrew Carnegie's college lectures : "Wealth and its uses;" "Business;" "How I served my apprenticeship." New York: F. Tennyson Neely, publisher, 114 Fifth avenue.

The institution — Chautauqua should be viewed primarily as an unconscious educational adaptation of the old Frankish idea of the folkmote or public open-air assembly   The historic survival of this ancient institution is seen in the American mass meeting, popular convention, or New England town meeting.   A religious outgrowth of the folkmote in the southern states was the camp meeting.   The Chautauqua lake assembly, established in 1874 at Fairpoint, on the site of an earlier Methodist camp meeting, still retains many religious and some political characteristics of the older assemblies.   Amid the multiform developments of modern Chautauqua, the observer should hold closely to the original and central idea of a summer meeting for popular educational and religious purposes.   The institution is a camp meeting for culture and religion. Bible study and the biblical training of Sunday school teachers were originally and still are dominant educational features.   When General Grant visited Chautauqua the chancellor publicly presented him with a Bible.   Grant took it but characteristically said nothing.   The control of the institution is in the hands of a legal corporation representing religious as well as secular interests.   The work is not carried on for pecuniary profit to the stockholders, but primarily for philanthropic purposes and for Christian popular education.

The highest exponent of the institution is its present chancellor, Dr. John H. Vincent, one of the two original founders.   He best represents the broad religious, and patriotic spirit of Chautauqua.   He infused into it the idea that all sound learning is sacred, and that the secular life may be pervaded by a religious spirit.   Accordingly he has added to biblical study and higher training for Sunday school teachers the greatest variety of allied subjects; for example, history, literature, languages (ancient and modern), art, science, music, elocution, physical culture ; in short, education in general.

The following tabular view of the Chautauqua system of

summer study and rational recreation at Chautauqua lake
and of home reading and study was published in bulletin
No. 29 of the University of the State of New York:

TABULAR VIEW

CHAUTAUQUA SYSTEM

HOME READING AND STUDY

1. *The Chautauqua Literary and Scientific Circle.* A four years' course of general reading. [Certificate granted. Does not count for degree.]

2. *Specialized Courses* for continued reading and study. [Certificate does not count for degree.]
   - History.
   - Literature.
   - Science.
   - Art.
   - Pedagogy. Teachers' Reading Union.

3. *School of Theology.* Correspondence instruction. [Degree B.D.] Rigid examinations personally supervised. [No honorary degrees.]
   - Hebrew and Old Testament.
   - Greek and New Testament.
   - Biblical and doctrinal theology.
   - Ecclesiastical history.
   - Homiletics and pastoral theology.
   - Christian science, life and literature.

4. *College of Liberal Arts.* Correspondence instruction in preparatory and college studies. [Degrees of B.A., etc.]
   - Latin, Greek, French, German, English, mathematics, psychology, political economy, history, physical science, geology and biology.
   - Sixteen courses and rigid personally-supervised examinations are required to secure the degrees of B.A., B.S., etc.

Correspondence and residence combined complete a system of academic study looking toward the degrees of B.A. and B.S.

SUMMER STUDY AND RATIONAL RECREATION AT CHAUTAUQUA

1. *College of Liberal Arts.* [No degrees except through Correspondence Department.]
   - Personal instruction by well-known men in all departments mentioned under (4) above.

2. *School of Methods in Teaching.*
   - Psychology.
   - Pedagogic principles.
   - Applications and methods.

3. *Schools of Sacred Literature.*
   - Study of the Bible as a great classic and inspired book.

4. *Classes in* art, music, physical culture, elocution, kindergarten, etc.

5. *Lecture Courses* on the University-Extension model.
   - Progressive courses by one lecturer. No extra fee is charged. The attendance is large.

6. *Public Lectures and Addresses* by men and women prominent in various departments of life.

7. *Recreative and æsthetic elements*, concerts, dramatic recitals, stereopticon entertainments, etc.

The passing visitor will, perhaps, form his opinion of
Chautauqua from the popular and recreative sides, but he
should know that, as in an American or English college,

which sometimes seems to exist exclusively for athletics and student amusement, there is a good deal of serious academic work. The bulletin above mentioned, says : " For the many there are popular lectures, concerts, entertainments ; for a somewhat less number there are philosophical, scientific and literary lectures in progressive courses ; for the comparatively few are provided means for careful study under able and well-known instructors. The Chautauqua assembly should be judged, not by its recreative exercises, but by its educational classes. The former attract the crowds from which the latter are recruited, and the revenue from the many supports the higher departments. All these elements combine to form a community life which, as a whole, makes for intelligence and arouses interest in higher education."

The Chautauqua literary and scientific circle (called, for short, the "C. L. S. C.,") was founded in 1878, and represents the first great popular differentiation from the original Chautauqua which was, and is still, a summer educational meeting on the Chautauqua lake shore. The C. L. S. C. is a well-directed system of home reading in literature and science carried on in connection with local reading circles, and practically aided by many good suggestions in a monthly magazine called *The Chautauquan*. The course of reading occupies four years, which are called respectively the Greek year, the Roman, the English and the American, from the relative prominence given to the history and literature of those four countries. An interesting feature of the course for 1899–1900 will be a so-called " Reading journey through France," published in *The Chautauquan*, and taking the reader on an imaginary journey through France, introducing him to the historical associations of the places visited, and thus forming an admirable preparation for a visit to the Paris exposition in 1900, or for a more extended study of France which the C. L. S. C. will take up two years hence.

The text books on England and the United States, Greece and Rome, and other subjects, social and economic, are prepared by good writers representing American colleges and universities. With all of the four regular courses in history are combined corresponding literary and cultural studies in art and religion. Natural science also forms a feature of every course. In the American year, the special subjects are, besides religion, American history, literature, government, diplomacy, social institutions and physiology. The entire expense for the required books and for the illustrated magazine is now about five dollars per annum. In former years the text books were purchased at reduced rates from regular publishers, but in recent years Chautauqua has maintained its own press and employed its own writers, who understand the special needs of a Chautauqua constituency. All readers are now registered at the central office of the C. L. S. C., in Cleveland.

The course of reading is carried on in leisure hours by Chautauquans at home, but once a week they come together in local circles in neighborhoods and villages all over the country and, under the best local guidance they can find devote an evening to the discussion of topics suggested by *The Chautauquan* and other private reading. The number of these local reading circles during the past twenty years has been about 10,000. The total enrollment of Chautauqua, readers has been about a quarter of a million. Of course, by far the larger number fail to complete the four years' course, but it is estimated that about one-half have done consecutive reading for two years. A saving remnant of perhaps 40,000 continue to the end and win a simple certificate testifying to the fact that they have completed the four years' course of Chautauqua reading. There is no degree awarded to the holders of these certificates, but the graduates of the C. L. S. C. are encouraged to form local educational clubs and to continue along lines of special historical and literary study. For example, this very year (1899) the writer, who is a member of the "educational council" of Chautauqua, was asked to recommend a course of reading in Russian history. There are literally scores of specialized courses for continued reading and study in history, literature, science, art, and education.

Schools — Next in importance to the C. L. S. C. are the summer classes or so-called "schools," wherein definite class instruction is carried on at Chautauqua by well-known college professors during the summer season. A great variety of regular and advanced work is offered. Work begun under competent direction at Chautauqua may be continued by correspondence with the professor or representative of the "school" throughout the year. This combined work done in residence and by correspondence may, in a few rare cases, lead to the degree of bachelor of arts or bachelor of science, conferred, however, only after searching tests. The degree giving power is vested in the regents of the University of the State of New York whose academic honors are better guarded by state examinations than by some academic corporations in America.

The various "schools" at the central Chautauqua are the following:

(1) School of English language and literature; (2) school of modern languages; (3) school of classical languages; (4) school of mathematics and science; (5) school of social sciences; (6) school of pedagogy; (7) school of religious teaching; (8) school of music; (9) school of fine arts; (10) school of expression; (11) school of physical education; (12) school of domestic science; (13) school of practical arts.

The Chautauqua idea — Much has been said and written concerning the "Chautauqua idea." Bishop Vincent is the best exponent of the original conception of the institution and he has attempted to define it in various publications. In a book entitled "The Chautauqua movement" and published by the Chautauqua press in 1886, Bishop Vincent said: "The full-orbed 'Chautauqua idea' must awaken in all souls a fresh enthusiasm in true living, and bring rich and poor, learned and unlearned in neighborship and comradeship, helpful and honorable to both. Education, once the peculiar privilege of the few, must in our best earthly estate become the valued possession of the many. * * * The theory of Chautauqua is that life is one and that religion belongs everywhere. Our people, young and old, should consider educational advantages as so many religious opportunities. Every day should be sacred. * * * Chautauqua pleads for universal education ; for plans of reading and study ; for all legitimate enticements and incitements to ambition, for all necessary adaptations as to time and topics ; for ideal associations, which shall at once excite the imagination and set the heart aglow. * * * Show people no longer young that the mind reaches its maturity long after the high school days end, and that some of the best intellectual and literary labor is performed in and beyond middle life. College halls are not the only places for prosecuting courses of study. College facilities are not the only opportunities for securing an education. A college is possible in everyday life if one choose to use it ; a college in house, shop, street, farm, market, for rich and poor, the curriculum of which runs through all of life, a college which trains men and women everywhere to read and think and talk and do ; * * * this is the ' Chautauqua idea.' "

Professor Albert S. Cook, of Yale university and a well-known Chautauqua lecturer, in an article on " Chautauqua : its aims and influence," published in *The Forum,* August, 1895, says of the " Chautauqua idea " : "As nearly as I can formulate it, it is something like this : A fraternal, enthusiastic, methodical, and sustained attempt to elevate, enrich, and inspire the individual life in its entirety, by an appeal to the curiosity, hopefulness, and ambition of those who would otherwise be debarred from the greatest opportunities of culture and spiritual advancement. To this end, all uplifting and stimulating forces, whether secular or religious, are made to conspire in their impact upon the person whose weal is sought. * * * Can we wonder that Chautauqua is a sacred and blessed name to multitudes of Americans ? "

Dr. Merrill E. Gates once said : " The true significance of

the Chautauqua movement seems to me not to lie chiefly in
the great summer gatherings, in the crowded lectures, the
enthusiastic conferences, and the inspiring commencement
address at Chautauqua itself, nor in the diplomas awarded
there. But the Chautauqua circles throughout the land
mean useful, wisely-directed home reading and intelligent
general conversation in the home circle wherever their influence extends. Not only is it true that neighborhoods which
have been stagnant for the lack of any common themes for
conversation higher than the local gossip have been stirred
to new intellectual life when the circles met to consider the
facts of science or history and the noble thoughts and perfect forms of the best literature of all time, but in the home
circle as well, in the family life of thousands of homes,
children and parents have new themes brought into their
horizon and talked about with a common interest at the
table and in the evening."

Principal A. M. Fairbairn, of Mansfield college, Oxford,
England, says: "The C. L. S. C. movement seems to me
the most admirable and efficient organization for the direction of reading, and in the best sense for popular instruction. To direct the reading during a period of years for so
many thousands is to affect not only their present culture,
but to increase their intellectual activity for the period of
their natural lives, and thus among other things, greatly to
add to the range of their enjoyment. It appears to me that
a system which can create such excellent results merits the
most cordial praise from all lovers of men."

Sir Joshua G. Fitch, for a long time her majesty's chief
inspector of the training colleges of England, said to an
audience of 5,000 people at Chautauqua: "It seems to me
that you have hit upon one of the most admirable and fruit-
ful devices ever yet adopted when, by means of reading circles and correspondence helps, the solitary student has
opened to him what he shall read and what use he shall
make of his reading when he has it. This is a great work
on which you have often invoked the divine blessing.

* * * I earnestly trust that it may continue to go on and prosper, that this great assembly may be one of the most notable agencies by which you may encourage the love of truth, the devotion to knowledge, and the help and guidance of the people of America."

Religion realized—It would be a fatal mistake for any observer to imagine that religion had been neglected amid the multiplication of departments, for in point of fact religion, in its spiritual ethical sense, is the very heart of Chautauqua. In these days of growing secularization and materialism, Chautauqua is a good object lesson in what might be called a religious survival or revival in concrete, wholesome, visible ways. Chautauqua, like Judaism in its best estate, is an institution for the promotion of the higher life, social and intellectual. "Holiness to the Lord" is an historic synonym for righteousness in all human relations, peace on earth, to men of good will. The Chautauqua idea, comprehensively stated, is religion realized in life and culture in practical, not merely in theoretical ways or barren creeds. Chautauqua cultivates faith and works.

The American library association held its annual conference at Lakewood-on-Chautauqua in July, 1898, where the president, Herbert Putnam, then librarian of the Boston public, now of the library of congress, paid the following deserved tribute to Chautauqua : "The Chautauqua system has a most intimate interest to us, as a system of practical and economic education, inaugurated by a sincere humanitarianism sustained by an enthusiastic missionary spirit, successful in reaching a vast body of individuals not reached by more formal processes of education, and successful also in bringing these — at least for a time, and even if but superficially — into touch with the highest in literature and achievement."

Local Chautauquas —There are now scattered throughout the United States and Canada more than 300 so-called "Chautauquas." They are federated with the parent "Chautauqua" only in filial ways like Greek colonies to their metropolis. The daughter educational societies follow the same methods and courses of reading as their *alma mater*, and gladly report to her their progress. Bishop Vincent every summer "swings around" at least part of the grand Chautauqua circle to encourage these local assemblies.

SELECT TYPES OF SUMMER SCHOOLS

Catholic summer school of America[1] — For nearly ten years the friends of higher education have maintained a Catholic summer school for the benefit of teachers and students. After meeting in various places, the school finally settled down at Plattsburg, New York, on Lake Champlain. In 1893, the regents of the University of the State of New York granted a charter by which this school became a legal corporation, and was classified in the system of public instruction devoted to university extension. By this charter certain advantages are acquired by summer school students who wish to prepare for the regents' or state's examinations.

The objects of the school, officially stated, are to increase the facilities for busy people as well as for those of leisure to pursue lines of study in various departments of knowledge. Opportunities for instruction are provided by lectures from eminent specialists. Courses are given in anthropology, history, literature, ethics, science, and religion.

The school itself is beautiful for situation and not far from the principal summer hotel on Lake Champlain. The Catholic Chautauqua has, however, its own cottage accommodations, a club or casino for social reunions, its lecture halls and local book store. The place, like the central Chautauqua, is an ideal summer resort and attracts many friends of education, both Catholic and Protestant.

It is pleasant to see the pictures of buildings on the lake shore and some of these summer gatherings of the clergy who are leading spirits in this popular movement. Dr.

---

[1] A special account of the origin of this new and remarkable movement may be found in the author's paper on "Chautauqua." See report of U. S. commissioner of education, 1894–95, pp. 1065, 1077.

Conaty who was long its faithful director is now the eloquent and progressive rector of the Catholic university of
America.

Catholic winter school[1] — Three or four sessions of the
Catholic winter school of America have been held at New
Orleans, one of the most catholic centers of American
education, secondary, higher and popular. With Tulane
university, the Howard memorial library and a fine system
of public schools, New Orleans, for its educational back-
ground, has a noble record of French Catholic spiritual and
intellectual activity extending through nearly two centuries,
from the time of the grand monarch under whose sovereignty
Louisiana was first colonized and named. The early Catholic movement in American education is well described by
Professor Fay in his History of education in Louisiana
(contributions to American educational history, published
by the U. S. bureau of education).

At the Catholic winter school of America popular education is naturally connected with religion. The school is
opened with pontifical high mass in St. Louis cathedral. A
bishop from Mexico officiated at the formal opening in February, 1898. It is noteworthy that the rector of the Catholic
university of America, Rev. Dr. Conaty, gave five lectures
on the relations of the church to the educational movement
of to-day. This former and well-beloved director of the
Catholic summer school of America at Cliff Haven, Plattsburg on Lake Champlain, has thus served as an educational
link between the north and the south, between the historic
shores of Lake Champlain and of the Gulf of Mexico.
Prof. Alcée Fortier, of Tulane university (one of the best
romance scholars in America), introduced the educational

---

[1] Dr. Weeks says (Education report, 1894-95, p. 1484): "As the summer was
originally chosen because of its comparative freedom and the greater suitability
of climate in the middle and northern states, so the idea has been reversed in the
extreme south and we have the Florida Chautauqua held in February and March,
and the Catholic winter school of America, which held its first session in New
Orleans, February 16 to March 14, 1896, and was a financial success." Winter
schools for adults would be expedient in Baltimore and Washington or some other
cities which are prevented by climatic reasons from attempting summer schools.

program. The distinguished novelist, F. Marion Crawford, also gave a course of literary lectures. In the public instruction given at summer schools by these traveled men and cosmopolitan spirits there is and must be a peculiar extension of the best international and catholic influences. What the *Congrés international de l'enseignement des sciences sociales* will probably represent at Paris in July, 1900 (the idea, namely, of an interchange of *personnel* between the universities and schools of different countries), is already realized in some measure by various American institutions, Harvard, Johns Hopkins, the Catholic university of America and by well-known American summer schools like Chautauqua and Philadelphia, some of which institutions every summer call over to this country celebrated European educationists and public lecturers, *e. g.*, Brunetière, Doumic, George Adam Smith, Principal Fairbairn, Professor Mahaffy, Michael Sadler, Professor Moulton, F. Marion Crawford and many others.

Columbian Catholic summer school — At Madison, Wis., one of the best centers of academic and popular education in the great northwest, there assembled in July, 1898, the Columbian Catholic summer school with lecturers from Washington, D. C., and other seats of educational extension. Noteworthy among these public teachers were the Rt. Rev. Thomas Gorman, Bishop Spalding, the Catholic historian from Peoria, Henry Austin Adams, from the Brooklyn institute, who lectures now on Lake Champlain, now in New Orleans and now in the lake district of Wisconsin.

Jewish Chautauqua — The third summer assembly of the Jewish Chautauqua at Atlantic City, from July 14 to July 30, offered the following general program of work, which continues throughout the year : (1) Popular lectures ; (2) Chautauqua circles for bible studies ; (3) Chautauqua circles for post-biblical studies ; (4) teachers' institute ; (5) general conferences ; (6) religious services ; (7) social entertainment ; (8) preparatory work ; (9) reunion of Chautauquans.

The Jewish Chautauqua now enrolls over 2,000 members in its various local circles in the United States and Canada. For summer assembly work it employs the most eminent American Hebrew scholars, *e. g.*, Professor Richard Gottheil, of Columbia university; Rev. Dr. Jastrow, of Philadelphia; Rev. Dr. Guttmacher, of Baltimore (a graduate student of the Johns Hopkins university) ; Rev. Dr. F. De Sola Mendes, of New York; Rev. Dr. Kohler, of New York; and D. W. Amram, of Philadelphia.   The Jewish Chautauqua also employs various Christian scholars of eminence, for example, Rev. Dr. Charles Cuthbert Hall, president of the Union theological seminary, New York; Professor Leon H. Vincent, the well-known Chautauqua lecturer on literary subjects, whose themes in 1899 were partially Jewish — "Heine" and "Zangwill." This combination of lecturers and subjects well illustrates the truly catholic influence of the Chautauqua idea. Much attention was paid to education, for example, Professor Bamberger, principal of the Jewish training school in Chicago, lectured on "Religious education from the view-point of pedagogy." The chancellor of the Jewish Chautauqua is the Rev. Dr. Henry Berkowitz, whose wholesome and liberalizing influence upon American education cannot be too highly praised.[1]

The original Chautauqua is undoubtedly the most popular and best-known type of American summer schools. Its example influenced the development of very many others, and, perhaps, suggested certain English summer meetings, *e. g.*, those of the National home-reading union, at Chester, London and other well-known places. The summer meetings of university extension and their friends at Oxford, Cambridge and Edinburgh are truly international in spirit. They are the most delightful summer schools in the English-speaking world, but Chautauqua remains after more than twenty-five years' experience the most democratic and largely-attended summer school. It is the earliest continu-

---

[1] A more elaborate account of "National Jewish educational work," by Charles S. Bernheimer, was published in the *American monthly review of reviews*, New York, April, 1897.

ous school of the kind in the world. Chautauqua was founded in 1874 as an educational assembly, with the primary idea of promoting higher and better Sunday-school work. While this idea is wisely retained, educational effort had been extended over many other fields. We may best characterize all Chautauquas as religious summer schools.

Summer schools of science — In July, 1873, Louis Agassiz, the Swiss naturalist, professor in Harvard university, opened a scientific summer school on Penikese island, about twenty-five miles from Newport. This experiment served to develop several young zoologists and gave rise to a succession of similar schools of natural science, for example, the Chesapeake zoological laboratory, the Marine stations at Newport, Wood's Hole and others. The Marine biological laboratory at Wood's Hole, Massachusetts, has completed its twelfth year, and is known as the clearing house of American scientists. Sooner or later the prominent workers appear at this interesting summer school and pay tribute by giving public lectures on the trend of their work. There are three main departments : (1) Zoology, in charge of Professor Whitman, of the University of Chicago; (2) physiology, Dr. Loeb ; and botany, Dr. Davis. See letter from Wood's Hole, dated August 12, 1899, in *Sunday Tribune*, following :

Types of summer schools — Dr. Stephen B. Weeks who prepared for the U. S. bureau of education (report of commissioner, 1894–95, pp. 1483–1503) a check list of American summer schools, says they "may be roughly divided into the following classes according to the phases of education, which they emphasize particularly : (1) Schools that teach special branches of knowledge as ancient and modern languages, literature, psychology, natural sciences, law, medicine ; (2) schools of the arts, as drawing, industrial art, music, oratory, etc. ; (3) professional, normal or schools of methods where the training of teachers is the main idea — summer schools of pedagogy ; (4) general, where all, or nearly all, the subjects in the general curriculum of education are treated; (5) Chautauqua, where the idea of study is united with that of rest and recreation, and where the Chautauqua course of reading (C. L. S. C.) is made the basis of the educational work.

"Again, from the standpoint of control, they may be divided into several classes: (1) Private, which range in scope from a school devoting itself to preparing students for college or to making up the deficiencies of common school teachers, to a private school of chemistry, law or Bible study; (2) college or university, which are usually more general in character; (3) state, which are generally devoted to the training of teachers, are more or less local and even migratory in character. In the matter of fees they range all the way from the private with fees sufficient to support the school to the public state schools which are free."

In the same report Dr. Weeks says: "The length of term varies in different schools from a few days to three months. The tendency to increase the length of time and make as much use of the vacation as possible is increasing, and there has been a material change in the character of the courses offered. At first it was the custom to give many short courses or single lectures. It is now the custom to make the courses of lectures as continuous and connected as possible."

University of Chicago — The most remarkable and most recent development of the summer school idea in America is that of the fourth quarter or summer term at the University of Chicago, where academic work goes straight on throughout the year (48 weeks) like any other business. President Harper, for many years principal of Chautauqua, was probably influenced by its example in devising his plan for a summer university course. The result of his excellent policy is that, while most American colleges and universities rest or go to sleep in summer time, Chicago is drawing students and professors from nearly all of them. Many Chicago professors arrange to take their long vacation in the winter or spring. Outside seekers after academic knowledge can, therefore, find good men at their Chicago post in the mid-summer term. Thus, the summer school idea has been fully incorporated by a vigorous and progressive American university.

"Continuous sessions for colleges and universities" was a subject presented to the Southern association of colleges and preparatory schools, in November, 1898, by Jerome H. Raymond, president of West Virginia university, where the Chicago system of the summer quarter was introduced that very year. President Raymond's favorable account of his West Virginia experiment and of its educational advantages is printed in the *School review*, University of Chicago press, February, 1899. Among the advantages enumerated are:

(1) The new system of four continuous sessions (with a week's recess between successive terms) enables a college or university to meet the needs of young men and women who are obliged to work their way by teaching during the winter months, and can recover lost academic ground by returning to college for the summer quarter.

(2) Professional teachers and others can get some advantage by a summer sojourn at a university of the West Virginia or Chicago type.

(3) Professors in such a university can take a vacation when other academic institutions are in full session and can profit by these outside courses.

(4) The Chicago system enables the student to complete his academic work more quickly.

(5) What business man would equip an extensive plant and allow it to lie idle for three months out of every twelve? "Shall we, then, be less zealous to make the greatest possible use of the great educational plants?"

Harvard summer school — By special request the following account of Harvard summer school in the July season of 1899, was contributed by Miss Elizabeth T. King, president of the Arundell club of Baltimore:

Cambridge possesses nearly every qualification for a summer school. The class rooms, laboratories and college library of 400,000 volumes are at hand. The zoological and mineralogical museums, the Fogg art museum, and the Peabody museum, with its unrivalled Central American, Semitic and other collections, are open to the student. The boarding houses and some halls are ready; the majestic and varied series of buildings in their beautiful setting of court and turf and trees; the historic and literary associations, not only of Cambridge but of all the neighboring region, stimulate the imagination and arouse enthusiasm.

The beginnings of the school were university lectures given on Saturdays to teachers as far back as 1863. Course after course has been added and developed, until now the university offers forty-seven different courses ranging from Greek through modern languages to history, psychology and science. There are this year over 700 students, mostly college graduates, teachers and special students. The work is arranged so that each student is expected to specialize in one or at the most two courses, and much outside work is required in addition to daily recitations.

The six weeks' work is equivalent to a half-year's course of three lectures a week, and it so counts for Harvard students. A certificate is given at the close which is useful to teachers in many states, especially in New York, where a summer school certificate is required.

The fee for each course varies from $15 to $25 and does not admit the student to any other advantages beside those included in his own work. There is none of the pleasant interchange of thought common to most summer schools. Even in more elementary work, the university spirit and seminary methods of a great center of learning are evident. There are, however, admirable general lectures given in the evening upon educational and literary topics, such as German secondary education, the drama of to-day, Dürer, the abbey of Cluny, the evolution of the conscience, etc.

At the close of the school an educational conference is held to which two students from each class are appointed and who prepare a program of conference and discussion.

The historic pilgrimages are by far the most interesting general feature. They are preceded by a lecture showing how the civic conscience can thus be cultivated, and encouraging students from distant states to go home and find their own Mayflowers and Bunker Hills. The connection between the literature and history of this rich region is pointed out, and twice a week most interesting and significant pilgrimages are made to surrounding places where the local historical societies and the antiquarians welcome the students.

This year a new feature has been added in a three weeks' course in the divinity school. It is intended for the "intellectual quickening of the clergy;" and that this purpose was realizable, was at once shown by the enrollment of more than 100 clergymen, although at first a very small attendance had been expected. Eight women have availed themselves of these advantages. Lectures are given on ethics and the ideal elements of religion; on Old Testament history including institutions, Babylonian parallels and methods of historical investigation; on church history and its development from primitive to Catholic christianity. The most distinguished scholars and theologians from Harvard and other divinity schools have in turn lectured to an enthusiastic body of workers and thinkers, and the course has been a conspicuous success.

In general it is remarkable to see what an admirable body of special students have been assembled at the school, especially from the south and west, and to hear from their teachers how good the quality of their work is. The result of disseminating the methods and influences of Harvard throughout the states and institutions thus brought into contact with it cannot fail to benefit both the university and the country. Much praise is due the earnest and disinterested men who give their time to it.

It is amusing to see how frankly co-educational Harvard becomes in summer, and the question naturally arises, if for six weeks in summer, why not for six months in winter?

The men and women students board at the same houses, work in the same laboratories, study in the same library without the slightest supervision — but human nature is so inconsistent that it will doubtless be some time before this logic is convincing. Summer schools are, however, quickly and gradually solving many educational problems, and their directness of methods, adaptation to practical needs of workers, absence of hampering conditions, and quickness of response to popular wants make them interesting laboratories for discovering solutions for the educational problems of democracy.

An equally significant feature is the eagerness for knowledge and desire for enlightened methods in education shown by representatives from every part of this great country which cannot fail to affect the life of the nation.

Melvil Dewey on summer schools — " Thousands testify after trial that the change of surroundings and occupation, the stimulus of cheerful companions interested in the same subjects, and the many provisions of our best summer schools for healthful recreation, are better preparation for hard work the next year than a vacation spent in idleness. In brief, it is evident that the tendency is growing among teachers to congregate for a few weeks during the long vacation."

UNIVERSITY EXTENSION

This subject was first publicly presented in the United States at a meeting of the American library association in their session upon one of the Thousand Islands in September, 1887. The well-known English system, as adapted to American local needs, was promptly taken up by public spirited American librarians in Buffalo,[1] N. Y., in Chicago and St. Louis. In all three cities and in many others, west and south, the idea was gradually developed and extended by the co-operation of university graduates with libraries, churches and other local institutions. The subject was first

---

[1] "An experiment in university extension," by J. N. Larned, *Library journal*, March-April, 1888.

publicly presented in Philadelphia, March 11, 1891, at the galleries of the Art club, Dr. James MacAlister presiding.

New York beginnings—In January, 1888, Melvil Dewey, then chief librarian of Columbia university, laid the plan before the regents of the University of the State of New York, and at the University convocation in Albany, July, 1888, advocated university extension in connection with public libraries. A year later he again brought the matter before convocation. In February, 1890, a committee of New York colleges and universities urged the regents to establish, under state supervision, a system of extension teaching. It was further urged that the state should work through existing colleges and institutions.

First state appropriation—In the spring of the following year, May 1, 1891, a bill was signed by the governor appropriating $10,000 for the state organization of university extension. This was on "university day," the historic anniversary of the granting of the original charter of the University of the State of New York, May 1, 1784. Fit augury of a new era of public control of the higher education of the people! This grant of $10,000 is absolutely the first case on record of a state appropriation for university extension.

It was stipulated by the bill of 1891 that no part of the grant should be used for the payment of lecturers, but only for purposes of organization, supervision and printing. The expense of local lectures was very properly to be defrayed by the local constituency. From this auspicious beginning there rapidly developed in the state of New York the double system of public instruction : (1) University extension from the Albany center or popular education by lecturers, accredited or controlled by university authority, and reporting results to the regents ; (2) library extension from Albany or popular education by means of well-selected, classified libraries suiting definite local needs in connection with local lectures or home-study clubs.

It is possible to follow out both of these lines of educational extension through the valuable and interesting extension and library bulletins issued by the University of the State of New York and exhibited by the same in illustration of this subject.

The University of the State of New York at first, in 1891, made "extension" one of five great departments: (1) Regents' office, executive, administrative and supervisory, through which educational charters are granted; (2) extension for lecture courses, study clubs, reading circles, for extending educational opportunities outside regular teaching institutions; (3) examinations; (4) state library; (5) state museum. The extension department included all agencies for higher education outside the regular teaching institutions. These agencies were at first distributed in four sections: (1) Public libraries and traveling libraries; (2) extension teaching, outside regular schools and colleges, or "university extension;" (3) study clubs, for associate study and discussion of a common series of topics; (4) summer schools.

Experience showed the necessity of some modification of the above organization.

The university has now (1899) six main departments: (1) Administrative; (2) college; (3) high school; (4) home education in distinction from schools and colleges; (5) state library; (6) state museum. These are all well illustrated in the bulletins and circulars of the University of the State of New York.

"Home education" includes the following six divisions: (1) Extension teaching; (2) study clubs; (3) exchanges; (4) traveling libraries; (5) public libraries; (6) library school. The term home education, as employed in the state of New York, comprehends that entire group of agencies which promote the higher education of adults at home and through life, in distinction from the work done by the regular teaching institutions such as the university, the college and the school. Mr. Melvil Dewey, in his director's report of the New York state library for 1897, p. 61, practically identifies "home education " with what the present writer prefers to call simply popular education or "educational extension," *e. g.*, from an institutional center like a university, a college, a state board of public instruction, a church, a public library or a people's institute. The published bulletins of the regents of the University of the State of New York, by their long use of the phrase "extension" have given sanction to the idea of established agencies proceeding from some central source, *e. g.*, Albany, towards the town, the village, the home and the individual.

Mr. Dewey on home education says: "Our extension or home education department has from the first been conducted in the rooms of the state librarian and under the supervision of its director. In the nature of the case this was necessary, and we should without hesitation have carried it on always under the library name had it not been thought desirable to use a distinctive name because of the initial appropriation of $10,000 for a fuller organization of this new work.[1]   Both in print and in addresses I have from the first impressed extension societies and conferences and those interested in other phases of home education that it was in itself naturally so closely allied to the public library that it would be folly to dissociate them in administration. The library has won its place as an essential part of our educational system, and every community of 500 inhabitants is coming to feel that it is discredited unless it has a free library as well as provision for instruction of its children in something more than the three R's.   In our own state we are quietly studying the distribution of institutions and look-

---

[1] "University extension" act was passed May 1, 1891. Home education as a descriptive term originated in Albany, 1897, and it was first publicly emphasized by Mr. Dewey at the Chautauqua meeting of the American library association, in 1898. Among the best known types and agencies of " home education " of an earlier date were, (1) the " home culture clubs," founded and promoted in Northampton, Mass., by George W. Cable, and by him extended throughout the country; and (2) the still earlier "Society for the encouragement of study at home," founded by Miss Ticknor of Boston, and long sustained by her circle of friends; (3) Catholic home reading circles; (4) the National home reading union of England. The more recent is the Chicago Record's " Home study circle."

ing forward to a not distant day when there shall be no village of 500 inhabitants in the state which does not have a regents school and a public library.   The most enthusiastic believer in the work of the study clubs, summer schools, extension lectures, correspondence teaching and other forms of home education will admit the folly of undertaking to organize a third educational center in the smaller communities.   The work will be done best and cheapest by associating it either with the high school or the library, and there is no question that the library as in itself the most important of the agencies for home education is the proper center around which the others should be grouped.   It has long been our habit to think and speak of the work of the state library and the extension department as being substantially one, and we couple it under the phrase of 'state library and home education.'   The reasons that led to giving this work an independent name in 1891 no longer hold good, and it would doubtless be better hereafter for us to make in form what we have in fact, a single department for the rapidly growing interests of home education.   Other states are sure to follow New York's leadership, and we shall set a more practical and convenient example if the administration is understood to belong with that of the library.

" While we are so much gratified with what has recently been accomplished in this great field, those who best understand its possibilities realize that this work is now only well begun.   The public are demanding more and more because they are learning that it is possible through the state library and home education department to secure more help educationally than has ever before been afforded by an equal expenditure of time and money."

Popular education — Undoubtedly a better name than " university extension " must be found to describe that class of extramural educational activities which Mr. Dewey includes under the domestic roof-tree of " home education." The objections to this latter term are : (1) The home idea does not comprehend the larger social and institutional ideas conveyed by extension teaching, study clubs, public libraries, library schools, and educational extension in general; home education is only a part of a larger public education. (2) Attention should not be diverted from the varied and universal sources of educational power, activity, or supply whether in nature, society, university, college, public library or peoples' institutes and monopolized by one of the local objects of popular education, the *home*. (3) Popular education, like freedom, health or salvation is living water springing up from many fountains, which cannot be grouped under two or three heads like "home," "school," "library," or even "university" although all of these terms and others are needed for purposes of educational extension. (4) Home education is a term not easily translated into a cosmopolitan language. Imagine a Frenchman resolving his lucid "*education populaire*" or "*education des adultes*" into "*education chez lui!*" (5) No descriptive term for the education of the people is worth considering if it requires debate and exposition; whatever term is finally chosen it must be perfectly clear, self-explanatory, and go straight to the mark as does the phrase "popular government." If "educational extension" is not sufficiently lucid, what is the objection to "popular education?" Dignify this familiar term by association and ennoble it as men are trying to ennoble democracy. *Noblesse oblige.*

> "'Tis in the advance of individual minds
> That the slow crowd should ground their expectation
> Eventually to follow; as the sea
> Waits ages in its bed till some one wave
> Out of the multitudinous mass, extends
> The empire of the whole, some feet perhaps,
> Over the strip of sand which could confine
> Its fellows so long time: thenceforth the rest,
> Even to the meanest, hurry in at once."
>
> BROWNING'S "*Paracelsus*"

Results in the United States—Limitations of time and space, in this connection, forbid more than a passing notice of the results of university extension in the United States. It has been tried and found wanting in many parts of this

country and Canada. The state universities of the west and
south, for public reasons, early entered their state fields and
some still hold their own with varying degrees of honor and
success ; but as an educational movement, university extension in America cannot be said to have accomplished all that
its friends at first hoped. It will probably not die, but
causes of its diminished zeal are not far to seek : (1) Lack
of suitable extension lecturers ; (2) lack of financial support ; (3) the vast distances to be traversed by university
men, already overworked ; (4) the necessity and greater
importance of academic service on college and university
premises ; and (5) the recognition of better and less expensive instrumentalities for popular education.

Among these better and cheaper agencies, which are to be
elsewhere considered by the present writer, are (1) free illustrated lectures for the people in town and county at city or
state expense ; (2) education at institutes ; (3) public
libraries ; (4) traveling libraries and traveling pictures ;
(5) educational clubs ; (6) vacation schools. All of these
popular educational movements are growing in America
more rapidly than is university extension and have already
surpassed it in practical efficiency.

Results in New York — Leaving for a more convenient
form of publication the history of the educational extension
movement in America, let us notice its three best surviving
phases, which may be associated with (1) the University of
the State of New York ; (2) the American society for the
extension of university teaching (Philadelphia) ; and (3) the
University of Chicago.

These three original head centers, Albany, Philadelphia
and Chicago, still remain the most active and influential
points of departure for American university extension. All
three strategic centers have permanently advanced the cause
in America and have given rise to other and better popular
educational agencies. The University of the State of New
York has organized " home education " and " study clubs,"
with the combined aid of traveling libraries, traveling pic-

tures, extension lecturers and state examiners. All work harmoniously and efficiently together under one central guidance at Albany.

The latest report of the extension teaching division of the University of the State of New York, June, 1899, shows that this organization now includes under the head of "extension teaching" whatever is under the immediate supervision of a teacher; *i. e.*, extension lecture courses, free lectures to the people, institutes both social and general, correspondence instruction in its various forms, summer schools, vacation and evening schools.

During the year 1898-99 there were maintained under Albany auspices 36 extension lecture courses at 12 different centers, as compared with 21 courses at 13 centers the year before. Extension methods were adopted to some extent by Dr. H. M. Leipziger in certain of the free lecture courses of the people of New York state; they are growing elsewhere in public favor. These extension features are of great pedagogical value: (1) Continuity of course on one great theme; (2) a printed outline of topics; (3) a class conference with the lecturer; (4) occasional written exercises; (5) final written examination; (6) certificate.

The greatest practical difficulties in New York, as elsewhere, are: (1) The local financial problem; (2) the discovery and engagement of satisfactory lecturers; (3) the absorption of university and college men in their own academic duties; (4) the extent of travel and extra work required from busy professors.

Result in Philadelphia — This city and the whole region round about have been quickened to new intellectual life and social activity by university extension since its organization in 1890. Noteworthy is the union of energy, enthusiasm, self-sacrifice and devotion to duty, quick insight and skillful direction on the part of the leaders of the American society for the extension of university teaching. Many experienced lecturers have been invited from England to lend expert service in the American popular educational cause. Progressive and public-spirited institutions have co-operated with well-trained, earnest lecturers and their classes of eager students. Generous and whole-souled citizens, men and women, have hitherto sustained the American society by voluntary subscriptions. Its various series of useful and readable publications, especially *The Citizen* and *The University extension magazine*, have united to promote the extension movement, which has accomplished noble, patriotic and helpful service in Philadelphia and throughout the middle and eastern states, where it will doubtless endure in many grateful and permanent ways.

Representatives of the American society justly maintain that there is a decided advantage in the contact of the speaker with the people whom he is teaching. " The living teacher is the center of inspiration. He gives them the best fruit of wide reading and systematic study ; he not only can tell them what to read, but he can rouse an interest by his personal conviction and enthusiasm, and he gives an opportunity after each lecture for the discussion of any questions that arise ; he examines the essays that are written, and guides the class study of those who do work between the lectures. Compared with fixed plants for doing the same sort of thing, university extension is more flexible, and has the advantage of mobility. It carries the teacher as well as the teaching to the people. The lecturer goes where he is needed, and uses any hall or room which will accommodate an audience."

According to the report published in the extension bulletin of the University of the State of New York, June, 1899, the American society last season gave lecture courses in 14 different places in Philadelphia, and in 29 different towns throughout Pennsylvania and adjoining states.

The University of Chicago was opened in October, 1892, and early made the university extension[1] division one of the

---

[1] Dr. William F. Poole was one of the fathers of the original Chicago society for university extension, and the Newberry library was one of its first centers. See article by Dr. Poole in *The Dial*, September 1, 1892.

main branches of educational effort.   Like Philadelphia, Chicago enjoyed the hearty co-operation of all friends and promoters of the extension movement.   The writer was present in Washington, D. C., when one of the most experienced English extension lecturers, Prof. R. G. Moulton, was engaged by President Harper for pioneer work in the west.   In the personality of President Harper Chicago has been singularly fortunate.   He inherited the administrative training of a professor, schooled at Yale university, Chautauqua and other summer schools, also in the American institute of sacred literature.   All of these institutions are democratic in their work and methods, national in their scope.   Dr. William R. Harper, a man from out of the west, educated in the east, patriotic in sentiment, fervent in spirit, serving in his generation "the god of things as they are," and expressing the higher criticism with prudent reservation and helpful suggestions, has been the maker of the University of Chicago, which was founded and is upheld by the lavish gifts of John D. Rockefeller.   The University of Chicago is liberal in spirit and municipal in name.   Its founder and trustees were wise enough not to burden an institution of learning with one man's name.   Cities and states are now lending themselves anew to municipal and state universities for baptismal and other public purposes, as cities and states have done for the local and national identification of the church in all ages of the world.

President Harper and his trustees early attracted to Chicago eminent professors from other institutions east and west, together with many home-wandering scholars from Europe.   At least two experienced directors of university extension work were called to Chicago from Philadelphia. The present head of the extension movement, which may be truthfully and tersely characterized as academic expansion, is the eminent economist, Professor E. J. James, founder of the American academy of political and social science.

Results of Chicago extension — In no small degree, by the aid of university extension, with its superior pedagogical methods and its marked adaptations to local needs, has Dr. Harper, of Chicago, built up his academic resources and a great federal university. Educational extension, lecture studies, correspondence courses, affiliation and coeducation, have made John D. Rockefeller's institution well known to Chicago people, and also to the towns, schools, colleges, libraries and churches round about. Under Dr. Harper's extension policy the University of Chicago is now surely developing a vast academic and national alliance, which will perhaps yet reach Washington, D. C., and include the Columbian university.

All non-resident work connected with the University of Chicago is conducted through the extension division, which provides for different methods : (1) Lecture study courses; (2) correspondence courses ; (3) study clubs, and (4) evening and Saturday classes for Chicago and vicinity. In the lecture study courses the university co-operates with existing literary organizations. During the year closing June 30, 1898, 141 such courses, each of six lecture studies, were given in 92 different centers, with an aggregate attendance of 30,315. To these different organizations or communities the university sent out small traveling libraries containing in all 3,562 books, which have been kept in constant local use. Local librarians recognize the beneficial influence of these traveling libraries in connection with lecture studies, and co-operate with the university in every possible way.

Benefit to the city — The University of Chicago also co-operates with the board of education, and has given in the city itself 17 courses of lectures in 13 different public school buildings. Of the total number, 10 were systematic university extension lecture studies, and the rest were arranged, as far as possible, in educational sections. 55 lectures were illustrated by the stereopticon.

The extension staff of the University of Chicago has been utilized by Professor E. J. James for the purpose of teaching public school teachers. Representative branches of knowledge, history, economics, political and matured science, have been taught as illustrating superior educational methods, and a teachers' college, at last accounts, had begun to develop in connection with the university.

Through university influences the board of education in Chicago lifted the famous Cook county normal school, with the experienced Col. F. W. Parker at its head, into the still more honorable position of the Chicago normal school. In order to raise the educational profession entirely above politics Mrs. Emmons Blaine endowed a school of pedagogy in Chicago and called to it from the Chicago normal school Col. Parker, who chose 17 well-trained teachers, who have been given a year's leave of absence for special study and preparation in Europe and elsewhere, for their new and responsible work. The avowed purpose of the new school of pedagogy is by institutional means to develop teachers who shall bring the public schools of Chicago to such excellence that private schools shall no longer be necessary.

Influence upon the country — The influence of the University of Chicago upon the whole country, east and west, is beyond present estimate. We are living in the era of federations. Colleges and universities in this country as well as in Canada and England, are coming into academic affiliation. In Chicago and New York great libraries are combining or associating together. Colleges and universities themselves in America must ultimately follow the federal trend of Anglo-American institutional development.

At the present time our American universities, particularly the state institutions and the church colleges, have their acknowledged spheres of influence. No one institution can swallow all its neighbors or establish a great academic trust. Historic colleges and universities will doubtless continue to live and let live in some capacity; but Chicago university has extended its power far beyond state lines, and the end is not yet.

Educational extension has a great future in the United States in connection with live colleges and state universities, people's institutes, public libraries, public schools, traveling libraries, traveling museums and traveling pictures. Lately a specimen French *musée scolaire* was brought to Brooklyn, where it has attracted great public attention. Like the earlier Scotch and English traveling libraries, the school museum has also come to stay and it will doubtless soon appear in our public schools and town museums. Already for years the national museum in Washington, D. C., has been distributing to local institutions of science and learning its surplus geological and ethnological specimens. The various tendencies in educational extension, local, state and federal, will undoubtedly merge in a broader current than any one university can possibly represent. Nothing will suffice, short of a national university, coextensive with the nation, like the University of France or its historic prototype the University of the State of New York.

Smithsonian institution — Of all distributing centers of historical and scientific knowledge in America, there is nothing comparable to the Smithsonian institution, that Washington clearing house of the publications of the American historical association and of the literary and scientific work of all our productive colleges, universities and learned academies. Nor is there any institution in the United States which can begin to accomplish so much for the educational and social betterment of the entire American people than do already the various national agencies in the federal city at Washington, beginning with congress and continuing through the departments of labor and agriculture, and all the social and educational ramifications of the United States government in its relations with the country at large.

Authorities — The best account published on " the extension of university teaching in England and America" is by James E. Russell, Ph. D., published by the University of the State of New York in 1895, and shown herewith. Dr. Russell well says: " New York takes pride in the fact that the first five significant steps in extension history in America were all in the empire state, viz. : The library meeting at the Thousand Islands, the work at Buffalo, Chautauqua, Brooklyn and at the capital in connection with the regents. New York also claims the distinction of being the first state in the world to make university extension an integral part of its educational system." Consciously or unconsciously this policy is an historical expansion of that Hamiltonian idea of university control which the empire state shares with the University of France.

For a detailed study of university extension in America the following bibliographical references have been supplied at the state library at Albany by Miss Avery.

1 **University of the State of New York** — The extension bulletins devoted to that subject and published from year to year since the beginning of the movement in America are the most comprehensive sources of information. The university early reprinted articles by H. B. Adams on "university extension and its leaders," *Review of reviews*, July, 1891, and "university extension in America," *The Forum*, July, 1891. See also Miss Katharine L. Sharp's regents' prize essay on "public libraries in relation to university extension," published in 1892, as a regents' bulletin, and republished by *University extension world*.

2 **Philadelphia** — In Philadelphia a magazine called *University extension* was started in 1891. For three years it was a news magazine, but in November, 1893, a second monthly, *The University extension bulletin*, was started, which gave the news side and left the other magazine free for discussion of problems connected with the work. In March, 1895, the publication of both was stopped and they were replaced by *The Citizen*, devoted to university extension in its widest sense. Practically the magazine dealt with subjects of interest to the Civic league, and incidentally with extension subjects. *The Citizen* rendered very great service to the educational cause and to the promotion of good literature as well as of good government. The suspension of the journal in 1898 was widely regretted.

3 **The Chicago University extension society**, a city organization antedating the organized extension work of the

university, published very early a periodical called *The university extension magazine*, which changed its form and character four times within a year and a half, and suddenly vanished out of existence. The result was a small collection of numbers of various sizes, volumed four times, with usually two monthly numbers to a volume. When the University of Chicago organized its extension division the Chicago magazine was practically replaced by the *University extension world*, which was first published as a quarto, and contained a good deal of local material. A change in the editorial staff resulted favorably for the reading matter and the size was reduced. Finally in 1894 the issue was changed from a monthly to a quarterly and printed on heavy glazed paper with wide margins. Cuts were frequently inserted and the magazine was changed to a high grade quarterly. Unfortunately with the issue for April, 1895, the magazine stopped, but the occasional publications of the university afford sufficient information regarding the continuation of extension work down to the present time.

SELECT BIBLIOGRAPHY

By FREDERICK WILLIAM ASHLEY, A. M., *New York State Library School, Albany*

I CHAUTAUQUA

Adams, Herbert B. Chautauqua, a social and educational study. (See U. S. — Education, Bureau of. Report for 1894–95, v. 1, p. 977–1077)

   A graphic account of what Chautauqua is and what it is doing; its outward features clearly pictured and its manifold activities comprehensively treated, from historical, social and educational standpoints. Also printed separately.

Bernheimer, Charles S. National Jewish educational work. (See *American monthly review of reviews*, Ap. 1897, 15:442–45)

   Includes brief account of the Jewish Chautauqua society. Portraits.

Boyesen, Hjalmar Hjorth. The Chautauqua movement. (See *Cosmopolitan*, June 1895, 19:147–58)

   Interesting judgment as to social and educational value. Illustrated.

Chautauqua assembly. Chautauqua year-book for 1895, an official publication of the Chautauqua system of education. 130 p. D. Chautauqua 1895.

   No more published.

Cook, Albert S. Chautauqua, its aims and influence. (See *Forum*, Aug. 1895, 19:689–706)
Extent and scope of the system fully outlined; objections considered.

Faxon, Frederick Winthrop, *comp.* Chautauqua, a bibliography of the lake and assembly. (See Bulletin of bibliography, July 1898, 1:86–87)

Fitch, J. G. The Chautauqua reading circle. (See *Nineteenth century*, Oct. 1888, 24:487–500)
A competent English authority's view of the work and its results.

Foster, Solemn, *ed.* Second summer assembly of the Jewish Chautauqua society; official account, issued by resolution of the executive committee. 63 p. Q. Phil. 1898. Jewish Chautauqua soc.
Includes brief review of the session, with abstracts of all addresses.

Habberton, John. Chautauqua, the most American thing in America. (See *Illustrated American*,   20:10–14)
Illustrated.

Hale, Edward Everett. Chautauqua. (See *Lend a hand*, Oct. 1891, 7:223–30; Sept. 1895, 15:163–67)
Discursive sketches of the work of the reading circles.

—— The Chautauqua literary and scientific circle. (See *Century magazine*, Nov. 1885, 31:147–50)
Outlines the general plan.

—— Chautauqua reading circles. (See *Unitarian review*, Sep. 1887, 28:233–48)
Good general view of plans and methods, including course of study for four years.

Harper, William R. The founder of the Chautauqua movement. (See *Outlook*, Sep. 1896, 54:546–50)
Appreciative judgment of Bishop Vincent's educational work. Illustrated.

Noble, Frederick Perry. Chautauqua as a new factor in American life. (See *New England magazine*, Mar. 1890, 8:90–101)
Good description of the several branches of the system with brief satisfactory consideration of the results accomplished. Illustrated.

Post, D. H. "Chautauqua". (See *Harper's magazine*, Aug. 1879, 59:350–60)
An interesting early account; well written; illustrated.

Tarbell, Ida. Bishop Vincent and his work. (See *McClure's magazine*, Aug. 1895, 5:240–56)
Excellent sketch; well illustrated.

Vincent, John H. *bp.*   Chautauqua, a popular university.   (See *Contemporary review*, May 1887, 51:725–35)

> Contains suggestions which led to the summer courses at Oxford and Cambridge in 1888.

—— The Chautauqua movement; with an introduction by President Lewis Miller. 9+308 p. D. Bost. 1886. Chautauqua press.

> The founder's story of Chautauqua's origin, development, aims and methods, with a candid discussion of objections. Condensed programmes and brief accounts of other assemblies are included. Invaluable.

Willoughby, Westel W.   Chautauqua.   (See U. S.— Education, Bureau of.   Report for 1891–92, v. 2, p. 921–45)

> Historical study, including short accounts of forty other "Chautauquas."

II   SUMMER SCHOOLS

Adams, Herbert B.   The Catholic summer school of America. (See U. S.— Education, Bureau of.   Report for 1894–95, v. 1, p. 1065–77)

> Clear, accurate and sympathetic account from the inception to the end of the fourth year.

Conventions and summer gatherings.   American summer schools, 1892–9.   (See *American monthly review of reviews*, May 1892, 5:421–22; May 1893, 7:539–42; May 1894, 9:539–43; May 1895, 11:530–34; May 1896, 13:553–55; May 1897, 15:554–55; May 1898, 17:540–41; May 1899, 19:583–85.

> Brief announcements of the more important schools; the contemporary outlook excellently presented from year to year. The first number is by Albert Shaw, the editor. Title varies slightly from the above in 1893, '96 and '97.

Innovations at the University of Chicago.   (See *Nation*, Oct. 1892, 55:255–56)

> Doubts the wisdom of the summer term.

Mosher, Warren F. & Conaty, Rev. T: J.   Retrospective and prospective views of the Catholic summer school of America. (See *Mosher's magazine*, July 1899, 14:161–70)

> Origin, development and purposes clearly stated, by the secretary and a former president.

Mosher's magazine; monthly, official organ of the Catholic summer school of America and Reading circle union. Jan. 1891–date. v. 1–date. O. Youngstown, Ohio, 1891–date.

> The Aug.-Sep. double number each year gives a detailed report of the sessions at Plattsburg, including abstracts of all lectures; with briefer accounts of the Madison school. v. 1–12 bear title *Catholic reading circle review*.

Mullaney, Rev. John F. Summer schools and their relation to higher education. (See N. Y. (state)—University. Proceedings of the 31st university convocation. 1893, p. 484–90)
The Catholic attitude toward the movement.

The new home of the Catholic summer school at Plattsburg. (See *Catholic world*, Ap. 1893, 57:67–84)
Very readable illustrated description of the place and its surroundings.

N. Y. (state)—Home education department. Summer schools, report of the summer schools division, 1894–99. O. Alb. 1894–99. (Home education bulletin nos. 8, 9, 13, 19, 25, 30)
Gives each year specific details of the more prominent schools, not only in New York but elsewhere in America and abroad ; with announcements of educational conferences, and summer school statistics. An admirable yearly survey of the entire field.

Raymond, Jerome H. Continuous sessions for colleges and universities. (See *School review*, Feb. 1899, 7:117–24)
Enthusiastic sketch of the plan in operation at West Virginia university.

The summer school. (See *Dial*, June 1895, 18:313–15)
Good brief historical statement.

Thwing, Charles F. Summer schools. (See *Harper's magazine*, Mar. 1878, 56:501–10)
Interesting early sketch of the scientific schools, with brief view of the whole movement. Illustrated.

Weeks, Stephen B. Check list of American summer schools. (See U. S.—Education, Bureau of. Report for 1894–95, v. 2, p. 1483–1503)
Includes excellent historical review, list of 319 schools arranged by states; bibliography, 2 p.

Willoughby, Westel W. History of summer schools in the United States. (See U. S.—Education, Bureau of. Report for 1891–92, v. 2, p. 893–959)
Comprehensive, scholarly monograph, specially valuable for earlier history. The schools are classified according to their fundamental character.

III UNIVERSITY EXTENSION

Adams, Herbert B. Progress of university extension. (See N. Y. (state)— Home education department. Extension bulletin, no. 5, p. 179–84)
Reprinted from *Congregationalist*, 25 Aug. 1892.
Brief but adequate statement of results accomplished in the United States.

—— Seminary libraries and university extension. 33 p. O. Balt. 1887. (Johns Hopkins university studies, v. 5, no. 11)
Early suggestions for popularizing seminary methods.

Adams, Herbert B. University extension and its leaders. (See *American monthly review of reviews*, July 1891, 3:593–609)

——— ——— 28 p. O. Alb. 1891. N. Y. state univ. (Extension circular no. 10)

——— ——— (See N. Y. (state) — Home education department. Extension bulletin no. 5, p. 199–224)

> Excellent historical statement of the work in England and its earlier phases in America. Received the highest award in competition for prize offered by the University of the state of New York. Illustrated in the *Review* with portraits of seventeen leaders, chiefly American.

——— University extension in America. (See *Forum*, July 1891, 11:510–23)

——— ——— 16 p. O. Alb. 1891. N. Y. (state) — Home education department. (Extension circular no. 2)

> Clear account of the genesis and early development.

American society for the extension of university teaching. Proceedings of the first annual meeting of the national conference on university extension, 1891 ; comp. by George Francis James. 292 p. O. Phil. 1892. Lippincott.

Bardeen, C. W. University extension. (See *School bulletin*, July 1891, 17:123–24)

——— ——— 8 p. O. Alb. 1891. N. Y. (state) — Home education department. (Extension circular no. 4)

——— ——— (See N. Y. (state) — Home education department. Extension bulletin no. 1, p. 44–48)

> Brief review of history and methods.

Boughton, Willis, and others. University extension, the new system in operation. (See *Book news*, Sep. 1891, 10:21–46)

> Fifteen articles descriptive of methods of organization, teaching and study.

Dewey, Melvil. The extension of the University of the state of New York. (See N. Y. (state) — University. Proceedings of the 27th annual convocation. 1889, p. 73–115)

——— ——— (See N. Y. (state) — University. Regents report 1889, p. 73–115)

> Outlines and discusses plans for extending the functions of the university through libraries, publications, museums and lectureships. Suggestive and valuable. Also printed separately.

——— New York's part in university extension. (See *Critic*, Aug. 1891, 19:90–91)

——— ——— 8 p. O. Alb. 1891. N. Y. (state) — Home education department. (Extension circular no. 7)

Dewey, Melvil. (See N. Y. (state) — Home education department. Extension bulletin no. 2, p. 69–74)

Lucid statement of the nature and limits of the work undertaken by the state.

Frost, William Goodell. University extension in Kentucky. (See *Outlook*, Sep. 1898, 60:73–79)

Interesting sketch of work among the " mountain whites." Illustrated.

Harris, William T. The place of university extension in American education. (See American society for extension of university teaching. Proceedings, 1892, p. 18–31)

———— —— 14 p. O. Phil. 1892. Lippincott.

———— —— (See U. S.— Education, Bureau of. Report for 1891–92, v. 2, p. 743–52)

Able discussion of the significance and bearings of the movement.

—— Statistics of university extension in the United States. (See U. S.— Education, Bureau of. Report for 1889–90, p. 207, 247, 827–35, 1159–61 ; 1890–91, p. 843–52 ; 1891–92, p. 742, 751, 983, 1206–15 ; 1892–93, p. 1613–17 ; 1893–94, p. 951–71 ; 1895–96, p. 2008–20)

Hart, Albert Bushnell. University participation, a substitute for university extension. (See *Educational review*, June 1893, 6:42–57)

Fair criticism; urges superior advantages of university courses for teachers, in specific subjects; proposes methods.

Henderson, C. Hanford. University extension. (See *Popular science monthly*, Nov. 1891, 40:1–15)

———— —— 15 p. O. N. Y. 1891. Appleton.

—— Nationalization of university extension. (See *Popular science monthly*, Feb. 1892, 40:500–6)

Favors government support and supervision.

James, Edmund J. University extension in the United States. (See *Our day*, Feb. 1892, 9:79–85)

The educational functions of the movement intelligently discussed.

—— New career for college men. (See *American monthly review of reviews*, June 1893, 7:578–80)

Presents the advantages, opportunities and requirements of extension lecturing as a profession.

James, George F. *ed.* Handbook of university extension no. 1 ; being v. 1 of *University extension*, July 1891–June 1892. 3+400 p. O. Phil. 1892. American society for extension of university teaching.

James, George F. *ed.* Ed. 2 enl. 19+425 p. O. Phil. 1893. American society for extension of university teaching.
Miscellaneous papers.

—— University extension in America. (See *American monthly review of reviews*, Jan. 1893, 6:701–12)
Supplements Dr. H. B. Adams's " *University extension* " *and its leaders*, bringing results down to close of 1892. Fifteen portraits.

Larned, J. N. An experiment in university extension. (See *Library journal*, Mar.–Ap. 1888, 13:75–76)
Interesting account of the first library course in the United States.

Moore, Charlotte McIlvain. University extension. (See *Catholic world*, Ap. 1893, 57:27–35)
Favorable Catholic view of the work. Illustrated.

Moulton, Richard G. The university extension movement. 19 p. O. Phil. n. d.

—— —— (See N. Y. (state) — Home education department. Extension bulletin no. 5, p. 185–98)
Clear statement of methods, purposes and spirit.

Moulton, Richard G. and others. University extension, a series of articles on various phases of the movement. (See *Book news*, May 1891, 9:339–80)

—— —— 44 p. Q. Phil. 1891. American society for extension of university teaching.
Present value mainly historical.

N. Y. (state) — Home education department. Development of university extension. p. 179–234, O. Alb. 1893. (Extension bulletin no. 5)
Contains Dr. H. B. Adams's *Progress of university extension*, his " *University extension* " *and its leaders*, and R: G. Moulton's *University extension movement*.

—— Report of extension teaching division, 1893–99. O. Alb. 1894–99. (Extension bulletin nos. 6, 12, 17, 22, 26, 28)
Details and statistics of work in New York, with annual review of progress elsewhere in America and abroad. No. 6 o. p.

Palmer, George Herbert. Doubts about university extension. (See *Atlantic monthly*, Mar. 1892, 69:367–74)
Presents the difficulties in the way of finding suitable teachers.

Problems of university extension. (See *Dial*, Nov. 1892, 13:297–98)
Forcible statement of present burdens of overworked professors.

Russell, James E. Extension of university teaching in England and America, a study in practical pedagogics. p. 147–253, O. Alb. 1895. N. Y. (state) — Home education department. (Extension bulletin no. 10)

Russell, James E.   Die volks-hochschulen in England & Amerika ; deutsch mit anmerkgn.   von Otto Wilhelm Beyer.   112 p. O. Lpz. 1895.   R. Voigtländer.   2m. 80pf.

> Results of Dr. Russell's observations as special commissioner of the University of the state of New York to visit Europe and report on whatever he might find of most importance to educational institutions in New York. Especially valuable for its statements of the results of twenty years of university extension, and its conclusions as to pedagogic value.

Sharp, Katharine Lucinda.   Local public libraries and their relation to university extension.   (See N. Y. (state) — Home education department.   Extension bulletin no. 4, p. 147–71)

> A study of plans of co-operation in use in typical libraries.   Awarded $100 prize as the most practical essay on the subjeet.   Contains list of authorities, 2 p.

Zeublin, Charles.   Results and prospects of university extension. (See *Dial*, Ap. 1897, 22:207–9)

> Later developments briefly and intelligently summed up.

DEPARTMENT OF EDUCATION

FOR THE

UNITED STATES COMMISSION TO THE PARIS EXPOSITION OF 1900

MONOGRAPHS ON EDUCATION

IN THE

UNITED STATES

EDITED BY

NICHOLAS MURRAY BUTLER

Professor of Philosophy and Education in Columbia University, New York

17

SCIENTIFIC SOCIETIES AND ASSOCIATIONS

BY

JAMES McKEEN CATTELL

Professor of Psychology in Columbia University, New York

THIS MONOGRAPH IS CONTRIBUTED TO THE UNITED STATES EDUCATIONAL EXHIBIT BY THE STATE OF NEW YORK

SCIENTIFIC SOCIETIES AND ASSOCIATIONS

The educational activity of a nation is not confined to its schools. Societies, journals, museums, laboratories and other institutions devoted to the advancement and diffusion of knowledge are an important part of the educational system of the United States. These agencies are on the one hand for the use of those who teach, and thus represent the most advanced educational work. On the other hand they extend the range of education widely among the people. The rapid development of the United States, its large area and scattered centers of culture, have in some respects favored and in other respects retarded the institutions with which we are concerned. They, however, show great activity and great progress, and the present review will indicate that they need not shun comparison with the similar institutions of the other great nations of the world.

SOCIETIES AND ACADEMIES

The National academy of sciences, corresponding to the Academy of sciences of Paris or the Royal society of London, was incorporated by act of congress in 1863. By the terms of this act the academy, whenever called upon by any department of the government, is required to investigate and report upon scientific questions. Thus a report has recently been presented to the department of the interior on a policy for the forested lands of the United States, and other reports have furnished the basis for important legislation. As a matter of fact the academy has not been as frequently employed by the government as was originally intended or as sound policy dictates. Established like our schools of agriculture and the mechanic arts when the country was involved in a great civil war, the academy represents a forward movement the importance of which can scarcely be

overestimated. Under the constitution of the United States
the executive, legislative and judicial functions of the government are defined and separated with remarkable foresight
and wisdom. But as science increases in range and in detail,
expert advice and decision as a basis for legislation become
more necessary. It is by no means unreasonable to look
forward to a time when the scientific or advisory department
of the government will rank co-ordinate with its executive,
legislative and judicial departments. But before the National
academy can undertake these duties it must consist, not of
the most eminent, but of the most efficient men of science
of the United States. In addition to its function as a scientific adviser of the government, the academy holds meetings
for the reading of scientific papers, publishes reports and
memoirs and administers certain funds for the promotion of
research and the awarding of medals. A stated meeting is
held annually at Washington in April, and migratory scientific sessions are held in the autumn. Reports are issued
annually and the memoirs are now in their eighth volume.
The academy administers the Bache, Watson, Draper, Smith,
Gibbs and Gould funds, yielding in all an annual income of
about $6,000 for the encouragement of scientific research.
The membership of the academy was originally limited to
fifty, but this limitation was removed in 1870, and at present
five members may be elected annually. There are now
eighty-six members distributed among the different sciences
as follows: Mathematics and mechanics, 3; astronomy, 9;
meteorology, 1; physics, including engineering, 19; mineralogy, 2; chemistry, 14; geology, 10; paleontology, 2;
zoology, 13; botany, 3; statistics, 1; anthropology, 3;
physiology and pathology, 6. The academy is thus larger
than the Paris academy (40 members), but smaller than the
Royal society (fifteen annual elections). Fifty foreign associates may be elected; there are at present twenty-five. The
present officers of the academy are: Wolcott Gibbs, president; Asaph Hall, vice-president; A. Agassiz, foreign secretary; Ira Remsen, home secretary, and John S. Billings,

treasurer. The past presidents have been A. D. Bache, 1863–1867; Joseph Henry, 1867–1878; Wm. B. Rogers, 1879–1882; O. C. Marsh, 1883–1895.

The American association for the advancement of science held its first meeting in 1848, being the continuation of the Association of American geologists and naturalists founded in 1840. The objects of the association are stated in its constitution to be "by periodical and migratory meetings, to promote intercourse between those who are cultivating science in different parts of America, to give a stronger and more general impulse and more systematic direction to scientific research, and to procure for the labors of scientific men increased facilities and wider usefulness." The association thus occupies the same field as the British association for the advancement of science (established in 1831), L'Association française pour l'avancement des sciences (established in 1864), Die Versammlurg deutscher Naturforscher und Aerzte (established in 1828), and similar societies in Switzerland, Russia and other countries. All these associations have performed a useful service in bringing men of science together and in attracting the attention of the general public to scientific work. With the increasing specialization of science, the establishment of special societies and journals, and the growth of university centers, the meetings have perhaps become relatively less important than formerly. But the division into sections for the different sciences has in part met the needs of modern specialization, and there is at present a movement to arrange for the meetings of special societies in affiliation with the association.

The American association is composed of members and fellows. All interested in science are eligible to membership, while the fellows are elected from such of the members as are engaged in advancing science. There are at present 949 members and 776 fellows and in addition two patrons, one corresponding member and one honorary member. The attendance at the meetings, which are held for a week, usually in August, varies considerably with the place and other circumstances, the average being about 400. The funds, the income of which is used to promote scientific investigation, are small, only about $7,000. The sections into which the association is divided are as follows: A. Mathematics and astronomy. B. Physics. C. Chemistry. D. Mechanical science and engineering. E. Geology and geography. F. Zoology. G. Botany. H. Anthropology. I. Social and economic science. The executive officer of the association is the permanent secretary, of whom there have been but four, Spencer F. Baird, 1851–1854; Joseph Lovering, 1854–1873; F. W. Putnam, 1873–1898, and L. O. Howard, since 1898. The president is elected annually, and as this is regarded as one of the chief honors that can be conferred upon American men of science the list may be given: Wm. B. Rogers, W. C. Redfield, Joseph Henry, A. D. Bache, Louis Agassiz, Benjamin Peirce, James D. Dana, John Torrey, James Hall, Alexis Caswell, J. W. Bailey, Jeffries Wyman, Stephen Alexander, Isaac Lea, F. A. P. Barnard, J. S. Newberry, B. A. Gould, J. W. Foster, T. Sterry Hunt, Wm. Chauvenet, Asa Gray, J. Lawrence Smith, Joseph Lovering, J. L. Le Conte, J. E. Hilgard, William B. Rogers, Simon Newcomb, O. C. Marsh, G. F. Barker, Lewis H. Morgan, G. J. Brush, J. W. Dawson, C. A. Young, J. P. Lesley, H. A. Newton, Edward S. Morse, S. P. Langley, J. W. Powell, T. C. Mendenhall, G. Lincoln Goodale, Albert B. Prescott, Joseph Le Conte, William Harkness, Daniel G. Brinton, E. W. Morley, Edward D. Cope, Wolcott Gibbs, F. W. Putnam, Edward Orton, G. K. Gilbert, R. S. Woodward.

The American philosophical society, "held in Philadelphia, for promoting useful knowledge," was organized in 1743 through the efforts of Franklin, who was its first secretary, and later until his death its president. It was situated in Philadelphia, but was intended to represent all "the British plantations," and this national character has to a certain extent been maintained, the membership extending over the country. The intended scope of the society, strictly utilitarian in accordance with Franklin's whole career and the general tendencies of the time, is thus defined in the original "proposal":

"That the subject of the correspondence be all new-discovered plants, herbs, trees, roots, their virtues, uses, etc.; methods of propagating them, and making such as are useful but particular to some plantations more general; improvement of vegetable juices, or ciders, wines, etc.; new methods of curing or preventing disease; all new-discovered fossils in different countries, as mines, minerals, and quarries; new and useful improvements in any branch of mathematics; new discoveries in chemistry, such as improvements in distillation, brewing, and assaying of ores; new mechanical inventions for saving labor, as mills and carriages, and for raising and conveying of water, draining of meadows, etc.; all new arts, trades and manufactures that may be proposed or thought of; surveys, maps, and charts of particular parts of the seacoasts or inland countries; course and junction of rivers and great roads, situation of lakes and mountains, nature of the soil, and productions; new methods of improving the breed of useful animals; introducing other sorts from foreign countries; new improvements in planting, gardening, and clearing land, and all philosophical experiments that let light into the nature of things, tend to increase the power of man over matter, and multiply the conveniences or pleasures of life."

The publication of transactions began in 1799 and of proceedings in 1838. 24 volumes of the former and 38 of the latter have been issued.

The American academy of arts and sciences, due largely to the efforts of Adams, was organized in Boston in 1780. Its object is said to be:

"To promote and encourage the knowledge of the antiquities of America and of the natural history of the country, and to determine the uses to which the various natural productions of the country may be applied; to promote and encourage medical discoveries, mathematical disquisitions, philosophical inquiries and experiments; astronomical, meteorological and geographical observations, and improvements in agriculture, arts, manufactures and commerce, and, in fine, to cultivate every art and science which may tend to advance the interest, honor, dignity and happiness of a free, independent and virtuous people."

As the names indicate, the Philosophical society followed the example set in Great Britain, while the American academy was influenced by French models, but their original intention and subsequent history have, in many respects, been parallel. The academy publishes memoirs in quarto, of which 16 volumes have been issued, and proceedings in octavo, now consisting of 33 volumes. Its library contains 25,000 volumes.

Societies and academies similar to the Philosophical society of Philadelphia and the Academy of arts and sciences of Boston are to be found in many of the larger cities of the United States. They have been established during the present century, many of them recently, and in their scope and influence are chiefly local or confined to a single state. These societies cover the field of the natural and exact sciences or of the natural sciences only, while special societies for different sciences have been founded in many cities. National societies have also been established for most of the sciences, and these are at the present time the most active of the scientific societies of the United States.

The New York academy of sciences, organized in 1817 as the Lyceum of natural history in the city of New York, is divided into four sections, each of which holds monthly meetings. These sections are: Astronomy and physics; geology and mineralogy; biology; anthropology, psychology and philology. The academy also holds general meetings and gives an annual reception and exhibition of scientific progress. It publishes annals in octavo and memoirs in quarto, and has a library numbering over 18,000 titles. In New York there is also a scientific alliance, including the academy and the following local societies: The Torrey botanical club, the New York microscopical society, the Linnæan society of New York, the New York mineralogical club, the American mathematical society, the New York section of the American chemical society, and the New York entomological society. Efforts are now being made for the erection of a central building for the societies composing the Scientific alliance.

Washington has recently become the chief scientific center of America, the government institutions and departments offering numerous and important positions for men of science. The **Philosophical society** was organized in 1871. This and the other societies of the city subsequently formed a joint alliance, which was transformed into the Washington academy of sciences in 1898. The societies united by the academy are : The Anthropological society of Washington, the Biological society of Washington, the Entomological society of Washington, the Geological society of Washington, the National geographic society, the Medical society of the District of Columbia, and the Philosophical society of Washington.   The academy and most of the separate societies publish proceedings.

In Philadelphia there are, in addition to the Philosophical society, several important institutions.   The Academy of natural sciences, organized in 1812, possesses large endowments, a fine museum and a good library (50,000 volumes). Meetings of its different sections are held weekly, and the proceedings are now in their — volume.   The Franklin institute was organized in 1824 for the promotion of the mechanic arts.   Its *Journal*, published continuously since 1826, is now in its 147th volume.   The institute has done much toward promoting industrial exhibitions, the development of the patent system of the United States, the laws on weights and measures, etc.   It has a large library, and conducts classes and lectures.   The Wagner free institute of science, organized in 1855, supports a museum and library, gives free lectures and instruction and publishes transactions.

The Boston society of natural history, founded in 1830, conducts a museum and a library, and publishes memoirs and proceedings.   The Boston scientific society holds meetings partly popular in character.   The Lowell lectures, endowed by Mr. John Lowell with $250,000, are an important foundation that may be mentioned in this connection.

Other cities of the Atlantic states possess academies, organized on the general lines of those already described. The Connecticut academy of arts and sciences at New Haven, founded in 1799 on the model of the Boston academy, is the oldest of these.   The Maryland academy of sciences at Baltimore dates from 1819.   Local academies, often with a museum and scientific library, or scientific societies, usually of more recent development than the academies, are to be found in many cities, including Salem, Worcester, Gloucester and Williamstown, Mass.; Portland and Augusta, Me.; Hanover and Keene, N. H.; Brattleboro, Vt.; Providence, R. I.; Hartford, Meriden, New Britain, Middletown and Bristol, Conn.; Albany, Buffalo, Rochester, Binghamton and Poughkeepsie, N. Y.; Reading and Media, Pa., and Wilmington, Del.

The conditions in the southern states before the civil war and in the years following were not favorable to the development of scientific institutions, but in recent years there has been much industrial progress, and educational and scientific institutions are increasing in number and in strength. An academy was established at Richmond, Va., in 1788, but scarcely survived its organization. There is an academy of sciences in New Orleans, La., and local societies at St. Augustine, Fla., at University, Ala., and at Chapel Hill, N. C.

The central states of the upper Mississippi valley maintain a population of high average intelligence, which is borne witness to by a great abundance of educational and scientific institutions. In several of the states — Ohio, Indiana, Wisconsin, Iowa, Minnesota, Kansas, Nebraska, Colorado — there are academies that hold winter meetings, with programs covering the different sciences. There are also academies in many cities. The Chicago academy of sciences maintains a museum and a library, publishes transactions and a bulletin and holds sectional meetings for the different sciences. There is a society of natural history at Cincinnati, Ohio, a scientific association at Detroit, Mich., and an academy of sciences at St. Louis, Mo. There are similar societies in other cities including Brookville and Terre Haute, Ind.; Elgin, Peoria and Princeton, Ill.; Davenport and Muscatine, Ia.; St. Paul, Minn., and Topeka, Kans. On the Pacific coast the California academy of sciences in San Francisco was organized in 1853. It possesses a museum and a scientific library and publishes proceedings, occasional papers, and memoirs. There are local scientific societies at Santiago and Santa Barbara, Cal., and at Tacoma, Wash., and an Alaskan society of natural history and ethnology has been founded at Sitka. California now possesses two of the important universities of the United States, and a rapid growth of scientific interest may be expected on the Pacific coast.

The societies and academies thus briefly reviewed suffer from the specialization which the growth of modern science requires. This has indeed been met in the larger centers by a subdivision into sections, but in many cases the societies are concerned only with natural history and often in an amateur and somewhat superficial manner. The differentiation in science which has interfered with societies covering a wide field has, however, been favorable to the establishment of local and national societies devoted to a single science, while professional and technical societies with definite interests to promote have in recent years grown greatly in number and in influence.

Of these societies the National educational association should be mentioned first. Its present name was assumed in 1870, but it was established as the National teachers' association in 1857, being then the outgrowth of the American institute of instruction, organized in 1830, and other societies.

The objects of the association, according to the preamble of its constitution, are "to elevate the character and advance the interests of the profession of teaching and to promote the cause of popular education in the United States." The association has been extremely successful in attaining these ends. The annual meetings have been held in different states and in Canada, and the attendance at recent meetings tends to be as large as 10,000 members. The finances have been so administered that a large permanent endowment has been secured, and the annual volumes of the *Proceedings* contain papers and discussions of great educational interest and value. Until 1870 topics were discussed before the whole association as a body, but subsequently special departments have been organized, including school superintendence, normal schools, kindergarten instruction, elementary education, secondary education, higher education, industrial education, art education, music education, and a national council of education. The council of education, consisting of sixty members elected from the association, has been the author of many important documents and reports.

There are in nearly every state and in many counties associations of teachers devoted to the improvement of the schools and the professional interest of the members. Meetings are usually held once a year, and are largely attended. There are also numerous local societies, which perform important scientific, professional and social functions. It cannot be expected that the general level of the papers and discussions before these societies should be much above the average of those who attend the sessions. But teaching is gradually becoming a profession co-ordinate with medicine, law and theology, and the numerous educational societies are contributing toward this end.

The physicians of the United States have numerous societies, which in part perform the functions of trades unions for the profession, and in part contribute to the advancement of medical science and practice. The American medical association holds an annual migratory meeting, and publishes an important monthly journal. The Association of American physicians and the American academy of medicine are also national associations covering the whole field of medicine. There are further national societies for different departments — neurology, ophthalmology, otology, gynæcology, dermatology, pediatry, climatology, etc. Then there are societies for different sections of the country, and nearly every state of the union has a special medical society holding an annual meeting. There are also numerous local societies which meet in sections and at frequent intervals. The Academy of medicine in New York city, and the College of physicians of Philadelphia, for example, own fine buildings and administer large libraries.

In addition to an American bar association there are several state and local societies of lawyers. These sometimes maintain a library, but their objects are strictly professional, so that they can scarcely be regarded as scientific societies even in the widest interpretation of the term. This holds also for the congresses and assemblies of different religious denominations. They are chiefly occupied with executive work and matters of discipline and but rarely discuss subjects that contribute to the advancement or diffusion of knowledge.

On the other hand the societies of technical science, while to a certain extent concerned with the professional interests of their members, are chiefly devoted to research. The societies are large in membership and in influence, representing one of the most important scientific developments of the present time and of the United States.

The American chemical society was the outgrowth of a meeting held in 1874 to celebrate the centennial of the discovery of oxygen. The society was organized in 1876, and now holds two general meetings annually, one during the Christmas holidays and one in the summer in connection with the American association. It maintains a monthly journal, and has recently established in New York city a club house in which its library is deposited. Local sections of the society, holding frequent meetings throughout the year, have been established in New York, Washington, Chicago, Rhode Island, Cincinnati, the Lehigh Valley, New Orleans, Nebraska, North Carolina and Columbus.

The American society of civil engineers is the oldest of the societies of applied science, having been organized and incorporated in 1852. It has headquarters in New York city and publishes monthly *Transactions*. The American institute of mining engineers was organized in 1871, the American society of mechanical engineers in 1880, and the American institute of electrical engineers in 1884. Each of these societies has a large membership, publishes transactions, and exercises an important influence on the development of applied science. In addition to these national societies there are in the United States numerous other technological associations. The Tekniker Verein of Washington is the headquarters of the National association of German-American technologists with nine branches. We have an Engineering association of the south, a Technical society of the Pacific coast, a Western society of engineers, and many local societies.

All the leading sciences now have national organizations. The American mathematical society, established as the New York mathematical society in 1888, publishes a monthly *Bulletin* and *Quarterly transactions*, holds regular meetings in New York and in Chicago, and a migrating meeting in the summer. A conference of astronomers and astrophysicists was held on the occasion of the dedication of the Yerkes observatory in 1897, and has since been made an annual meeting. A physical society is now in course of organization. An American metrological society was established in 1873 and has exerted much influence toward the adoption of the metric system and the definition of units of measure. The American chemical society has already been described.

The Geological society of America was organized in 1888. It holds two annual meetings and publishes a *Bulletin*. The American geographical society of New York and the National geographic society of Washington, though from one point of view local, are national in their influence. Each publishes a journal, and does much to arouse popular interest in geographical exploration. The New York society has a new building in course of erection.

The American society of naturalists, organized in 1883, largely with a view to the discussion of educational questions, holds winter meetings during the Christmas holidays, which serve as a center for several societies devoted to the natural sciences. These are the Association of American anatomists, the Society for plant morphology and physiology, the American morphological society, the American physiological society, the American psychological association, the American folklore society, and section H, anthropology, of the American association for the advancement of science. Some two hundred papers are annually presented before these affiliated societies representing a high level of scientific research. The American ornithologists' union, organized in 1883, always has a valuable program for its annual meetings, and publishes a quarterly journal — *The Auk*. The American microscopical society (1878) and the American entomological society (1859) complete the list of national scientific societies, but there are in addition to these a large number more local in character. The Astronomical society of the Pacific, organized in 1889, issues a bi-monthly *Publication*. There are in San Francisco two geographical societies and Philadelphia has an important geographical society. Local clubs, especially of botany, ornithology and microscopy are widely scattered over the country. They are often somewhat amateur in character, but useful in many ways.

In history and economics there are several national societies of importance. The American historical association, organized in 1884, issues reports and papers. Its principal office is at Washington, but it holds migratory meetings. The American economical association (1885), and the American academy of political and social science (1889), are both active associations issuing important publications. There are further to be mentioned the American statistical association and the American social science association. The Massachusetts historical society, organized in 1791 and incorporated in 1794, is one of the oldest historical societies in the world. The New York historical society was organized in 1804, and the Historical society of Pennsylvania in 1824. Historical societies, chiefly for the collection of material relating to a single state, county or locality, are very numerous. There are also many genealogical, memorial and patriotic societies which scarcely fall within the limits of this review.

The Archæological institute of America has sent out various expeditions and published the results. The American antiquarian society, organized in 1812 in Worcester,

Mass., has had a long and useful career. There is an American numismatic and archæological society and several local archæological and antiquarian societies.

In philology the American philological association (1869), the American oriental society (1842), the American dialect society (1889), the American folklore society (1888), the Modern language association of America (1883), and the Spelling reform association (1876), are the most important societies. In this connection may also be mentioned the American library association, although its objects are largely professional. We have an American Dante society, and numerous local Shakespeare clubs and literary societies.

In the fine arts there are important associations, such as the National academy of design, in New York, and the Pennsylvania academy of the fine arts in Philadelphia, which hold annual exhibitions. A National league of mineral painters was organized in 1892.

JOURNALS

The dispersion of American students over a great area and the lack of a single center of culture, such as foreign nations possess in London, Paris and Berlin, gives especial importance to journals as a means of intercommunication. The differentiation of science in recent years has lead to the rapid multiplication of special journals, but at the same time increases the need of journals that will keep the sciences in touch with each other.

The American journal of science was the earliest of our scientific journals, having been established at Yale university by the elder Silliman in 1818. *The Journal of the Franklin institute* began as the *American mechanic's magazine* in 1825; other technical journals were established and various scientific journals came and went, but the *American journal of science* for fifty years sufficed for the publication of the scientific work of the country. The *American naturalist* was founded by Professors Packard, Morse, Hyatt and Putnam in 1867. *The Popular science monthly*

was begun in 1872.   Dr. A. Graham Bell and the late Gar-
diner G. Hubbard established *Science*, a weekly journal, in
1883.   Numerous journals devoted to special sciences have
recently been founded, largely under the auspices of universities, Johns Hopkins and Chicago accomplishing the most
in this direction.

A representative educational journal was lacking until the
establishment of the *Educational review* by Professor
Nicholas Murray Butler in 1891.   We have some four hundred medical journals, only a few of which surpass medio-
crity.   Among literary journals the *Atlantic monthly* has
had the most honorable history, while the *Nation*, including
politics in its scope, has been an influential weekly journal.
The North American review and *The Forum* do not equal
the journals of Great Britain and France devoted to literature and public affairs.   On the other hand, the monthly
illustrated journals have been extremely successful and have
contributed much to the popularization of literature, art and
science.

The more important of the scientific and learned journals
of the United States (proceedings of societies and technical
and trade journals being omitted), are as follows:

General science

American journal of science (1818).   E. S. Dana.   New Haven,
monthly.

Science (1883).   J. McKeen Cattell.   New York, weekly.

Appletons' popular science monthly (1872).   W. J. Youmans.   New
York, monthly.

Scientific American (1846).   New York, weekly.

Scientific American supplement (1876).   New York, weekly.

Mathematics

American journal of mathematics (1878).   S. Newcomb.   Baltimore,
quarterly.

Bulletin of the American mathematical society (1893).   Thomas S.
Fiske, F. N. Cole, Alexander Ziwet, Frank Morley, E. O. Lovett.   New
York, monthly.

Annals of mathematics (1884).   Ormond Stone, H. S. White, W. E.
Byerly, H. F. Osgood, Maxime Bocher.   Cambridge.

Astronomy

Astronomical journal (1849). Seth C. Chandler. Cambridge.

Astrophysical journal (1895). George E. Hale and James E. Keeler. Chicago, monthly.

Popular astronomy (1893). Wm. W. Payne. Northfield, Minn., monthly.

Physics

Physical review (1893). E. L. Nichols, Ernest Merritt, Frederick Bedell. New York, monthly.

Terrestrial magnetism and atmospheric electricity (1895). L. A. Bauer. Baltimore, quarterly.

Chemistry

American chemical journal (1879). Ira Remsen. Baltimore, monthly.

Journal of the American chemical society (1887). Edward Hart. Easton, Pa., monthly.

Journal of physical chemistry (1896). W. D. Bancroft, J. E. Trevor. Ithaca, N. Y., nine numbers.

Geology and geography

American geologist (1888). N. H. Winchell. Minneapolis, monthly.

Journal of geology (1893). T. C. Chamberlin. Chicago, semi-quarterly.

National geographic magazine (1888). John Hyde. Washington, monthly.

Bulletin of the American geographical society (1892). Librarian. New York, five numbers.

Natural science

American naturalist (1867). Boston, monthly.

Biological bulletin (1897). C. O. Whitman. Boston, irregular.

Zoology

Journal of morphology (1887). C. O. Whitman. Boston, irregular.

The Auk (1876). J. A. Allen. New York, quarterly.

Botany

Bulletin of the Torrey botanical club (1870). L. M. Underwood. New York, monthly.

Botanical gazette (1876).   John M. Coulter, Charles R. Barnes, J. C. Arthur. Chicago, monthly.

Physiology and pathology

American journal of physiology (1898). Wm. T. Porter. Boston, monthly.

Journal of comparative neurology (1890). C. L. and C. J. Herrick, Granville, O., quarterly.

Journal of experimental medicine (1895). W. H. Welch. New York, bi-monthly.

American journal of insanity (1843). Henry M. Hurd. Baltimore. quarterly.

Anthropology

The anthropologist (1888). F. W. Hodge. New York, quarterly.

Journal of the American folklore society (1888). W. W. Newell. Boston, quarterly.

Psychology

American journal of psychology (1887). G. Stanley Hall. Worcester, quarterly.

Psychological review (1894). J. McKeen Cattell, J. Mark Baldwin. New York, bi-monthly.

Education

Educational review (1891). Nicholas Murray Butler. New York, ten numbers.

Pedagogical seminary (1892). G. Stanley Hall. Worcester, quarterly.

The School review (1893). Charles H. Thurber. Chicago, ten numbers.

Philosophy

The Philosophical review (1891). J. G. Schurman, J. E. Creighton, James Seth. New York, bi-monthly.

The Monist (1890). Paul Carus. Chicago, quarterly.

The International journal of ethics (1890). Philadelphia, quarterly,

History and archæology

The American historical review (1895). John Franklin Jameson. New York.

The American journal of archæology (1885). John H. Wright. New York, bi-monthly.

Political economy and sociology

Political science quarterly (1885). The Faculty of political science of Columbia university. Boston, quarterly.

Journal of political economy (1892). J. Lawrence Laughlin. Chicago, quarterly.

Quarterly journal of economics (1886). F. W. Taussig. Boston, quarterly.

American journal of sociology (1894). Albion W. Small. Chicago, bi-monthly.

Philology

American journal of philology (1879). B. L. Gildersleeve. Baltimore, quarterly.

Modern language notes (1886). A. M. Elliott. Baltimore, eight numbers.

MUSEUMS AND OTHER SCIENTIFIC INSTITUTIONS

The Smithsonian institution at Washington is unique both in its history and in its objects. James Smithson, an Englishman, who died at Genoa in 1829, left a will containing the clause, " In the case of the death of my said nephew without leaving a child * * * I then bequeath the whole of my property * * * to the United States of America, to found at Washington, under the name of the Smithsonian institution, an establishment for the increase and diffusion of knowledge among men." In 1838 the United States government received somewhat more than $500,000 in accordance with the terms of this will. The character of the institution that should be established with the bequest was for eight years the subject of discussion in congress. The final result exactly fulfilled the intention of Smithson ; an institution was founded for "the increase and diffusion of knowledge," which has exercised an important influence on the development of science in America.

The board of regents of the institution has wisely left the administration to the secretary, who appoints all officers and is responsible for expenditures. They have been particularly fortunate in the secretaries they have selected, Joseph Henry, 1846–1878 ; Spencer Fullerton Baird, 1878–1887, and Samuel Pierpont Langley since 1887. The scope of the institution was outlined by the first secretary, and its policy was shaped by him during a long administration. Henry believed that the Smithsonian institution should not continue to do anything that could be done equally well by other agencies, and it was largely through this wise policy and under the guidance of the institution that the government of the United States has undertaken to develop the resources of the country and advance science to a greater degree than any other nation. On these objects the sum of over $8,000,000 is spent annually, and over 5,000 officers are employed.

The library of the Smithsonian institution was early transferred to the library of congress, and was the most important step towards making a great national library. The museum, though still administered by the institution, is now supported by the government. The meteorological observations, reported with the aid of the electric telegraph, to which Henry's researches had so largely contributed, were transferred to a separate bureau, now under the department of agriculture. The geological survey and the coast and geodetic survey, the beginnings of which were chiefly due to President Jefferson, were aided by the institution. They have now become well established as separate departments, while the bureau of American ethnology has been placed under the administration of the institution. The work on the fisheries, begun by Secretary Baird, has developed into a separate commission. Adams strenuously urged the application of the income from Smithson's bequest to the establishment of a national observatory, and the naval observatory founded at the time may perhaps be regarded as an indirect result of this bequest, while an astrophysical observatory has been made under Secretary Langley a part of the institution. When the National zoological park was established in 1889 it was placed under the direction of the institution.

The primary objects of the institution have been largely carried out by its publications, which include annual reports, contributions to knowledge and miscellaneous collections, in addition to the publications of the National museum and the Bureau of American ethnology. The publications now number 250 volumes, and by exchange the library, amounting to some 400,000 volumes and pamphlets, has been chiefly collected. The system for exchange of publications now corresponds with some 25,000 libraries and individuals, and acts as a medium of exchange for the government and other institutions as well as for the publications of the institution.

The building of the institution was erected from the income of the bequest, and further savings from the income amount to $100,000. By a gift of $200,000 from Thomas G. Hodgkin in 1891 and smaller bequests, the funds of the institution now amount to nearly one million dollars. These are deposited with the government which guarantees an income of 6 per cent. The Hodgkin's fund is, in part, for investigations of the atmosphere, and has contributed to research in different directions.

The United States national museum, as has been stated, is at present under the administration of the Smithsonian institution, but is supported by an annual government grant of somewhat over $200,000. The museum began with Smithson's cabinet of minerals and various miscellaneous collections housed in the patent office, and has grown by collections made under different government bureaus and by gifts. It is inadequately exhibited in a building that cost only $250,000, and, while containing much of value, is by no means equal to the national museums of Europe. Under the administration of G. Brown Goode, assistant secretary of the Smithsonian institution, the organization was greatly improved. At present it contains three main departments, anthropology, biology and geology.

The American museum of natural history, incorporated in 1869, has been provided by the city of New York with a fine building which is being continually enlarged, and about $100,000 annually is appropriated for maintenance. The museum is administered by a board of trustees who are responsible for the increase of the collections. About $75,000 is spent yearly for expeditions and collections. The museum includes a department of public instruction which provides frequent and largely attended lectures.

The Brooklyn institute of arts and sciences, first organized in 1823, in addition to an extensive provision for lectures and popular instruction, has a museum, for which a new building was recently erected.

The Field Columbian museum of Chicago was opened in 1894. It was established through the gifts of Mr. Marshall Field and other citizens of Chicago after the exposition of 1893, from which it received its building and some of its collections. The museum has enjoyed a rapid growth, its various departments of natural history and technology are well established, and it has begun several series of publications contributing to different departments of science.

There is a State museum at Albany, N. Y., but the museums at Washington, New York and Chicago are the only important independent institutions. There are, however, several museums conducted by societies and universities. Of the former the museums of the Academy of natural sciences of Philadelphia, of the Boston society of natural history and of the San Francisco academy of sciences have already been mentioned. Harvard university possesses the most extensive academic museums, including the Museum of comparative zoology, founded by Agassiz, and the Peabody museum of archæology and ethnology. Yale university has in its Peabody museum one of the most important collections of paleontology in the world. The University of Pennsylvania has good archæological and other collections. The recently-established commercial museums of Philadelphia represent a departure new to America, while the Army medical museum at Washington is an important institution, liberally supported by the government.

The United States possesses several of the greatest astronomical observatories of the world. The three most important are associated with universities, but are used exclusively for research, not for instruction. These are the Harvard, Lick and Yerkes observatories. The Harvard observatory, founded in 1843, is especially engaged in photography and astrophysical research. It has a branch near Arequipa, Peru, at an elevation of 8,000 feet, and is affiliated with the Blue Hill meteorological observatory. Professor

E. C. Pickering is the director, and forty assistants take part in the work of the observatory. The Lick observatory, established in 1875 by James Lick on Mount Hamilton, California, is a department of the University of California. Its great telescope (36 inches), at an elevation of 4,449 feet, has led to many important discoveries. Professor James E. Keeler is the present director. The Yerkes observatory of the University of Chicago, situated at Williams Bay, Wis., was opened in 1897. It has the largest refracting telescope (40 inches) so far made, and, under the direction of Professor George E. Hale, promises important work. The United States naval observatory at Washington, established in 1845, and removed to its present fine building in 1893, has charge of the Nautical almanac and the time service, and has carried out research in various directions. There are special observatories at Albany and Geneva, N. Y., and elsewhere, and nearly all the larger universities and many of the small colleges possess observatories. Among the more active of these are those at Princeton, Allegheny, Madison and Philadelphia.

There is no evident reason why there should not be in the United States great physical and chemical laboratories corresponding to the astronomical observatories, independently endowed, affiliated with universities or under the government, but the time for these institutions appears to have not yet come. The United States, however, must follow the example set by Germany and less adequately by Great Britain and France, and the increasing manufactures and commerce of the country will probably lead to a great development of research in pure and applied physics and chemistry during the twentieth century. It should, however, be mentioned that there are under the national government laboratories and divisions engaged in physical and chemical research, in addition to several private laboratories and the well-equipped laboratories of the universities.

The great unexplored regions of the country and the importance of its mining interests led early to the establishment of geological and topographical surveys under the government. The national survey has an extremely efficient organization, and is allowed an annual appropriation of over $800,000. It co-operates with the surveys established in many of the states, which are also liberally supported.

A botanical garden was begun in Philadelphia by John Bartram in 1728, and is still maintained somewhat as originally planned. A second garden was established in New York city at the beginning of the century by David Hosack, of Columbia university. It became at one time the property of the state, but was not continued. Nearly a hundred years later a great botanical garden has been established in New York city in affiliation with Columbia university. The city has set aside in Bronx park, 250 acres of land — about equal to the area of the Royal botanic gardens at Kew — and liberal sums for construction and equipment have been provided from public funds and by private gifts. The buildings are now being constructed and the grounds laid out under the supervision of the director, Dr. N. L. Britton. The Missouri botanical garden was established at St. Louis in 1889, through a large bequest from Henry Shaw. It possesses over 600 acres, only part of which is required by the garden, while the rest gives an ample endowment. Dr. William Trelease is the director. The garden, which is affiliated with Washington university, issues annual *Reports* and special *Contributions*. In addition to a botanical garden at Buffalo, established in 1897, several universities possess botanical gardens, of which by far the most important are the Botanic garden and Arnold aboretum of Harvard university. There are well-arranged gardens, especially for teaching purposes, at the University of Pennsylvania, at the University of California, at Smith college and at the Michigan agricultural college. Lastly the botanic gardens and the gardens of the U. S. department of agriculture at Washington may be mentioned. A vast amount of important scientific and economic work in botany, forestry and agriculture is carried out under the auspices of the department, and plans are being made for the establishment of great botanical gardens at Washington.

The Zoological society of Philadelphia began the construction of a zoological garden in Fairmount park in 1872 ; the collection of animals has been the best in the United States, and scientific research has not been neglected. In 1874 a flourishing zoological garden was established in Cincinnati, and San Francisco, Pittsburg and other cities have recently secured similar foundations. But the most important advance in this direction has been the recent establishment of great zoological parks in Washington and in New York city. The National zoological park was established by act of congress in 1889, was provided with about 166 acres of land and placed under the direction of the Smithsonian institution. The collections are not very extensive, but the large area of the park allows the animals to live under conditions more nearly natural than is usual in zoological gardens. The park is under the scientific direction of Dr. Frank Baker. A menagerie has been maintained in Central park, New York city, since 1860, but one among the notable scientific advances of the city in recent years has been the establishment of a zoological society and the setting aside by the city in 1897 of 261 acres for a zoological park. It is in Bronx park, near the botanical gardens, and is being developed with resources almost unequalled, under the direction of Mr. W. T. Hornaday, with Professor H. F. Osborn of Columbia university as chairman of the executive committee.

Biological laboratories, beginning with Louis Agassiz's school at Penikese have enjoyed an important development in the United States. These are maintained during the summer, usually in affiliation with a university, and like the university combine research with instruction. The Marine biological laboratory at Woods Holl, Mass., was incorporated in 1888, and under the direction of Dr. C. O. Whitman has grown continually in size and importance. In the laboratory and in the station of the fish commission at

Woods Holl about 100 investigators are engaged each summer, a larger number of students of biology, probably, than will be found elsewhere in the world. Courses of instruction are also given. There are well-organized marine laboratories at Cold Spring Harbor, Long Island, and on the Bay of Monterey, California. The former is administered by the Brooklyn institute of arts and sciences and is under the direction of Dr. Charles B. Davenport. The latter is part of Stanford university and is directed by members of its faculty. There are at least three important freshwater biological stations conducted, respectively, by the University of Indiana, the University of Illinois and the Ohio state university. Numerous special laboratories have also been established, including stations in Bermuda and the Bahamas.

The establishment of a national board of health has often been recommended, but has not as yet been carried into effect. There are, however, numerous state and local boards which carry on important statistical and experimental investigations. We have as yet no well-endowed institutes of pathology or bacteriology, but special laboratories are being founded in connection with municipalities, hospitals and universities. A pathological laboratory has been established for New York state, and it may be expected that the near future will witness a great increase in institutes of experimental and preventative medicine.

There is no previous publication covering the ground of this monograph and in its preparation I have been especially indebted to the officers of societies and institutions who have supplied the information needed. The most useful publications of a general character have been: "Preliminary list of American learned and educational societies," in the report of the commissioner of education for 1893-94; "Catalogue of scientific and technical periodicals," by Dr. H. Carrington Bolton, published by the Smithsonian institution; and "Minerva, Jahrbuch der gelehrten Welt," published at Strasburg.

DEPARTMENT OF EDUCATION

FOR THE

UNITED STATES COMMISSION TO THE PARIS EXPOSITION OF 1900

MONOGRAPHS ON EDUCATION

IN THE

UNITED STATES

EDITED BY

NICHOLAS MURRAY BUTLER

Professor of Philosophy and Education in Columbia University, New York

18

EDUCATION OF THE NEGRO

BY

BOOKER T. WASHINGTON

Principal of the Tuskegee Institute, Tuskegee, Alabama

THIS MONOGRAPH IS CONTRIBUTED TO THE UNITED STATES EDUCATIONAL EXHIBIT BY THE STATE OF NEW YORK

EDUCATION OF THE NEGRO

I could make no more fitting introduction to this monograph — dealing with a race which has grown from twenty
native Africans imported into the country as chattel slaves
in 1619, to fully 10,000,000 of free men, entitled under the
federal constitution to all the rights, privileges and immu-
nities of citizens of the United States, in 1899 — than to
reproduce here in part the eloquent remarks of President
William McKinley, made at Chicago, October 9, 1899, showing in the fewest possible words the national growth in population, in territory and in material wealth, a growth which
has no parallel in the various history of the human race,
only comprehending, as it does, a little more than a century
of national life.   President McKinley said:

"On the reverse side of the great seal of the United
States, authorized by congress, June 20, 1782, and adopted
as the seal of the United States of America after its formation under the Federal constitution, is the pyramid, signify-
ing strength and duration.

" The eye over it and the motto allude to the many signal
interpositions of Providence in favor of the American cause.
The date underneath, 1776, is that of the declaration of
independence, and the words under it signify the beginning
of a new American era which commences from that date.
It is impossible to trace our history since, without feeling
that the Providence which was with us in the beginning, has
continued to the nation His gracious interposition.   When,
unhappily, we have been engaged in war He has given us
the victory.

"Fortunate, indeed, that it can be said we have had no
clash of arms which has ended in defeat, and no responsibility resulting from war is tainted with dishonor.   In peace
we have been signally blessed, and our progress has gone

on unchecked and even increasing in the intervening years. In boundless wealth of soil and mine and forest nature has favored us, while all races of men of every nationality and climate have contributed their good blood to make the nation what it is. From 3,929,214 in 1790 our population has grown to upward of 62,000,000 in 1890, and our estimated population to-day made by the governors of the states is 77,803,241.

"We have gone from thirteen states to forty-five. We have annexed every variety of territory, from the coral reefs and cocoanut groves of Key West to the icy regions of Northern Alaska — territory skirting the Atlantic, the Gulf of Mexico, the Pacific and the Arctic and the islands of the Pacific and Carribean sea — and we have extended still further our jurisdiction to the faraway islands in the Pacific. Our territory is more than four times larger than it was when the treaty of peace was signed in 1783. Our industrial growth has been even more phenomenal than that of population or territory. Our wealth, estimated in 1790 at $462,000,000, has advanced to $65,000,000,000.

"Education has not been overlooked. The mental and moral equipment of the youth upon whom will in the future rest the responsibilities of government have had the unceasing care of the state and the nation. We expended in 1897–98 in public education, open to all, $202,115,548; for secondary education, $23,474,683; and for higher education for the same period, $30,307,902. The number of pupils enrolled in public schools in 1896–97 was 14,652,492, or more than 20 per cent of our population. Is this not a pillar of strength to the republic?

"Our national credit, often tried, has been ever upheld. It has no superior and no stain. The United States has never repudiated a national obligation either to its creditors or to humanity. It will not now begin to do either. It never struck a blow except for civilization, and has never struck its colors. Has the pyramid lost any of its strength? Has the republic lost any of its virility? Has the self-governing principle been weakened? Is there any present menace to our stability and duration?

"These questions bring but one answer. The republic is sturdier and stronger than ever before. Government by the people has been advanced. Freedom under the flag is more universal than when the Union was formed. Our steps have been forward, not backward. From Plymouth Rock to the Philippines the grand triumphant march of human liberty has never paused. Fraternity and union are deeply imbedded in the hearts of the American people. For half a century before the civil war disunion was the fear of men of all sections. That word has gone out of the American vocabulary. It is spoken now only as an historical memory. North, south, east and west were never so welded together, and while they may differ about internal policies they are all for the Union and the maintenance of the integrity of the flag."

II DEVELOPMENT OF POPULAR EDUCATION

As the early efforts to educate the Negroes of the sixteen southern states, after the war of the rebellion, in 1865,— they were declared no longer to be slaves, but human beings with souls to be saved and intellects to be cultivated, to the end that they might be the better prepared to discharge the serious obligations of manhood and citizenship,— are intimately connected with the development of the common school system of New England, it will be necessary here to describe in as brief a manner as possible the growth of popular education in those states. If this principle of popular education had not been so firmly rooted in the heart and conscience of the people of the New England states by the Pilgrim fathers, the history of education of the Negroes would have been distinctly different and, perhaps, not possible at all. The spirit which actuated these sturdy pioneers from the old world, who have blazed the way for American civil and religious liberty and the development of a system of popular education which has come to permeate the entire republic — forty-five mighty states, each sovereign in all

matters of its internal policy — was prophesied by Bishop
Berkeley, in the lines that follow, which have endeared
their author's memory to all lovers of education and liberty
in America :

> The Muse, disgusted at an age and clime
>   Barren of every glorious theme,
> In distant lands now waits a better time
>   Producing subjects worthy fame.
>
> In happy climes, where from the genial sun
>   And virgin earth such scenes ensue,
> The force of art by Nature seems outdone,
>   And fancied beauties by the true;
>
> In happy climes, the seat of innocence,
>   Where Nature guides and virtue rules,
> When men shall not impose for truth and sense
>   The pedantry of courts and schools —
>
> There shall be sung another golden age,
>   The rise of empire and of arts,
> The good and great inspiring epic rage,
>   The wisest heads and noblest hearts.
>
> *   *   *   *   *   *
>
> Westward the course of Empire takes its way;
>   The first four acts already past,
> A fifth shall close the drama with the day.
>   Time's noblest offspring is the last.

Our country is now divided into four distinct groups of
states — the New England, the middle, the southern and
western states — but it can of truth be said that all of them
have drawn their theories of education, of theology and
statesmanship, from the ten states in the middle and New
England group, especially from the latter. The sixteen
states in the southern group have not profited so much from
this source as the nineteen states in the central and western
group, but they have been influenced in a very marked way
since the war of the rebellion, and are being more and more
influenced now, by the work of New England men and
women engaged in the active work of education among the
Negroes of the southern states.

The development of the common-school principle kept
pace with that of the population in New England from the

earliest settlement of the colonies, through the period of the revolutionary war, and for some time after the colonies had achieved their independence of Great Britain and established the Federal Union. During this period many academies and colleges, notably Harvard and Yale, were founded, to meet the growing demand for higher and more thorough education of the people. But from 1810 to 1830 there was a notable decline in the character, extent and efficiency of the public school system in New England. Massachusetts and Connecticut had always been foremost in the maintenance of the system. As far back as 1647 a Massachusetts statute " compelled every township of 50 families to establish a public school for all children, and every town of 100 families to set up a grammar school, where youth might be fitted for Harvard college." This was the first law ever passed by which a self-governing community was authorized to offer the elements of knowledge to all children and youth. In 1683 every town of 500 families was required to sustain two grammar and two writing (or elementary) schools. On this broad foundation the original people's common school of the colony of Massachusetts Bay stood during the one hundred and thirty-eight years of colonial life, until the organization of the commonwealth of Massachusetts, in 1780.

" The support of the common school through all the grades, including the university at Cambridge, was incorporated in the constitution of 1780. By a constitutional amendment in 1855 it was ordered that no public money should be used for the support of the schools of any religious sect."

There was continuous development of the public school system in New England in this direction up to 1834, when the general school fund of Massachusetts was established.

Dr. A. D. Mayo, M. A., LL. D., among the most reliable and popular authorities on educational subjects in the United States, from whom I have quoted in the preceding paragraphs, says further:

" It is plain from this brief record that the American common school was as practically organized in all essential respects in 1837 as to-day, when the state assumed additional responsibility by establishing the first board of education, of which Horace Mann became the first secretary. This fact disposes of the statement, somewhat industriously propogated, that Horace Mann virtually created the present common school system of the country by his administration of twelve years as secretary of the Massachusetts board of education, from 1837 to 1849. There was, doubtless, ample need that Mann and his illustrious group of co-workers should accomplish the reformation of the public schools of that day. But the foundation had been laid, and there was no call for the destruction of anything ; only for the return to the original habit of town supervision, additional legal authorization of all that then existed, and especially the waking of the people to the call of the new time for the more vital and generous support of their own system of public education, reorganized according to the improved methods of a progressive age. In nothing was the educational statesmanship of Horace Mann more evident than in his immediate grasp of the solution, his estimate of the points of attack, and his commanding influence over the foremost public men and wise manipulation of the legislature of the commonwealth during his entire administration."

The honors which belong to Horace Mann, as head of the educational system of Massachusetts, in awakening among the people renewed interest in their common schools, and in securing such legislation as was necessary to place the system upon an effective and assured foundation, were shared by some of the best and ablest men in the commonwealth. Their combined enthusiasm and labors aroused popular interest in the cause of public education throughout the New England and the middle states, which gradually spread to the splendid states of the western group.

What Horace Mann accomplished in the public school system of Massachusetts Henry Barnard accomplished in perfecting the systems of Connecticut and Rhode Island, both of which he was instrumental in reorganizing and perfecting. The great republic has produced no two men whose life work has wrought more for national education, and, therefore, for national strength, than that of Horace Mann and Henry Barnard.

But, strangely enough, little provision was made in this great and far-reaching revival in these free states, from 1830 to 1860, for public school education for the children of those who were termed in those days " free people of color," although the anti-slavery contest, which was to end in the war of the rebellion, and its sequence of inestimable benefits to all the people, the bondsman and the free man, was in its height during this educational revival which was to give new life and energy to the republic. The Negro's social and political status in the free states was of the most unsatisfactory sort. In the matter of educational and religious instruction he had, in a large measure, to shift for himself, and in many localities, when he did this, the hoodlum element of the white population molested and terrorized him at its pleasure, in some instances wrecking and destroying the modest schools he or his friends had provided for his benefit. But what he did for himself and what his friends did for him in the matter of education during the trying years preceding the war of the rebellion, will be more extensively related under the next heading of this monograph. What relation the labors of Horace Mann and Henry Barnard sustained to the inauguration of public education in the sixteen southern states after the war will be seen when we come to treat of that phase of the subject.

III EDUCATION OF NEGROES BEFORE 1860

It was the general policy of the sixteen slave-holding states of the south to prohibit by fine, imprisonment and whipping the giving of instruction to blacks, mulattoes or other descendants of African parentage, and this prohibition was extended in most of the slave states to " free persons of color " as well as to slaves.

But it has been the general policy of the slave system in all ages to keep the slaves in ignorance as the safest way to perpetuate itself. In this respect the American slave system followed the beaten path of history, and thus furnished the strongest argument for its own undoing. The ignorance of the slave is always the best safeguard of the system of slavery, but no such theory could long prevail in a democracy like ours. There were able and distinguished men among the slaveholders themselves who rebelled against the system and the theories by which it sought to perpetuate itself. Such southern men as Thomas Jefferson, Henry Clay, Cassius M. Clay, and hundreds of others, never became reconciled to the system of slavery and the degradation of the slave.

The general character of the laws enacted on this subject by the slave states can be inferred from the following law, passed by the state of Georgia in 1829:

"If any slave, Negro, or free person of color, or any white person shall teach any slave, Negro or free person of color to read or write either written or printed characters, the said free person of color or slave shall be punished by fine and whipping, at the discretion of the court; and if a white person so offend, he, she or they shall be punished with a fine not exceeding $500 and imprisonment in the common jail, at the discretion of the court."

There were no laws in the slave code more rigidly enforced than those prohibiting the giving or receiving instruction by the slaves or "free persons of color." And yet in nearly all the large cities of the southern states — notably in Charleston, Savannah and New Orleans — there were what were styled "clandestine schools," where such instruction was given. Those who maintained them and those who patronized them were constantly watched and often apprehended and "beaten with many stripes," but the good work went on in some sort until 1860, when the war that was to be "the beginning of the end" of the whole system of slavery, put a stop to all such effort for the time being.

There is no more heroic chapter in history than that which deals with the persistence with which the slaves and "free persons of color" in the slave states sought and secured a measure of intellectual and religious instruction ; for they were prohibited from preaching or receiving religious instruction except by written permit and when at least five "white men of good reputation" were present at such gatherings.   But there has never been a time in the history of mankind when repressive laws, however rigidly enforced, could shut out the light of knowledge or prevent communion with the Supreme Ruler of the universe by such as were determined to share these noblest of human enjoyments. True, only a few, a very few, of the blacks and "free people of color" were able to secure any appreciable mental instruction ; but the fact that so many of them sought it diligently in defiance of fines and penalties is worthy of notice and goes far towards explaining the extraordinary manner in which those people crowded into every school that was opened to them after the war of the rebellion had swept away the slave system and placed all the children of the republic upon equality under the Federal constitution.   Nor was this yearning for mental instruction spasmodic ; thirty-four years after the war all the school houses, of whatever sort, opened for these people are as crowded with anxious pupils as were the modest log school houses planted by New England men and women while the soldiers of the disbanded armies of the north and south were turning their faces homeward.   A race so imbued with a love of knowledge, displayed in slavery and become the marvel of mankind in freedom, must have reserved for it some honorable place in our national life which God has not made plain to our understanding. In His own good time He will make plain His plans and purposes with regard to this people who were allowed to serve an apprenticeship of 250 years of slavery in a democratic republic.

In the free states of the north very little more provision was made, as late as 1830, by the state for the education of the Negro population than by the slave states.   There was no prohibition by the state against such instruction, but there was a very pronounced popular sentiment against it, when prosecuted by benevolent corporations and individuals. In 1833 the Connecticut legislature enacted the following black law, for the purpose of suppressing a "school for colored misses" which Miss Prudence Crandall had been forced to open in self-defense, at Canterbury :

"Whereas, attempts have been made to establish literary institutions in this state for the instruction of colored persons belonging to other states and countries, which would tend to the great increase of the colored population of the state, and therefore to the injury of the people ; therefore,

"Be it enacted, etc., that no person shall set up or establish in this state any school, academy, or other literary institution for the instruction or education of colored persons, who are not inhabitants of this state, or harbor or board, for the purpose of attending or being taught or instructed in any such school, academy or literary institution, any colored person who is not an inhabitant of any town in this state, without the consent in writing, first obtained, of a majority of the civil authority, and also the selectmen of the town, in which such school, academy or institution is situated, etc.

"And each and every person who shall knowingly do any act forbidden as aforesaid, or shall be aiding or assisting therein, shall for the first offense forfeit and pay to the treasurer of this state a fine of $100, and for the second offense $200, and so double for every offense of which he or she shall be convicted ; and all informing officers are required to make due presentment of all breaches of this act."

The cause of this law was the acceptance' by Miss Crandall of a young colored girl into her select school for young ladies.   The parents of the white students insisted upon the dismissal of Miss Harris, the bone of contention, but Miss Crandall refused to do so, when the white students were withdrawn.   Miss Crandall then announced that she would

open her school for "young ladies and little misses of color."
The people of Canterbury protested against this course, and
persecuted legally and otherwise Miss Crandall and her 20
pupils. When they found that they could not intimidate
the brave woman the legislature was appealed to, and the law
I have quoted was enacted. Under it Miss Crandall was
arrested and placed in the common jail. The following day
she was bailed out by Rev. Samuel J. May and others. The
case was tried three times in the inferior courts, and was
argued on appeal before the court of errors, July 22, 1834.
The court reserved its decision and has not yet rendered it.
Several attempts were made to burn Miss Crandall's house,
and finally, September 9, 1834, about 12 o'clock at night,
"her house was assaulted by a number of persons with
heavy clubs and iron bars, and windows were dashed to
pieces.[1] The school work was abandoned after this upon
the advice of Rev. Mr. May and other friends. The obnox-
ious law was repealed in 1838.

All this sounds rather odd when it is remembered that the
citizens of no state in the republic have contributed as many
of their sons and daughters to the educational work among
the Negroes of the south since the war, with the possible
exception of Massachusetts, as Connecticut, and that two of
her citizens, John F. Slater and Daniel Hand, contributed
each the princely sum of one million dollars for the education of the Negroes of the southern states. Surely this all
indicates one of the most remarkable revolutions in the public opinion of a state of which we have any record.

Schools established for the education of Negro youth were
assaulted and wrecked in other free states, but the good work
steadily progressed. Private schools sprang up in all the middle and New England states, Pennsylvania, New York and
Massachusetts leading in the work, their white citizens contributing largely to their support. There were many of
these schools, some of them of splendid character, in Boston, Providence, New York, Philadelphia, Washington and

---

[1] Williams' History of the Negro race, vol. IV, p. 156.

Cincinnati. They were gradually absorbed into the public school system, and none of them now exist in an independent character, except the Institute for colored youth at Philadelphia, Lincoln university, in Chester county, and Avery institute at Allegheny City, all in Pennsylvania.

In 1837 Richard Humphreys left $10,000 by will, with which the Institute for colored youth was started, thirty members of the Society of Friends forming themselves into an association for the purpose of carrying out the wishes and plans of Mr. Humphreys. A remarkable feature of the constitution adopted by the trustees, in view of the present consideration of the subject by those concerned in Negro education, is the following preamble :

" We believe that the most successful method of elevating the moral and intellectual character of the descendants of Africa, as well as of improving their social condition, is to extend to them the benefits of a good education, and to instruct them in the knowledge of some useful trade or business, whereby they may be enabled to obtain a comfortable livelihood by their own industry ; and through these means to prepare them for fulfilling the various duties of domestic and social life with reputation and fidelity, as good citizens and freemen."

The measure of progress which has been made in public opinion and in the educational status of the Negro race in the middle and New England states can easily be estimated by the fact that as recently as 1830 no Negro could matriculate in any of the colleges and other schools of this splendid group of states, and that now not one of them is closed against a black person, except Girard college at Philadelphia, whose founder made a perpetual discrimination against people of African descent in devising his benefaction ; that Negro children stand on the same footing with white children in all public school benefits ; that the separate school system has broken down entirely in the New England states and is gradually breaking down in the middle states, New Jersey and Pennsylvania being the only states in the latter

group which still cling to the principle ; and that in many
of the public schools of both groups of states Negro teachers are employed and stand upon the same footing as
white teachers.   Indeed, Miss Maria L. Baldwin, an accomplished black woman, is principal of the Agassiz school, at
Cambridge, Mass., and in the large corps of teachers
under her, not one of them, I believe, is a member of her
own race.

All this is a very long stride from the condition of the
public mind in the middle and New England states when
Negro children were not allowed to attend any public school
or college and when a reputable white woman was persecuted, jailed and her property destroyed, in 1834, for accepting a young colored woman into her select school.   This
remarkable change in public sentiment argues well for the
future of the Negro race and for the republic, which for
more than a century has agonized over this race problem,
and is still anxious about it in the sixteen southern states,
where a large majority of the Negroes reside and will, in all
probability, continue to reside for all time to come.

IV PUBLIC SCHOOL EDUCATION IN THE SOUTH AFTER THE WAR

Dr. A. D. Mayo, M. A., LL.D., one of the best authorities on educational matters in the United States, says that
"it is still a favorite theory of a class of the representatives
of the higher university and college education to proclaim
the invariable legitimate descent of the secondary and even
elementary schooling of the people always and everywhere
from this fountain head," the southern states, and that, "in
one sense, this assertion is 'founded on fact.'"   But, although
most of the southern states were committed to the theory
of public education, the system of slavery stood in the way
of the development of the theory.   Popular education and
slavery, like oil and water, will not mix.   The educational
energy of the south expanded rather along academic and
collegiate than common school lines.   The slave-holding
aristocrary drew the social line against the poor whites as

well as the slave blacks, and while dooming the latter to
mental darkness by stringent laws, rigidly enforced, the same
result was accomplished in the case of the former by the
steady development of the old English theory of academy
education, chartered for the most part by the state but supported almost wholly by their patrons, and therefore inaccessible to the children of the poor whites. It was due to this
fact that so very large a percentage of the southern white
population figured in the first census after the war of the
rebellion as illiterate and so figure to a large extent even
to-day, twenty-nine years after the beneficent operation of
the public school system in all of the states of the south.

If the south, because of the existence of the slave system
more than anything else, drifted away from the theory of
public school education, prior to 1860, it has nobly rectified
its mistake since 1870. Upon this point Dr. Mayo says,
speaking of Virginia, which has always set the pace for her
sister states of the south — and especially in the matter of
education, under the leadership of Dr. W. H. Ruffner (from
1870 to 1882), who has been appropriately styled the Horace
Mann of the south :

" But the condition of the educational destitution in which
the state found itself in 1865, in the hour of its dire extrem-
ity, was the logical result of the narrow English policy it
has pursued in this as in other directions ; and, in 1870, the
cry went up, from the sea sands to the most distant recesses
of the western mountains, for the establishment of the
American people's common school.

" In nothing has the really superior class of Virginia more
notably declared its soundness, persistence, and capacity to
hold fast to a great idea than in the way in which it stood
by the educational ideas of Jefferson through the one hundred turbulent years from the outbreak of the war of the
revolution to the inauguration of the people's common
school in 1870."

As it was with Virginia, so it was with the other southern
states. A revival was begun in public or common school

education, in 1870, which is still in progress, such as swept over New England and the middle states from 1830 to 1860. Broken in fortune and bowed with defeat in a great civil war, the south pulled itself together as a giant rouses from slumber and shakes himself and began to lay the basis of a new career and a new prosperity in a condition of freedom of all the people and in the widest diffusion of education among the citizens through the medium of the common schools. Perhaps no people in history ever showed a more superb public spirit and self-sacrifice under trying circumstances than the people of the south have displayed in the gradual building up of their public school system upon the ruins of the aristocratic academy system. The work had to be done from the ground up, from the organization of the working force to the building of the school houses and the marshalling of the young hosts. The work has required in the aggregate, perhaps, the raising by taxation of $514,922,268, $100,000,000 having been expended in maintaining the separate schools for the Negro race. This must be regarded as a marvelous showing when the impoverished condition in which the war left the south in 1865 is considered. But it is a safe, if a time-honored saying, that "where there is a will there is a way." The southern people found a way because they had a will to do it; and it is not too much to claim that the industrial prosperity which the south is now enjoying is intimately connected with the effort and money expended in popular education since 1870.

The statistical tables will show more eloquently than could be done by words the growth of the public school system in the southern states since 1870. These tables are furnished at the conclusion of the monograph, together with other tables showing the growth in other directions in secondary, academic, collegiate and industrial education.

It is interesting to note that the total enrollment of the sixteen southern states and the District of Columbia for the year 1896–97 was 5,398,076, the number of Negro children being 1,460,084; the number of white children 3,937,992.

The estimated number of children in the south from 5 to 18 years of age was 8,625,770, of which 2,816,340 or 32.65 per cent were children of the Negro race, and 5,809,430 or 67.35 per cent were white children.   The number of Negro children enrolled was 51.84 per cent of the Negro population and 67.79 of the white population.   When the relative social and material condition of the former is contrasted with that of the latter, it must be admitted that the children of the former slaves are treading closely upon the heels of the children of the former master class in the pursuit of knowledge as furnished in the public school system.

During the year 1896–97 it is estimated that $31,144,801 was expended in public school education in the sixteen southern states and the District of Columbia, of which, it is estimated, $6,575,000 was expended upon the Negro schools.

Since 1870 it is estimated that $514,922,268 have been expended in the maintenance of the public school system of the southern states, and that at least $100,000,000 have been expended for the maintenance of the separate public schools for Negroes.   The total expenditure for each year and the aggregate for the twenty-seven years, as well as the common school enrollment of white and colored children for each year since 1876 are shown in table 2 at the end of the monograph.

The significance o₁ the racts contained in the two foregoing paragraphs will be appreciated by Europeans as well as Americans.   The fact that 2,816,340 children of former slaves were in regular attendance in the public schools of the late slave-holding states of the south for the year 1896–97, and that $6,575,000 was expended for their maintenance, gathered entirely from public taxation and funds for educational purposes controlled by the states, should be regarded as the strongest arguments that could be presented to Americans or to foreigners to prove that the race problem in the United States is in satisfactory process of solution. That there is grave doubt at home and abroad upon this subject I freely acknowledge; but judging entirely from

such facts as are here recited, and from observation in the
black belt covering a period of eighteen years, I am free to
say I have no doubts whatever as to the ultimate outcome.
The people of the southern states, the old slave-holding class,
have not only accepted in good faith the educational burden
placed upon them, in the addition of 8,000,000 of people to
their citizenship, but they have discharged that burden in a
way that must command the admiration of the world.
That my own people are discharging their part of the obligation is shown in the statistics of school attendance I have
given, and in the further fact that it is estimated they have
amassed since their emancipation $300,000,000 of taxable
property.   While this may seem small as a taxable value as
compared to the aggregate of taxable values in the southern
states, it is large, indeed, when the poverty of the Negro
race in 1865, with all the advantages and disadvantages of
slave education and tradition to contend with, are considered.   When a race starts empty-handed in the serious business of life, what it inclines to and amasses in a given period
is valuable almost wholly as a criterion upon which to base
a reasonable deduction as to its ultimate future.

In all matters affecting my race and its future in the
United States, I indulge an optimism which I endeavor to
keep within the bounds of reasonable hopefulness.   I have
this faith because of the facts in the situation, because I
have faith in the possibilities of my race and in the humanity
and self-interest of my white fellow-citizens, not only of the
south, but of the north and the west as well, and because
as a historical fact social revolutions seldom if ever go backwards.   The Negro race is compelled to go forward in the
social scale because it is surrounded by forces which will not
permit it to go backwards without crushing the life out of
it, as they crushed the life out of the unassimilable aborigi-
nal Indian races of North America.   In this matter of statistics I have presented, it is clearly to be seen that the
Negro race, in its desire for American education, possesses
the prime element of assimilation into the warp and woof of

American life, and if its desire for the Christian religion be added we have the three prime elements of homogenous citizenship as defined by Prof. Aldrini, viz. : Habitat, language and religion.

It seems well to me to say this much, adduced from the statistics of common school education in the late slave states of the sixteen southern states and the District of Columbia, where the bulk of the Negro people reside, as a logical conclusion in a problematical situation, concerning which many wise men are disposed to indulge a pessimism which confuses them as well as those who have to deal immediately with the perplexing condition of affairs. I submit that the common school statistics of the southern states leave no room for doubt as to the ultimate well-being of the Negroes residing in those states.

V GROUND WORK EDUCATION IN THE SOUTH

In the preceding chapter the extraordinary development of the public school system of the sixteen southern states and the District of Columbia has been hastily recorded from 1870 to 1896–97. It is a record worthy of the proud people who made it,— people who have from the foundation of the republic been resourceful, courageous, self-reliant ; rising always equal to any emergency presented in their new and trying circumstances, surrounded on every side, as they were, by a vast undeveloped territory, and by a hostile Indian population, and fatally handicapped by a system of African slavery, which proved a mill stone about the neck of the people until it was finally abolished, amid the smoke and flame and death of a hundred battles, in 1865. There are none so niggardly as to deny to the southern people the full measure of credit which they deserve for the splendid spirit with which they put aside their prejudices of more than two centuries against popular common school education on the one hand, and their equally prescriptive prejudice against the education of the Negro race under any circumstances on the other. Few if any people in the various history of mankind have so completely overcome two such prejudices. On this point Dr. Mayo says :

" Almost one hundred years ago young Thomas Jefferson drew up a scheme for the education of the people of Virginia, which, had it been adopted, would have changed the history of that and of every southern state and the nation. He proposed to emancipate the slaves and fit them, by industrial training, for freedom ; to establish a free school for every white child in every district of the colony ; to support an academy for boys within a day's horseback ride of every man in the Old Dominion, and to crown all with a university, unsectarian in religion, elective in its curriculum, teaching everything necessary for a gentleman to know. This plan received the indorsement of many of the most eminent men of the day, and exalts the fame of Jefferson as an educator even higher than his reputation as a statesman."

All that Jefferson dreamed and outlined for the people of Virginia and of the south has been more than accomplished for both races in Virginia and in the south. The possibilities of a common school, collegiate and industrial education have been placed in easy reach of all the people, and the people are justifying the splendid faith of the Sage of Monticello by the earnestness with which they are taking advantage of the opportunities provided for them by the states and a munificent Christian philanthropy — a philanthropy which has given fully $40,000,000 of money and thousands of devoted men and women teachers to illuminate the mental darkness generated by the system of slavery. Surely no better monument than this philanthropy could be erected to perpetuate the memory of Horace Mann and Henry Barnard, in relighting the fires of popular education in the middle and New England states, for without their labors and sacrifices in this cause that philanthropy would not have been possible. Truly,

> "God moves in a mysterious way
> His wonders to perform ;
> He plants his footsteps in the sea
> And rides upon the storm."

But the public school system of the southern states had to have other and more substantial foundation than was offered at the close of the war of the rebellion, in 1865, by the academy and college system which had been fostered and developed as best adapted to a social condition whose corner stone was the slave system. Without this foundation, firmly and wisely laid in the fateful years from 1865 to 1870, by the initiative of the Federal government, magnificently sustained by the philanthropy and missionary consecration of the people of the New England and middle states, the results which we have secured in the public school system of the south from 1870 to the present time would not have been possible. All the facts in the situation sustain this view.

It is creditable to the people of the New England and middle states that they, who had been engaged for four years in a Titanic warfare with their brethren of the southern states, should enter the southern states in the person of their sons and daughters, and with a voluntary gift of $40,000,000, or more, to plant common schools and academies and colleges, in the devastation wrought by the civil war, upon the sites where the slave auction block had stood for 250 years, thereby lifting the glorious torch of knowledge in the dense mental darkness with which the slave system had sought to hedge its power ; nor is it less creditable that the southern people accepted this assistance and builded upon it a public school system which promises to equal that in any of the other sections of the republic.

In anticipation of the condition of affairs that would arise when hostilities should cease, as early as the spring of 1865, before the war was over, an act was passed by congress providing for the relief of the destitute of the south. The act was entitled " an act to establish a bureau for the relief of freedmen and refugees." May 20, 1865, Major-General O. O. Howard was appointed commissioner of the Freedmen's bureau. General Howard,— who founded the institution which bears his name at Washington and gave it a princely endowment,[1]— "gave," says the historian Williams, "great attention to the subject of education; and after planting schools for the freedmen throughout a greater portion of the south, in 1870, five years after the work was begun, he made a report. It was full of interest. In five years there were 4239 schools established, 9,307 teachers employed, and 247,333 pupils instructed. In 1868 the average attendance was 89,396, but in 1870 it was 91,398, or 79 3-4 per cent of the total number enrolled. The emancipated people sustained 1324 schools themselves, and owned 592 school buildings. The Freedmen's bureau furnished 654 buildings for school purposes."

In 1879, according to the same authority, "there were 74 high and normal schools, with 8,147 students, and 61 intermediate schools, with 1,750 students in attendance. In doing this great work,— for buildings, repairs, teachers, etc., — $1,002,896.07 was expended. Of this sum the freedmen raised $200,000. This was conclusive proof that emancipation was no mistake."

Mr. Williams says further (p. 393) that it appears from the reports of the Freedmen's bureau that the earliest school for freedom was opened by the American missionary association, at Fortress Monroe, Va., September, 1861, and before the close of the war Hampton and Norfolk were leading points where educational operations were conducted; but after the cessation of hostilities teachers were sent from the northern states and schools for freedmen were opened in all parts of the south. During the five years of its operations the bureau made a total expenditure of $6,513,955.55. No money was ever more wisely or beneficently expended. While a goodly portion of it was expended in food and clothing, and the like, for the destitute freedmen, by far the most of it went into school houses and into the salaries of school teachers, and finally became the basis if not the inspiration of the public school system of the southern states; it certainly did become the inspiration and the

---

[1] History of the Negro race, p. 385.

foundation of the 178 schools for secondary and higher education which exist to-day independently of the public school system or of state control, although many of them are recipients of state assistance.

While the Federal government was planting these schools among the freedmen, the people of the middle and New England states were sending thousands of dollars into the south and sending an army of devoted men and women to back up and carry forward the educational work among the freed people. In the extent of it, it was and it continues to be the most striking example of Christian brotherhood and benevolence in the annals of mankind. Through the agency of the Federal government and northern philanthropy, schools for the freed people were planted everywhere, and grew and prospered, and continue to grow and prosper, as such schools never have done before.

Writing on this subject in the *Southern workman* (January, 1898), the organ of the Hampton institute, T. Thomas Fortune said :

" It is true that the public and private interest which aroused the north especially, to the importance of lifting into the glorious sunlight of knowledge the great mass of Afro-Americans who had so long stumbled and fallen and grovelled in the darkness of ignorance and superstition and immorality, with which the institution of slavery was compelled to hedge itself about in order to insure existence, has no parallel in the history of mankind. We seek in vain for philanthropy so instant and generous and continuous, and for missionary spirit so noble and capable and self-sacrificing, as that which answered the Macedonian cry that came out of the log cabins of the south,

" 'When the war drums throbbed no longer, and the battle flags were furled,
    In the parliament of man, the federation of the world.' "

" And what a herculean task was theirs ! The New England men and women who went into the waste places of the south, following closely upon the heels of the warlike host that stacked their arms at Appomattox court house, formed an army as heroic as ever went forth under the standard of the cross to 'redeem the human mind from error.' No wealth could have purchased the service and the sacrifice they undertook for God and humanity, and no memorial of affection or granite shaft can ever adequately commemorate their works. There are some services and sacrifices which it is impossible to reward. These evangels went into a hostile country, armed with Puritan faith and New England culture, and by singleness of purpose and gentleness of character disarmed the prejudice of the whites and won the respect and confidence of the suspicious blacks, who had been educated in the school of slavery to distrust all Greeks, even those bearing gifts. But in the progress of time all this was changed, and prejudice and suspicion were transformed into respect and confidence.

"What have been the results? After thirty years of effort there are 25,615 Afro-American teachers in the schools of the south, where there was hardly one when the work began ; some 4,000 men have been prepared, in part or in whole, for the work of the Christian ministry, and a complete revolution has been effected in the mental and moral character of Afro-American preachers, a service which no one can estimate who is not intimately informed of the tremendous influence which these preachers exercise everywhere over the masses of their race ; the professions of law and medicine have been so far supplied that one or more representatives are to be found in every large community of the south, as well as in the north and west, graduates for the most part of the schools of the south ; and all over the south I have found men engaged in trade occupations whose intellects and characters were shaped for the battle of life by the New England pioneers who took up the work where their soldier brothers laid it down at the close of the war. But the influence of these teachers upon the character, the home life, of the thousands who are neither teaching, preaching nor engaged in professional or commercial pursuits, but are devoted to the making of domestic comfort and happiness for their husbands and children, in properly training the future citizens of the republic, was one of the most necessary and far-reaching that was exercised, and the one which to-day holds out the promise for the best results in the years to come."

It was these New England men and women who labored all over the south from 1865 to 1870 who made possible the splendid public school results so eloquently depicted in the statistical tables given at the end of this monograph. Their labors did not end in the field of primary education in 1870; they remained at their posts until they had prepared the 25,000 Negroes necessary to take their places. "When shall their glory fade?" And even unto to-day hundreds of them are laboring in some one of the 169 schools of secondary and higher education maintained for the freed people.

VI BEQUESTS FOR SOUTHERN EDUCATION

In the inauguration and development of the educational work in the southern states and the District of Columbia there have been other potential agencies than those already enumerated. It has been shown that the Federal government, operating through the Freedmen's bureau, of which Major-General O. O. Howard was commissioner, between 1865 and 1870 established 4,239 schools, employing 9,307 teachers, with an enrollment of 247,333 pupils, at a total expense of $1,002,896.07, of which the freedmen themselves raised $200,000; that the American missionary association, founded in 1846, was among the first agencies to enter the southern educational work, as it has since been the most active and effective; and that the southern states, from 1870, when they assumed control of the common school system, to 1896–97, spent in primary education, $514,922,268, of which at least $100,000,000 was devoted to the free education of the slaves. These enormous expenditures (see table 2) were largely supplemented by private benevolence, estimated at a total of $40,000,000, much of which went into primary school buildings and education, the buildings in most instances having been gradually relinquished to the states.

As the American missionary association was among the first to enter the southern school work, it is proper to give it a conspicuous place in this monograph. The extent of its operations in the southern field can be inferred from the fifty-third annual report of the executive committee (September 30, 1899). From this report it appears that the association has in the southern educational work of secondary and higher education 5 chartered institutions, 45 normal and graded schools, 26 common schools, being 76 schools, with 414 instructors and 12,428 pupils. The receipts for the current work for the year (1898–99) were $297,681.98; expenditures, $296,810.84. The total receipts for all purposes for the year were $370,963.44, of which $71,960.50 is credited to income from the Daniel Hand fund. The work of this association has been inestimable.

At the annual meeting of the American missionary association, at Providence, R. I., October 23–25, 1888, it was announced that Mr. Daniel Hand, of Guilford, Connecticut, had given the association $1,000,894.25, in trust, to be known as the "Daniel Hand educational fund for colored people," the income of which shall be used for the purpose of educating needy and indigent colored people of African descent, residing, or who may hereafter reside, in the recent slave states of the United States." In addition to this princely gift Mr. Hand provided that his residuary estate, amounting to the sum of $500,000, should be devoted to the same purpose, to be disbursed through the association. Mr. Hand made his wealth in the south, where he settled in Augusta, Ga., in 1818, and he, therefore, had an intimate knowledge of the educational needs of the emancipated people. He was a man of devout nature.

But the fund which had the most influence upon the development of the primary and secondary education of the southern states was that of $2,000,000 established by George Peabody, of Danvers, Mass. (the first gift of $1,000,000 being made February 7, 1867, the second $1,000,000 being added July 1, 1869). In addition, $1,100,000 in bonds, indorsed by Mississippi, and $384,000 Florida bonds were given to the trustees appointed to administer the trust, but these bonds were ultimately repudiated by Mississippi and Florida, although both of them were beneficiaries of the trust,— Mississippi by $86,878 and Florida by $67,375, from 1868 to 1897. The general purposes of the trust, as Mr. Peabody stated it, in his letter to the sixteen trustees designated by him, were that "the income thereof should be applied in your discretion for the promotion and encouragement of intellectual, moral or industrial education of the young of the more destitute portions of the southern and southwestern states of our union; my purpose being that the benefits intended shall be distributed among the entire population, without other distinction than their needs and the opportunities of usefulness to them."

Mr. Peabody laid the foundation of his immense fortune in Georgetown, D. C., and Baltimore, from 1812 to 1837. In the latter year he permanently settled in London, England, and began business there, where his benefactions equalled those he made in the United States, of which the trust fund for educational purposes was the most considerable, but by no means the only one. Mr. Peabody started life as a poor boy, but he had a natural genius for making money, and, what is far rarer, as the poor of London and our southern states can testify, a natural genius for so devoting his wealth to public uses as to accomplish the most good.

The trustees of the Peabody fund, of which the Hon. Robert C. Winthrop was chairman, were particularly fortunate in securing as the first general agent Dr. B. Sears, then president of Brown university. In 1848 Dr. Sears had succeeded Horace Mann as secretary of the Massachusetts board of education and as its executive agent, and served in that capacity until 1855, when he was called to the presidency of his *alma mater*. He was still president of Brown university when called to the work of the Peabody fund,

April 9, 1867. He had been grounded in the common school theories of Horace Mann and Henry Barnard and in the work of higher education as president of a great university. He was eminently fitted, therefore, to do much towards shaping the public school system of the southern states.

Dr. J. L. M. Curry, the present able general agent of the fund, says of Dr. Sears (who died July 6, 1880), in his "History of the Peabody fund" (page 67):

"The highest commendation of his work is to be found in the persuasive, potential influence he exerted in behalf of popular education. School superintendents bore their strong and cheerful testimony to his rare insight into the educational needs of the south, and to his influence in stimulating to proper and wise action."

Dr. Curry succeeded Dr. Sears February 2, 1881, and with the exception of three years, when he was minister plenipotentiary and envoy extraordinary to Spain, he has been the working force in shaping the policy of the fund to the present time. Dr. Curry,— himself a southern man,— learned, eloquent, an indefatigable worker, and passionately devoted to the highest educational ideas and to the cause of southern education, as the representative of the Peabody fund and the Slater fund, has done equally as much as Dr. Ruffner and Dr. Sears in shaping the southern educational movement. In speaking of the general effects of the fund, Dr. Curry says (History of the Peabody education fund, p. 25):

"The fund has been a most potent agency in creating and preserving a bond of peace and unity and fraternity between the north and the south. It instituted an era of good feeling; for the gift, as Mr. Winthrop said, 'was the earliest manifestation of a spirit of reconciliation toward those from whom we had been so unhappily alienated and against whom we of the north had been so recently arrayed in arms.' No instrumentality has been so effective in the south in promoting concord, in restoring fellowship, in cultivating a broad and generous patriotism, and apart from its direct connection with schools, it has been an unspeakable blessing in cementing the bonds of a lately dissevered union."

From 1868 to 1897 the income of the fund amounted to $2,478,527.13, of which $248,562.25 was expended in maintaining the Normal college for whites at Nashville, Tenn., and $398,690.88 for scholarships at the same college. The remainder was expended in rendering aid to the needy public schools of the south and in stimulating normal and industrial education for both races.

March 4, 1882, Mr. John Fox Slater, of Norwich, Conn., created a trust fund of $1,000,000, stating that the " general object which I desire to have exclusively pursued is the uplifting of the lately emancipated population of the southern states and their posterity by conferring on them the blessings of Christian education." He declared in the same relation : " The disabilities formerly suffered by these people and their singular patience and fidelity in the great crisis of the nation, establish a just claim on the sympathy and good will of humane and patriotic men. I cannot but feel the compassion that is due in view of their prevailing ignorance which exists by no fault of theirs."

" But it is not only for their own sakes," Mr. Slater said further, " but also for the safety of our common country, in which they have been invested with equal political rights, and I am desirous to aid in providing them with the means of such education as shall tend to make them good men and good citizens — education in which the instruction of the mind in the common branches of secular learning shall be associated with training in just notions of duty toward God and man in the light of the Holy Scriptures."

The fund is administered by a trustee board, and like the Peabody fund, composed of some of the most distinguished citizens of the republic. The Slater fund is used almost exclusively at the present time in promoting industrial education at a number of the largest institutions for colored people.

These princely donations by three private citizens, aggregating a fund of $4,000,000, have been supplemented by
millions of dollars more from private citizens which have
gone to the building up of the educational waste places of
the south, to which all of the great church denominations
have contributed, and still contribute, more or less as organized bodies.   As the outgrowth of all the benefactions and
effort since 1865 there are now, according to Dr. Mayo, 169
schools of secondary and higher education in the southern
states maintained for the Negro people.   They are fed constantly by the common schools, and all the agencies working together are fast reducing the ignorance bequeathed as
a terrible legacy by the slave system to the southern states.
We shall search history in vain for a parallel to the munificence, the Christian charity and the personal sacrifice which
the people of the great republic have contributed since 1865
to the education of the lately enslaved people of the Negro
race.

VII PRESENT EDUCATIONAL STATUS

It was natural and to have been expected, after the New
England men and women who had graduated out of the
white heat of the high educational enthusiasm created by
Horace Mann, Henry Barnard, Dr. Sears, and others, from
1830 to 1860, had laid the foundation of the primary education among the emancipated people of the southern states,
that they would then turn their attention to the secondary
and higher education of the same people.   That is what
they did.   As fast as they prepared young men and women
to take their places as school teachers (and at the present
time there are more than 25,000 such teaching in the public
schools of the south), these New England men and women
retired from the field as public school teachers.   They were
actuated almost wholly by Christian missionary spirit.   They
heard the loud " Macedonian cry " and responded to it with
a devotion and self-sacrifice which will always remain one
of the most luminous and striking pages in missionary
effort.

But there was another and a splendid work for them to do in laying the foundation of the secondary and higher education as the necessary supplement of the primary educational work. At the present time there are 169 such schools in the sixteen southern states and the District of Columbia. Some of them are magnificent seats of learning ; such, for example, as Howard university, at Washington ; Atlanta university, at Atlanta ; Fisk university, at Nashville ; Wiley university, at Marshall, Texas, and the like, so that the southern state which has no such school of higher learning is poor indeed. And these schools were founded, for the most part, and are maintained in the main by northern philanthropy — a philanthropy of which George Peabody, John F. Slater and Daniel Hand are the most striking examples. The money value and the income of these schools is set forth in table 8 of the appendix ; while the character, teachers and students are set forth in tables 3 to 7 inclusive. The fact that the income of these 169 schools in 1896–97 was $1,045,278, that $540,097 of it was derived from unclassified sources, that the several states and municipalties contributed $271,839, and that the students paid in tuition fees $141,262, shows that all the best forces of the republic — the state, the Christian philanthropist and the grateful beneficiary — are all working harmoniously together to prepare the children of the former slaves for the proper and high duties of citizenship. The public school system,— with 1,460,084 pupils enrolled of Negroes, in 1896–97, as against an enrollment of only 571,506 in 1876–77,— is a fixture and serves as a constant feeder of the 169 schools of higher learning. Thus the whole system, it will be seen, of primary, secondary and higher education, is in harmonious relationship and must grow stronger and stronger every year.

It should not be overlooked, however, that besides the splendid advantages offered the Negroes by these 169 schools of higher learning, all of the colleges and universities of the northern and western states are accessible to Negro students who prefer them, color distinctions not being recognized or tolerated in the management of these schools. The white colleges and universities of the southern states, like the public school system, are conducted rigidly upon lines of race separation.

It was a natural development of the educational effort in the southern states that when the schools of secondary and higher education had become fixed facts that a desire should have grown up for other institutions whose principal object should be the industrial education of such of the Negroes as desire that sort of education. Of late years industrial schools have sprung up all over the southern states, and they are growing constantly in favor with the masses, because of their economic condition and the growing demand for skilled workmen in all avenues of industry. In the early days of the educational work of the southern states little stress was laid upon the industrial training of the people. Mental and moral and religious training was considered the all-important thing. Perhaps it was,— to a people who had dwelt in mental, moral and religious darkness from 1620 to 1865. They needed the great light of mental, moral and religious truths as a firm and sure foundation upon which was to be built a structure of technical education, out of which should naturally grow the industrial and commercial rehabilitation of the people, without which there can be no character, no strength, no prosperity in an individual or a race. This principle was recognized by the 30 members of the Society of Friends, who established the Institute for colored youth at Philadelphia, in 1837, to which reference has already been made.

The good Friends were very much in advance of their time, and a great many good people of both races have not caught up with their idea as yet. However, there has been a very great and satisfactory awakening all over the republic during the past decade, among all races of the population, as to the vital importance of technical education. The fact that 13,581 Negro students were receiving industrial training

in schools of the south, in 1896–97 (see table 7), speaks volumes, as compared to the 2,108 who were receiving collegiate
education (see table 3), and the 2,410 who were receiving
classical instruction (see table 4), and the 1,311 who were
taking the professional course (see table 6) in the same
year ; making a total of 5,829 taking the higher education,
or 7,752 fewer than were taking the industrial course.
Indeed, the growth of the industrial theory of education
among Negroes in the past decade has not only been
phenomenal but it is by all odds the most encouraging fact
in a situation not without its discouraging features.

It is a rare compliment to one of the wisest and best of
the New England men who engaged in the southern educational work that his theory of industrial training has taken
such a firm root in a rich soil. This good and wise man
was General Samuel Chapman Armstrong. While other
men and women were devoting themselves to the necessary
work of founding schools of secondary and higher education for the freed people, General Armstrong, in 1868, busied
himself in founding and developing the Hampton normal
and agricultural institute at Hampton, Va., which, says the
historian of the work, " beginning in 1868 with two teachers
and 15 students in the old barracks left by the civil war, the
Hampton school has grown, until at the beginning of the
present year (1899) there were on the grounds 1,000 students. Of these 135 are Indians, representing ten states
and territories. Of the 80 officers, teachers and assistants,
about one-half are in the industrial departments. Instead
of the old barracks there are now fifty-five buildings."

The Hampton normal and agricultural institute is without doubt at the present time the center of all that is best,
wisest and most permanent in the educational development
of the black man in the south. It is by far the largest and
most important seat of learning in the country for the
development of the Negro. It has a large property now
valued at over half a million of dollars, and has in constant
operation all the industries by which the colored people find

it necessary to make a living. Under the wise supervision of Dr. H. B. Frissell, the successor of General Armstrong, this institution is constantly growing, broadening and deepening its influence among the people. The work of the Hampton institute has not only resulted in turning the attention of the Negro population to the importance of industrial education, but has had a marked influence in shaping the education of the white south in the same direction.

It was the constant aim of General Armstrong to educate the head, the heart and the hand of the student, to make strong school teachers and skilled mechanics and agriculturalists, and his aims have been amply justified by results. General Armstrong was born of missionary parents in Hawaii. He was educated in this country. He was a soldier in the war for the preservation of the union and commanded a regiment of black soldiers. His was a pious and lovable nature which delighted to do the Master's work by reaching out the hand of assistance to the lowest and most needy of the Master's children.

Out of the Hampton institute has grown the Tuskegee normal and industrial institute, located at Tuskegee, Ala., in the black belt of the south. The Tuskegee institute has grown from a log cabin to an institution possessing 42 buildings with 2,300 acres of land, 88 instructors and about a thousand students. It gives instruction in about twenty-six different industries, in addition to giving training in academic and religious branches. A large number of graduates of Tuskegee are turned out every year and are at work in various portions of the south as teachers in class rooms, instructors in agricultural, mechanical and domestic pursuits. Quite a number of these graduates and students cultivate their own farms or man their own industrial establishments. The property owned by the Tuskegee normal and industrial institute is valued at $300,000, and the buildings have been very largely built by the labor of the students themselves. One rather unique feature of the Tuskegee normal and ndustrial institute is that the institution is wholly officered by members of the Negro race.   Aside from Hampton, Tuskegee is one of the largest and most important centers of education in the south, especially in the direction of industrial development.

The work of the Hampton institute and Tuskegee is not only proving itself valuable in showing the rank and file of the colored people how to lift themselves up, but it is equally important in winning the friendship and co-operation of the southern white people.   The influence of the young men and women turned out from these two institutions, as well as from other institutions, is gradually softening the prejudice against the education of the Negro, and in many striking instances bringing about the active co-operation and help of the southern white man in the direction of elevating the Negro.

There have been many other schools than the Tuskegee institute founded on the Hampton idea, and the number is increasing every year.   Nearly all the southern states are now maintaining industrial schools not only for the blacks but for the whites as well, for the education that is good and necessary for the black is equally so for the white boy.

From the facts and conclusions set forth, hastily withal, in this monograph it will readily be seen that from the educational point of view the Negro race has, since 1865, taken full advantage of its splendid opportunities, and that the present affords splendid promise that the future, which so many dread, will, in the providence of God, take care of itself.

TABLE I — *Common school statistics, classified by race, 1896–97*

STATE	ESTIMATED NUMBER OF PERSONS, 5 TO 18 YEARS OF AGE		PERCENTAGE OF THE WHOLE		PUPILS ENROLLED IN THE PUBLIC SCHOOLS.		PER CENT OF PERSONS 5 to 18 YEARS ENROLLED		AVERAGE DAILY ATTENDANCE		PER CENT OF ENROLLMENT		NUMBER OF TEACHERS	
	White	Colored	White	Colored	White	Colored	White	Colored	White	Colored	White	Colored	White	Colored
Alabama	334 700	286 000	53.84	46.16	198 605	120 921	59.34	42.15	b 130 230	b 82 770	65.57	68.45	4 725	2 398
Arkansas	331 700	128 500	72.08	27.92	234 078	82 192	70.57	63.96	144 532	50 977	61.75	62.02	5 617	1 564
Delaware (1891–92)	39 850	8 080	81.61	18.39	28 316	4 858	71.06	54.10	b 19 746	b 2 947	69.73	60.66	734	106
District of Columbia	45 440	25 000	64.51	35.49	27 797	15 198	61.17	60.79	21 783	11 530	28.36	75.87	715	356
Florida	92 240	73 660	55.80	44.20	65 913	39 502	71.46	54.07	43 623	25 854	66.38	65.45	2 016	642
Georgia	369 000	346 300	51.59	48.41	266 991	179 180	72.36	51.74	156 504	90 179	58.62	50.33	6 014	3 247
Kentucky (1895–96)	557 400	95 400	85.39	14.61	337 618	62 508	60.57	65.52	247 203	39 658	73.23	63.44	8 727	1 482
Louisiana	206 500	220 000	48.42	51.58	103 868	66 079	50.30	30.36	75 384	48 739	72.58	73.76	2 630	1 052
Maryland	268 000	77 200	77.64	22.36	186 416	43 531	69.56	56.39	111 208	22 419	59.66	51.50	4 062	774
Mississippi (1894–95)	212 700	309 800	40.71	59.29	162 830	187 785	76.55	60.61	99 048	103 635	60.83	55.19	4 591	3 264
Missouri	890 300	54 200	94.26	5.74	641 237	31 915	72.02	58.88	468 611	21 820	73.08	68.37	14 176	762
North Carolina (1895–96)	389 700	233 700	62.51	37.49	244 376	126 544	62.71	54.15	155 899	75 826	63.79	59.92	5 129	2 756
South Carolina (1895–6)	176 700	296 900	37.34	62.66	110 027	139 156	67.36	46.93	82 627	82 213	69.42	71.81	2 928	2 045
Tennessee (1895–6)	480 300	162 000	74.78	25.22	386 483	95 102	80.47	58.70	272 963	65 213	70.63	68.57	7 557	1 878
Texas (1895–96)	800 500	245 500	74.53	25.47	481 419	135 149	60.14	55.05	349 913	90 336	72.68	66.84	10 470	2 747
Virginia	340 100	242 000	58.43	41.57	244 583	123 234	71.92	50.92	145 218	68 203	59.37	55.34	6 448	2 127
West Virginia (1895–96)	274 300	11 300	90.04	9.96	208 435	7 230	75.99	63.98	135 614	4 467	65.54	61.78	6 219	235
Total	5 809 430	2 816 340	67.35	32.65	3 937 992	1 460 084	67.79	51.84	2 661 106	904 505	67.58	61.95	92 458	27 435
Total, 1889–90	a 5 132 948	a 2 510 847	67.15	32.85	3 402 420	1 296 959	66.29	51.65	2 165 249	813 710	63.64	62.74	78 903	24 072

a United States census.   *b* Approximately.

TABLE 2 — *Sixteen former slave states and the District of Columbia*

YEAR	COMMON SCHOOL ENROLLMENT		Expenditures (both races)
	White	Colored	
1870–71			$10 385 464
1871–72			11 623 238
1872–73			11 176 048
1873–74			11 823 775
1874–75			13 021 514
1875–76			12 033 865
1876–77	1 827 139	571,506	11 231 073
1877–78	2 034 946	675 150	12 093 091
1878-79	2 013 684	685 942	12 174 141
1879–80	2 215 674	784 709	12 678 685
1880–81	2 234 877	802 374	13 656 814
1881–82	2 249 263	802 982	15 241 740
1882–83	2 370 110	817 240	16 363 471
1883–84	2 546 448	1 002 313	17 884 558
1884–85	2 676 911	1 030 463	19 253 874
1885–86	2 773 145	1 048 659	20 208 113
1886–87	2 975 773	1 118 556	20 821 969
1887–88	3 110 606	1 140 405	21 810 158
1888–89	3 197 830	1 213 092	23 171 878
1889–90	3 402 420	1 296 959	24 880 107
1890–91	3 570 624	1 329 549	26 690 310
1891–92	3 607 549	1 354 316	27 691 488
1892–93	3 697 899	1 367 515	28 535 738
1893–94	3 835 593	1 424 995	29 223 546
1894–95	3 845 414	1 441 282	29 372 990
1895–96	3 861 300	1 429 713	30 729 819
1896–97	3 937 992	1 460 084	31 144 801
Total			$514 922 268

TABLE 3 — *Teachers and students in institutions for the colored race in 1896-97*

STATE	Number of schools	TEACHERS			STUDENTS											
		Male	Female	Total	ELEMENTARY			SECONDARY			COLLEGIATE			TOTAL		
					Male	Female	Total	Male	Female	Total	Male	Female	Total	Male	Female	Total
Alabama	13	104	111	215	1 131	1 427	2 558	1 223	1 008	2 231	38	12	50	2 392	2 447	4 839
Arkansas	8	20	29	49	593	696	1 289	253	210	463	23	7	30	869	913	1 782
Delaware	1	3	0	3				24	6	30	10	2	12	34	8	42
District of Columbia	4	85	31	116	144	148	292	408	590	998	342	82	424	894	820	1 714
Florida	5	10	15	25	250	329	579	67	96	163				317	425	742
Georgia	20	71	153	224	1 354	2 416	3 770	629	1 049	1 678	174	16	190	2 157	3 481	5 638
Illinois	1	1	1	2				16	24	40	0	0	0	16	24	40
Indiana	2	8	10	18	26	27	53	35	50	85				61	77	138
Kentucky	7	34	40	74	453	784	1 237	466	586	1 052	98	80	178	1 017	1 450	2 467
Louisiana	6	48	50	98	841	1 193	2 034	186	181	367	49	21	70	1 076	1 395	2 471
Maryland	6	8	20	28	60	183	243	93	186	279	10	0	10	163	369	532
Mississippi	9	42	52	94	415	561	976	520	334	854	105	72	177	1 040	967	2 007
Missouri	5	17	16	33	236	247	483	171	218	389	5	0	5	412	465	877
New Jersey	1	3	5	8	11	7	18	17	16	33				28	23	51
North Carolina	23	84	90	174	983	1 661	2 644	672	860	1 532	201	60	261	1 856	2 581	4 437
Ohio	2	14	9	23	71	79	150	82	97	179	47	15	62	200	191	391
Pennsylvania	3	17	8	25	111	156	267	236	137	373	48	0	48	395	293	688
South Carolina	12	48	75	123	1 202	1 270	2 472	410	524	934	14	3	17	1 626	1 797	3 423
Tennessee	14	49	101	150	1 772	2 272	4 044	570	601	1 171	193	179	372	2 535	3 052	5 587
Texas	10	40	59	99	568	1 006	1 574	349	440	789	84	31	115	1 001	1 477	2 478
Virginia	14	70	123	193	1 458	1 745	3 203	433	941	1 374	85	2	87	1 976	2 688	4 664
West Virginia	3	11	10	21	94	111	205	84	105	189				178	216	394
Total	169	787	1 008	1 795	11 773	16 318	28 091	6 944	8 259	15 203	1 526	582	2 108	20 243	25 159	45 402

TABLE 4—*Classification of colored students, by courses of study, 1896–97*

STATE	STUDENTS IN CLASSICAL COURSES			STUDENTS IN SCIENTIFIC COURSES			STUDENTS IN ENGLISH COURSES			STUDENTS IN BUSINESS COURSES		
	Male	Female	Total	Male	Female	Total	Male	Female	Total	Male	Female	Total
Alabama	11	3	14	2	1	3	392	497	889	9	6	15
Arkansas	52	29	81	32	38	70	168	229	397	7	0	7
Delaware	3	0	3	5	2	7	2	0	2	0	0	0
District of Columbia	129	218	347	....	....	....	....	....	....	52	49	101
Florida	121	150	271	46	68	114	233	326	559	0	0	0
Georgia	0	0	0	0	0	0	735	1 359	2 094	0	0	0
Illinois	35	50	85	....	....	....	16	24	40	....	....	....
Indiana	73	161	234	3	12	15	....	....	....	2	1	3
Kentucky	47	35	82	53	28	81	70	170	240	10	7	17
Louisiana	40	107	147	0	0	0	330	422	752	....	....	....
Maryland	41	30	71	21	6	27	57	237	294	0	0	0
Mississippi	19	11	30	64	111	175	129	187	316	....	....	....
Missouri	0	0	0	....	....	....	18	20	38	0	0	0
New Jersey	....	....	....	0	0	0	0	0	0	0	0	0
North Carolina	175	14	189	33	55	88	533	696	1 229	69	25	94
Ohio	14	3	17	15	9	24	56	40	96	15	2	17
Pennsylvania	165	29	194	35	29	64	56	29	85	5	6	11
South Carolina	67	31	98	12	17	29	678	658	1 336	10	20	30
Tennessee	218	176	394	55	50	105	486	775	1 261	0	0	0
Texas	40	7	47	57	44	101	186	237	423	0	0	0
Virginia	44	36	80	14	57	71	522	767	1 289	0	0	0
West Virginia	18	8	26	....	....	....	....	....	....	0	0	0
Total	1 312	1 098	2 410	447	527	974	4 667	6 673	11 340	179	116	295

TABLE 5 — *Number of colored normal students and graduates in 1896–97*

STATE	STUDENTS IN NORMAL COURSES			GRADUATES OF HIGH SCHOOL COURSES			GRADUATES OF NORMAL COURSES			GRADUATES OF COLLEGIATE COURSES		
	Male	Female	Total	Male	Female	Total	Male	Female	Total	Male	Female	Total
Alabama	828	669	1 497	8	10	18	308	281	589	2	0	2
Arkansas	103	61	164	7	4	11	6	7	13	3	1	4
Delaware												
District of Columbia												
Florida	75	79	154	27	58	85	26	36	62	5	0	5
Georgia	17	10	27	0	2	2	7	3	10	0	0	0
Illinois	114	240	354	44	71	115	3	41	44	9	5	14
Indiana	0	0	0	1	4	5				0	0	0
Kentucky	77	144	221	6	10	16	4	13	17			
Louisiana	12	60	72	14	19	33	8	17	25	5	0	5
Maryland	17	33	50	11	19	30	1	11	12	2	0	2
Mississippi	85	156	241	14	4	18	24	26	50	3	0	3
Missouri	61	57	118	14	23	37	6	5	11	2	0	2
New Jersey	0	0	0	0	0	0	0	0	0	0	0	0
North Carolina	221	232	453	44	14	58	33	36	69			
Ohio	29	54	83	7	20	27	2	12	14	11	2	13
Pennsylvania	54	29	83				5	6	11	7	3	10
South Carolina	102	223	325	37	58	95	14	43	57	30	0	30
Tennessee	266	365	631	55	111	166	31	60	91	0	0	0
Texas	137	138	275	24	30	54	14	24	38	16	2	18
Virginia	108	65	173	20	54	74	36	89	125	5	1	6
West Virginia	76	84	160	0	2	2	9	9	18	3	0	3
Total	2 382	2 699	5 081	333	513	846	537	719	1 256	103	14	117

TABLE 6—Colored professional students and graduates in 1896–97

STATE	Male	Female	Total	Theology Students	Theology Graduates	Law Students	Law Graduates	Medicine Students	Medicine Graduates	Dentistry Students	Dentistry Graduates	Pharmacy Students	Pharmacy Graduates	Nurse training Students	Nurse training Graduates
Alabama	107	25	132	107	6									25	0
Arkansas															
Delaware															
District of Columbia	295	0	295	73	14	79	25	106	22	20	4	17	8	0	0
Florida															
Georgia	154	39	193	151	11	3	0	0	0	0	0	0	0	39	2
Illinois	0	0	0	0	0	0	0	0	0	0	0	0	0	0	0
Indiana	0	0	0	0	0	0	0	0	0	0	0	0	0	0	0
Kentucky	13	0	13	13	0	0	0	0	0	0	0	0	0	0	0
Louisiana	38	5	43	0	2	0	0	38	8	0	0	0	0	5	0
Maryland	2	0	2	2	1	0	0	0	0	0	0	0	0	0	0
Mississippi	5	52	57	5	0	0	0	0	0	0	0	0	0	52	8
Missouri	4	0	4	4	0	0	0	0	0	0	0	0	0	0	0
New Jersey	0	0	0	0	0	0	0	0	0	0	0	0	0	0	0
North Carolina	116	6	122	43	7	11	3	51	7	0	0	11	8	6	0
Ohio	15	0	15	13	1	2	0	0	0	0	0	0	0	0	0
Pennsylvania	48	0	48	48	16	0	0	0	0	0	0	0	0	0	0
South Carolina	50	36	86	47	0	3	0	0	0	0	0	0	0	36	22
Tennessee	221	0	221	36	1	6	2	150	34	18	6	11	4	0	0
Texas	4	9	13	4	1	0	0	0	0	0	0	0	0	9	0
Virginia	65	2	67	65	8	0	0	0	0	0	0	0	0	2	3
West Virginia	0	0	0	0	0	0	0	0	0	0	0	0	0	0	0
Total	1 137	174	1 311	611	68	104	30	345	71	38	10	39	20	174	35

TABLE 7—Industrial training of colored students in 1896-97

STATE	PUPILS RECEIVING INDUSTRIAL TRAINING			STUDENTS TRAINED IN INDUSTRIAL BRANCHES												
	Male	Female	Total	Farm or garden work	Carpentry	Bricklaying	Plastering	Painting	Tin or sheet metal work	Forging	Machine-shop work	Shoemaking	Printing	Sewing	Cooking	Other trades
Alabama	1 117	988	2 105	294	195	17	17	17	8	45	12	38	69	542	125	687
Arkansas	132	182	314	40	29	0	0	0	0	14	9	3	23	119	83	13
Delaware	34	6	40	14	20			1			2		3			
District of Columbia	151	74	225		88				10	11	13			43		
Florida	76	118	194	44	68	9		44	0		11	1	10	112	63	
Georgia	251	1 272	1 523	23	165		9	7				0	66	956	85	283
Illinois																
Indiana																
Kentucky	20	201	221	18	7	10	1	21	60	10	48	0	2	81	81	120
Louisiana	394	433	827	73	78						4	4	45	319	70	209
Maryland	48	207	255	0	8							47	57	164	147	75
Mississippi	360	432	792	90	94			5			12			416	160	104
Missouri	65	140	205	0	31					22	12			140		
New Jersey	28	23	51	15	28	0	0	0	0		0		0	23	23	15
North Carolina	442	1 116	1 558	66	142	0	20	14	2	80	5	0	65	941	446	236
Ohio	83	133	216	0	38	26	0	0	0	0	0	31	46	67	65	0
Pennsylvania	28	88	116	0	28	0			0			18	16		88	96
South Carolina	667	1 042	1 709	53	182	18	79	26	0	22	76	18	42	995	196	93
Tennessee	142	416	558	5	41	79		4	4			5	92	407	116	6
Texas	421	693	1 114	167	125	7	10	10		19	16	18	36	517	214	2
Virginia	452	915	1 367	125	77		8		1	4	40		42	760	318	814
West Virginia	59	132	191		52					4	40		4	126	69	
Total	4 970	8 611	13 581	1 027	1 496	166	144	149	85	227	248	185	689	6 728	2 349	2 753

TABLE 8 — *Financial summary of the 169 colored schools.*

STATE	Value of benefactions or bequests, 1896-97	Volumes in library	Value of library	Value of grounds, buildings, furniture and scientific apparatus.	Amount of state or municipal aid	Amount received from tuition fees	Amount received from productive funds	Amount received from sources unclassified	Total income for the year 1896-97
Alabama	$35 377	16 125	$15 970	$552 247	$14 730	$7 271	$7 766	$36 778	$60 545
Arkansas	1 020	5 660	2 935	170 200	8 200	5 807	2 100	4 145	20 252
Delaware	200	...	...	17 800	4 000	...	...	4 200	8 200
District of Columbia	0	17 319	14 500	965 000	32 600	...	9 000	11 000	60 514
Florida	15	2 376	2 350	70 500	11 500	7 914	0	145	11 937
Georgia	10 703	33 770	29 659	1 324 262	17 300	292	5 700	81 115	127 129
Illinois	...	169	190	18 000	...	23 014	...	...	...
Indiana	...	212	200	2 500	...	...	...	...	...
Kentucky	133	18 567	17 025	294 203	29 220	5 094	4 578	8 173	47 065
Louisiana	2 600	10 700	8 800	326 236	9 000	4 054	6 440	22 610	42 104
Maryland	...	5 000	4 400	110 000	12 900	3 200	1 240	11 610	28 950
Mississippi	8 110	16 820	24 400	431 500	9 750	7 313	10 000	23 222	50 285
Missouri	200	2 910	2 159	166 300	18 000	1 761	125	2 996	22 882
New Jersey	...	100	75	1 000	3 000	0	0	0	3 000
North Carolina	24 464	17 250	16 035	523 710	17 889	8 588	725	49 857	77 059
Ohio	0	6 600	6 500	108 000	16 400	1 822	1 323	8 771	28 316
Pennsylvania	...	14 000	14 000	214 000	...	...	...	...	...
South Carolina	1 745	8 475	5 680	212 500	3 100	8 485	1 000	37 633	50 218
Tennessee	47 538	18 166	17 330	904 400	3 100	24 958	2 800	38 633	69 491
Texas	1 950	7 575	6 700	324 600	20 600	23 683	500	25 134	69 917
Virginia	167 480	17 400	11 223	888 000	25 550	7 681	37 224	164 406	234 861
West Virginia	3 515	5 600	3 600	110 000	15 000	1 325	1 559	9 669	26 553
Total	$305 050	224 794	$203 731	$7 714 958	$271 839	$141 262	$92 080	$540 097	$1 045 278

DEPARTMENT OF EDUCATION

FOR THE

UNITED STATES COMMISSION TO THE PARIS EXPOSITION OF 1900

MONOGRAPHS ON EDUCATION

IN THE

UNITED STATES

EDITED BY

NICHOLAS MURRAY BUTLER

Professor of Philosophy and Education in Columbia University, New York

19

EDUCATION OF THE INDIAN

BY

WILLIAM N. HAILMANN

Superintendent of Schools, Dayton, Ohio

THIS MONOGRAPH IS CONTRIBUTED TO THE UNITED STATES EDUCATIONAL EXHIBIT BY THE STATE OF NEW YORK

EDUCATION OF THE INDIAN

INTRODUCTION

The first successful attempts to colonize America on the part of the Anglo-Saxons were made during the first quarter of the seventeenth century. Immediately the struggle set in between brutal greed and a certain irrepressible spirit of fair play on the part of the intruding race in their intercourse with the Indians. Greed saw in the Indian a hateful obstacle in the way of its advance in the acquisition of territory. Fair play, aided by a nascent spirit of broad Christianity and genuine philanthropy, emphasized in the Indian his essential humanity and labored to lead him, for the sake of his own salvation, to a recognition of the fatherhood of God and to lift him into a condition that would render him worthy of being received as a full equal into the brotherhood of man. This struggle is still going on with shifting success. Yet, on the whole, humanity and fair play are steadily gaining.

The intellectual and spiritual upheavals of the sixteenth century, which had culminated in Bacon and Luther, had directed thought to education as the chief reliance in the liberation of the race from the trammels of superstition, and in leading him out of the worship of physical prowess to the recognition of his duty to God and man. Naturally, therefore, those who sought the conversion and uplifting of the Indian directed their attention primarily to efforts for his education. The very charters, granted to the colonizing companies, breathed the hope that their work might bring about " the enlargement of God's kingdom among the heathen people."

The present system of Indian education, under the direction of the government of the United States, is in no way the outcome of a deliberate and carefully-conceived plan on the part of Washington officials. It is descended directly from the first attempts in Indian education on the part of Virginia, and more particularly on the part of New England. Here its seeds were planted. From these it derives certain inherent, vital principles, rooted in a broad Christianity and a fervent philanthropy which have enabled it to withstand blights of partisanship, of greed and rapacity on the part of spoilsmen, of incompetence on the part of teachers, of race prejudice on the part of settlers and other unfavorable conditions of environment and policy.

JOHN ELIOT

A remarkable pioneer work, and of a typical character, was done by Rev. John Eliot in Massachusetts. Mr. Eliot was actuated by motives of broadest Christianity and purest philanthropy. His simple measures were chosen with consummate wisdom. In the first place he familiarized himself with the language, disposition and character of his Indians. Then, by according them the same, he secured their confidence and respect and stimulated in their hearts reverence and a sincere desire for the industry and thrift, the godliness and purity of life, of which New England communities afforded the example. Those who would follow him he gathered in towns, where he taught them the liberties and responsibilities of township government and the devices and institutions of civilized life, among which the church and the school naturally occupied places of honor. A number of "choice Indian youths" he induced to attend English schools that they might prepare themselves for missionary work as teachers and catechists among their own people.

He was warmly supported in his work by "the corporation for the propagation of the Gospel in foreign parts," by the general court of Massachusetts and, particularly, by Mr. Daniel Gookins, the official superintendent of the Indians in Massachusetts. Mr. Eliot began his work in 1646. In 1674 there were fourteen towns of "praying Indians" whose schools and churches, in the majority of instances, were administered by educated natives. At the same time, an

Indian college had been founded at Cambridge. Yet, in due time, this success was swept away by the fears and prejudices which developed under the baneful influences of the Indian wars. Similar successful work under the direction of Revs. John Cotton and Richard Bourne in Plymouth colony shared the same fate.

SERGEANT AND WHEELOCK

Other memorable efforts in the eighteenth century were robbed of their fruits by similar causes, intensified by a number of disorganizing factors incident to the revolutionary period. Prominent among these is the work of Rev. John Sergeant at Stockbridge in Massachusetts and that of Rev. Eleazer Wheelock in Connecticut and New Hampshire.

The work of Mr. Sergeant, which involved the establishment of day schools, of a boarding school and an experimental "outing system," was almost ideal in conception, but ended with the deportation of his Indians to the west. Dr. Wheelock's labors led to the establishment of an effective training school and, indirectly, to the creation of Dartmouth college "for the education and instruction of youths of the Indian tribes in this land in reading, writing, and all parts of learning which shall appear necessary and expedient for civilizing and christianizing the children of pagans, as well as in all liberal arts and sciences, and also of English youths and any others." Only the last purpose was destined for achievement.

PERSISTENCE OF SPIRIT OF WORK

It is interesting to note that, in spite of practically total external failure, the spirit and even much of the form of these early enterprises persisted. Their impress is observable to-day in almost every prominent feature of the Indian school organization of the United States.

Among these I would point out the establishment of day schools in or near Indian villages or settlements and their organization as a means for the domestic and industrial uplifting of Indian family and village life, as well as for the instruction of children; the establishment of industrial boarding schools in territory occupied by Indians, with their opportunities for introducing among the young a taste for the amenities and refinements, as well as for the duties and responsibilities of civilization; the establishment in civilized English-speaking communities of advanced training schools for the fuller equipment of "choice Indian youths" for full citizenship in white communities or for missionary work in the ideals, institutions, and arts of civilization among their own people; the universal stress in all schools upon instruction of boys in the arts of husbandry and certain trades and of girls in the domestic arts; the "outing system" which places partially educated Indian girls and boys as paid helpers in suitable English-speaking families and affords them instruction in the ordinary public schools; the importance attached to religious and ethical training.

SHORTCOMINGS

On the other hand, it is to be deplored that a number of valuable features of the early schools have been abandoned and even supplanted by opposite tendencies. Among the latter are to be reckoned the unintelligent warfare waged against the Indian idiom; the introduction of certain brutalities of military discipline under the influence of soldiers who for a time controlled Indian schools; an equally unintelligent effort on the part of some schools to wean Indian youth from Indian association by throwing contempt upon the Indian and by stimulating a feeling akin to hatred of Indian family ties; and a variety of measures and devices inspired by a policy of compulsion and repression, rather than by a spirit of development and benevolent helpfulness.

Serious harm came to the government schools from time to time from the fact that until 1893 patronage and partisanship entered as a weighty, perhaps the weightiest, factor in the appointment of officers and employees. Thanks to the constant vigilance of the Indian rights association, the Mohonk conference and a number of other societies earn-

estly interested in the welfare of the Indians, these evils are
steadily yielding. They have been greatly reduced since
1893 by the application of civil service rules to school
employees, and it is hoped that in these matters every new
dawn will bring a better day.

PERIOD OF INACTION

Before entering upon a descriptive account of the Indian
school work of the present day, it is desirable to indicate in
a few words the successive steps that have led to their
organizatiqn.

After the revolution, congress and the country as a whole
were so much absorbed with the duties of self-establishment
that little heed was paid to Indian education. A number of
minor appropriations are recorded on the basis of treaties
with a few tribes, and at a few points missionary zeal continued a fitful activity. During the first quarter of the nineteenth century, however, a great religious revival again
directed general attention to Indian education as a Christian
and national duty.

RESUMPTION OF WORK

Missionary bodies took up the work with renewed zeal.
Congress responded in 1819 with an appropriation of $10,000
in addition to certain treaty obligations.   In 1820 the president was authorized to apply this sum annually in aid of
societies and individuals engaged in the education of Indians.
In 1823 the sum of $80,000 was expended in 21 schools
maintained by missionary bodies ; $12,000 of this amount
had been contributed by the government.

In 1825 the number of such schools had risen to 38, the
entire expenditure for these to $202,000, of which the gov-
ernment, directly and indirectly, had contributed $25,000.
In 1848 there were reported in operation 16 manual training
schools, 87 boarding schools and other schools.

These schools continued to increase in number and
efficiency up to 1873. They were under the control of missionary bodies with such scanty aid from the government as

the small appropriations afforded. Only a few small day schools had been established by the government directly under treaty provisions.

GOVERNMENTAL ZEAL

After this time, however, the government entered upon an era of almost feverish activity in the establishment of strictly government schools; first, day schools, then boarding schools and industrial training schools. Congress kept pace with this zeal in the liberality of its appropriations.

In 1877 it appropriated for schools, outside of treaty provisions, $20,000, in 1880 $75,000, in 1885 $992,800, in 1890 $1,364,568, in 1895 $2,060,695, in 1899 $2,638,390. During this period the average attendance rose in similar ratio from 3,598 in 1877 to 19,648 in 1898.

The increased appropriations by congress for the education of Indians naturally stimulated a desire on the part of the government to control the expenditures directly and in detail. Possibly this desire was much enhanced by the fact that such expenditure opened to the party in power a rich field for patronage.

At the same time it was discovered that the constitution, by implication at least, forbade the appropriation of public funds for denominational purposes. Concurrent conclusions, unfavorable to government support of missionary schools, were further strengthened by the fact that the Roman Catholic church had gradually outstripped the Protestant missionary bodies and was absorbing the lion's share of government support.

DECAY OF MISSIONARY EFFORT

During the first half of the century the Protestant missionary organizations had had well nigh a monopoly of government support; but, later on, the Roman Catholics had wrested from them the preponderance. In 1889 the Catholic church drew from the appropriations for this purpose $347,672, as against $128,518 drawn by Protestant bodies. In 1892 these amounts had risen to $394,756 for the Catholics and $160,874 for the Protestants. In 1893 the Methodist Episcopal church withdrew from participation in government aid without, however, abandoning its schools. In 1895 this example was followed by the Presbyterians and Congregationalists, in 1896 by the Friends, and in 1897 by the remaining Protestant denominations. This left only the Catholics in the field with an appropriation of $198,228.

This process was aided by congress which, in 1894, had declared its policy of gradually abandoning all support of denominational schools. This policy has since been followed, so that in 1899 the appropriation was reduced to $116,862.

PRESENT ORGANIZATION

In their present organization the Indian schools under government control are designated as day schools, as reservation boarding schools, non-reservation boarding schools, and as industrial and normal training schools.

Day schools — Day schools are located in Indian villages or near Indian camps or settlements. They are, as a rule, in charge of a male teacher and his wife, who acts as housekeeper, or — more particularly in the pueblos of New Mexico and in the Indian villages of Southern California — of a lady teacher and an Indian housekeeper. The children spend from five to eight hours during five days of the week under the care of these employees and return to their homes in the evening. At noon they are furnished a substantial luncheon, except in the pueblos of New Mexico and in the villages of Southern California, where they generally return to their homes during the noon recess.

The instruction is of the simplest character. The children are taught to speak, read and write the English language within narrow limits, to cipher, to draw and to sing. In addition they get some rudimentary notions of geography, of natural history and of United States history. The methods are borrowed largely from the kindergarten and from object teaching.

Much stress is laid upon habits of cleanliness and order,

mutual kindliness and prompt obedience.   The boys receive
some instruction in the use of tools, in gardening and in
some instances, in the care of cows.   The girls are taught
sewing, cooking and other arts of housekeeping.

While day schools, as a rule, accomplish comparatively
little in conventional school-room work, they achieve much
in bringing to the Indians among whom they are located,
the message and desire of better ways of living.   The
school as such serves as a concrete illustration of a civilized
Christian home which the Indians learn to respect and in an
appreciable degree to emulate.   Where the teacher and
housekeeper, at the same time, possess the inclination and
the skill to attract to themselves the older Indians, to secure
their confidence and to instruct them unobtrusively in the
simpler arts of thrift and home-making, these schools become
invaluable factors in the uplifting of the race.   Moreover,
they reconcile the Indian with the idea of sending his children to school, and render him more willing in due time to
intrust them to the care of boarding schools, as well as more
ready to appreciate and to accept the lessons of civilization
that radiate from these centers of education.

According to the report of the commissioner of Indian
affairs the government operated in 1898 142 day schools.
The most successful of these are located in Wisconsin (16),
in North Dakota (11), and in South Dakota (54) ; the least
successful, probably, among the pueblos of New Mexico
(14).   This comparative lack of success, however, is not to
be attributed to the teachers who are devoted and capable.
It is due rather to the fact that these Indians live in a state
of half-civilization which they owe to their Mexican and
Spanish antecedents.   This condition fully satisfies their
ideals, and, consequently, they do not care to exchange it
for the ways of their teachers.

The life of the day-school teacher is one of extreme isolation from the amenities and refinements of civilization.   It
argues on their part a degree of self-denial and devotion
which even with persons of only ordinary goodness is sure to

emphasize the best traits and impulses of the soul. It is not rare, therefore, to find among them sanctified men and women whose very presence is an inspiration. I have no doubt that to this is due much of their benign influence upon the Indians among whom their lot is cast. It is an observation much to the credit of human nature that only rarely a teacher is found of a character so corrupt as to take advantage of the people and the children intrusted to his care.

The day schools are kept open for ten months. The salaries paid vary from $600 to $800 for the teacher and from $300 to $480 for the housekeeper, according to location.

Reservation boarding schools — These schools are located within the territory reserved for some tribe of Indians. They are in charge of a superintendent, assisted by a matron and such teachers, industrial and domestic helpers as the capacity and character of the school may require. In addition to the required number of school teachers, the school is provided with a cook, a seamstress, and a laundress whose office it is not only to supervise their respective departments, but also to instruct the girls in these arts. Similarly, there is for the instruction of the boys a farmer, an industrial teacher, and, at larger schools, a tailor, a shoe and harness maker, a carpenter and blacksmith. An experiment to provide for more methodical instruction in the use of tools by expert manual training teachers failed because the Indian office would not afford a salary for this position, sufficient to attract competent men.

In 1894 the experiment of connecting kindergartens with these schools was tried. The experiment proved eminently successful. The children entered into the work and the games with zest and intelligence. Their traditional shyness and reticence yielded naturally and readily to their objective interest in the exercises. They acquired the English idiom with much ease and learned to express their ideas freely and with eagerness. At the present time, there are forty kindergartens connected with boarding schools. Moreover, the use of kindergarten methods and of kindergarten material has entered the primary classes in practically all these schools and in many of the day schools with similar good results.

The children spend from one and a-half to two hours each half-day with the kindergarten. Other children, in the majority of these schools, spend half a day — forenoon or afternoon — in the school room and the other half-day in domestic or industrial work of a character suited to their age. In a number of schools, however, which are lacking in facilities or in skill and good will on the part of the respective employees, the smaller children are detained in the school room during the entire day, much to their physical, intellectual and moral deterioration.

Indeed, experience has proved that half-day instruction which at first was forced upon the schools as an expedient, is one which every consideration of wisdom and prudence would commend. The sedentary life of the more or less crowded school room becomes irksome to these children accustomed to an active outdoor life ; the interests of the school room are foreign to their heredities and traditions. The industrial features of the work, on the other hand, appeal more or less forcibly to their habits and tastes and stimulate practical interests which the parents can appreci-ate and which induce them to look with favor upon the school and to aid it in its work. The school room itself finds in these interests material for practice and discussion directly welcome to the pupil ; it can thus more readily overcome aversion and secure an appreciative and sympa-thetic attitude on the part of the pupils. It adds to the work of the schools in a large measure all the advantages of mental stimulation which manual training yields. It is, consequently, not astonishing that the children in schools in which the half-day practice has not been adopted make less rapid progress, are backward in physical and intellectual development, and morally less earnest and responsible than the children of half-day schools.

The aim of the school, in so far as instruction is con-cerned, is to give to the pupils ability to read and write

English within the limits of ordinary primary school work, practical control of arithmetic for the needs of ordinary daily life, clear rudimentary notions of geography and United States history, drawing and singing, a knowledge of the laws of hygienic living, garden work, the cultivation of fruits and vegetables, and familiarity with the simpler requirements of agricultural and domestic industries suited to the locality. Moreover, in a few of the larger schools, the larger boys have much opportunity to acquire skill in carpentry, blacksmithing, tailoring and shoemaking.

It has already been indicated that these institutions are to the children not only school, but also home and community. The institution gives them shelter, food and clothing ; it accustoms them to habits of cleanliness and decency ; it cultivates their æsthetic tastes ; it labors to secure right moral attitude and, at least in its Sunday school, seeks to impart the plainer truths of Christianity and to stimulate the religious life of the children.

In these last efforts, it is true, the schools are much handicapped by denominational jealousies which are ever ready to suspect proselyting, and which have forced the government into an attitude of indifference and inactivity in all matters that affect religion. In a number of reservations, however, missionary establishments, which are impartially encouraged by the government, supplement the work of the schools to a certain extent in matters of religion.

The superintendent of the reservation boarding school is subject in his work to the control of the Indian agent, who, as representative of the government, administers the affairs of the reservation. To this agent he makes requisition for whatever the school may need ; through him he makes his reports and requests to the Indian office at Washington and receives replies and directions ; through him he makes his recommendations, if any, for the appointment or dismissal of employees ; from him he and his subordinates receive their pay.

Inasmuch as these agents are selected on partisan

grounds, usually at the suggestion of local politicians and as a reward for partisan service, this arrangement is fraught with much danger to the true interests of these schools. Until 1893 — when superintendents, matrons and teachers were placed under civil service protection — all employees at these schools were at the mercy of the Indian agents, dismissals for partisan or patronage reasons were the order of the day, scandals of every description were frequent, and the schools accomplished good only when the agent happened to be a good man.   After 1893 there came some improvement. Yet with reference to employees in the domestic and industrial service and in minor positions the same evils continued practically unabated.   With reference to these the superintendents and even the Indian office were powerless, and frequently good superintendents were forced out of the service by combinations against them among the appointees of the agent or through the aid and influence of unscrupulous partisan inspectors or supervisors.

In 1896, at last, all employees of the school service were placed under civil service protection, and since that time there has been marked improvement in the conditions and work of these schools.

Nevertheless, from the very inertia of things — moral as well as material — the superintendents of these schools are frequently ignored, recommendations are made by agents without even the knowledge of the superintendents and honored by Washington officials.   In a number of agencies, where the agent has practically no duties save those connected with the school service, this relation is peculiarly oppressive and acts generally as a hindrance in the development of the school.

As a remedy for these evils, friends of the Indians and of good government have repeatedly proposed the relief of these superintendents from the control of agents and the abolishment of unnecessary agencies, but the propositions have as repeatedly been " turned down" by spoilsmen in control at Washington.

On the other hand, there has been decided gain in the equipment, in the sanitary condition, in the general character of employees, and in the conduct of these schools. Employees are learning to look to efficiency as their chief reliance for continuance in office and for promotion, rather than to the favor of some patron.   The consequent increase in self-respect on their part has operated as a barrier to a number of abuses which thereby became simply impossible, and have secured a spirit of genuine devotion to the work of the school on the part of the employees.

At the same time the Indian office has been relieved of attention to office-seekers and their patrons, which had occupied so much of the time of officials.   It has, consequently, been enabled to pay increased attention to the schools themselves, to their equipment, their sanitary condition, their management.   The new schools, erected within the last few years, are models in their way, and most of the older schools have in all these matters been greatly improved.

According to the report of the commissioner of Indian affairs there were in operation in the year 1898 seventy-five of these schools with a capacity of 8,825, an enrollment of 8,877, and an average attendance of 7,532 pupils.   There were employed in their conduct 1,247 persons, including Indian cadets and apprentice assistants who are paid at the rate of $60 per year.   The cost of these schools to the government was $1,149,155.90.

The life of the employees is comparatively pleasant and affords many social amenities.   In many instances, towns inhabited by white people are within easy access.   Where this is not the case there is, as a rule, a sufficient number of employees at the school to preclude the isolation and loneliness of day-school life.   Usually a pleasant room is set aside and neatly furnished as an employees' sitting room.   The employees are furnished quarters at the schools, but provide for their food.   For this purpose they are organized in a common mess.   Their expenses for board rarely reach $12 per month, and more frequently fall below $10.

They are employed for the year; but are granted thirty days leave of absence, and on occasion thirty days of sick leave without deduction of pay.   Instruction continues through forty weeks; but in many instances a portion of the children are kept at the school throughout the year.

Superintendents are paid from $900 to $1,200; matrons from $500 to $720, according to the size of the school. Teachers receive from $450 to $720, according to experience; farmers and other industrial employees from $600 to $800; heads of domestic industries $400 to $600; their assistants $300 to $500; Indian apprentice assistants from $60 to $240.   Promotion is based usually on experience and merit.

Non-reservation boarding schools— Of these there are at present twenty-five.   Seven of them are distinguished as industrial training schools and three others as industrial and normal training schools.

The remaining fifteen, in their original scope of work, differed little from the reservation boarding schools.   Differences in organization, however, as well as differences in environment, have exercised a salutary influence upon them, and have lifted them in aims and attainments far above the latter.

In the first place the superintendents of these schools are bonded and directly responsible to the Indian office.   There is between them and the authorities at Washington no intervening Indian agency with its demoralizing possibilities. Their authority in the management of the schools is complete. The consequent sense of responsibility and self-respect in the head of the school finds its reflection in the attitude of his subordinates, as well as in the attitude of the pupils. Undivided loyalty on the part of the employees does away largely with factional hindrances.   Efficiency and devotion to duty have a vastly greater share in appointments, in tenure and in promotion.

The beneficial influence of this better condition of affairs is further enhanced in the majority of instances by the environment of these schools. They are, as a rule, located at a distance from the Indian country and in the vicinity of civilized American towns which afford the schools — teachers and pupils — the stimulus of constant contact with the ideals and amenities of civilized life. The work thereby gains in every respect — in scope, in depth, in intensity, in vitality, in permanence of influence upon the pupils.

The pupils at these schools are on an average more advanced in years than those at reservation schools. Frequently, they have had some previous training in day schools or reservation boarding schools. They are, because far away from their Indian homes, more constant and more regular in attendance ; and, for the same reason and because of their vicinity to English-speaking communities, they gain a better control of the English idiom.

Their class-room work is, therefore, more thorough and more extended, and reaches far into the advanced grammar school courses of study, laying special stress upon language practice, arithmetic, geometry, geography, history, nature study, drawing, and civil government.

Their facilities for training pupils in the domestic and industrial arts are much greater than in reservation schools ; and the effectiveness of their instruction in these arts is much enhanced by the fact that pupils have frequent opportunities to observe the practical applicability and value of these arts in the environment of the schools.

The superintendents are paid from $1,200 to $1,500 per annum. Other employees are paid on the same scale as in reservation schools.

The most noted and successful of these schools are located at Flandreau in South Dakota, Pipestone in Minnesota, Mount Pleasant in Michigan, Fort Mojave in Arizona, Carson in Nevada, Perris in California, Tomah in Wisconsin, Wittenberg in Wisconsin, Fort Lewis in Colorado, and Pierre in South Dakota.

Industrial training schools — These schools are located at Carlisle in Pennsylvania, Chemawa near Salem in Oregon,

Chilocco in Oklahoma, Genoa in Nebraska, Albuquerque in New Mexico, Lawrence in Kansas (the Haskell institute), Grand Junction in Colorado, Santa Fe in New Mexico, Phœnix in Arizona, Fort Shaw in Montana.

In the essential features of their organization tnese schools are similar to the schools just described. In the scope of their work, however, in equipment and in cultural facilities they excel, as a rule, in a high degree.

With a view of training teachers systematically and in greater number for the work of teaching, the government in 1894 added to three of these schools normal departments. This was done at Carlisle, at the Haskell institute and at Santa Fe, and these schools were henceforth distinguished as industrial and normal training schools. The experiment proved fairly successful with Carlisle where, indeed, similar work had been previously done, and, more especially, with the Haskell institute. The school at Santa Fe during the first years accomplished little in this direction, but of late has begun to gain success under a gifted superintendent.

Haskell institute — The following sketch of the work of Haskell institute will afford an idea of the scope of these schools, as well as of the possibilities of Indian education under government control :

Haskell institute is located near the city of Lawrence, in the state of Kansas. The school was opened in 1884. It has now a capacity of 550 pupils. The main buildings are substantial stone structures. The dormitories, school building and some other buildings, are heated by steam, lighted by electricity, provided with hot and cold water, and supplied with modern sanitary conveniences. The entire plant consists of about thirty buildings and has its own water works. A farm of 650 acres is attached to the institution.

The institution is under the direction of a superintendent, aided by an assistant superintendent, who acts also as physician, and by three clerks. In their daily movements the pupils are under the supervision of a disciplinarian — exclusively for the boys — and a corps of six matrons and housekeepers. The academic department of the school is administered by a principal teacher, assisted by fifteen teachers, suitably assigned to the kindergarten, the model school, the normal department, the commercial department, and the department of music — vocal and instrumental.

In addition there are the departments of manual training and of domestic science, and a printing office, each under competent leadership.

In the girls' industrial department, sewing, cooking, laundering, and other features of housekeeping, are taught and practiced in supplying the needs of the institution in these matters.

Similarly, in the boys' industrial department, farming, gardening and dairying, carpentering, blacksmithing, masonry and plastering, steamfitting and engineering, wheelwrighting, painting, harnessmaking, tailoring, shoemaking and baking are taught and practiced.

In a well-equipped hospital the physician and two nurses take care of the sick.

In a number of departments, graduates and other advanced pupils are employed as assistants at salaries ranging from $60 to $120 per annum. In 1898 there were 18 of these.

Much attention is paid throughout the institution to music, vocal and instrumental. In addition to general singing exercises, the school has organized special choruses, glee clubs, a string orchestra, and an orchestra of mixed instruments, all of which render music very creditably.

For purposes of study and for the stimulation of self-culture, the institution is provided with a carefully-selected reference library, as well as with magazines and other periodicals placed at the disposal of pupils in a comfortable and well-lighted reading room.

Religious nurture is provided in a Sunday school on Sunday forenoon; in a short, undenominational religious service on Sunday afternoon, and in certain devotional exercises connected with the daily movements of the school. Moreover, pupils who may wish to do so are given opportunity to attend religious service in the city on Sunday morning in the churches with which they may be affiliated. Pupils enrolled in the Young Men's Christian association and in the Young Women's Christian association hold their meetings at the school on Sunday evenings. They welcome all non-members who may wish to attend.

The model school is arranged in eight grades and is planned for eight years of work. In scope and content it compares satisfactorily with the ordinary public school courses for elementary schools, and is fully abreast with the times in matter and method.

The model course is followed by a preparatory course, intended for pupils who may desire to enter the normal or commercial course. It embraces a general review of arithmetic, the first rudiments of algebra, the systematic study of English grammar, the reading of literary master-pieces, composition work, English history, zoology, botany and music.

The normal course, planned for two years, deals with the rudiments of algebra and geometry, with elementary physics, general history, rhetoric, American and English literature, and — on the professional side — with psychology, history of pedagogy, pedagogics, discussion of methods, and practice teaching under the direction of a critic teacher.

The commercial course, planned also for two years, affords instruction and practice in stenography, typewriting, com-mercial arithmetic, commercial law, parliamentary rules, bookkeeping, business correspondence, banking, penman-ship and business practice.

Graduates of the normal department are offered the oppor-tunity to devote one additional year to preparation for kindergarten work under the direction of the kindergartner of the institution, and in connection with a well-equipped kindergarten, where they are permitted to observe the work and occasionally to assist in it.

Members of the three special departments are exempt from industrial training; they devote their entire time to class-room work. All others give one-half of the day to class-room work and the other half to manual and industrial training. In both of these they acquire a commendable degree of skill and efficiency.

The fact that the Kansas state university is located at Lawrence exerts a stimulating influence upon the institution. The professors of the university take an active personal interest in its welfare and favor it from time to time with courses of lectures adapted to the needs of the pupils. As a result the desire grows in their hearts to secure for themselves university training after graduation from Haskell. At present there are two graduates of the institution in the law school of the university.

Quite a number of acceptable teachers have gone forth from the normal department of the institution in the years of 1896, '97 and '98, and have found employment in Indian schools. With very few exceptions, these have shown a commendable degree of judgment, devotion, progressiveness and continuity in their work, repelling by their conduct the pessimistic allegation made by detractors of the Indian character, that they would prove capricious and unreliable.

Of the 25 normal graduates put out by the institution in the three years, 14 are now acting as teachers, one as principal teacher, one as disciplinarian, one as lumber inspector, two as clerks, one as farmer and dairyman, one as assistant matron. One has entered the training school for kindergartners, one the high school in a western city, and one the law school of the university.

Carlisle — The organization of the Indian school at Carlisle, in the state of Pennsylvania, is, in its main features, similar to that of Haskell institute. It differs, however, in many details of management, because of the strong personal characteristics of its superintendent.

The school has a capacity of 800 pupils. This, however, may be nearly doubled with the aid of the excellent " outing system," which is a distinctive feature of the institution.

By this system the Carlisle school requires its students to

spend one or more years of their school life away from the school in carefully selected white families, under the supervision of the school. For their services in these families they receive current wages, but are required to attend public schools for four or more months during the winter. Thus they gain direct, personal experience in self-support by honest work and an insight into the responsibilities and amenities of civilized family and institutional life in its best and most attractive forms, while at the same time they are reasonably protected against the demoralizing factors of white civilization which are so much in the way of success in the outlying districts near the Indian country.

The growth of this system has been quite remarkable and emphasizes its value. It began tentatively with a few pupils in 1880. In 1898 the superintendent reported that "an average of 250 remained out during the winter attending the public schools, and 600 were out during the vacation." "Each pupil," he continues, "earned wages according to ability, the boys' earnings aggregating $13,541.30, of which they saved $5,208.61, and the girls' earnings aggregating $8,184.20, of which they saved $3,098.50."

Other distinctive features of this school are found in its excellent department of music, its art school, and, more particularly, in its systematic attention to physical training. The school has a well-equipped gymnasium in which both girls and boys receive instruction and training. The football team of Carlisle has a national reputation for clean and vigorous play; it receives and meets with credit challenges from the best colleges of the land.

Contract schools — In addition to maintaining these strictly government schools, the Indian office pays $108 per pupil to 25 Catholic mission boarding schools for the education of 1,098 children; $30 per pupil for 21 children in two Catholic day schools, and $167 per pupil for 200 pupils in Lincoln institute at Philadelphia, and for 120 pupils in Hampton institute, located at Hampton, in the state of Virginia.

Of these, Hampton institute deserves special mention. It was originally established with the help of northern philanthropists for the industrial and normal training of negroes in 1868. Its support to-day is derived from small endowment funds, liberal annual contributions from the north, and $10,000 annually paid to it in its capacity as an agricultural school by the state of Virginia.

In 1878 seventeen young Indians were brought to it from Florida, where they had for three years been kept as prisoners of war. From this was developed the present Indian department of the institution, superior in equipment and in the spirit that controls its work. Here, too, originated the outing system which, subsequently, grew into an educational factor of vast importance at Carlisle.

The distinctive feature of this school, however, is its broad missionary spirit. Bound to no particular denomination, yet respecting all and respected by all, it is deeply religious in spirit and work, and labors to inculcate its own missionary zeal in the hearts of its students.

In its young Indian students it stimulates a keen sense of responsible manhood and womanhood. It teaches them to experience and to appreciate the advantages of the intelligent Christian civilization of which it furnishes them the example. It stimulates and nurtures in them a deep sympathy with their own people in their sufferings and needs, and a fervent desire to bring to these in due time the blessings of which they themselves have become participants.

There are still a number of independent schools that receive no support whatever from the government. Some of these do much good so that it would be a gratifying task to give a detailed account of their organization and work. Nothing, however, could be gained by this for the presentation of the subject in its general bearings. On the whole they are similarly organized, with the exception that they pay more direct and persistent attention to religious training, inasmuch as they are affiliated with particular religious denominations.

Supervision — The direction and supervision of the Indian schools rests with the Indian office which, in its turn, is under the direction and supervision of the secretary of the interior. In the Indian office the details of the work are intrusted to the education division, now probably the most important division under its control. The education division consists of a chief clerk, with a corps of subordinate clerks, stenographers and copyists. To this division all reports are made; by it all directions and orders are drafted and issued.

The education division is aided in its work by the superintendent of Indian schools and by five supervisors, assigned in their work to five districts respectively. These officials constitute a branch of the Indian school service which occupies a very uncertain position, which can be designated neither as subordinate nor as co-ordinate, and which in its effectiveness depends wholly on the force of character of the incumbents and the good will of the commissioner. They have duties, but no rights; and even their efforts to perform these duties may be rendered practically nugatory by the ill-will of the education division or of the commissioner.

A similarly anomalous relation exists between the commissioner and the secretary of the interior with regard to all matters which the latter may wish to control directly. For this purpose the secretary has established under his direct control an Indian division, independent of the Indian office, and to which all orders and directions which the secretary may designate must be referred by the Indian office for approval. The power of this Indian division is further reinforced by a corps of inspectors in the field appointed on partisan grounds and responsible to him alone.

Here too, therefore, the effectiveness of the commissioner in his work depends wholly upon the good will of the secretary of the interior, who may reduce the commissioner to practical non-existence in so far as the judgment and the conscience of the latter are concerned.

It is true that technically the superintendent of Indian schools may appeal from the commissioner to the secretary of the interior, and the commissioner from the decision of the secretary to the president of the United States. In view, however, of the hopelessly autocratic relation that runs through the chain, that is practically out of the question, as it would tend to increase ill-will.

Under these conditions the fact that Indian education has prospered reflects credit upon all concerned. It argues, on the part of the subordinates, a commendable degree of force of character and on the part of superiors an equally commendable degree of moderation and sense of justice.

CONCLUSION AND OUTLOOK

There can be no doubt that an education which inculcates the tastes and establishes the ideals of current civilization constitutes the proper first step in the work of introducing the Indians into American citizenship. It is equally evident that the cultivation of these tastes and ideals is well nigh impossible under the conditions and influences of tribal life on Indian reservations.

The mere recital of a few of the leading differences between the two civilizations will sufficiently emphasize these difficulties. The Indian civilization looks upon the tribe or family as the unit; with us it is the individual. With the Indian he is richest who gives most; with us it is he who keeps most. The Indian claims hospitality as a right until the means of his host are exhausted; and this hospitality is freely granted. To the Indian, land is as free as the water he drinks; proprietorship continues only so long as the land is tilled or otherwise in use. The Indian prizes the worthless pony, whilom his companion and friend in the lost occupations of the chase and war. The cow is to him only a poor substitute for the buffalo; he knows nothing of her value as a giver of milk and a breeder of cattle. Woman in Indian civilization is a producer and possesses in full Indian life an economic value and independence to which in our civilization she is largely a stranger. His religious rights and ceremonies afford the Indian, in addition to a certain degree of spiritual elevation, opportunities for intense social enjoyment for which he looks in vain in the new civilization.   Add to this that the wants of the Indian are few and easily gratified by simple forms of homely skill in which the industries and other acquirements of the Indian school find little application; that chiefs and medicine-men in the very nature of things look with distrust and disdain upon a civilization which robs them of power and influence; that time-honored tradition imposes upon the young Indian silence and obedience,— and you have an array of adverse conditions which is appalling.

Against these odds the Indian schools are pitted.   The government, it is true, made an effort to come to their aid in a well-intentioned allotment scheme.   In this, a certain amount of land was allotted to each member of a tribe for purposes of agriculture or stock-raising.   The allotment was to be held by the respective allotees inalienably for a period of twenty-five years, and it carried with it under certain conditions rights of citizenship.

In most instances, however, this well-meant measure developed into a new obstacle to the work of the schools. The Indians are gregarious; they live in bands and villages. The isolation of farm life is distasteful to them.   They prefer, therefore, to lease their lands to white farmers and to enjoy the meagre income from this source and from certain government annuities in tribal bands and villages as heretofore.

Nevertheless the schools are steadily gaining ground even against this added difficulty, partly through their direct influence in day schools and reservation boarding schools, partly through the medium of "returned students" from the more advanced non-reservation schools.

Honor and grateful admiration is due the young heroes and heroines who annually go forth from the Indian schools pitting their lives against adamantine walls of tradition and superstition, wresting victory for themselves and their unwilling people from conditions which seem all but hopeless.   It

is not to be wondered that of these soldiers of a new dispen-
sation some fall by the wayside or succumb in the unequal
struggle; but the misfortune, rather than dishonor, of these
should not render us blind to the steady valor of the young
men and women who are steadily pushing ahead, gaining
new ground inch by inch, until even now the observer who
looks beneath the surface sees victory assured. So great,
indeed, has been the gain already achieved that in many
instances where twenty years ago Indian savagery ruled
supreme, it would be difficult now to find any of its features
as enumerated above clearly manifest. The busy farmer,
the thrifty housewife, the skillful artisan, the careful trades-
man are no longer rare; on a number of reservations they
are beginning to be respected as marks of superiority to
which all should aspire. The Indian schools can point with
satisfaction to fervent missionaries, devoted teachers, physicians, lawyers, field matrons, nurses and trained workers
in other fields who owe the impulse to their career, and
much of their equipment to the work and influence of these
schools.

In response to the outcry against the efficiency of Indian
education on the part of superficial observers and prejudiced
detractors of the Indian, the Indian office a few years ago
gathered statistics as to the success in life and fidelity to the
"white man's ways" on the part of "returned students."
As a result it was enabled to announce that fully seventy-five
per cent of these could be rated as excellent or good; that
less than ten per cent were poor or bad, and the remainder
fair or indifferent. Surely an encouraging showing.

Schools of Indian territory — The schools of the so-called
"five civilized tribes" of Indian territory are not included in
the above sketch. Indian territory comprises more than
40,000 square miles of rich, arable land, with valuable coal
and asphalt deposits. It was set aside in 1832 for certain
Indian tribes who formerly occupied the southern and gulf
states. The five civilized tribes of to-day include 30,000
Cherokees, 14,500 Choctaws, 10,000 Creeks, 6,990 Chicka-

saws and 2,000 Seminoles.   In addition there are in the territory 18,500 freed men and 200,000 whites.

Missionary zeal availed itself promptly of this new field for its efforts.   Substantial boarding schools were erected, more particularly by the Presbyterians, Methodists and Baptists.

Much good radiated from these centers of civilization.   In due time, however, the Indian authorities began to make appropriations for these schools.   Ultimately, they took entire charge of them.   Unfortunately, administrative affairs were largely in the hands of whites who, by intermarriage or bribery, had been adopted into the tribes, and there came over the schools, as well as over all other public interests, the blight of extreme partisanship and nepotism which rapidly degraded them in character and efficiency.

In 1898, therefore, the government at Washington found itself compelled to come to the rescue and to assume supervisory control over the affairs of all these tribes except the Seminoles.

Under the act by which this was done, the conduct of the schools and orphan asylums in the four tribes involved was placed under the direction of a "superintendent of schools in Indian territory," appointed by the secretary of the interior.   Under him there is for each of the tribes or nations a "supervisor of schools," whose duty it is to inspect the educational institutions in his district and to assist in their organization and conduct.   The superintendent reports to the commissioner of Indian affairs at Washington through the United States inspector for the Indian territory, who is his immediate superior.

The initial report of the superintendent shows that there are in the four tribes 24 boarding schools, with an enrollment of 1,758 pupils, and an average attendance of 1,480, taught and cared for by 234 employees at an annual expense of $236,824.   This does not include 363 neighborhood schools, in which more than 10,000 children are taught at an annual expense of $113,380.   In character and equipment, however, these schools are very poor.

STATISTICAL TABLES

TABLE I — *Number of Indian schools and average attendance from 1877 to 1898*[1]

YEAR	BOARDING SCHOOLS		DAY SCHOOLS [2]		TOTALS	
	Number	Average attendance	Number	Average attendance	Number	Average attendance
1877................................	48	....	102	....	150	3 598
1878................................	49	....	119	....	168	4 142
1879................................	52	....	107	....	159	4 448
1880................................	60	....	109	....	169	4 651
1881................................	68	....	106	....	174	4 976
1882................................	71	3 077	76	1 637	147	4 714
1883................................	80	3 793	88	1 893	168	5 686
1884................................	87	4 723	98	2 237	185	6 960
1885................................	114	6 201	86	1 942	200	8 143
1886................................	115	7 260	99	2 370	214	9 630
1887................................	117	8 020	110	2 500	227	10 520
1888................................	126	8 705	107	2 715	233	11 420
1889................................	136	9 146	103	2 406	239	11 552
1890................................	140	9 865	106	2 367	246	12 232
1891................................	146	11 425	110	2 163	256	13 588
1892................................	149	12 422	126	2 745	275	15 167
1893................................	156	13 635	119	2 668	275	16 303
1894................................	157	14 457	115	2 639	272	17 220
1895................................	157	15 061	125	3 127	282	18 188
1896................................	156	15 683	140	3 579	296	19 262
1897................................	145	15 026	143	3 650	288	18 676
1898................................	148	16 112	147	3 536	295	19 648

1 Some of the figures in this table as printed prior to 1896 were taken from reports of the superintendent of Indian schools. As revised, they are all taken from the reports of the commissioner of Indian affairs. Prior to 1882 the figures include the New York schools.

2 Indian children attending public schools are included in the average attendance, but the schools are not included in the number of schools.

TABLE 2 — *Enrollment and average attendance at Indian schools, 1897 and 1898, showing increase in 1898; also number of schools in 1898*

KIND OF SCHOOL	ENROLLMENT			AVERAGE ATTENDANCE			Number of schools
	1897	1898	Increase	1897	1898	Increase	
Government schools:							
Non-reservation boarding.	5 723	6 175	452	4 787	5 347	560	25
Reservation boarding.....	8 112	8 887	765	6 855	7 532	677	75
Day......................	4 768	4 847	79	3 234	3 286	52	242
Total...................	18 603	19 899	1 296	14 876	16 165	1 289	342
Contract schools:							
Boarding.................	2 579	2 509	1 70	2 313	2 245	1 68	2 29
Day......................	208	96	1 112	142	68	1 74	3
Boarding, specially appropriated for..........	371	394	23	23	326	1 4	2
Total...................	3 158	2 999	1 159	2 785	2 639	1 146	34
Public.....................	303	315	12	194	183	1 11	(3)
Mission boarding 4.........	813	737	1 76	741	662	1 79	17
Mission day................	87	54	1 33	80	22	1 58	2
Aggregate...............	22 964	24 004	1 040	18 676	19 671	995	295

TABLE 3 — *Annual appropriations made by the government since the fiscal year 1877 for the support of the Indian schools*

YEAR	Appropriation	Per cent increase	YEAR	Appropriation	Per cent increase
1877.........................	$20 000	....	1889......................	$1 348 015	14
1878.........................	30 000	50	1890......................	1 364 568	1
1879.........................	60 000	100	1891......................	1 842 770	35
1880.........................	75 000	25	1892......................	2 291 650	24.3
1881.........................	75 000	....	1893......................	2 315 612	.9
1882.........................	135 000	80	1894......................	2 243 497	1 3.5
1883.........................	487 200	260	1895......................	2 060 695	1 8.87
1884.........................	675 200	38	1896......................	2 056 515	1 .2
1885.........................	992 800	47	1897......................	2 517 265	22.45
1886.........................	1 100 065	10	1898......................	2 631 771	4.54
1887.........................	1 211 415	10	1899......................	2 638 390	.0025
1888.........................	1 179 916	1 2.6			

1 Decrease.

2 Three schools transferred to the government and contracts made for two schools which were paid by vouchers in previous year.

3 Thirty-one public schools in which pupils are taught not enumerated here.

4 These schools are conducted by religious societies, some of which receive from the government for the Indian children therein such rations and clothing as the children are entitled to as reservation Indians.

TABLE 4 — *Location and capacity of government day schools, June 30, 1898*

LOCATION	Capacity	LOCATION	Capacity
Arizona :		**New Mexico — Continued.**	
Hualapai—		Pueblo — Continued.	
Kingman	50	San Ildefonso	40
Hackberry	60	San Juan....................	50
Suppai	60	Santo Domingo	30
Navajo—		Taos........................	40
Little Water................	30	Zia	35
Oreiba......................	40	Zuni........................	60
Polacco	40	**North Dakota :**	
Second Mesa................	40	Devil's Lake, Turtle Mountain, 3	
California :		schools......................	140
Big Pine....................	30	Standing Rock, 4 schools........	130
Bishop	40	Fort Berthold, 4 schools.........	150
Hat Creek..................	30	**Oklahoma :**	
Independence...............	30	Kiowa......................	30
Manchester	40	Whirlwind..................	20
Mission, 11 schools..........	319	**South Dakota :**	
Potter Valley...............	50	Cheyenne River, 3 schools.......	67
Ukiah.......................	30	Pine Ridge, 31 schools...........	1 085
Upper Lake.................	30	Rosebud, 20 schools.............	631
Michigan :		**Utah :**	
Baraga	40	Shebit......................	30
Bay Mills	50	**Washington :**	
Minnesota :		Colville, 2 schools...............	80
Birch Cooley...............	36	Tulalip—	
White Earth—		Lummi....................	40
Gull Lake.................	30	Swinomish	40
Montana :		Neah Bay—	
Tongue River...............	40	Neah Bay.................	56
Nebraska :		Quillehute................	60
Santee—		Puyallup—	
Ponca......................	34	Jamestown	30
Nevada :		Port Gamble..............	25
Walker River	34	Chehalis..................	40
New Mexico :		Quinaielt.................	40
Pueblo—		Skokomish................	40
Acoma	50	**Wisconsin :**	
Cochita	30	Green Bay, Stockbridge.........	50
Isleta......................	50	Oneida, 5 schools..............	140
Jemez......................	40	La Pointe, 10 schools 1	502
Laguna.....................	40		
Pahuate....................	30	Total capacity 1............	5 164
Santa Clara................	30		
San Felipe..................	30	Total number of schools 1..	142

TABLE 5 — *Location, capacity and date of opening of government reservation boarding schools*

LOCATION	Capacity	Date of opening	Remarks
Arizona :			
Colorado river..................	80	Mar, —, 1879	
Keams canyon..................	90	— —, 1887	
Navajo.........................	120	Dec. —, 1881	
Pima.	150	Sept. —, 1881	
San Carlos,.....................	100	Oct. —, 1880	
White Mountain Apache........	65	Feb. —, 1894	

1 Including **Lac Court d'Oreilles No. 3 day**, which was a contract school for **seven months during** this fiscal year.

TABLE 5 — *Continued.*

LOCATION	Capacity	Date of opening	Remarks
California:			
Fort Yuma......................	250	Apr. —, 1884	
Hoopa Valley.................	200	Jan. 21, 1893	
Round Valley...................	70 {	Aug. 15, 1881	Suspended after July,
		Sept. 12, 1893	1883, by burning of
Idaho:			building
Fort Hall......................	150	—— —, 1874	
Fort Lapwai....................	250	Sept. —, 1886	
Lemhi	40	Sept. —, 1885	
Indian Territory:			
Quapaw	90	Sept. —, 1872	
Seneca, Shawnee and Wyandotte.	130	June —, 1872	Begun by Friends as orphan asylum in 1867 under contract with tribe
Kansas:			
Kickapoo....	30	Oct. —, 1871	
Pottawatomie................	80	—— —, 1873	
Sac and Fox and Iowa..........	40 {	—— —, 1871	Iowa
		Sept. —, 1875	Sac and Fox
Minnesota:			
Leech Lake.....................	50	Nov. —, 1867	
Pine Point.....................	100	Mar. —, 1892	Prior to this date a contract school opened in November, 1888
Red Lake......................	50	Nov. —, 1877	
White Earth....................	40	—— —, 1871	Building burned in February, 1895
Wild Rice River...............	65	Mar. —, 1892	Prior to this date a contract school opened in November, 1888
Montana:			
Blackfeet......................	125	Jan. —, 1883	
Crow..........................	160	Oct. —, 1884	
Fort Belknap..................	110	Aug. —, 1891	
Fort Peck.....................	200	Aug. —, 1881	
Nebraska:			
Omaha.....	75	—— —, 1881	
Santee.........................	80	Apr. —, 1874	
Winnebago.....................	100	Oct. —, 1874	
Nevada:			
Pyramid Lake..................	120	Nov. —, 1882	
Western Shoshone..........	50	Feb. 11, 1893	Previously a semi-boarding school
New Mexico:			
Mescalero......................	100	Apr. —, 1884	
North Carolina:			
Eastern Cherokee..............	160	Jan. 1, 1893	Prior to this date a contract school opened in 1885
North Dakota:			
Fort Berthold [1]...........	90	Nov. 21, 1894	
Fort Totten....................	350 {	—— —, 1874	At agency
		Jan. —, 1891	At Fort Totten
Standing Rock, agency..........	120	May —, 1877	
Standing Rock, agricultural.....	100	—— —, 1878	
Standing Rock, Grand River....	80	Nov. 20, 1893	
Oklahoma;			
Absentee Shawnee..............	75	May —, 1872	
Arapaho.......................	130	Dec. —, 1872	
Cheyenne......................	200	—— —, 1879	
Fort Sill......................	125	Aug. —, 1891	

[1] Building burned March 30, 1898.

TABLE 5 — *Continued.*

LOCATION	Capacity	Date of opening	Remarks
Oklahoma — *Continued.*			
Kaw.........................	60 {	Dec. —, 1869	In Kansas
		Aug. —, 1874	In Indian territory
Osage.........................	180	Feb. —, 1874	
Oteo.........................	75	Oct. —, 1875	In Nebraska
Pawnee.........................	125 {	—— —, 1865	In Nebraska
		—— —, 1878	In Indian territory
Ponca.........................	100	Jan. —, 1883	
Rainy Mountain................	50	Sept. —, 1893	
Red Moon.....................	75	Feb. —, 1898	
Riverside (Wichita)............	100	Sept. —, 1871	
Sac and Fox...................	120 {	—— —, 1868	In Kansas
		Apr. —, 1872	In Indian territory
Seger.........................	120	Jan. 11, 1893	
Oregon:			
Grande Ronde................	100	Apr. —, 1874	
Klamath......................	140	Feb. —, 1874	
Siletz..........................	80	Oct. —, 1873	
Umatilla......................	100	Jan. —, 1883	
Warm Springs.................	160	Nov. —, 1897	
Yainax.........................	100	Nov. —, 1882	
South Dakota:			
Cheyenne River................	130	Apr. 1, 1893	At new agency. At old agency school for girls opened in 1874 under missionary auspices in government buildings school for boys opened in 1880
Crow Creek, Agency............	140	—— —, 1874	
Crow Creek, Grace Mission......	50	Feb. 1, 1897	Prior to this date a contract school opened in 1888
Hope (Springfield).............	60	Aug. 1, 1895	Prior to this date a contract school opened in 1882
Lower Brule....................	140	Oct. —, 1881	
Pine Ridge....................	200	Dec. —, 1883	Suspended February 8, 1894, when building was burned. Reopened in new building February 7, 1898
Sisseton	130	—— —, 1873	
Rosebud......................	200	Sept. —, 1897	
Yankton......................	150	Feb. —, 1882	
Utah:			
Ouray	80	Apr. —, 1893	
Uintah.........................	90	Jan. —, 1881	
Washington:			
Puyallup	200	June —, 1871	
Yakima.........................	140	—— —, 1860	
Wisconsin:			
Lac du Flambeau.........	160	July 10, 1895	
Menomonee	160	—— —, 1876	
Oneida.......................	120	Mar. 27, 1893	
Wyoming:			
Shoshone.....................	200	Apr. —, 1879	
Total.......	8825		

TABLE 6—*Location, average attendance, capacity, etc., of non-reservation training schools during fiscal year ended June 30, 1898*

LOCATION OF SCHOOL	Date of opening	Number of employees	Rate per annum	Capacity	Enrollment	Average attendance
Carlisle, Pa..........	Nov. 1, 1879	82	$167	[1] 800	961	851
Chemawa, Oreg.......	Feb. 25, 1880	57	167	400	354	330
Chilocco, Okla........	Jan. 15, 1884	66	167	450	331	271
Genoa, Neb..........	Feb. 20, 1884	41	167	350	293	277
Albuquerque, N. Mex.	Aug. —, 1884	84	167	300	312	302
Haskell institue, Kans.	Sept. 1, 1884	67	167	500	553	463
Grand Junction, Colo.	—— —, 1886	23	167	170	171	158
Santa Fe, N. Mex.....	Oct. —, 1890	60	167	200	260	210
Fort Mojave, Ariz....	Oct. —, 1890	38	167	150	156	151
Carson, Nex..........	Dec. —, 1890	24	167	150	166	144
Pierre, S. Dak........	Feb. —, 1891	17	167	150	173	146
Phœnix, Ariz.........	Sept. —, 1891	60	167	400	480	418
Fort Lewis, Colo.	Mar. —, 1892	44	....	300	314	285
Fort Shaw, Mont.	Dec. 27, 1892	40	....	250	300	280
Perris, Cal...........	Jan. 9, 1893	22	167	150	180	171
Flandreau, S. Dak....	Mar. 7, 1893	27	167	200	304	204
Pipestone, Minn......	Feb. —, 1893	19	167	90	150	102
Mount Pleasant, Mich.	Jan. 3, 1893	26	167	160	186	150
Tomah, Wis..........	Jan. 19, 1893	20	167	125	146	114
Wittenberg, Wis. [2]....	Aug. 24, 1895	19	....	130	133	116
Greenville, Cal.[2]......	Sept. 25, 1895	6	....	50	57	35
Morris, Minn.[2]........	Apr. 3, 1897	15	.. ..	100	92	79
Clontarf, Minn.[2]......	Apr. 4, 1897	8	....	80	42	33
Chamberlain, S. Dak..	Mar. —, 1898	10	167	80	37	36
Fort Bidwell, Cal.....	Apr. 4, 1898	5	....	150	24	21
Total.........		880	.. ..	5 885	6 175	5 347

[1] 1,500 with outing system.   [2] Previously a contract school.

TABLE 7 — *Schools conducted under contract, with number of pupils contracted for, rate per capita, and total amount of contract for fiscal years ending June 30, 1895, and June 30, 1899*

NAME AND LOCATION OF SCHOOL	1895			1899		
	Number allowed	Rate	Amount	Number allowed	Rate	Amount
Banning, California.............	100	$125	$12 500	52	$108	$5 616
Baraga, Michigan...............	45	108	4 860	19	108	2 052
Blackfeet, Montana.......... ..	100	125	12 500	34	108	3 762
Bayfield, Wisconsin.............	30	125	3 750	19	108	2 052
Bernalillo, New Mexico..........	60	125	7 500	34	108	3 672
Colville, Washington..	65	108	7 020	34	108	3 672
Cœur d'Alene, Idaho............	70	108	7 560	41	108	4 428
Crow Creek, South Dakota......	60	108	6 480	......	....	....
Crow, Montana.................	85	108	9 180	34	108	3 672
Devils Lake, North Dakota......	130	108	14 040	72	108	7 776
Flathead, Montana..........	300	150	45 000	161	108	17 388
Fort Belknap, Montana....	135	108	14 580	49	108	5 292
Harbor Springs, Michigan......	95	108	10 260	34	108	3 672
Odanah, Wisconsin, boarding....	50	108	4 400	34	108	3 672
Odanah, Wisconsin, day..	15	30	450	......	....	....
Lac Court d'Oreilles, Wisconsin, day	40	30	1 200	......	....	....
Osage, Okla., St. Louis.........	50	125	6 250	......	....	....
Osage, Okla., St. Johns..........	40	125	5 000	......	....	....
Pine Ridge, South Dakota.......	140	108	15 120	86	108	9 288
Rosebud, South Dakota.........	95	108	10 260	61	108	6 588
San Diego, California..	95	108	11 875	51	108	5 508
Shoshone, Wyoming............	65	108	7 020	34	108	3 672
Tongue River, Montana.........	40	108	4 320	26	108	2 808
Tulalip, Washington............	100	108	10 800	50	108	5 400
White Earth, Minn., St. Benedict.	90	108	9 720	51	108	5 508
White Earth, Minn., Red Lake..	40	108	4 320	27	108	2 916
Pinole, California.............	20	30	600	10	30	300
Hopland, day, California........	20	30	600	11	30	330
St. Turubius, California........	30	108	3 240	6	108	648
Green Bay, Wisconsin..........	130	108	14 040	45	108	4 860
Kate Drexel, Oregon............	60	108	6 000	24	100	2 400
Bay Mills, Michigan............	20	30	600	......	....	....
Shoshone mission, Wyoming....	20	108	2 160	20	108	2 160
Total	2 435	....	$274 205	[2] 1 119	....	$119 022
Hampton institute, Virginia[1]...	120	167	20 040	120	167	20 040
Lincoln institution, Philadelphia, Pa.[1]...................	200	167	33 400	200	167	33 400
Grand total................	2 755	....	$327 645	1 439	....	$172 462

[1] Specially appropriated for by congress.

[2] Not including the two schools of Osage and two Pottawatomie schools at Sac and Fox agencies, Okla., nor one day school at La Pointe agency, which was converted into a government school during year.

TABLE 8—*Amounts set apart for education of Indians in schools under private control for the fiscal years 1890 to 1899, inclusive*

	1890	1891	1892	1893	1894	1895	1896	1897	1898	1899
Roman Catholic	$356 957	$363 349	$394 756	$375 845	$389 745	$359 215	$308 471	$198 228	$156 754	$116 862
Presbyterian	47 650	44 850	44 310	30 090	36 340					
Congregational	28 459	27 271	29 146	25 736	10 825					
Episcopal	24 876	29 910	23 220	4 860	7 020	7 020	2 160			
Friends	23 383	24 743	24 743	10 020	10 020	10 020				
Mennonite	4 375	4 375	4 375	3 750	3 750	3 750	3 125			
Unitarian	5 400	5 400	5 400	5 400	5 400	5 400				
Lutheran, Wittenberg, Wis.	7 560	9 180	16 200	15 120	15 120	15 120				
Methodist	9 940	6 700	13 980	6 480						
Mrs. L. H. Daggett	600						600			
Miss Howard		1 000	2 000	2 500	3 000	3 000	3 000	3 500		
Special appropriation for Lincoln institution	33 400	33 400	33 400	33 400	33 400	33 400	33 400	33 400	33 400	33 400
Special appropriation for Hampton institute	20 040	20 040	20 040	20 040	20 040	20 040	20 040	20 040	20 040	20 040
Woman's National Indian Association					2 040	4 320				
Point Iroquois, Mich.					900	600				
Plum Creek, Leslie, S. Dak.						1 620		600	600	
John Roberts								2 160	2 160	2 160
Total	$562 040	$570 218	$611 570	$533 241	$537 600	$463 505	$370 796	$257 928	$212 954	$172 462

INDEX

A

Adams, Herbert B., *Summer schools and university extension*, 823

Agricultural colleges, 606; classification of, 618; courses of study, 621, 627; expenses of students, 629; land-grant colleges, 611; military instruction, 628; requirement for admission, 620; report of committee, 622

Agricultural education, 595; interest of Washington, 596; struggles of early farmers, 595

Agricultural experiment stations, 640

Agricultural extension work, 629; co-operative experiments, 631; institutes, 630; instruction by correspondence, 631; itinerant schools, 632; Nixon bill, 632

Agricultural schools, 600

Agricultural societies and fairs, 597; first society, 597; Massachusetts society, 598; New York society, 598

Agriculture in the common schools, 632; nature teaching, 633

Agriculture, U. S. department of, 603

Allen, Edward Ellis, *Education of defectives*, 771

American academy of arts and sciences, 871

American art annual, 726 (see note)

American association for advancement of science, 869

American chemical society, 877

American library association, 833

American mathematical society, 878

American museum of natural history, 886

American philosophical society, 870

American society of civil engineers, 877

American society of naturalists, 878

Annals of the deaf, 783

Armour institute, 572, 687

Art and industrial education, 707; advocacy of, by Dr Barnard, 710; Albany capitol building, 760; condition in 1874, 720; development from 1874 to 1876, 725; influence of centennial of 1876, 725, 753; Massachusetts the first state to act, 720; method of Mr Fowle, 709; method of the Misses Peabody, 710; paucity of institutions, 723; progress, 709; work of John Brainard, 711; William Minifie, 710

Art and industry, summary of report, 749

Art departments in colleges and universities, 722

Art development, influence of localities, 717

Art loan exhibitions, 722

Art museums and galleries, 722

Art schools, 721

Art training, American facilities, 717

B

Bar, admission to, 498

Bell, Dr, influence of, 783

Biological laboratories, 890

Blind, 786; bibliography, 812; early schools, 788; education of, 787; embossed books, 792; embossed libraries, 795; North Carolina school, 789; schools, why started, 787; Sloyd, 791; statistics, 797

Boston society of natural history, 873

Botanical gardens, 889

Brooklyn institute of arts and sciences, 886

Business schools, 656; classes, 656; courses, 665; regents of the university of the state of New York, 664; tuition fees, 669

Business training, aim of, 669

Date Due
